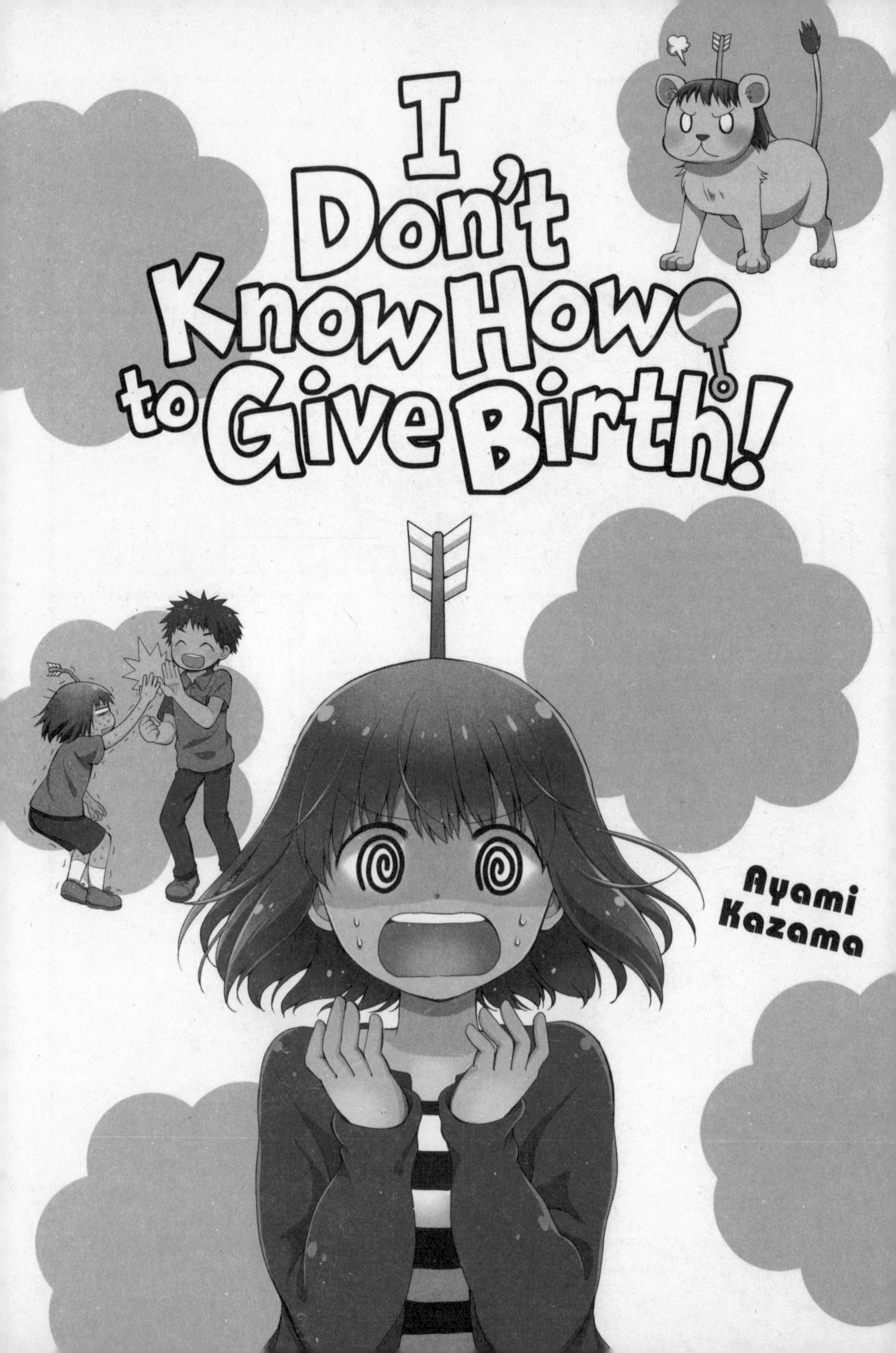
I Don't Know How to Give Birth!
Ayami Kazama

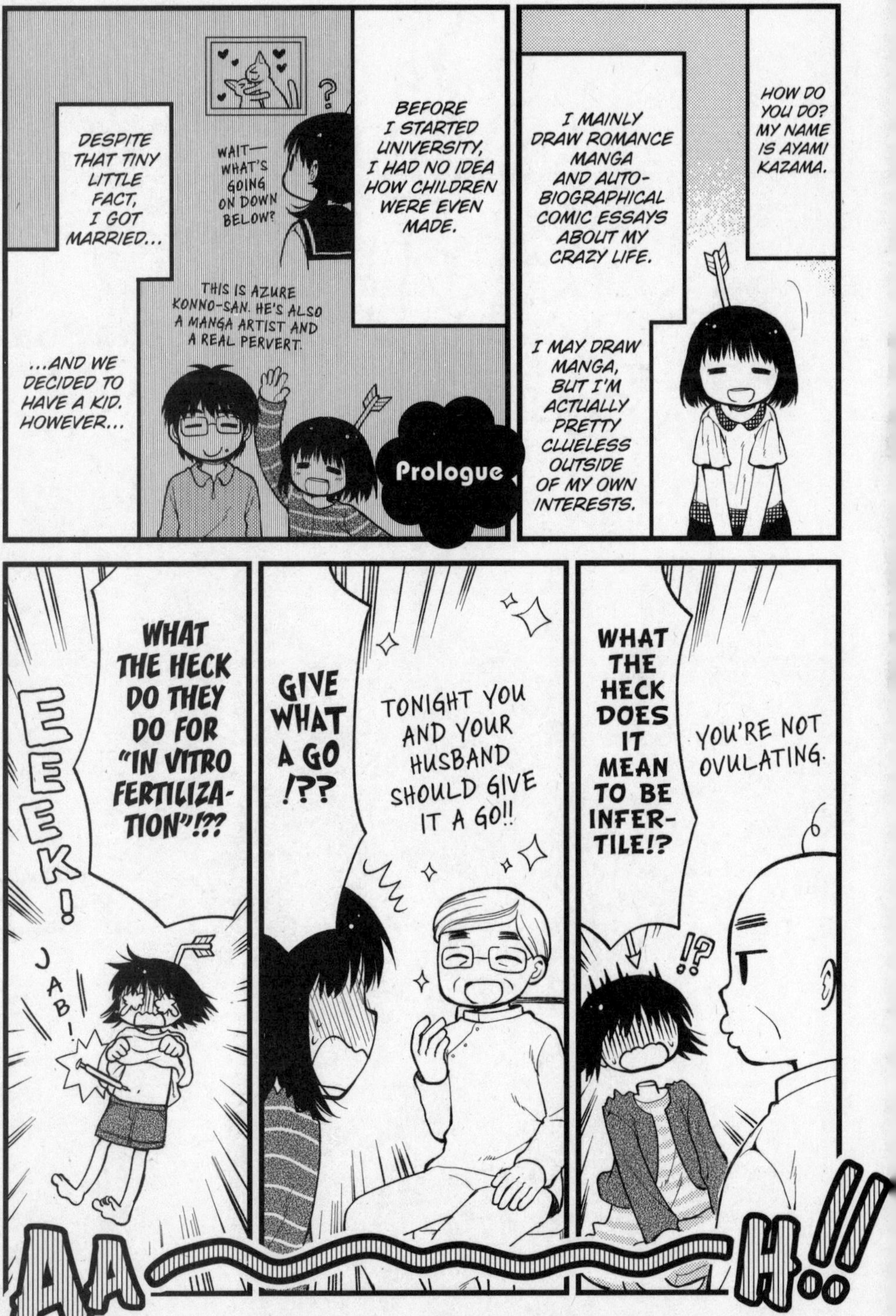
HOW DO YOU DO? MY NAME IS AYAMI KAZAMA.
I MAINLY DRAW ROMANCE MANGA AND AUTO-BIOGRAPHICAL COMIC ESSAYS ABOUT MY CRAZY LIFE.
I MAY DRAW MANGA, BUT I'M ACTUALLY PRETTY CLUELESS OUTSIDE OF MY OWN INTERESTS.
Prologue
BEFORE I STARTED UNIVERSITY, I HAD NO IDEA HOW CHILDREN WERE EVEN MADE.
WAIT— WHAT'S GOING ON DOWN BELOW?
DESPITE THAT TINY LITTLE FACT, I GOT MARRIED...
THIS IS AZURE KONNO-SAN. HE'S ALSO A MANGA ARTIST AND A REAL PERVERT.
...AND WE DECIDED TO HAVE A KID. HOWEVER...
YOU'RE NOT OVULATING.
WHAT THE HECK DOES IT MEAN TO BE INFERTILE!?
!?
TONIGHT YOU AND YOUR HUSBAND SHOULD GIVE IT A GO!!
GIVE WHAT A GO !??
WHAT THE HECK DO THEY DO FOR "IN VITRO FERTILIZATION"!??
EEEEK!
JAB!
AA—H!!

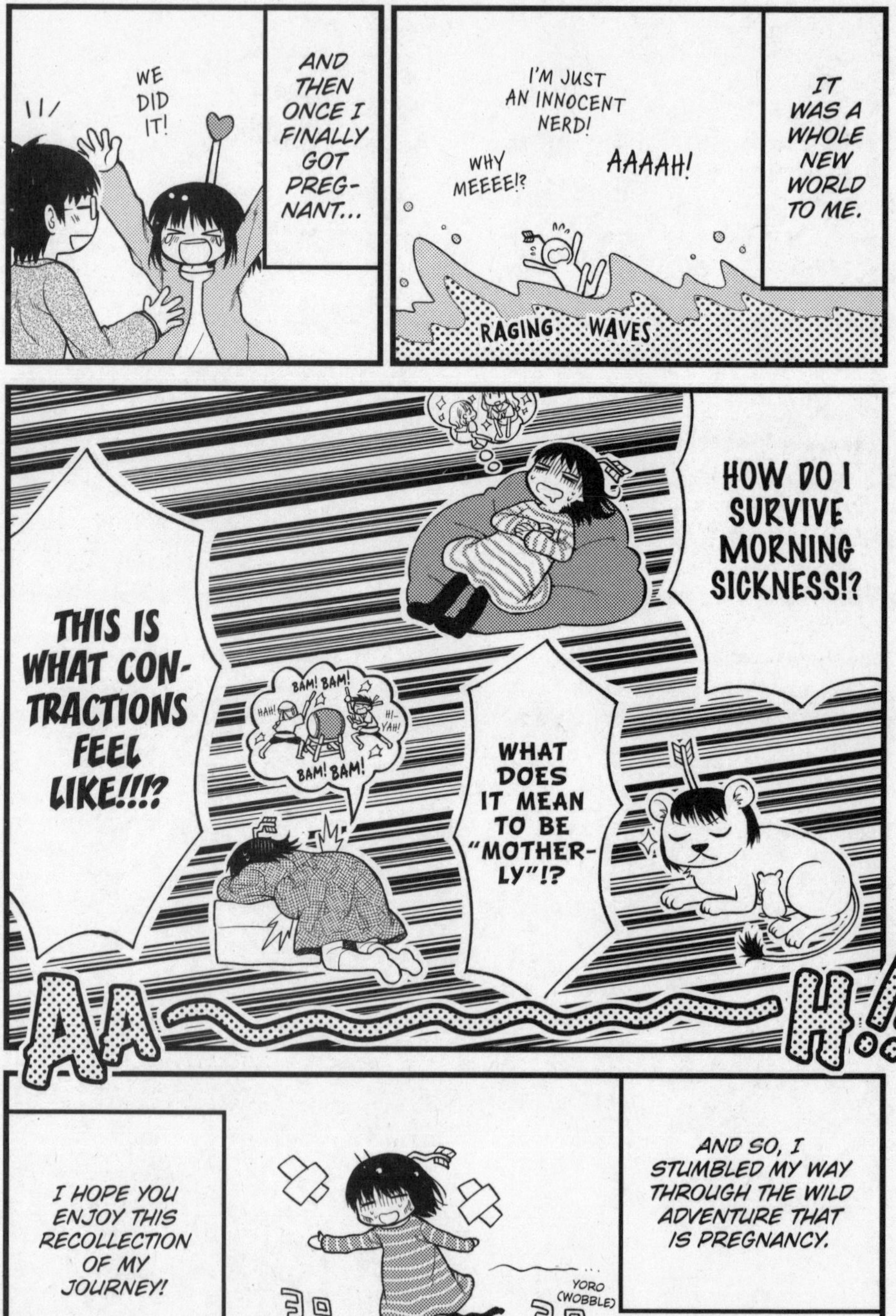
!!/
WE DID IT!
AND THEN ONCE I FINALLY GOT PREG-NANT...
I'M JUST AN INNOCENT NERD!
WHY MEEEE!?
AAAAH!
RAGING WAVES
IT WAS A WHOLE NEW WORLD TO ME.
HOW DO I SURVIVE MORNING SICKNESS!?
THIS IS WHAT CON-TRACTIONS FEEL LIKE!!!?
BAM! BAM!
HAH!
HI-YAH!
BAM! BAM!
WHAT DOES IT MEAN TO BE "MOTHER-LY"!?
AA——————H!!!
AND SO, I STUMBLED MY WAY THROUGH THE WILD ADVENTURE THAT IS PREGNANCY.
I HOPE YOU ENJOY THIS RECOLLECTION OF MY JOURNEY!
YORO
YORO (WOBBLE)

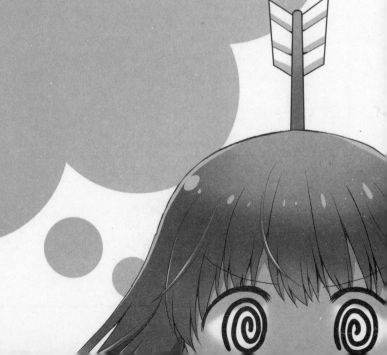

C O N T E N T S

I Don't Know How to Give Birth! Presented by Ayami Kazama

The content of this book is solely based on the personal experiences of the author and is not intended to substitute for professional medical advice, diagnosis, or treatment. Always seek the advice of a physician or other qualified healthcare provider with any questions regarding a medical condition. Please consult your physician for personalized medical advice.

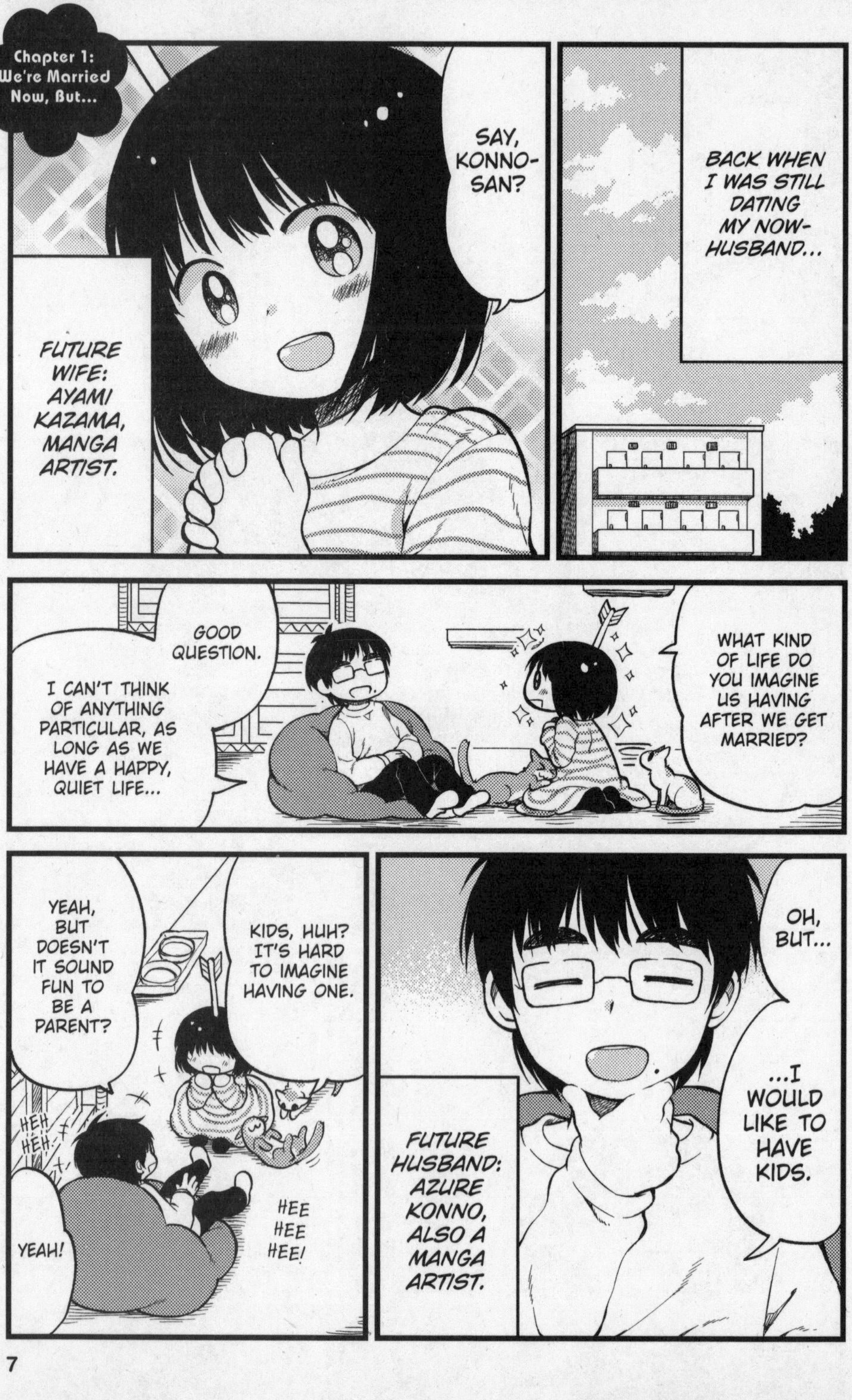
Chapter 1: We're Married Now, But...
BACK WHEN I WAS STILL DATING MY NOW-HUSBAND...
SAY, KONNO-SAN?
FUTURE WIFE: AYAMI KAZAMA, MANGA ARTIST.
WHAT KIND OF LIFE DO YOU IMAGINE US HAVING AFTER WE GET MARRIED?
GOOD QUESTION.
I CAN'T THINK OF ANYTHING PARTICULAR, AS LONG AS WE HAVE A HAPPY, QUIET LIFE...
OH, BUT...
...I WOULD LIKE TO HAVE KIDS.
FUTURE HUSBAND: AZURE KONNO, ALSO A MANGA ARTIST.
KIDS, HUH? IT'S HARD TO IMAGINE HAVING ONE.
YEAH, BUT DOESN'T IT SOUND FUN TO BE A PARENT?
HEH HEH
YEAH!
HEE HEE HEE!

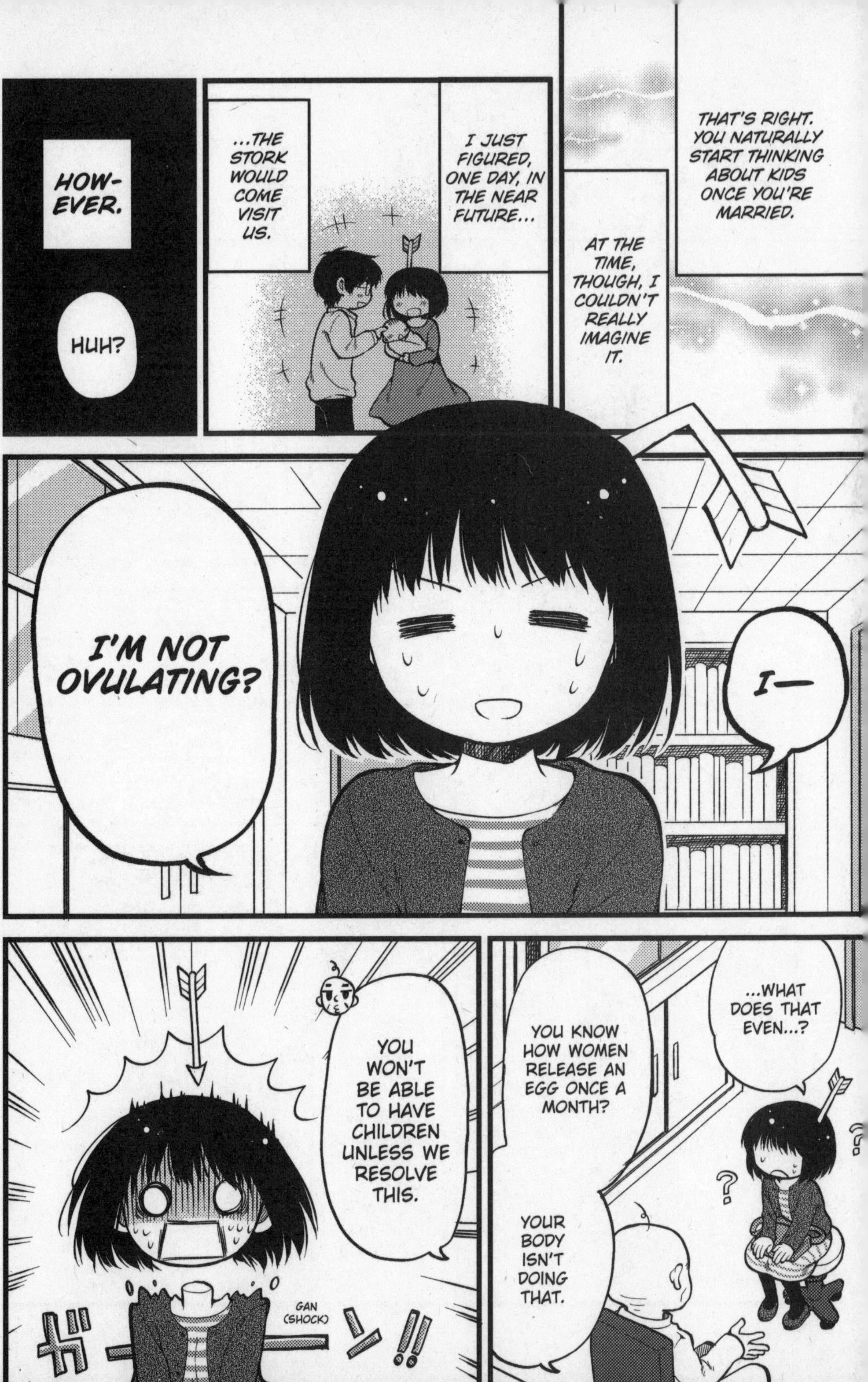
THAT'S RIGHT. YOU NATURALLY START THINKING ABOUT KIDS ONCE YOU'RE MARRIED.
AT THE TIME, THOUGH, I COULDN'T REALLY IMAGINE IT.
I JUST FIGURED, ONE DAY, IN THE NEAR FUTURE...
...THE STORK WOULD COME VISIT US.
HOW-EVER.
HUH?
I—
I'M NOT OVULATING?
...WHAT DOES THAT EVEN...?
YOU KNOW HOW WOMEN RELEASE AN EGG ONCE A MONTH?
YOUR BODY ISN'T DOING THAT.
YOU WON'T BE ABLE TO HAVE CHILDREN UNLESS WE RESOLVE THIS.
GAN (SHOCK)

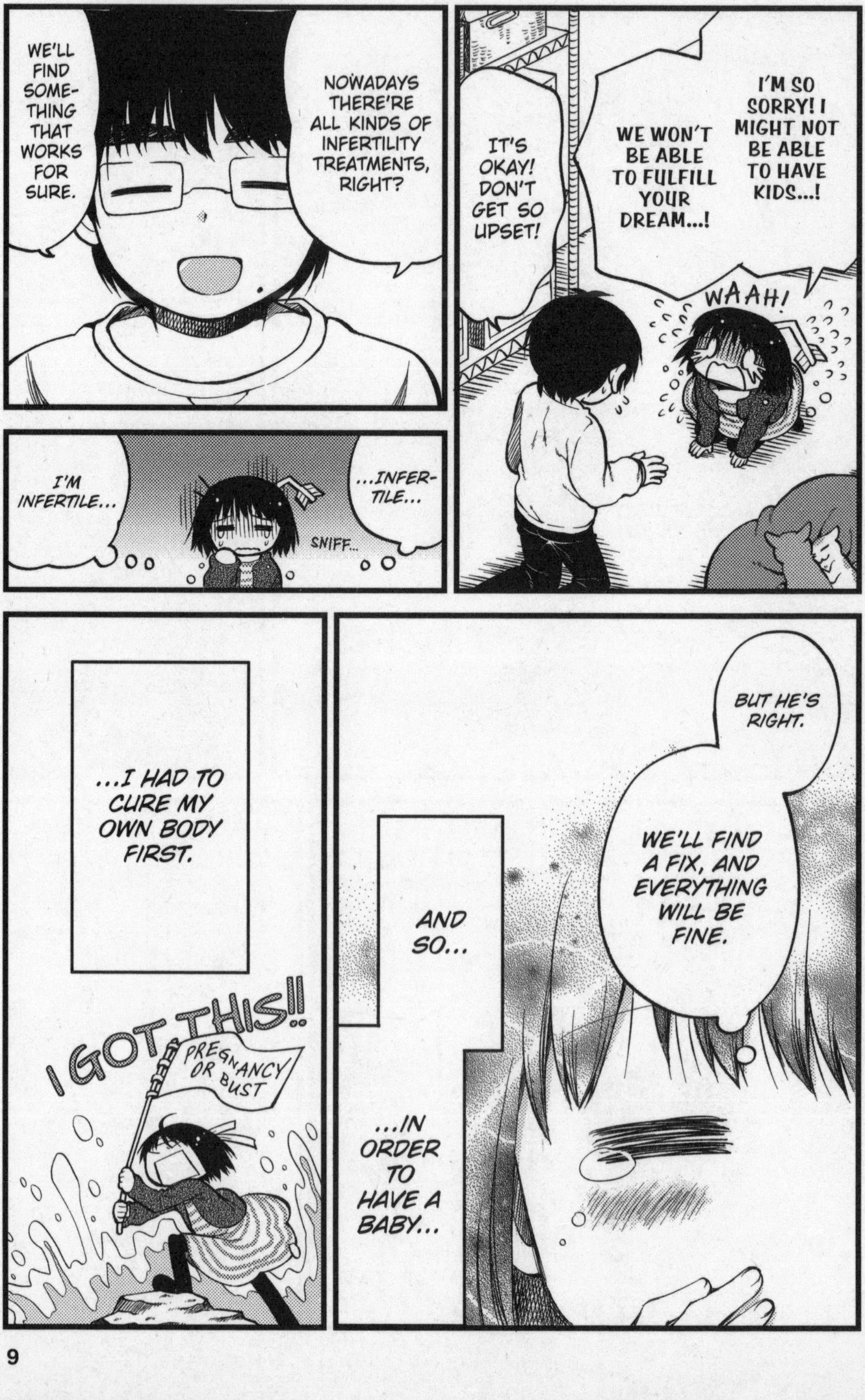
I'M SO SORRY! I MIGHT NOT BE ABLE TO HAVE KIDS...!
WE WON'T BE ABLE TO FULFILL YOUR DREAM...!
IT'S OKAY! DON'T GET SO UPSET!
WAAH!
NOWADAYS THERE'RE ALL KINDS OF INFERTILITY TREATMENTS, RIGHT?
WE'LL FIND SOMETHING THAT WORKS FOR SURE.
...INFERTILE...
SNIFF..
I'M INFERTILE...
BUT HE'S RIGHT.
WE'LL FIND A FIX, AND EVERYTHING WILL BE FINE.
AND SO...
...IN ORDER TO HAVE A BABY...
...I HAD TO CURE MY OWN BODY FIRST.
I GOT THIS!!
PREGNANCY OR BUST

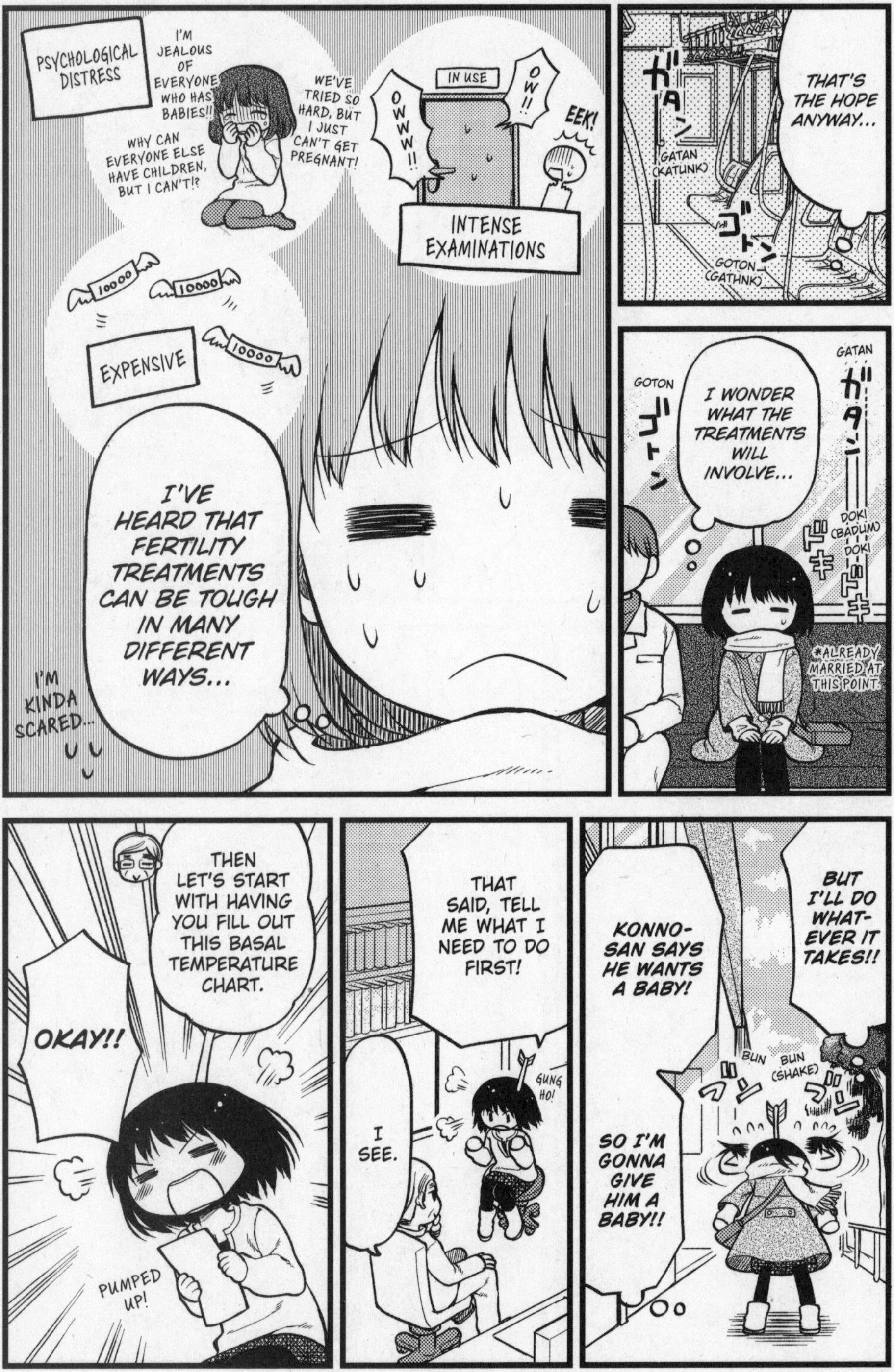
THAT'S THE HOPE ANYWAY...
ガタン
GATAN (KATUNK)
ゴトン
GOTON (GATHNK)
GATAN
ガタン
I WONDER WHAT THE TREATMENTS WILL INVOLVE...
GOTON
ゴトン
DOKI (BADUMP) DOKI
ドキドキ
*ALREADY MARRIED AT THIS POINT.
PSYCHOLOGICAL DISTRESS
I'M JEALOUS OF EVERYONE WHO HAS BABIES!!
WE'VE TRIED SO HARD, BUT I JUST CAN'T GET PREGNANT!
WHY CAN EVERYONE ELSE HAVE CHILDREN, BUT I CAN'T!?
IN USE
OW!!
OWWW!!
EEK!
INTENSE EXAMINATIONS
10000
10000
10000
EXPENSIVE
I'VE HEARD THAT FERTILITY TREATMENTS CAN BE TOUGH IN MANY DIFFERENT WAYS...
I'M KINDA SCARED...
BUT I'LL DO WHATEVER IT TAKES!!
KONNO-SAN SAYS HE WANTS A BABY!
SO I'M GONNA GIVE HIM A BABY!!
BUN BUN (SHAKE)
ブンブン
THAT SAID, TELL ME WHAT I NEED TO DO FIRST!
GUNG HO!
I SEE.
THEN LET'S START WITH HAVING YOU FILL OUT THIS BASAL TEMPERATURE CHART.
OKAY!!
PUMPED UP!

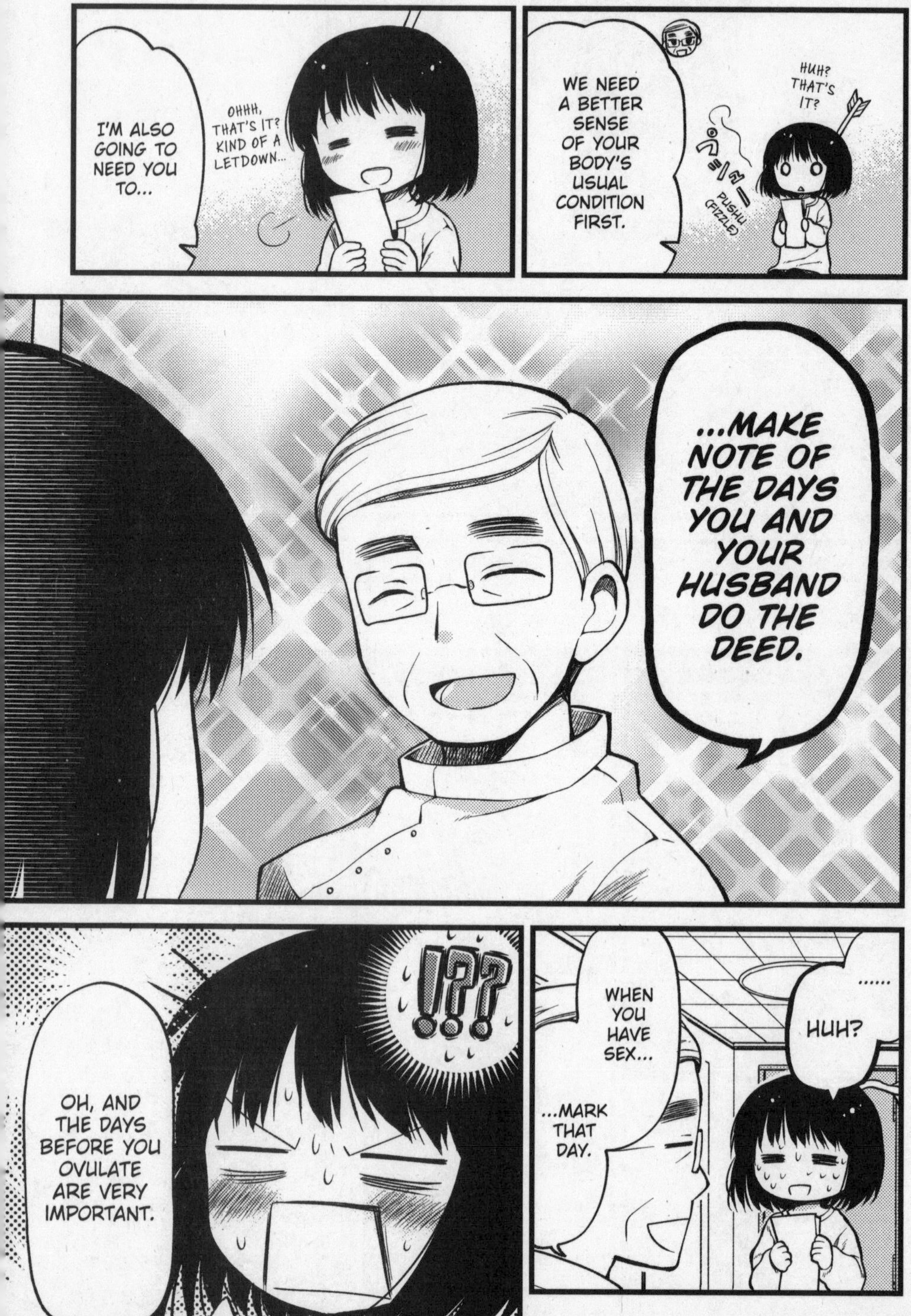
WE NEED A BETTER SENSE OF YOUR BODY'S USUAL CONDITION FIRST.
HUH? THAT'S IT?
PUSHU (FIZZLE)
OHHH, THAT'S IT? KIND OF A LETDOWN...
I'M ALSO GOING TO NEED YOU TO...
...MAKE NOTE OF THE DAYS YOU AND YOUR HUSBAND DO THE DEED.
......
HUH?
WHEN YOU HAVE SEX...
...MARK THAT DAY.
!??
OH, AND THE DAYS BEFORE YOU OVULATE ARE VERY IMPORTANT.

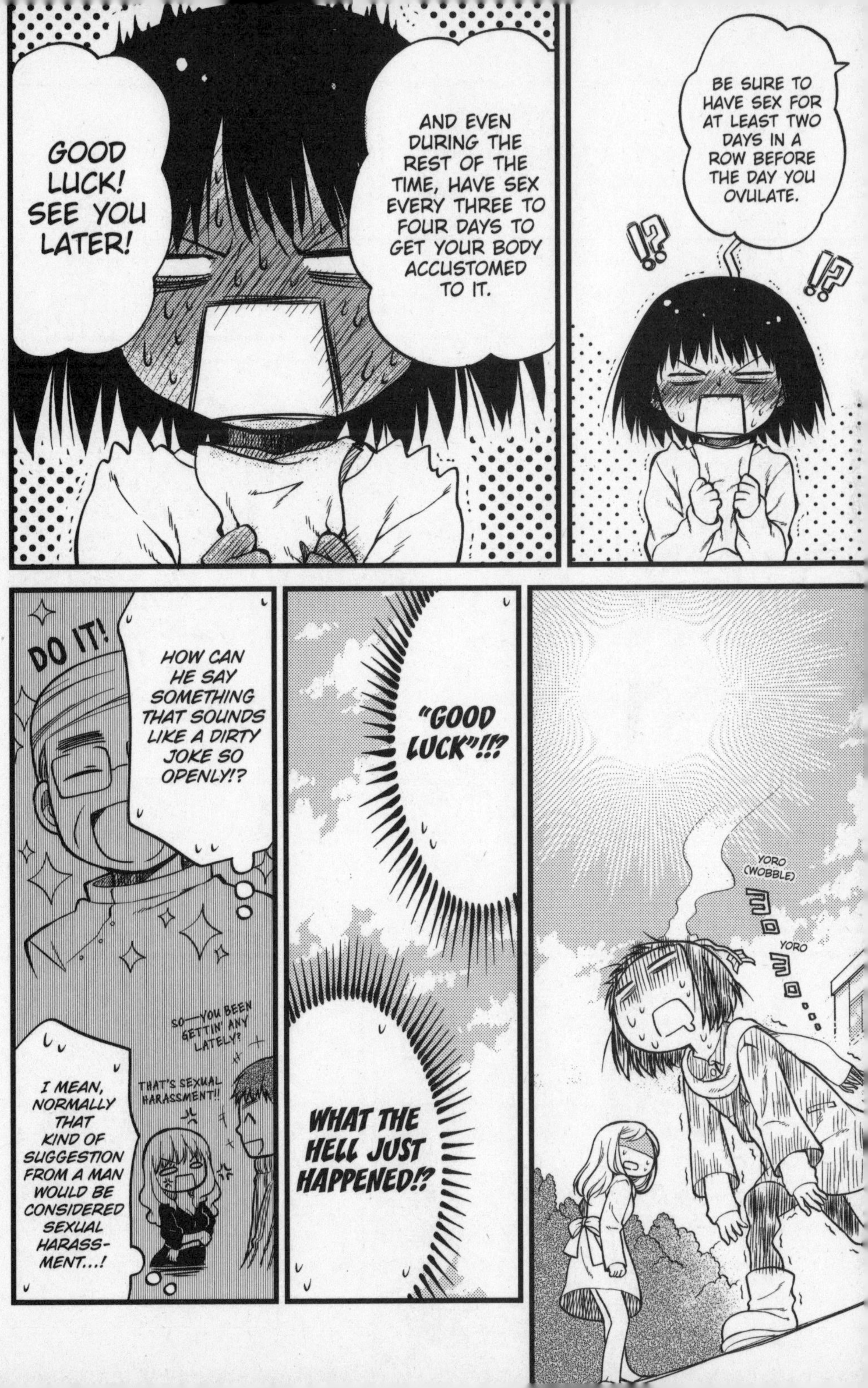
BE SURE TO HAVE SEX FOR AT LEAST TWO DAYS IN A ROW BEFORE THE DAY YOU OVULATE.
!?
!?
AND EVEN DURING THE REST OF THE TIME, HAVE SEX EVERY THREE TO FOUR DAYS TO GET YOUR BODY ACCUSTOMED TO IT.
GOOD LUCK! SEE YOU LATER!
YORO (WOBBLE)
YORO
"GOOD LUCK"!!?
WHAT THE HELL JUST HAPPENED!?
DO IT!
HOW CAN HE SAY SOMETHING THAT SOUNDS LIKE A DIRTY JOKE SO OPENLY!?
SO—YOU BEEN GETTIN' ANY LATELY?
THAT'S SEXUAL HARASSMENT!!
I MEAN, NORMALLY THAT KIND OF SUGGESTION FROM A MAN WOULD BE CONSIDERED SEXUAL HARASS-MENT...!

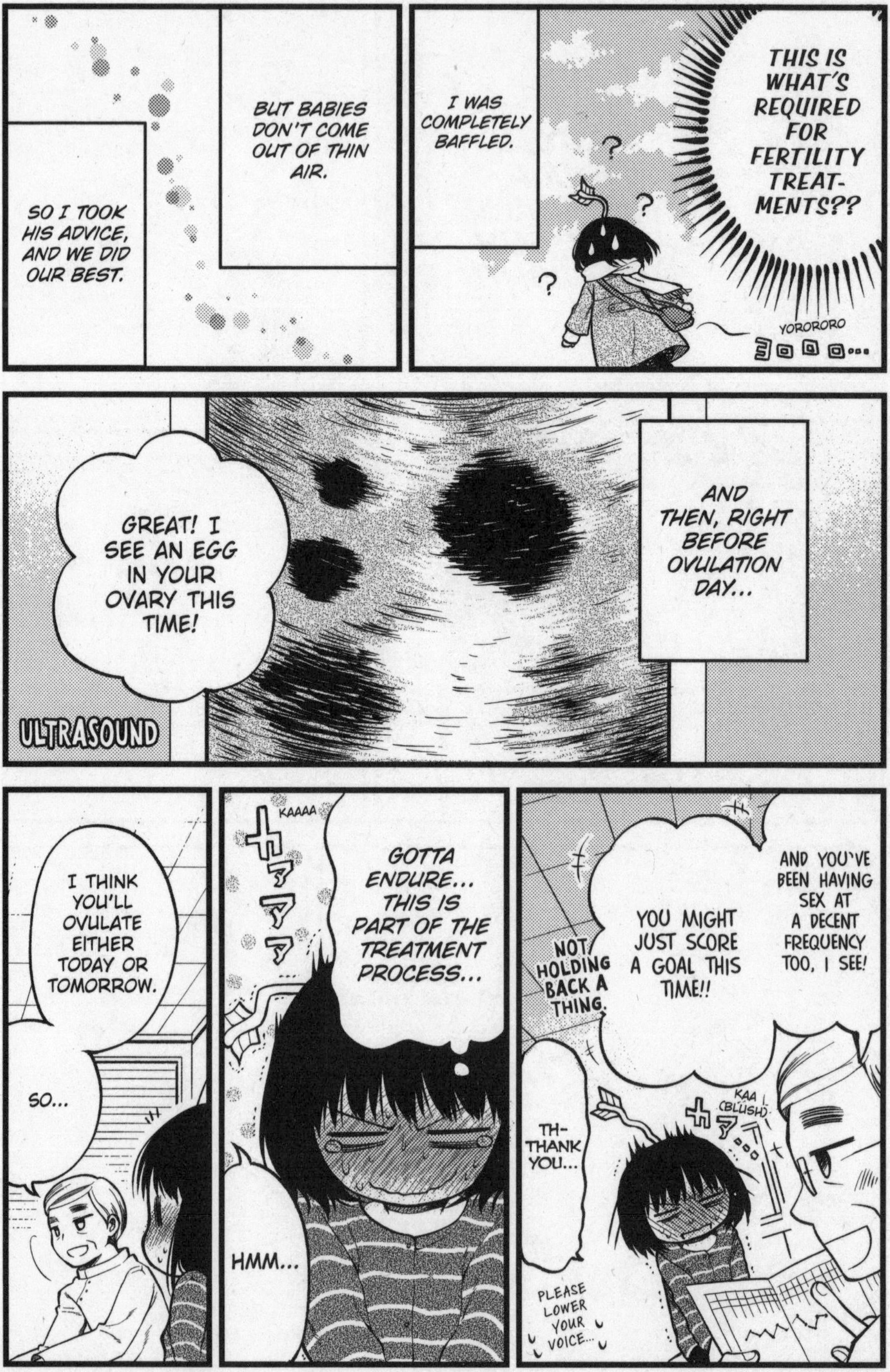
SO I TOOK HIS ADVICE, AND WE DID OUR BEST.
BUT BABIES DON'T COME OUT OF THIN AIR.
I WAS COMPLETELY BAFFLED.
THIS IS WHAT'S REQUIRED FOR FERTILITY TREAT-MENTS??
YORORORO
AND THEN, RIGHT BEFORE OVULATION DAY...
GREAT! I SEE AN EGG IN YOUR OVARY THIS TIME!
ULTRASOUND
I THINK YOU'LL OVULATE EITHER TODAY OR TOMORROW.
SO...
HMM...
KAAAA
GOTTA ENDURE... THIS IS PART OF THE TREATMENT PROCESS...
AND YOU'VE BEEN HAVING SEX AT A DECENT FREQUENCY TOO, I SEE!
YOU MIGHT JUST SCORE A GOAL THIS TIME!!
NOT HOLDING BACK A THING.
TH-THANK YOU...
KAA (BLUSH)
PLEASE LOWER YOUR VOICE...

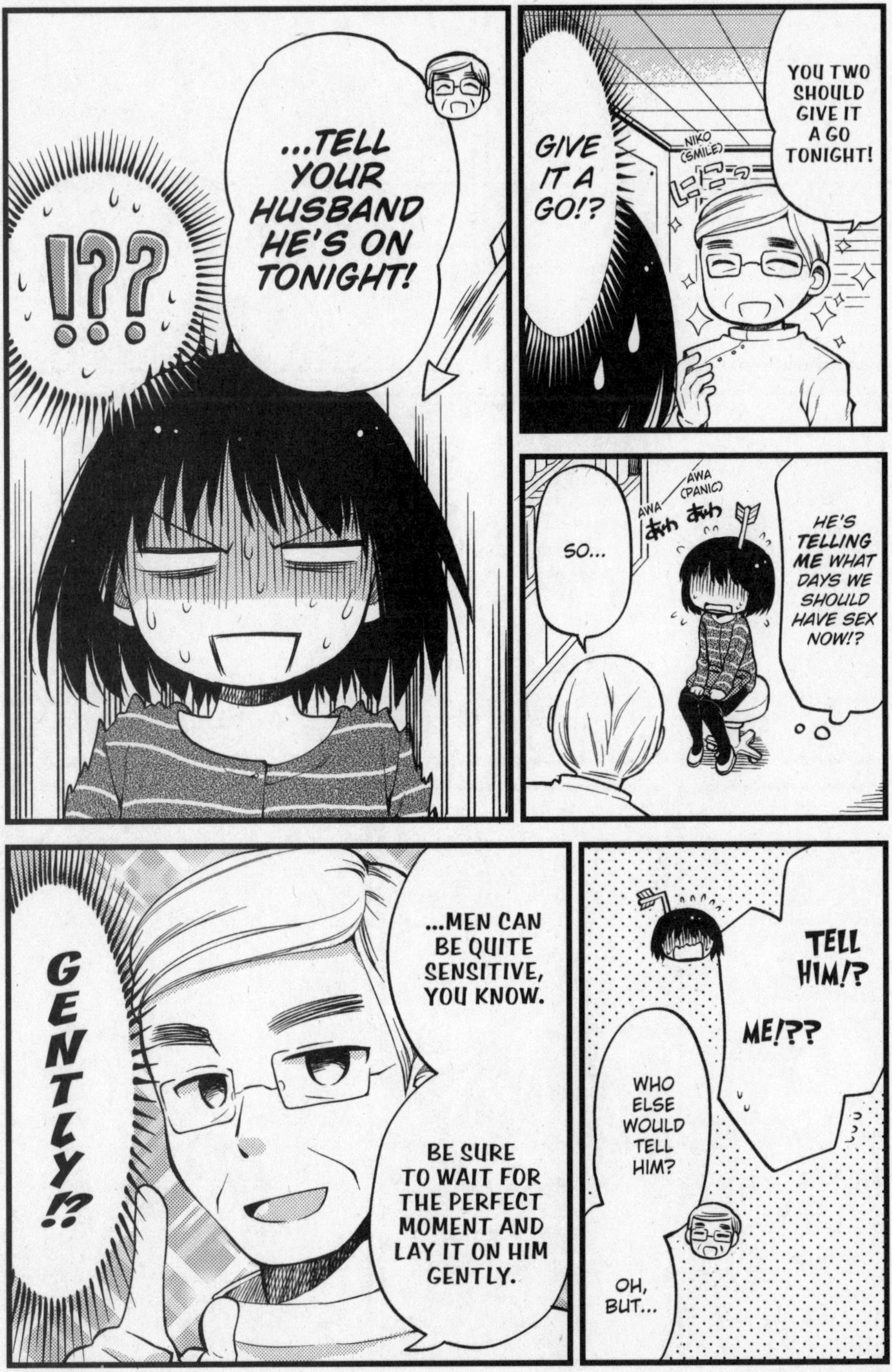
YOU TWO SHOULD GIVE IT A GO TONIGHT!
NIKO (SMILE)
GIVE IT A GO!?
HE'S TELLING ME WHAT DAYS WE SHOULD HAVE SEX NOW!?
AWA (PANIC)
AWA
SO...
...TELL YOUR HUSBAND HE'S ON TONIGHT!
!??
TELL HIM!?
ME!??
WHO ELSE WOULD TELL HIM?
OH, BUT...
...MEN CAN BE QUITE SENSITIVE, YOU KNOW.
BE SURE TO WAIT FOR THE PERFECT MOMENT AND LAY IT ON HIM GENTLY.
GENTLY!?

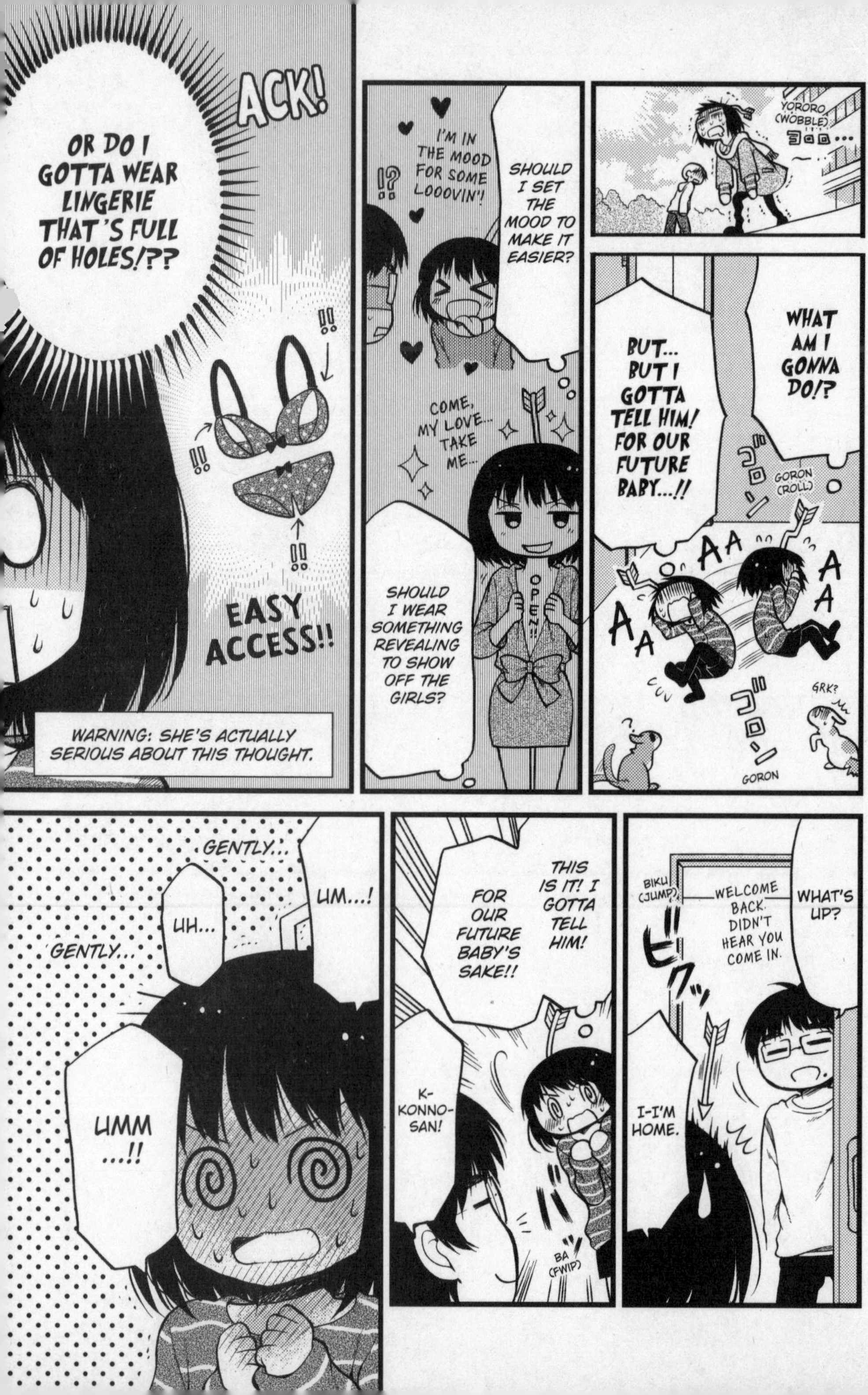
YORORO (WOBBLE)
ヨロロ…
WHAT AM I GONNA DO!?
BUT... BUT I GOTTA TELL HIM! FOR OUR FUTURE BABY...!!
GORON (ROLL)
ゴロン
AA AA
AA
AA
GRK?
ゴロン
GORON
SHOULD I SET THE MOOD TO MAKE IT EASIER?
I'M IN THE MOOD FOR SOME LOOOVIN'!
!?
COME, MY LOVE... TAKE ME...
OPEN!!
SHOULD I WEAR SOMETHING REVEALING TO SHOW OFF THE GIRLS?
ACK!
OR DO I GOTTA WEAR LINGERIE THAT'S FULL OF HOLES!??
!!
!!
!!
EASY ACCESS!!
WARNING: SHE'S ACTUALLY SERIOUS ABOUT THIS THOUGHT.
WHAT'S UP?
WELCOME BACK. DIDN'T HEAR YOU COME IN.
BIKU (JUMP)
I-I'M HOME.
THIS IS IT! I GOTTA TELL HIM!
FOR OUR FUTURE BABY'S SAKE!!
K-KONNO-SAN!
BA (FWIP)
UM...!
GENTLY...
UH...
GENTLY...
UMM ...!!

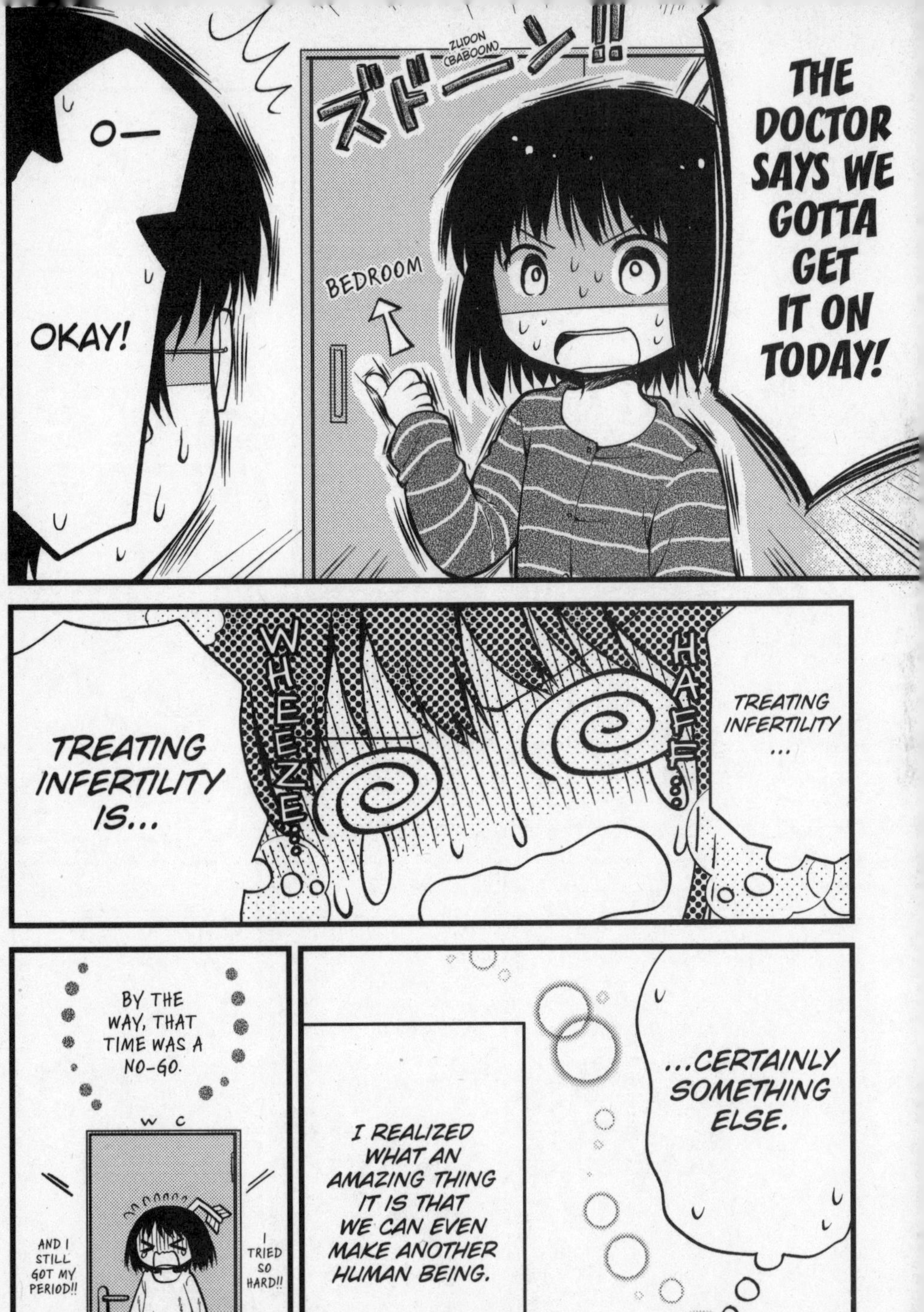
THE DOCTOR SAYS WE GOTTA GET IT ON TODAY!
ZUDON (BABOOM)
ズドーン!!
BEDROOM
O—
OKAY!
TREATING INFERTILITY ...
HAFF...
WHEEZE...
TREATING INFERTILITY IS...
...CERTAINLY SOMETHING ELSE.
I REALIZED WHAT AN AMAZING THING IT IS THAT WE CAN EVEN MAKE ANOTHER HUMAN BEING.
BY THE WAY, THAT TIME WAS A NO-GO.
W C
I TRIED SO HARD!!
AND I STILL GOT MY PERIOD!!

Chapter 1: We're Married Now, But...

Bonus manga by Azure Konno

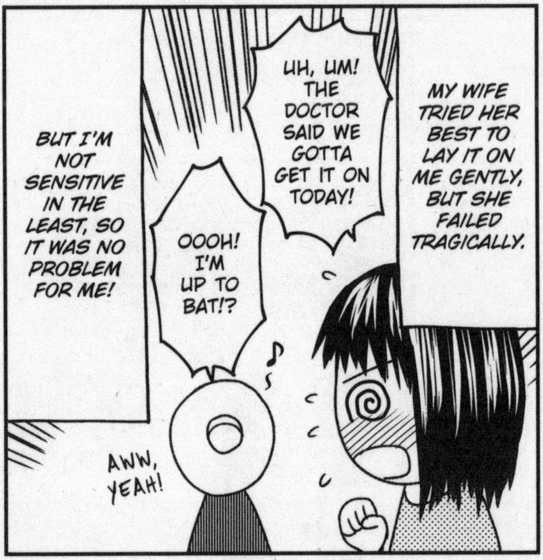
MY WIFE TRIED HER BEST TO LAY IT ON ME GENTLY, BUT SHE FAILED TRAGICALLY.
UH, UM! THE DOCTOR SAID WE GOTTA GET IT ON TODAY!
OOOH! I'M UP TO BAT!?
AWW, YEAH!
BUT I'M NOT SENSITIVE IN THE LEAST, SO IT WAS NO PROBLEM FOR ME!

I'm the husband whose stock skyrocketed thanks to Kazama-san.
By exploiting what she calls "my unique fetish" (I don't think it's that unique, though), we had no issues, but I'm sure there are couples out there who don't have such harmonious sex lives.
The first thing to do is have a heart-to-heart with your husband to find out what his secret preferences are.
He might not want to admit what turns him on, so you'll have to go excavating. He's almost certainly got something particular that gets him going.
You might find your husband's fantasies a bit shocking, but try not to jump and call him a "pervert." Instead, you should respond by exploring those areas with him.
Indulging him like that is the surest way to get that sperm. Now go have that chat!

Chapter 1: We're Married Now, But...

Bonus manga by Ayami Kazama

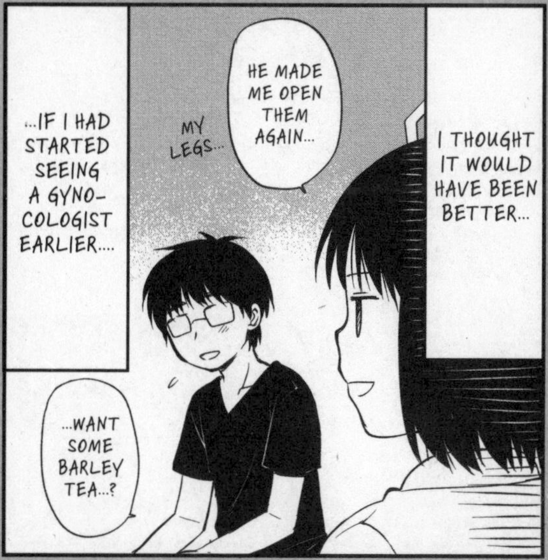
I THOUGHT IT WOULD HAVE BEEN BETTER...
HE MADE ME OPEN THEM AGAIN...
MY LEGS...
...IF I HAD STARTED SEEING A GYNO-COLOGIST EARLIER....
...WANT SOME BARLEY TEA...?

Up until I was about thirty years old, I had never once been to a gynecologist.
It was a long while before I got used to it, and every time the doctor examined between my legs, I'd be in a kind of daze as I made my way home.
I have a feeling I might make some readers scared about seeing a gynecologist by talking about them like this, but don't worry...You will get used to it...
Age might not have anything to do with it, but I think it's good to start seeing one regularly before you get worked up thinking about it too hard. Really.

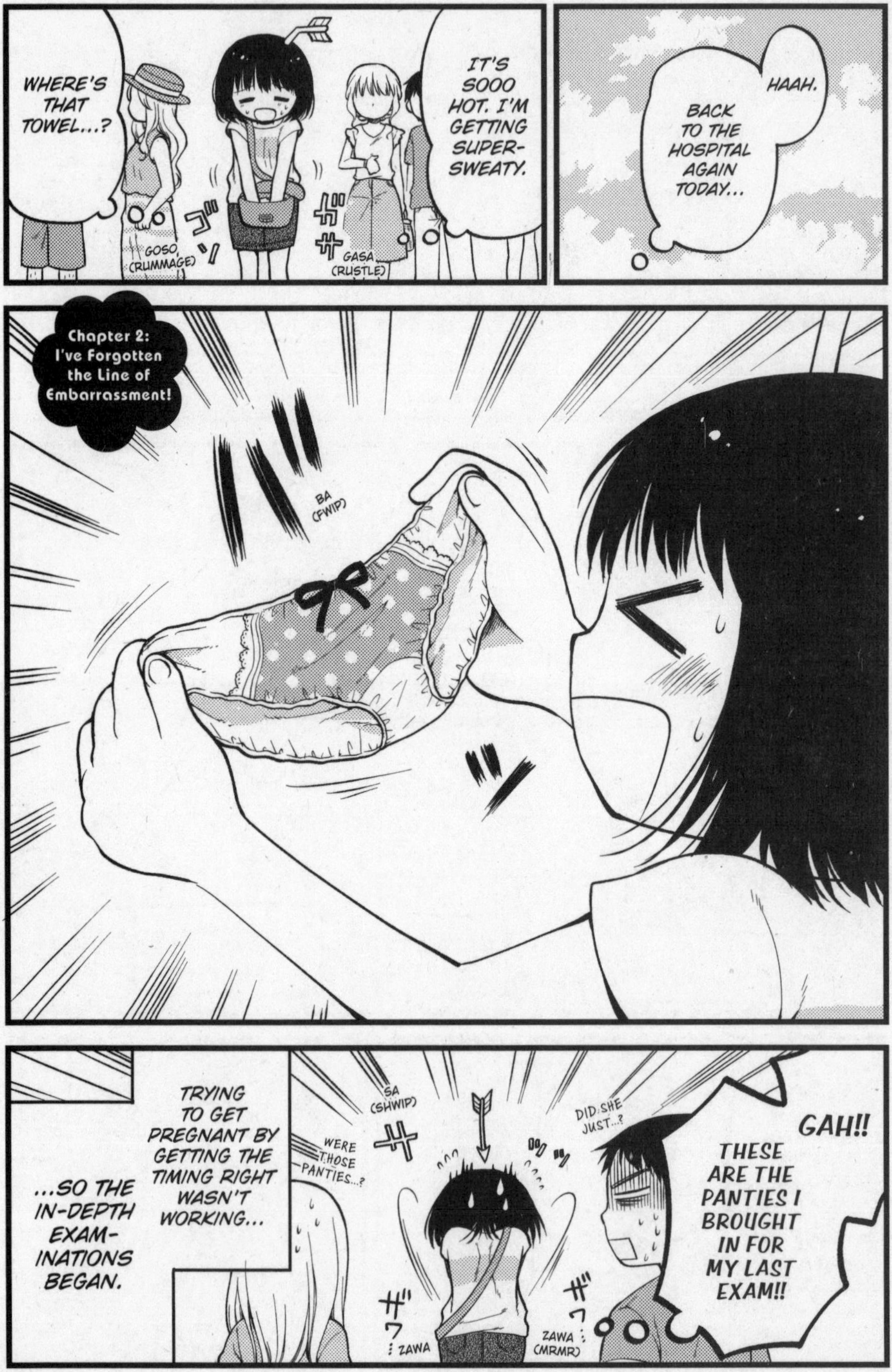
HAAH.
BACK TO THE HOSPITAL AGAIN TODAY...
IT'S SOOO HOT. I'M GETTING SUPER-SWEATY.
GASA (RUSTLE)
GOSO (RUMMAGE)
WHERE'S THAT TOWEL...?
Chapter 2: I've Forgotten the Line of Embarrassment!
BA (FWIP)
GAH!!
THESE ARE THE PANTIES I BROUGHT IN FOR MY LAST EXAM!!
DID SHE JUST...?
ZAWA (MRMR)
SA (SHWIP)
WERE THOSE PANTIES...?
ZAWA
TRYING TO GET PREGNANT BY GETTING THE TIMING RIGHT WASN'T WORKING...
...SO THE IN-DEPTH EXAM-INATIONS BEGAN.

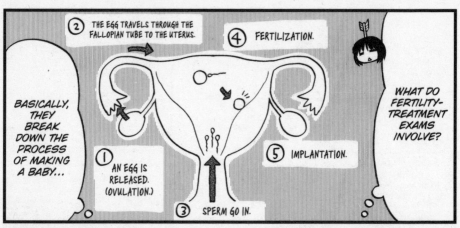

WHAT DO FERTILITY-TREATMENT EXAMS INVOLVE?
4 FERTILIZATION.
2 THE EGG TRAVELS THROUGH THE FALLOPIAN TUBE TO THE UTERUS.
5 IMPLANTATION.
1 AN EGG IS RELEASED. (OVULATION.)
3 SPERM GO IN.
BASICALLY, THEY BREAK DOWN THE PROCESS OF MAKING A BABY...
...AND LOOK AT EACH STEP VEEERY CLOSELY.
GOT 'EM!!
3 EXAM TO CHECK HUSBAND'S SPERM.
LIQUID INSERTED.
2 EXAM TO CHECK IF THE FALLOPIAN TUBES ARE BLOCKED.
JUST RELAX.
1 ULTRASOUND TO CHECK IF EGGS HAVE BEEN MATURING.
PERIOD BLOOD SAMPLE COLLECTION
TEST TO CHECK THE BACTERIA IN THE UTERUS.
URINE SAMPLE
TESTS TO CHECK HORMONE LEVELS.
BLOOD TEST
BUSURI (PSSK)
BLOOD TEST TO CHECK NUTRITIONAL LEVELS.
I CAN'T BELIEVE HOW MANY TESTS WE'VE DONE...
THIS HAS COST A TON OF MONEY TOO.
AND A LOT OF IT ISN'T COVERED BY HEALTH INSURANCE.
PLUS...
THIS NEXT TEST IS CALLED THE HUHNER TEST.
WE'LL EVALUATE HOW MANY SPERM ACTUALLY MAKE IT THROUGH THE CERVICAL MUCUS, SO...

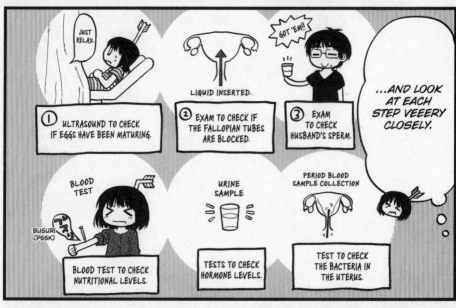

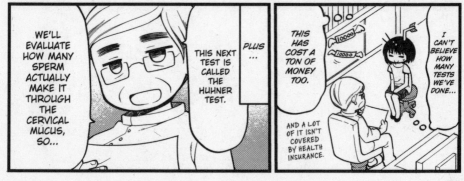

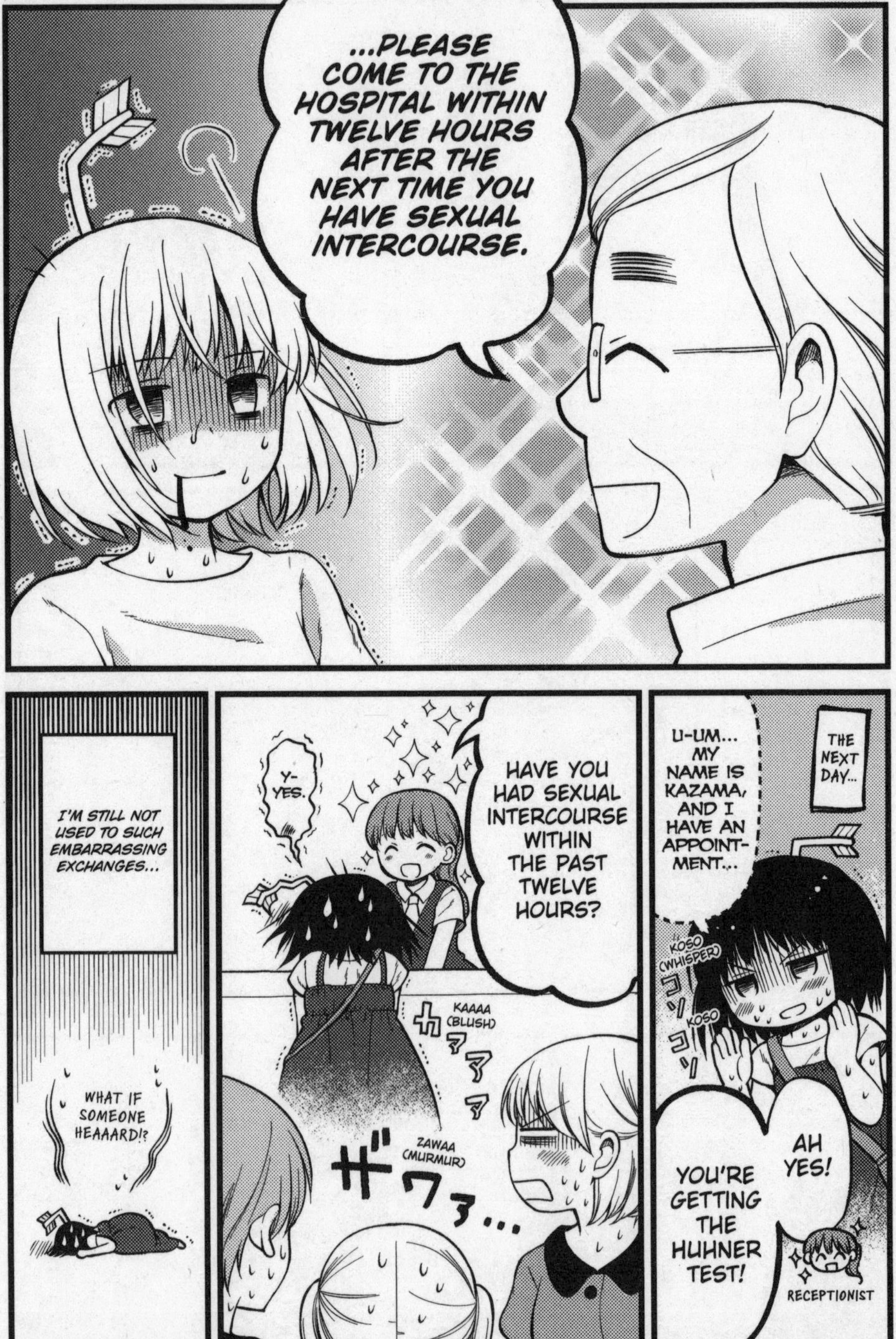
...PLEASE COME TO THE HOSPITAL WITHIN TWELVE HOURS AFTER THE NEXT TIME YOU HAVE SEXUAL INTERCOURSE.
THE NEXT DAY...
U-UM... MY NAME IS KAZAMA, AND I HAVE AN APPOINTMENT...
KOSO (WHISPER)
KOSO
AH YES!
YOU'RE GETTING THE HUHNER TEST!
RECEPTIONIST
HAVE YOU HAD SEXUAL INTERCOURSE WITHIN THE PAST TWELVE HOURS?
Y-YES.
KAAAA (BLUSH)
ZAWAA (MURMUR)
I'M STILL NOT USED TO SUCH EMBARRASSING EXCHANGES...
WHAT IF SOMEONE HEAAARD!?

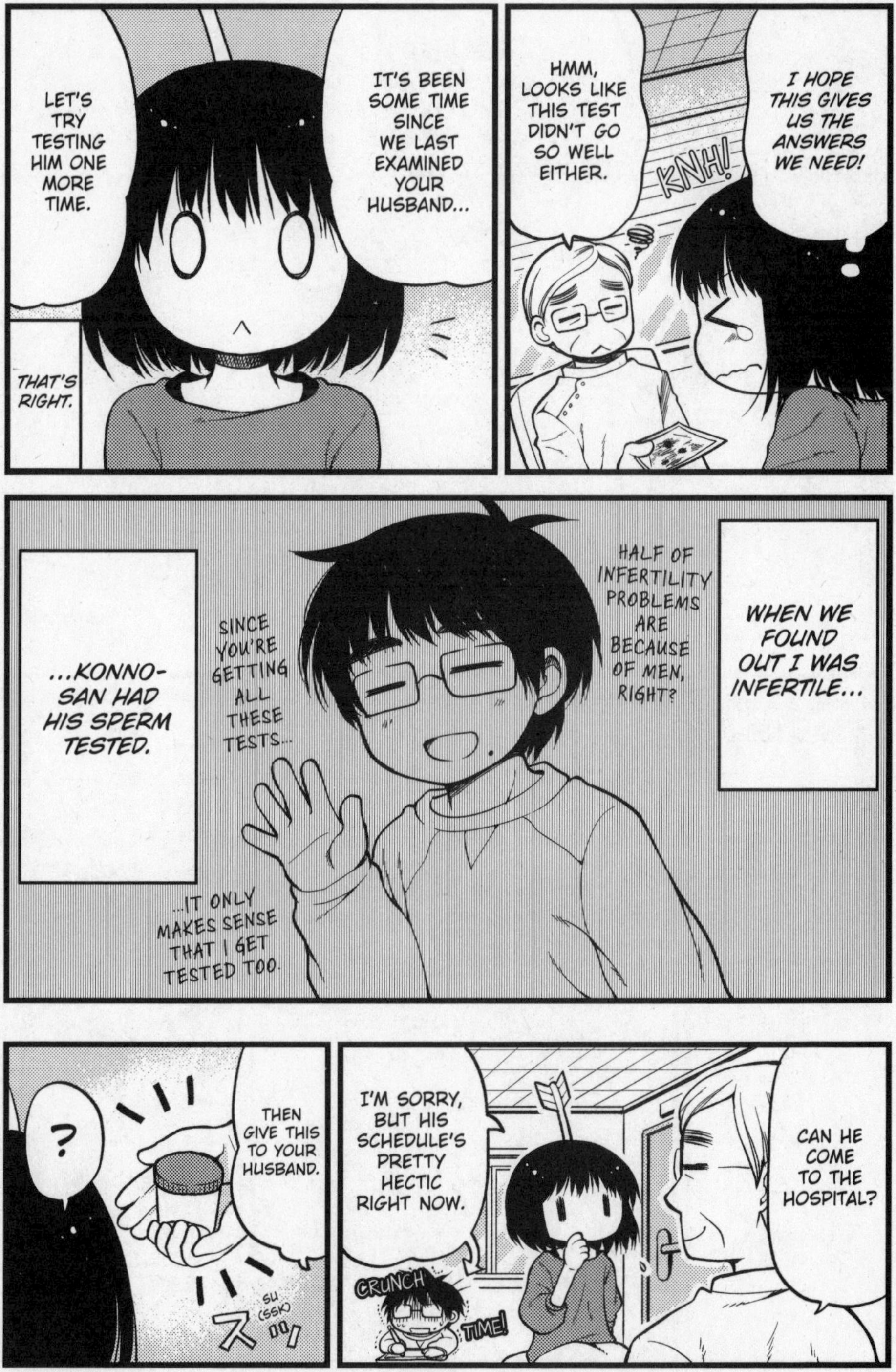
I HOPE THIS GIVES US THE ANSWERS WE NEED!
KNH!
HMM, LOOKS LIKE THIS TEST DIDN'T GO SO WELL EITHER.
IT'S BEEN SOME TIME SINCE WE LAST EXAMINED YOUR HUSBAND...
LET'S TRY TESTING HIM ONE MORE TIME.
THAT'S RIGHT.
WHEN WE FOUND OUT I WAS INFERTILE...
HALF OF INFERTILITY PROBLEMS ARE BECAUSE OF MEN, RIGHT?
SINCE YOU'RE GETTING ALL THESE TESTS...
...KONNO-SAN HAD HIS SPERM TESTED.
...IT ONLY MAKES SENSE THAT I GET TESTED TOO.
CAN HE COME TO THE HOSPITAL?
I'M SORRY, BUT HIS SCHEDULE'S PRETTY HECTIC RIGHT NOW.
CRUNCH
TIME!
THEN GIVE THIS TO YOUR HUSBAND.
?
ス
SU (SSK)

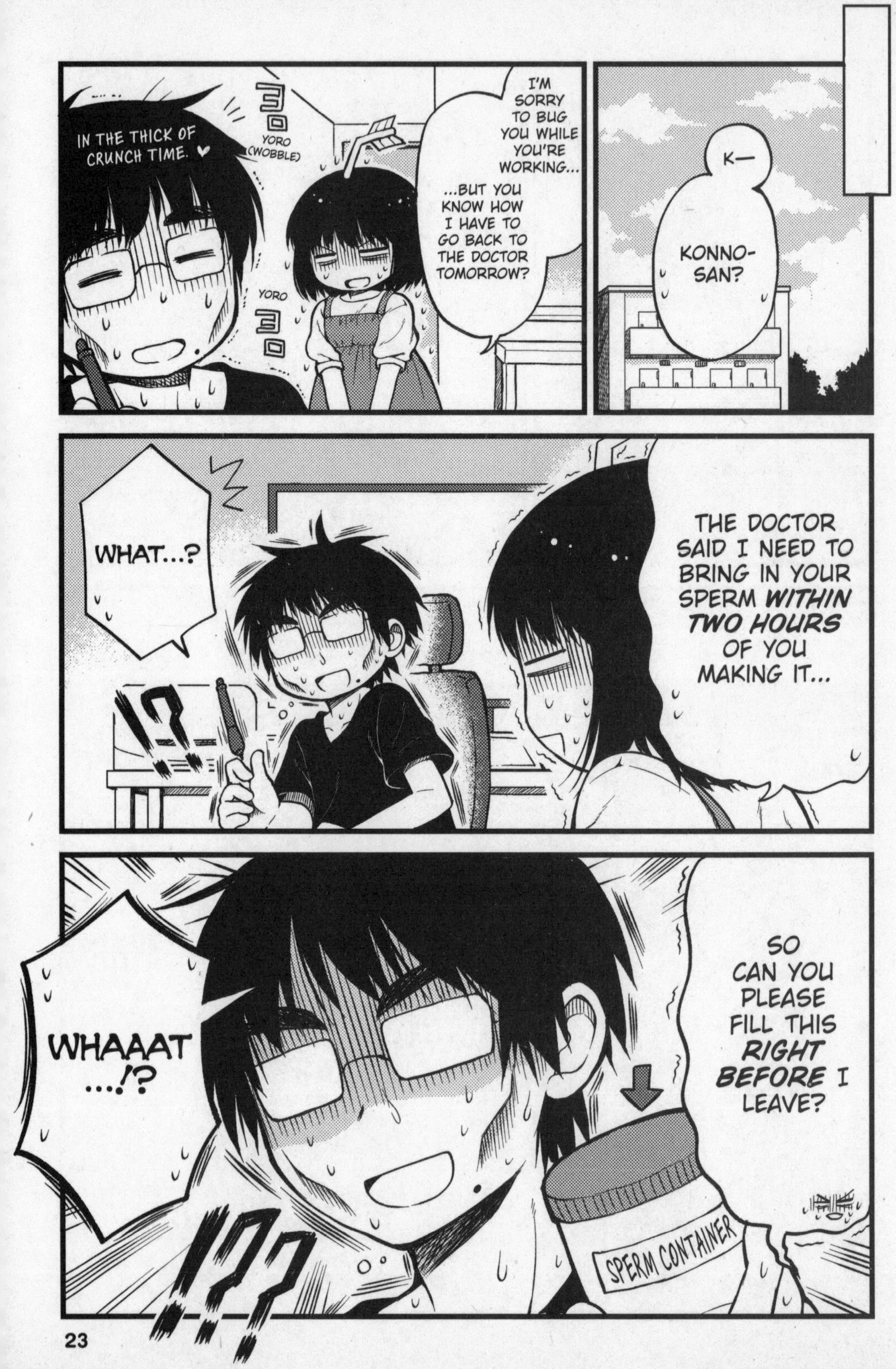
K—
KONNO-SAN?
I'M SORRY TO BUG YOU WHILE YOU'RE WORKING...
...BUT YOU KNOW HOW I HAVE TO GO BACK TO THE DOCTOR TOMORROW?
YORO (WOBBLE)
YORO
IN THE THICK OF CRUNCH TIME. ♥
THE DOCTOR SAID I NEED TO BRING IN YOUR SPERM ***WITHIN TWO HOURS*** OF YOU MAKING IT...
WHAT...?
!?
SO CAN YOU PLEASE FILL THIS ***RIGHT BEFORE*** I LEAVE?
SPERM CONTAINER
WHAAAT ...!?
!??

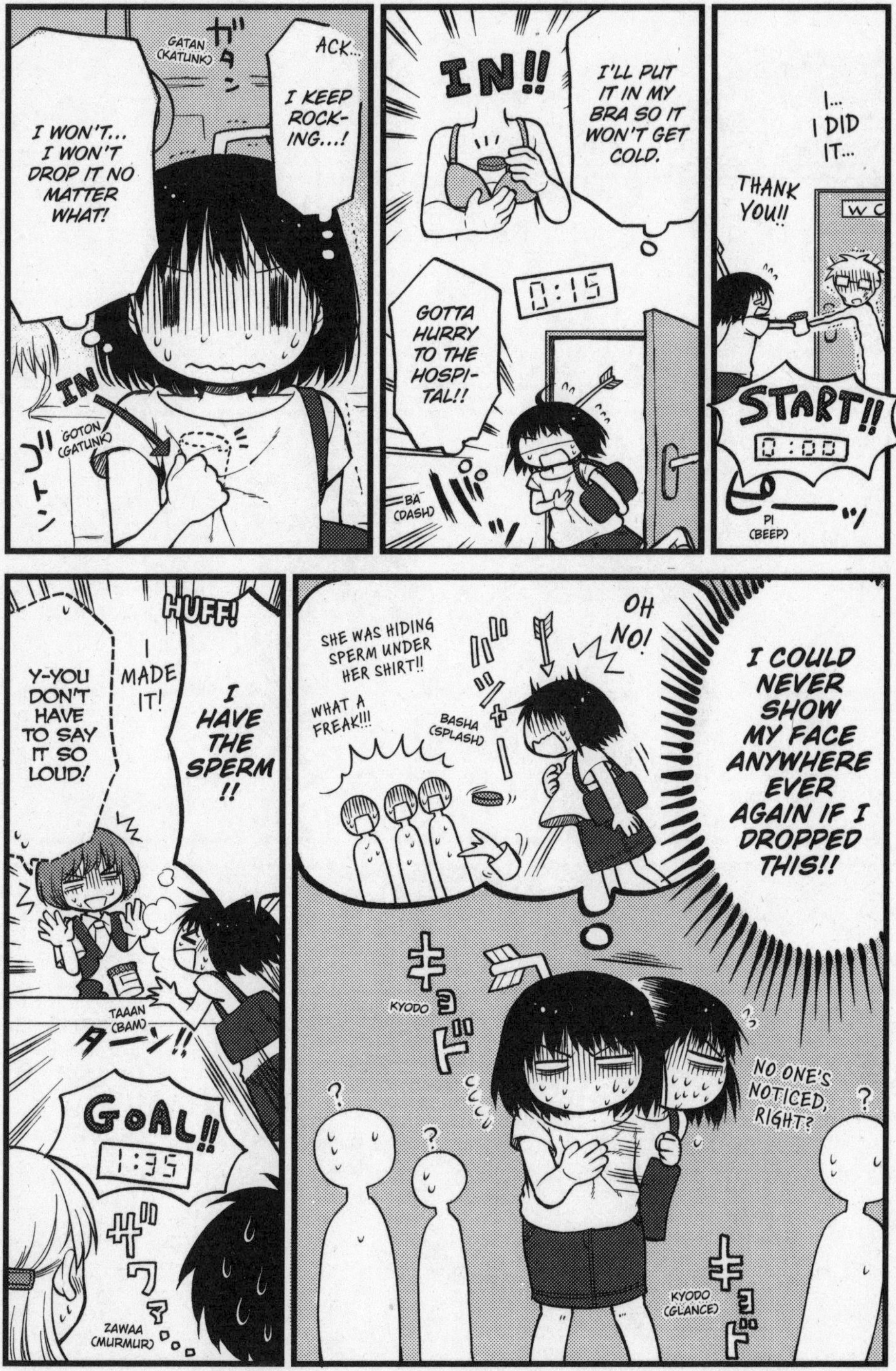
I... I DID IT...
THANK YOU!!
START!!
0:00
PI (BEEP)
IN!!
I'LL PUT IT IN MY BRA SO IT WON'T GET COLD.
0:15
GOTTA HURRY TO THE HOSPITAL!!
BA (DASH)
GATAN (KATUNK)
ACK...
I KEEP ROCKING...!
I WON'T... I WON'T DROP IT NO MATTER WHAT!
IN
GOTON (GATUNK)
I COULD NEVER SHOW MY FACE ANYWHERE EVER AGAIN IF I DROPPED THIS!!
OH NO!
SHE WAS HIDING SPERM UNDER HER SHIRT!!
WHAT A FREAK!!!
BASHA (SPLASH)
KYODO
NO ONE'S NOTICED, RIGHT?
KYODO (GLANCE)
HUFF!
I MADE IT!
I HAVE THE SPERM!!
Y-YOU DON'T HAVE TO SAY IT SO LOUD!
TAAAN (BAM)
GOAL!!
1:35
ZAWAA (MURMUR)

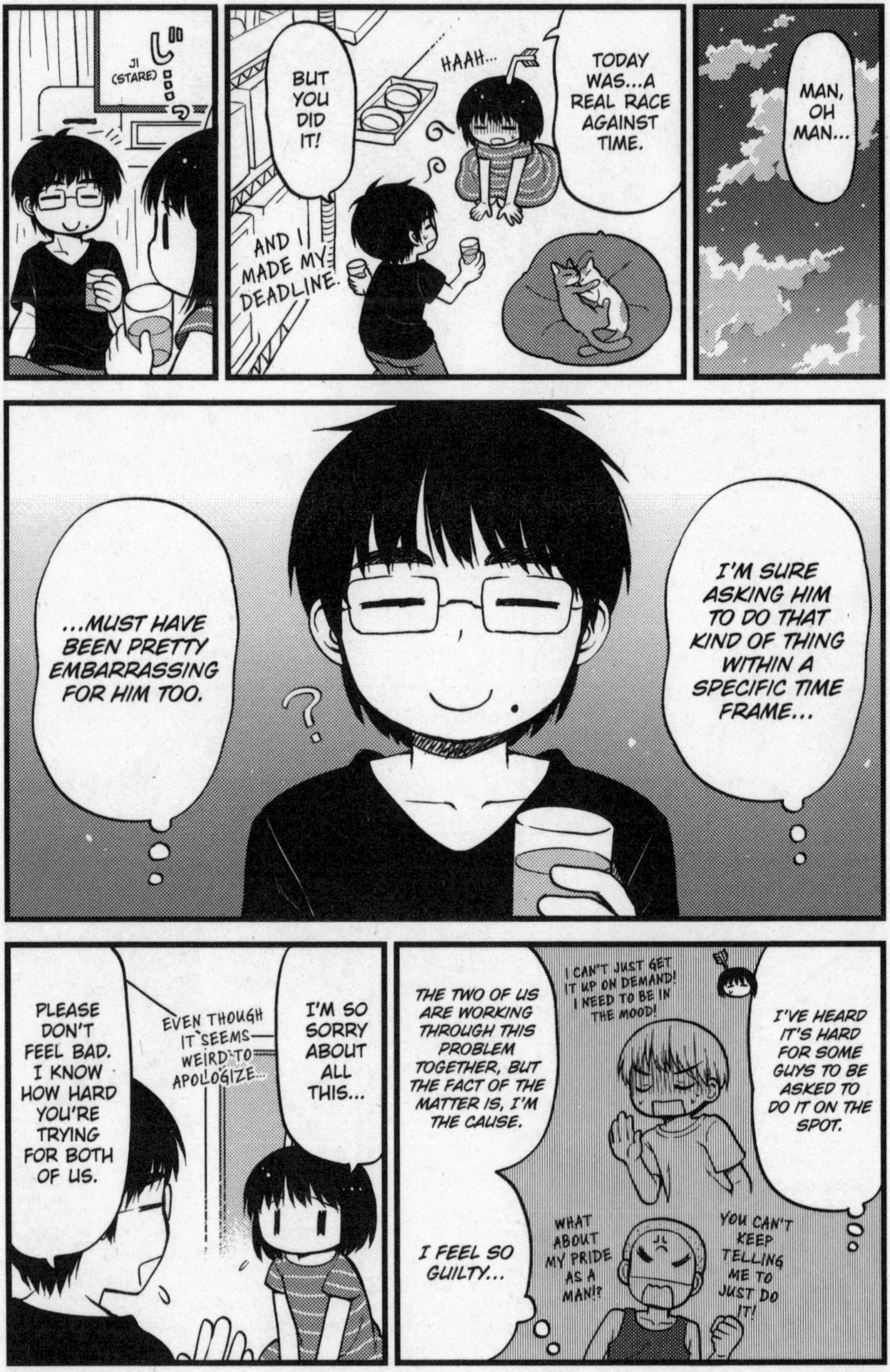
MAN, OH MAN...
TODAY WAS...A REAL RACE AGAINST TIME.
HAAH...
BUT YOU DID IT!
AND I MADE MY DEADLINE.
JI (STARE)
I'M SURE ASKING HIM TO DO THAT KIND OF THING WITHIN A SPECIFIC TIME FRAME...
...MUST HAVE BEEN PRETTY EMBARRASSING FOR HIM TOO.
I'VE HEARD IT'S HARD FOR SOME GUYS TO BE ASKED TO DO IT ON THE SPOT.
I CAN'T JUST GET IT UP ON DEMAND! I NEED TO BE IN THE MOOD!
THE TWO OF US ARE WORKING THROUGH THIS PROBLEM TOGETHER, BUT THE FACT OF THE MATTER IS, I'M THE CAUSE.
YOU CAN'T KEEP TELLING ME TO JUST DO IT!
WHAT ABOUT MY PRIDE AS A MAN!?
I FEEL SO GUILTY...
I'M SO SORRY ABOUT ALL THIS...
EVEN THOUGH IT SEEMS WEIRD TO APOLOGIZE...
PLEASE DON'T FEEL BAD. I KNOW HOW HARD YOU'RE TRYING FOR BOTH OF US.

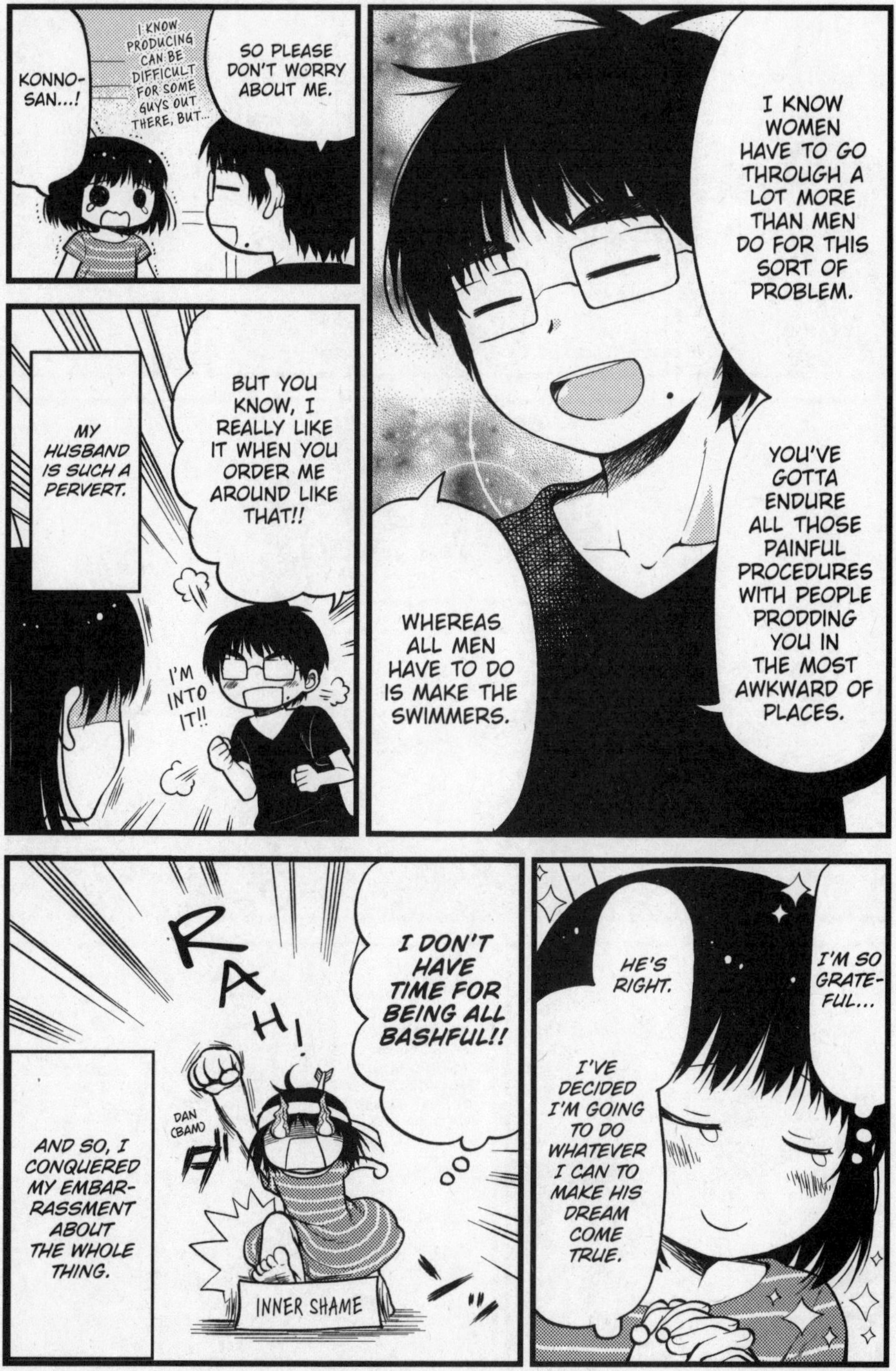
I KNOW WOMEN HAVE TO GO THROUGH A LOT MORE THAN MEN DO FOR THIS SORT OF PROBLEM.
YOU'VE GOTTA ENDURE ALL THOSE PAINFUL PROCEDURES WITH PEOPLE PRODDING YOU IN THE MOST AWKWARD OF PLACES.
WHEREAS ALL MEN HAVE TO DO IS MAKE THE SWIMMERS.
I KNOW PRODUCING CAN BE DIFFICULT FOR SOME GUYS OUT THERE, BUT...
SO PLEASE DON'T WORRY ABOUT ME.
KONNO-SAN...!
BUT YOU KNOW, I REALLY LIKE IT WHEN YOU ORDER ME AROUND LIKE THAT!!
I'M INTO IT!!
MY HUSBAND IS SUCH A PERVERT.
HE'S RIGHT.
I'M SO GRATEFUL...
I'VE DECIDED I'M GOING TO DO WHATEVER I CAN TO MAKE HIS DREAM COME TRUE.
RAH!
I DON'T HAVE TIME FOR BEING ALL BASHFUL!!
DAN (BAM)
INNER SHAME
AND SO, I CONQUERED MY EMBARRASSMENT ABOUT THE WHOLE THING.

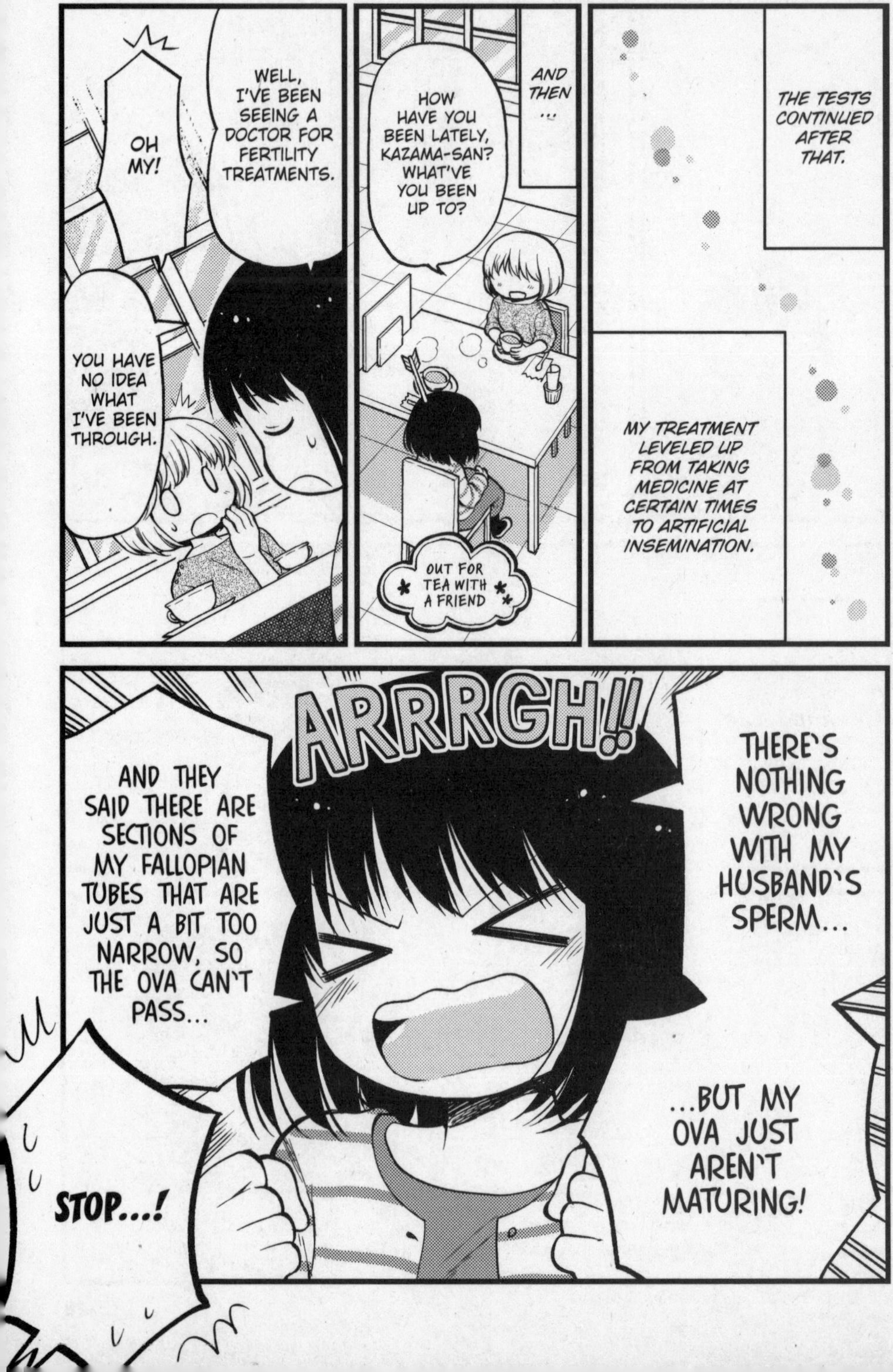
THE TESTS CONTINUED AFTER THAT.
MY TREATMENT LEVELED UP FROM TAKING MEDICINE AT CERTAIN TIMES TO ARTIFICIAL INSEMINATION.
AND THEN ...
HOW HAVE YOU BEEN LATELY, KAZAMA-SAN? WHAT'VE YOU BEEN UP TO?
OUT FOR TEA WITH A FRIEND
WELL, I'VE BEEN SEEING A DOCTOR FOR FERTILITY TREATMENTS.
OH MY!
YOU HAVE NO IDEA WHAT I'VE BEEN THROUGH.
THERE'S NOTHING WRONG WITH MY HUSBAND'S SPERM...
ARRRGH!!
AND THEY SAID THERE ARE SECTIONS OF MY FALLOPIAN TUBES THAT ARE JUST A BIT TOO NARROW, SO THE OVA CAN'T PASS...
...BUT MY OVA JUST AREN'T MATURING!
STOP...!

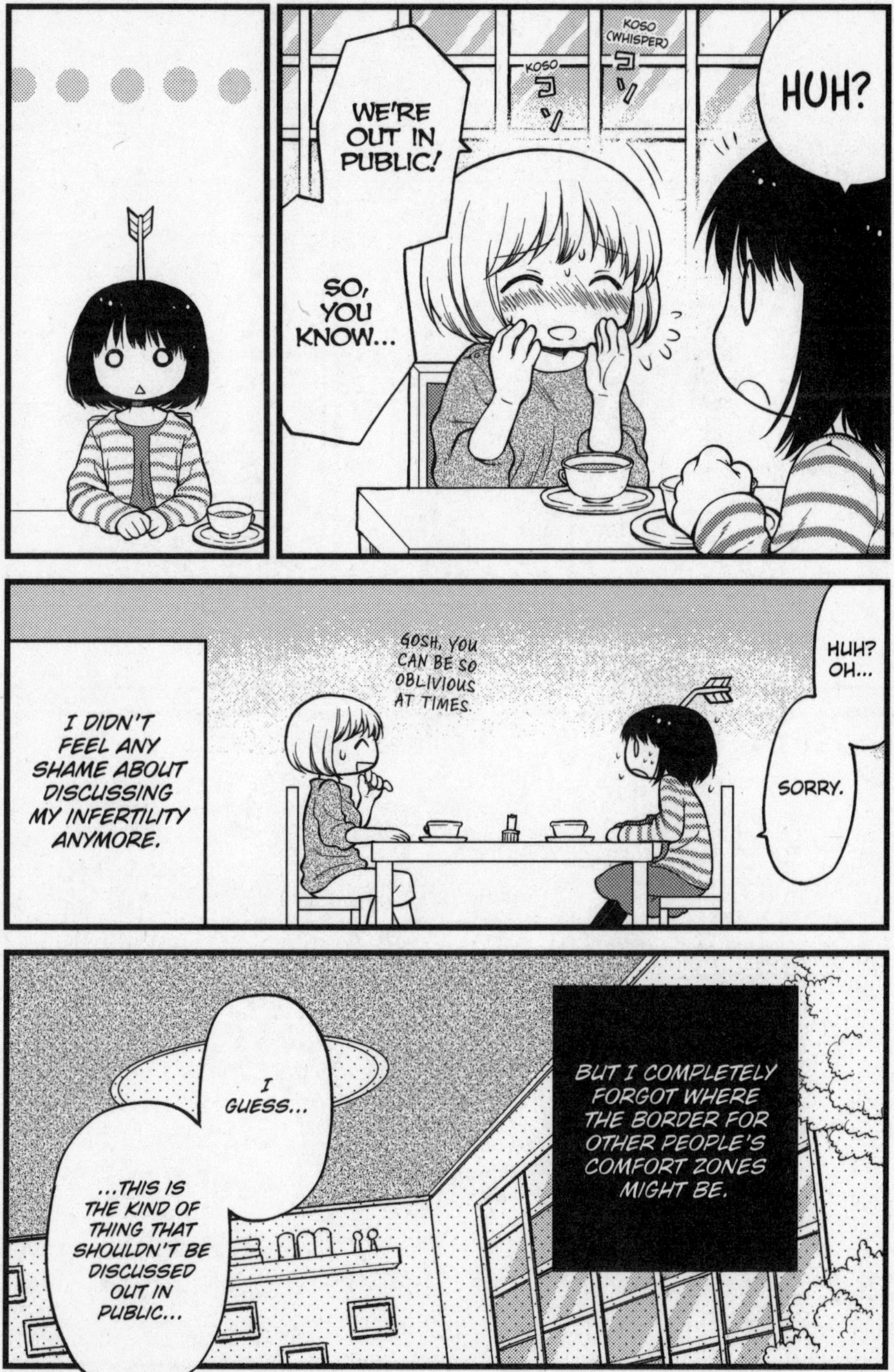

HUH?
KOSO (WHISPER)
KOSO
WE'RE OUT IN PUBLIC!
SO, YOU KNOW...
HUH? OH...
SORRY.
GOSH, YOU CAN BE SO OBLIVIOUS AT TIMES.
I DIDN'T FEEL ANY SHAME ABOUT DISCUSSING MY INFERTILITY ANYMORE.
BUT I COMPLETELY FORGOT WHERE THE BORDER FOR OTHER PEOPLE'S COMFORT ZONES MIGHT BE.
I GUESS...
...THIS IS THE KIND OF THING THAT SHOULDN'T BE DISCUSSED OUT IN PUBLIC...

Chapter 2:
I've Forgotten the Line of Embarrassment!

Bonus manga by Azure Konno

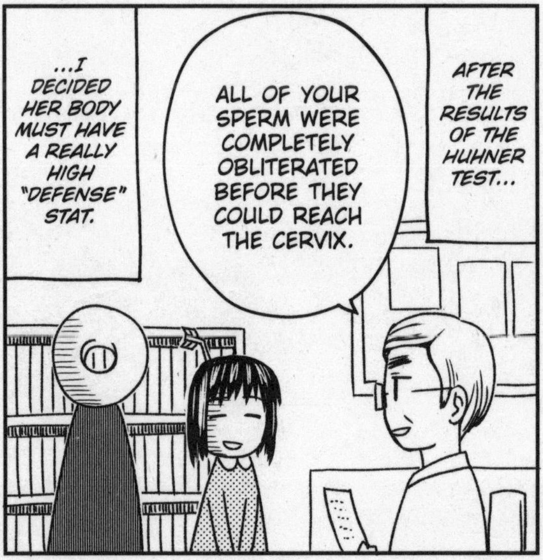
AFTER THE RESULTS OF THE HUHNER TEST...
ALL OF YOUR SPERM WERE COMPLETELY OBLITERATED BEFORE THEY COULD REACH THE CERVIX.
...I DECIDED HER BODY MUST HAVE A REALLY HIGH "DEFENSE" STAT.

I've seen her pull a lot of things out of her bag in the past. For example, she once pulled out a battery when she meant to take out her lip balm.
The fertility clinic has a room they call the "collection room." It's not that big, but it has a couch, porn DVDs, books, and a few other amenities.
This is where you're supposed to produce the sample.
I'm sure there are some who would rather not talk about how they felt in one of these rooms. But I actually got pretty excited about it.
"This is a room just for me to jerk off in? That's kinda hot! Awesome!!"
Kazama-san was a little weirded out by my excitement, though.

Bonus manga by Ayami Kazama

Chapter 2: I've Forgotten the Line of Embarrassment!

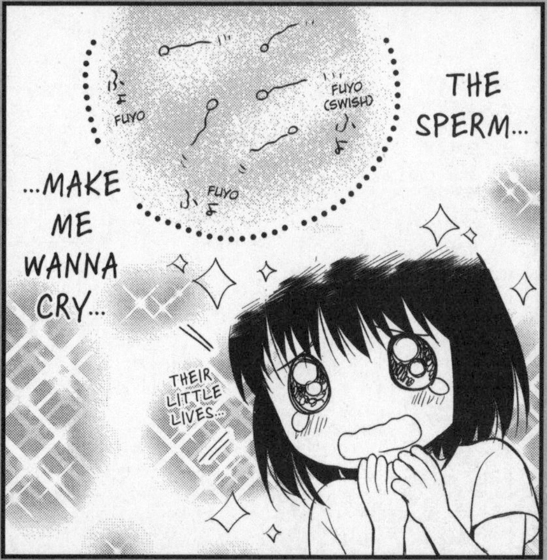
THE SPERM...
FUYO (SWISH)
FUYO
FUYO
...MAKE ME WANNA CRY...
THEIR LITTLE LIVES...

I saw sperm for the first time during my fertility treatments! It felt so surreal.
There were some that were happily swimming around, and others were just sitting still. I felt almost as if each of them was an individual child. I couldn't help but find them adorable.
But only one of them can survive...
And even then you don't know if the sperm will successfully fertilize the egg, and even if it is fertilized, will the egg be able to implant?
Once I thought about it that way, I got to thinking how all humans alive today were born because they made it through this fierce struggle for survival, and the thought made me break down and cry for some reason.
The fact that we're alive is amazing. Absolutely amazing.
When someone is depressed, I'm thinking of telling them that they were born because they beat out over a hundred million sperm and that they are actually pretty amazing. Just kidding. I think it might scare them off.

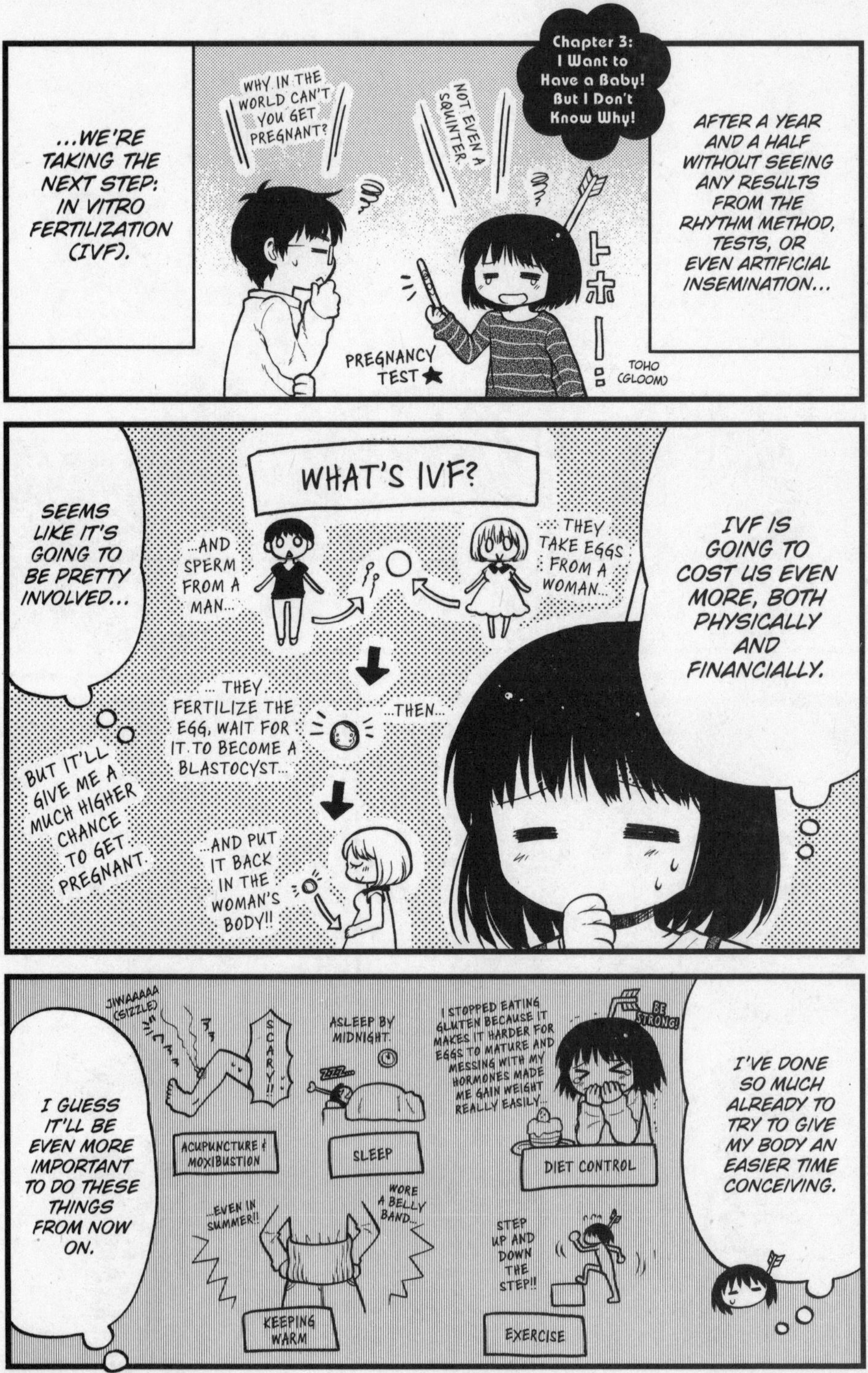
AFTER A YEAR AND A HALF WITHOUT SEEING ANY RESULTS FROM THE RHYTHM METHOD, TESTS, OR EVEN ARTIFICIAL INSEMINATION...
Chapter 3: I Want to Have a Baby! But I Don't Know Why!
NOT EVEN A SQUINTER.
WHY IN THE WORLD CAN'T YOU GET PREGNANT?
トホー!
TOHO (GLOOM)
PREGNANCY TEST★
...WE'RE TAKING THE NEXT STEP: IN VITRO FERTILIZATION (IVF).
IVF IS GOING TO COST US EVEN MORE, BOTH PHYSICALLY AND FINANCIALLY.
WHAT'S IVF?
THEY TAKE EGGS FROM A WOMAN...
...AND SPERM FROM A MAN...
...THEN...
...THEY FERTILIZE THE EGG, WAIT FOR IT TO BECOME A BLASTOCYST...
...AND PUT IT BACK IN THE WOMAN'S BODY!!
BUT IT'LL GIVE ME A MUCH HIGHER CHANCE TO GET PREGNANT.
SEEMS LIKE IT'S GOING TO BE PRETTY INVOLVED...
I'VE DONE SO MUCH ALREADY TO TRY TO GIVE MY BODY AN EASIER TIME CONCEIVING.
BE STRONG!
I STOPPED EATING GLUTEN BECAUSE IT MAKES IT HARDER FOR EGGS TO MATURE AND MESSING WITH MY HORMONES MADE ME GAIN WEIGHT REALLY EASILY...
DIET CONTROL
ASLEEP BY MIDNIGHT.
SLEEP
SCARY!!
JIWAAAAA (SIZZLE)
ACUPUNCTURE & MOXIBUSTION
STEP UP AND DOWN THE STEP!!
EXERCISE
WORE A BELLY BAND...
...EVEN IN SUMMER!!
KEEPING WARM
I GUESS IT'LL BE EVEN MORE IMPORTANT TO DO THESE THINGS FROM NOW ON.

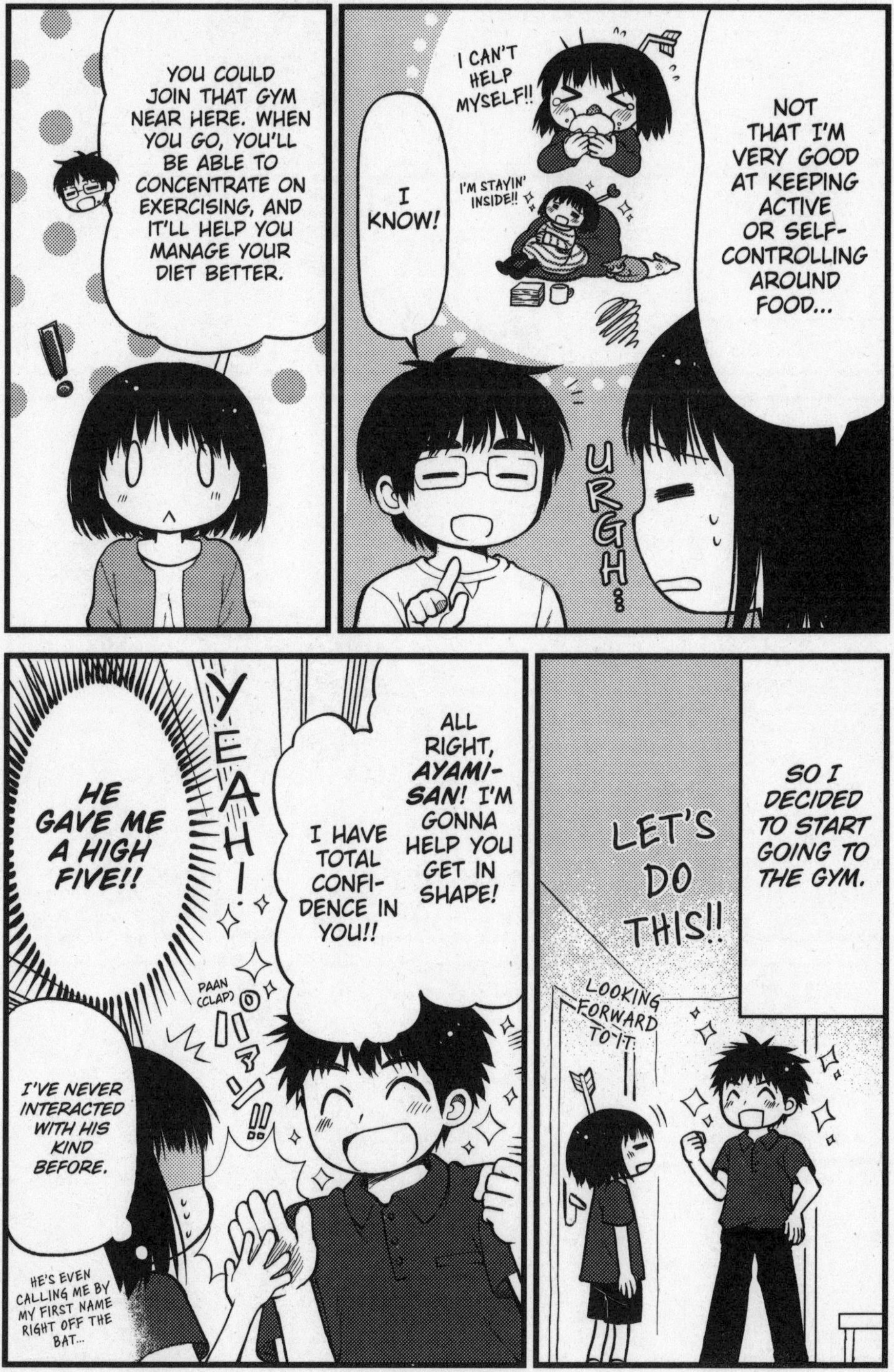
NOT THAT I'M VERY GOOD AT KEEPING ACTIVE OR SELF-CONTROLLING AROUND FOOD...
I CAN'T HELP MYSELF!!
I'M STAYIN' INSIDE!!
I KNOW!
URGH..
YOU COULD JOIN THAT GYM NEAR HERE. WHEN YOU GO, YOU'LL BE ABLE TO CONCENTRATE ON EXERCISING, AND IT'LL HELP YOU MANAGE YOUR DIET BETTER.
SO I DECIDED TO START GOING TO THE GYM.
LET'S DO THIS!!
LOOKING FORWARD TO IT.
ALL RIGHT, *AYAMI-SAN*! I'M GONNA HELP YOU GET IN SHAPE!
I HAVE TOTAL CONFIDENCE IN YOU!!
YEAH!
PAAN (CLAP)
HE GAVE ME A HIGH FIVE!!
I'VE NEVER INTERACTED WITH HIS KIND BEFORE.
HE'S EVEN CALLING ME BY MY FIRST NAME RIGHT OFF THE BAT...

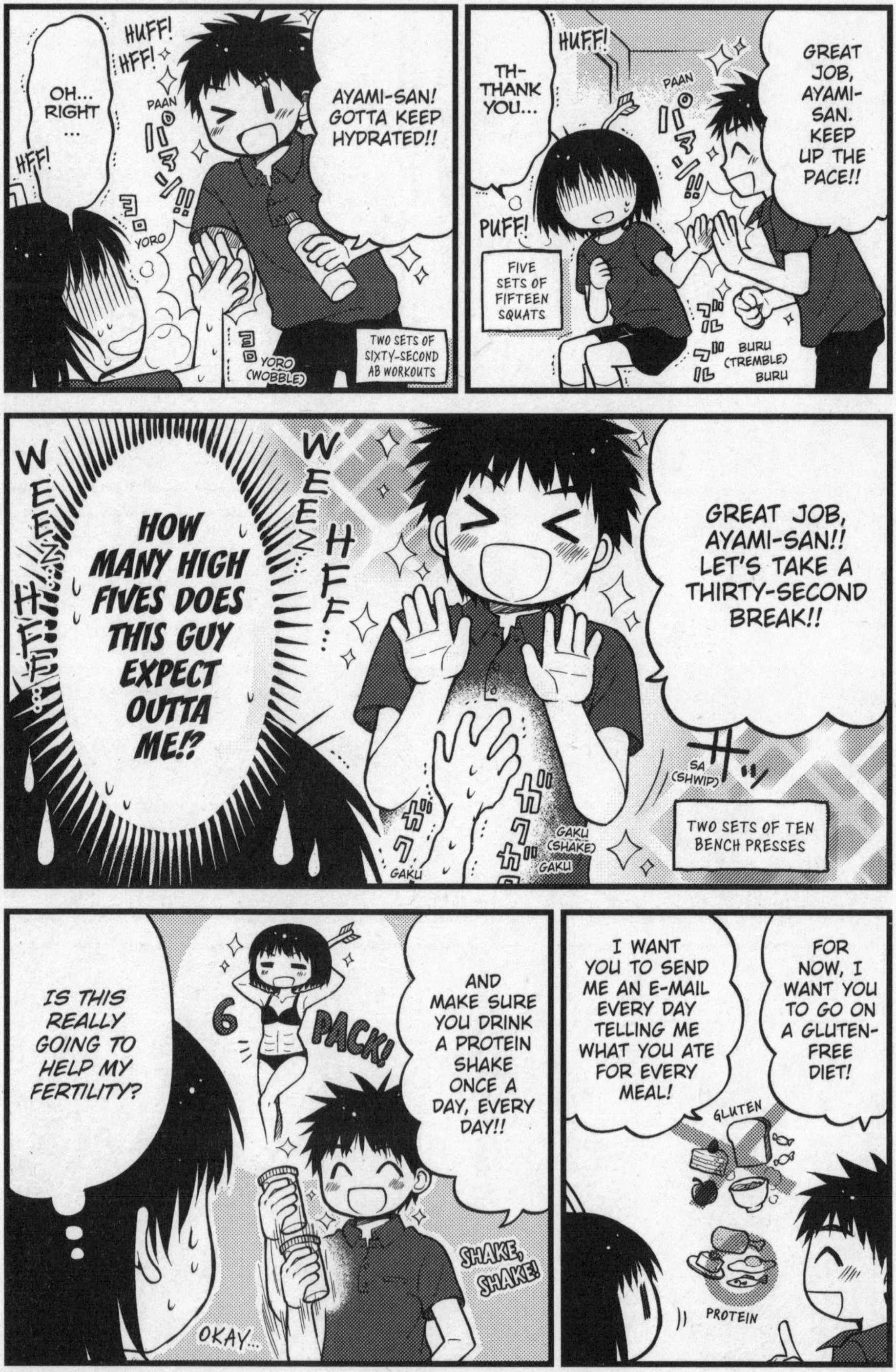
GREAT JOB, AYAMI-SAN. KEEP UP THE PACE!!
HUFF!
TH-THANK YOU...
PAAN
PUFF!
FIVE SETS OF FIFTEEN SQUATS
BURU (TREMBLE) BURU
AYAMI-SAN! GOTTA KEEP HYDRATED!!
HUFF! HFF!
OH... RIGHT ...
PAAN
HFF!
YORO
YORO (WOBBLE)
TWO SETS OF SIXTY-SECOND AB WORKOUTS
GREAT JOB, AYAMI-SAN!! LET'S TAKE A THIRTY-SECOND BREAK!!
SA (SHWIP)
TWO SETS OF TEN BENCH PRESSES
GAKU (SHAKE) GAKU
GAKU
WEEZ... HFF...
HOW MANY HIGH FIVES DOES THIS GUY EXPECT OUTTA ME!?
WEEZ... HFF...
FOR NOW, I WANT YOU TO GO ON A GLUTEN-FREE DIET!
I WANT YOU TO SEND ME AN E-MAIL EVERY DAY TELLING ME WHAT YOU ATE FOR EVERY MEAL!
GLUTEN
PROTEIN
AND MAKE SURE YOU DRINK A PROTEIN SHAKE ONCE A DAY, EVERY DAY!!
6 PACK!
SHAKE, SHAKE!
IS THIS REALLY GOING TO HELP MY FERTILITY?
OKAY...

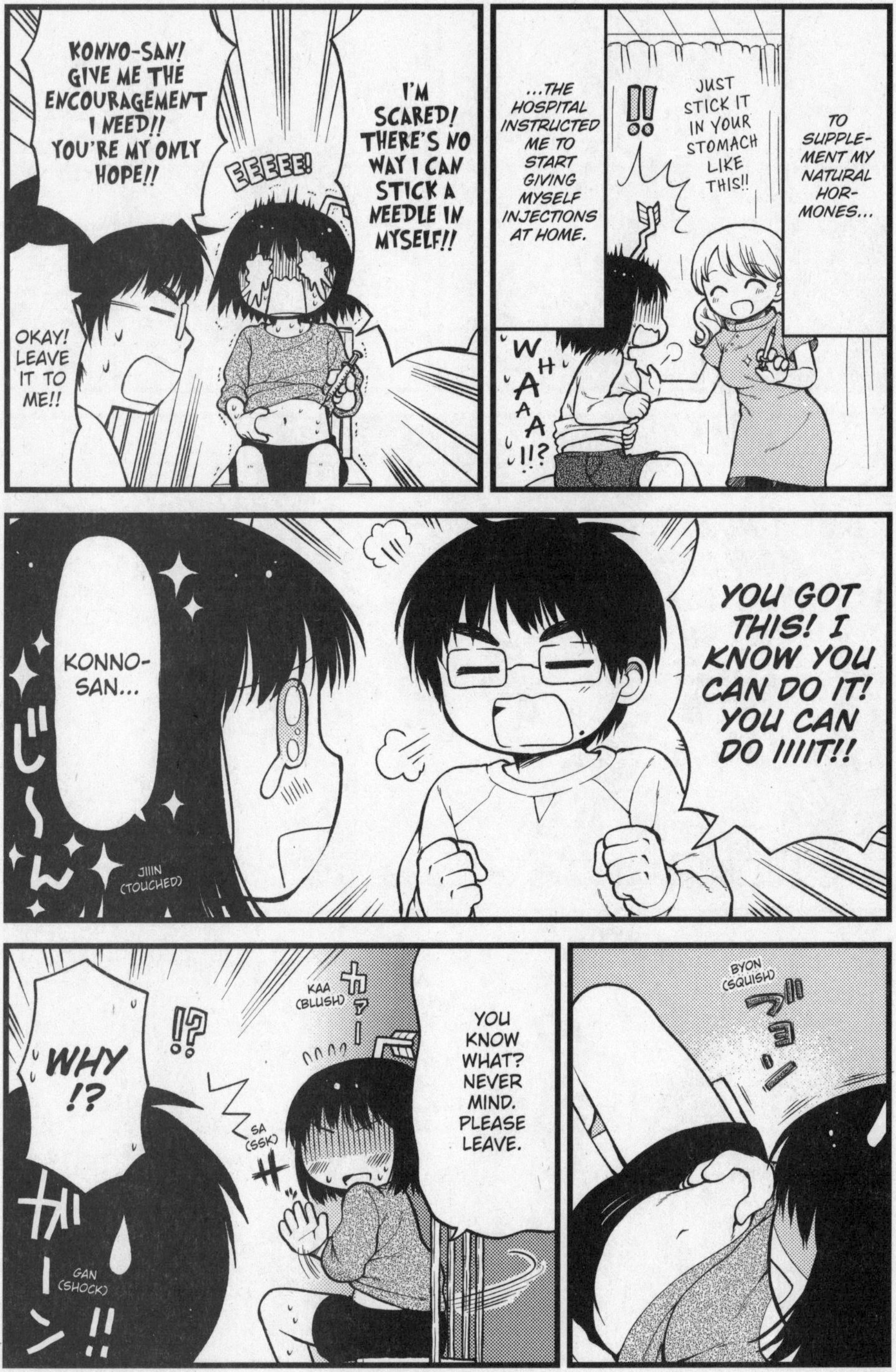
TO SUPPLEMENT MY NATURAL HORMONES...
JUST STICK IT IN YOUR STOMACH LIKE THIS!!
!!
...THE HOSPITAL INSTRUCTED ME TO START GIVING MYSELF INJECTIONS AT HOME.
WHAAAA!!?
I'M SCARED! THERE'S NO WAY I CAN STICK A NEEDLE IN MYSELF!!
EEEEE!
KONNO-SAN! GIVE ME THE ENCOURAGEMENT I NEED!! YOU'RE MY ONLY HOPE!!
OKAY! LEAVE IT TO ME!!
YOU GOT THIS! I KNOW YOU CAN DO IT! YOU CAN DO IIIIT!!
KONNO-SAN...
JIIIN (TOUCHED)
BYON (SQUISH)
YOU KNOW WHAT? NEVER MIND. PLEASE LEAVE.
KAA (BLUSH)
SA (SSK)
!?
WHY!?
GAN (SHOCK)

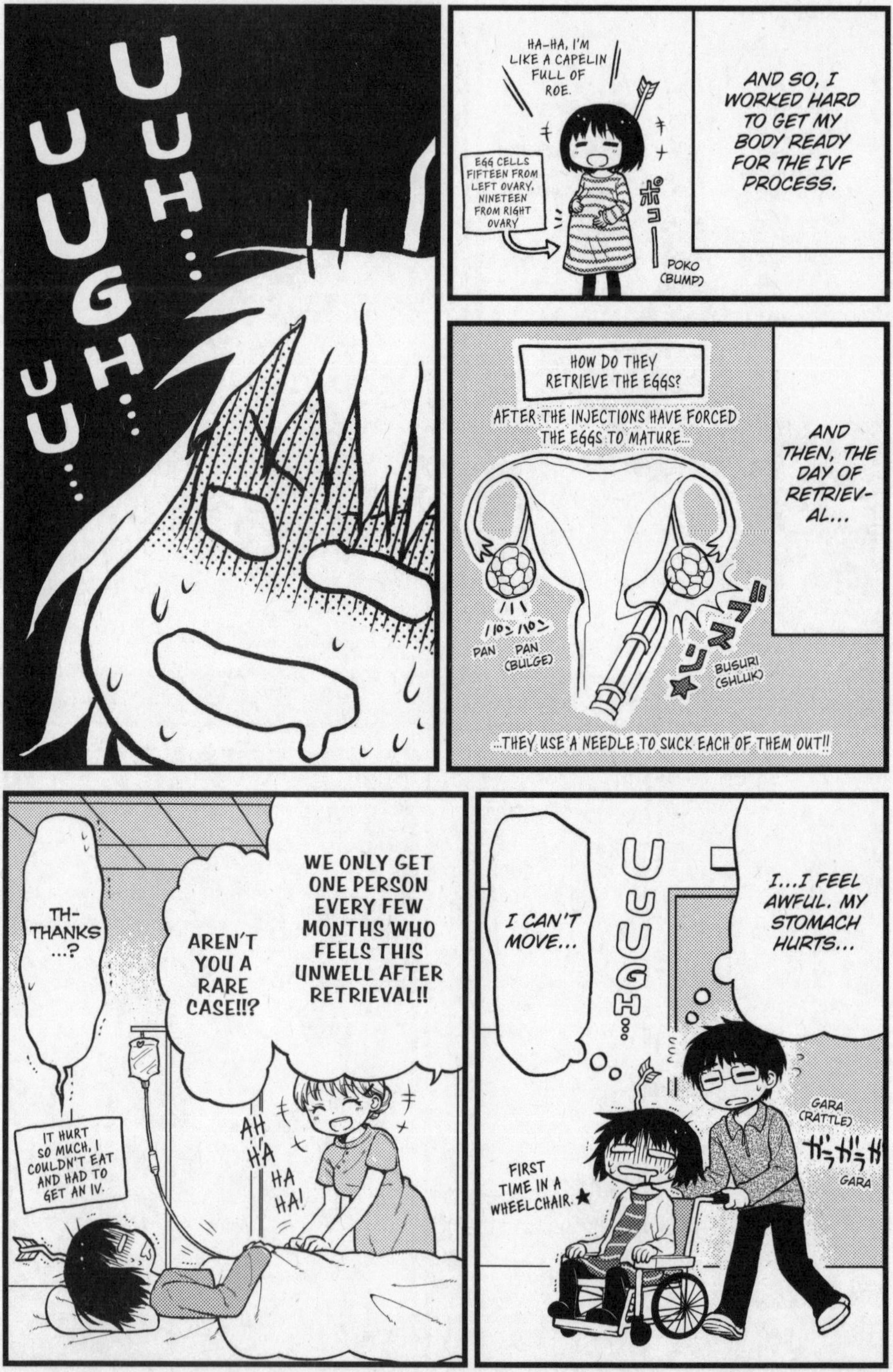
AND SO, I WORKED HARD TO GET MY BODY READY FOR THE IVF PROCESS.
HA-HA, I'M LIKE A CAPELIN FULL OF ROE.
EGG CELLS FIFTEEN FROM LEFT OVARY, NINETEEN FROM RIGHT OVARY
POKO (BUMP)
AND THEN, THE DAY OF RETRIEV-AL...
HOW DO THEY RETRIEVE THE EGGS?
AFTER THE INJECTIONS HAVE FORCED THE EGGS TO MATURE...
PAN PAN (BULGE)
BUSURI (SHLUK)
...THEY USE A NEEDLE TO SUCK EACH OF THEM OUT!!
UUH...
UUGH...
UU...
I...I FEEL AWFUL. MY STOMACH HURTS...
UUUGH...
I CAN'T MOVE...
GARA (RATTLE) GARA
FIRST TIME IN A WHEELCHAIR.
WE ONLY GET ONE PERSON EVERY FEW MONTHS WHO FEELS THIS UNWELL AFTER RETRIEVAL!!
AREN'T YOU A RARE CASE!!?
TH-THANKS ...?
AH HA HA HA!
IT HURT SO MUCH, I COULDN'T EAT AND HAD TO GET AN IV.

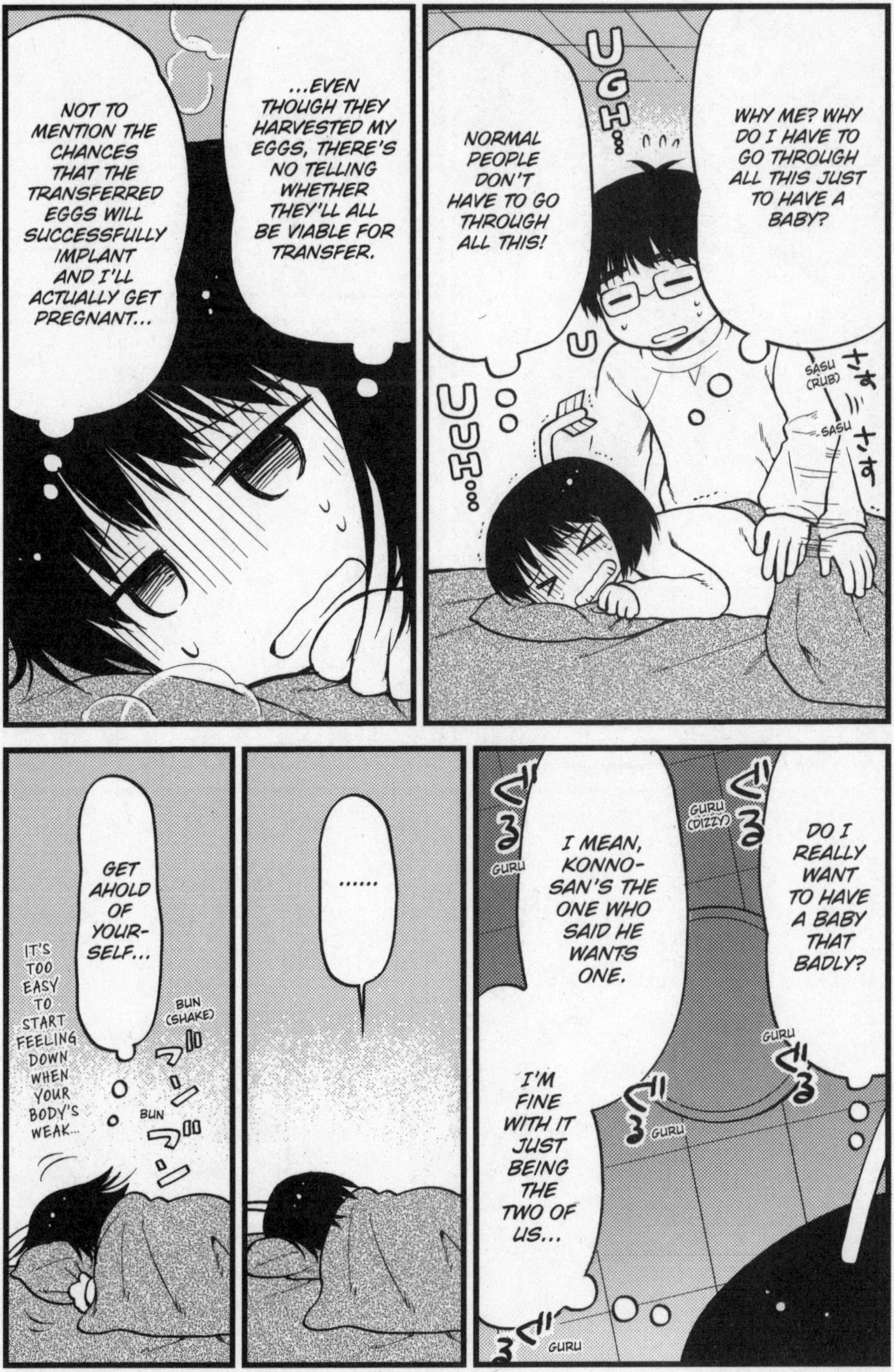
WHY ME? WHY DO I HAVE TO GO THROUGH ALL THIS JUST TO HAVE A BABY?
NORMAL PEOPLE DON'T HAVE TO GO THROUGH ALL THIS!
UGH...
U
UUH...
SASU (RUB)
さす
SASU
さす
...EVEN THOUGH THEY HARVESTED MY EGGS, THERE'S NO TELLING WHETHER THEY'LL ALL BE VIABLE FOR TRANSFER.
NOT TO MENTION THE CHANCES THAT THE TRANSFERRED EGGS WILL SUCCESSFULLY IMPLANT AND I'LL ACTUALLY GET PREGNANT...
DO I REALLY WANT TO HAVE A BABY THAT BADLY?
GURU (DIZZY)
ぐる
I MEAN, KONNO-SAN'S THE ONE WHO SAID HE WANTS ONE.
GURU
ぐる
GURU
ぐる
GURU
ぐる
I'M FINE WITH IT JUST BEING THE TWO OF US...
GURU
ぐる
......
GET AHOLD OF YOURSELF...
IT'S TOO EASY TO START FEELING DOWN WHEN YOUR BODY'S WEAK...
BUN (SHAKE)
BUN

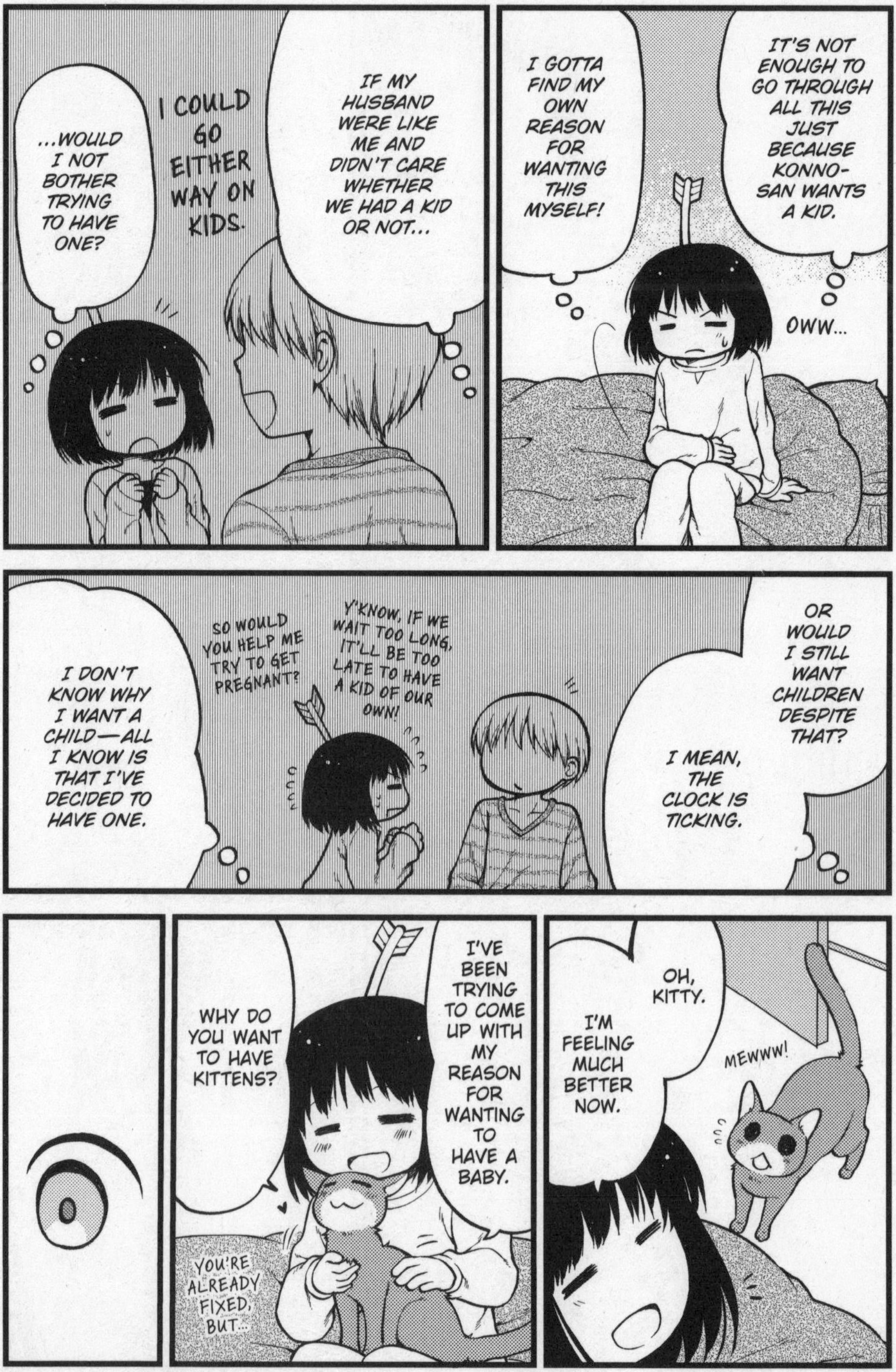
IT'S NOT ENOUGH TO GO THROUGH ALL THIS JUST BECAUSE KONNO-SAN WANTS A KID.
I GOTTA FIND MY OWN REASON FOR WANTING THIS MYSELF!
OWW...
IF MY HUSBAND WERE LIKE ME AND DIDN'T CARE WHETHER WE HAD A KID OR NOT...
I COULD GO EITHER WAY ON KIDS.
...WOULD I NOT BOTHER TRYING TO HAVE ONE?
OR WOULD I STILL WANT CHILDREN DESPITE THAT?
I MEAN, THE CLOCK IS TICKING.
Y'KNOW, IF WE WAIT TOO LONG, IT'LL BE TOO LATE TO HAVE A KID OF OUR OWN!
SO WOULD YOU HELP ME TRY TO GET PREGNANT?
I DON'T KNOW WHY I WANT A CHILD—ALL I KNOW IS THAT I'VE DECIDED TO HAVE ONE.
OH, KITTY.
I'M FEELING MUCH BETTER NOW.
MEWWW!
I'VE BEEN TRYING TO COME UP WITH MY REASON FOR WANTING TO HAVE A BABY.
WHY DO YOU WANT TO HAVE KITTENS?
YOU'RE ALREADY FIXED, BUT...

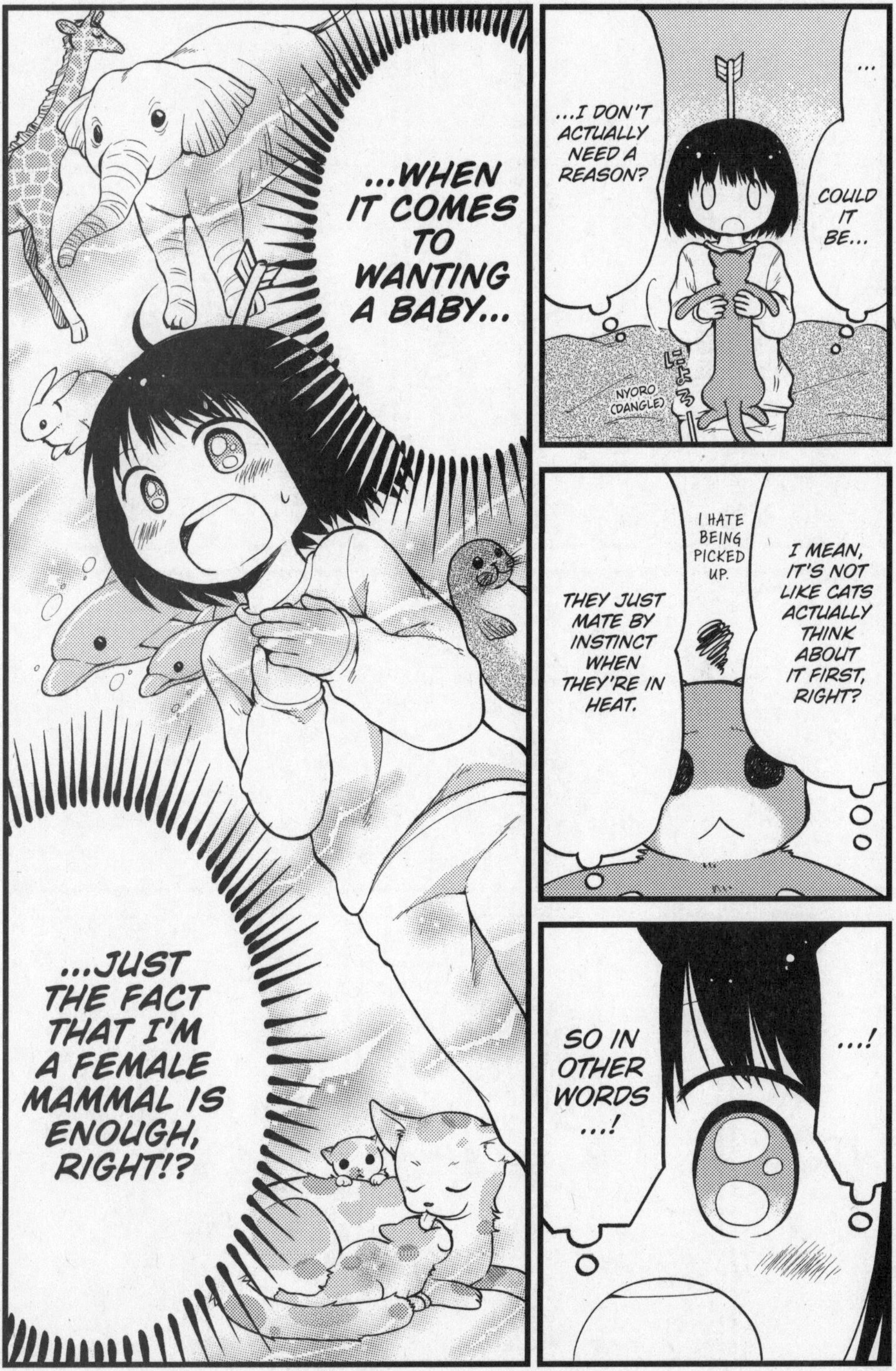
...
COULD IT BE...
...I DON'T ACTUALLY NEED A REASON?
にょろ
NYORO (DANGLE)
I MEAN, IT'S NOT LIKE CATS ACTUALLY THINK ABOUT IT FIRST, RIGHT?
I HATE BEING PICKED UP.
THEY JUST MATE BY INSTINCT WHEN THEY'RE IN HEAT.
...!
SO IN OTHER WORDS ...!
...WHEN IT COMES TO WANTING A BABY...
...JUST THE FACT THAT I'M A FEMALE MAMMAL IS ENOUGH, RIGHT!?

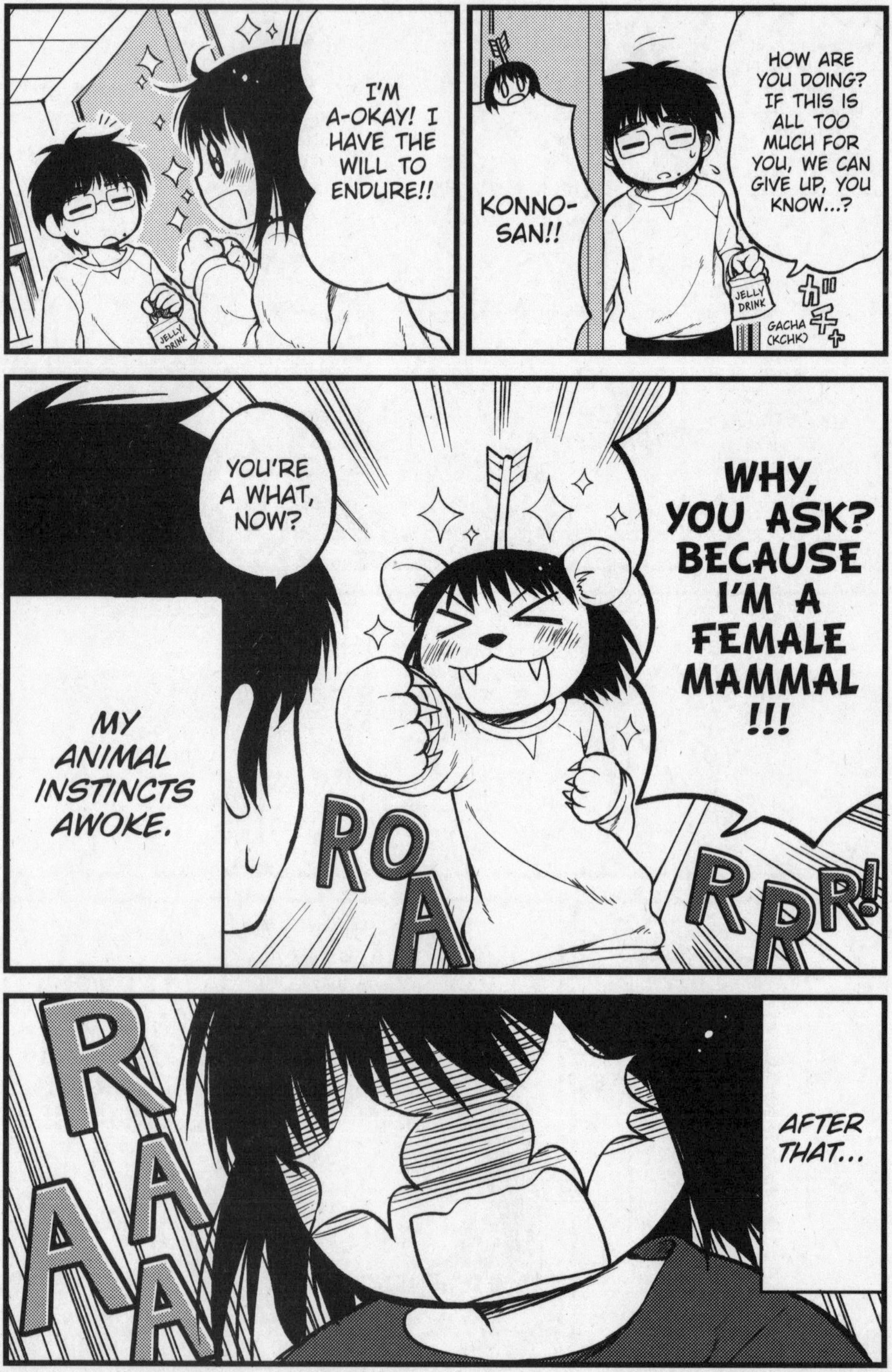

HOW ARE YOU DOING? IF THIS IS ALL TOO MUCH FOR YOU, WE CAN GIVE UP, YOU KNOW...?
GACHA (KCHK)
KONNO-SAN!!
JELLY DRINK
I'M A-OKAY! I HAVE THE WILL TO ENDURE!!
JELLY DRINK
WHY, YOU ASK? BECAUSE I'M A FEMALE MAMMAL!!!
YOU'RE A WHAT, NOW?
MY ANIMAL INSTINCTS AWOKE.
ROARRRR!
AFTER THAT...
RAAAA

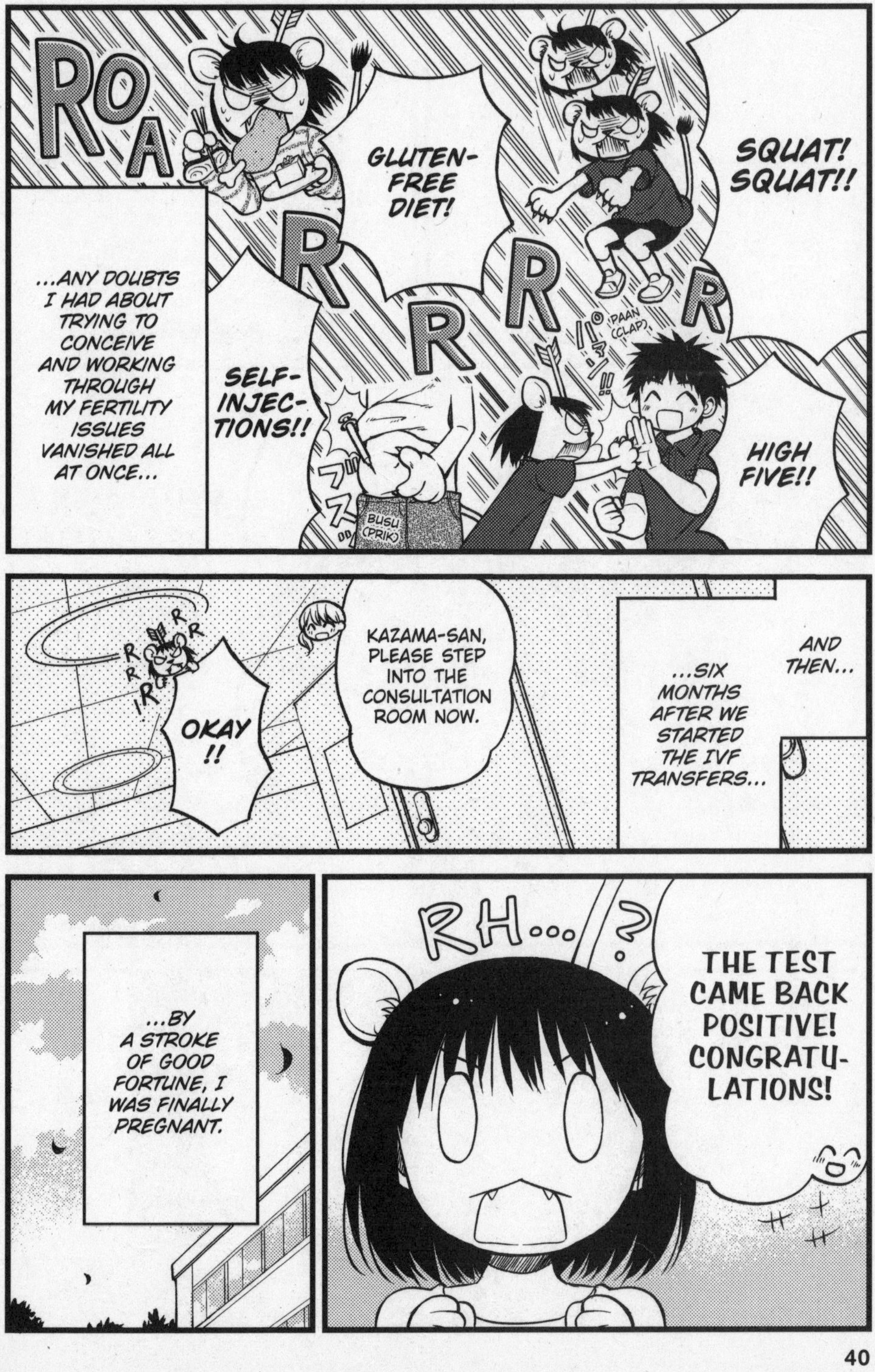
SQUAT! SQUAT!!
GLUTEN-FREE DIET!
ROARRRRR
HIGH FIVE!!
PAAN (CLAP)
SELF-INJECTIONS!!
BUSU (PRIK)
...ANY DOUBTS I HAD ABOUT TRYING TO CONCEIVE AND WORKING THROUGH MY FERTILITY ISSUES VANISHED ALL AT ONCE...
AND THEN...
...SIX MONTHS AFTER WE STARTED THE IVF TRANSFERS...
KAZAMA-SAN, PLEASE STEP INTO THE CONSULTATION ROOM NOW.
RRRRR
OKAY!!
THE TEST CAME BACK POSITIVE! CONGRATULATIONS!
RH...?
...BY A STROKE OF GOOD FORTUNE, I WAS FINALLY PREGNANT.

Chapter 3: I Want to Have a Baby! But I Don't Know Why!

Bonus manga by Azure Konno

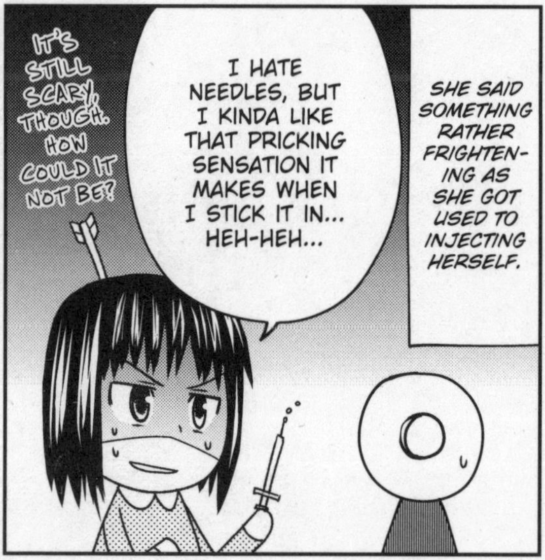
SHE SAID SOMETHING RATHER FRIGHTENING AS SHE GOT USED TO INJECTING HERSELF.
I HATE NEEDLES, BUT I KINDA LIKE THAT PRICKING SENSATION IT MAKES WHEN I STICK IT IN... HEH-HEH...
IT'S STILL SCARY, THOUGH. HOW COULD IT NOT BE?

It's surprising to hear that a diet high in gluten can affect the growth of egg cells, isn't it?
Rice, udon, okonomiyaki, bread, cakes—Kazama-san sure loves her carbs, so I think restricting her diet was the hardest thing for her.
She would pout and say, "A life without cake wouldn't be worth living at all. Ha-ha-ha-ha!"
I went to the gym with her too, but I wound up having to drop out after a while. (I discovered that weight training gave me headaches.)
Despite that, I'm the one who wound up losing more weight, which really pissed her off.
It's a sad turn of events.

Bonus manga by Ayami Kazama

Chapter 3: I Want to Have a Baby! But I Don't Know Why!

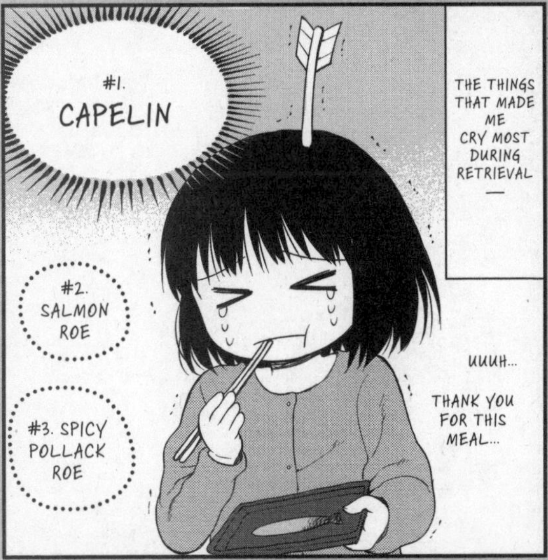
THE THINGS THAT MADE ME CRY MOST DURING RETRIEVAL —
#1. CAPELIN
UUUH...
THANK YOU FOR THIS MEAL...
#2. SALMON ROE
#3. SPICY POLLACK ROE

The hormone shots I was taking to prepare for the IVF retrieval made the follicles in my ovaries very lumpy.
And what do you think they look like? A capelin with roe.
That's why I got super emotional over the capelin I was having for dinner, and I ate it with tears streaming down my face without a care for what anyone else thought.
It's just...right as those healthy babies were on the verge of coming out into the world, full of the hope of living happy, fishy lives, they were robbed of their futures and eaten...!
Isn't that just the saddest thing ever?
I would like to mention that they were delicious, though.

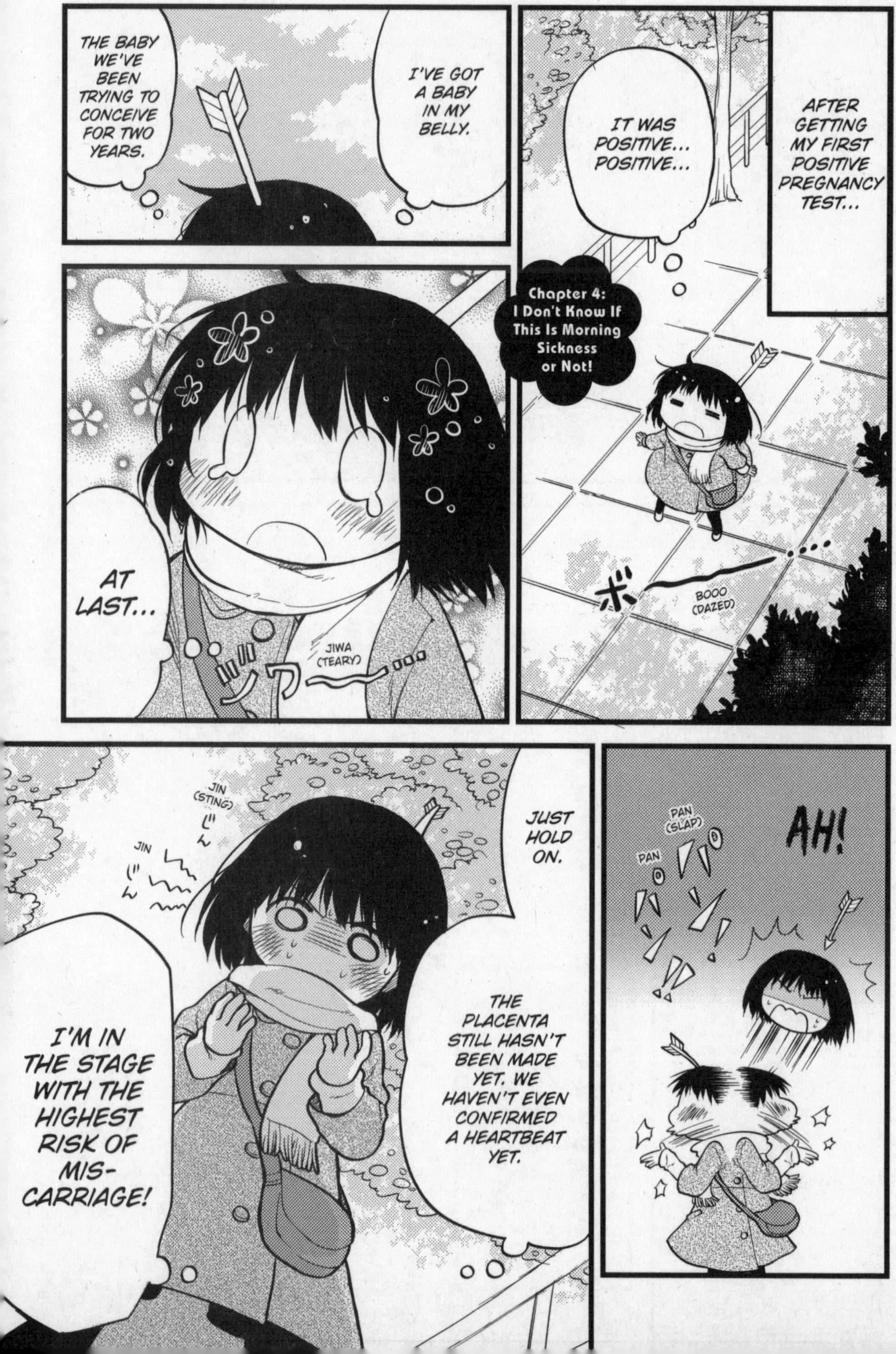
AFTER GETTING MY FIRST POSITIVE PREGNANCY TEST...
IT WAS POSITIVE... POSITIVE...
Chapter 4: I Don't Know If This Is Morning Sickness or Not!
...
ボ〜
BOOO (DAZED)
I'VE GOT A BABY IN MY BELLY.
THE BABY WE'VE BEEN TRYING TO CONCEIVE FOR TWO YEARS.
AT LAST...
ジワ〜…
JIWA (TEARY)
AH!
PAN (SLAP)
PAN
JUST HOLD ON.
JIN (STING)
じん
JIN
じん
THE PLACENTA STILL HASN'T BEEN MADE YET. WE HAVEN'T EVEN CONFIRMED A HEARTBEAT YET.
I'M IN THE STAGE WITH THE HIGHEST RISK OF MIS-CARRIAGE!

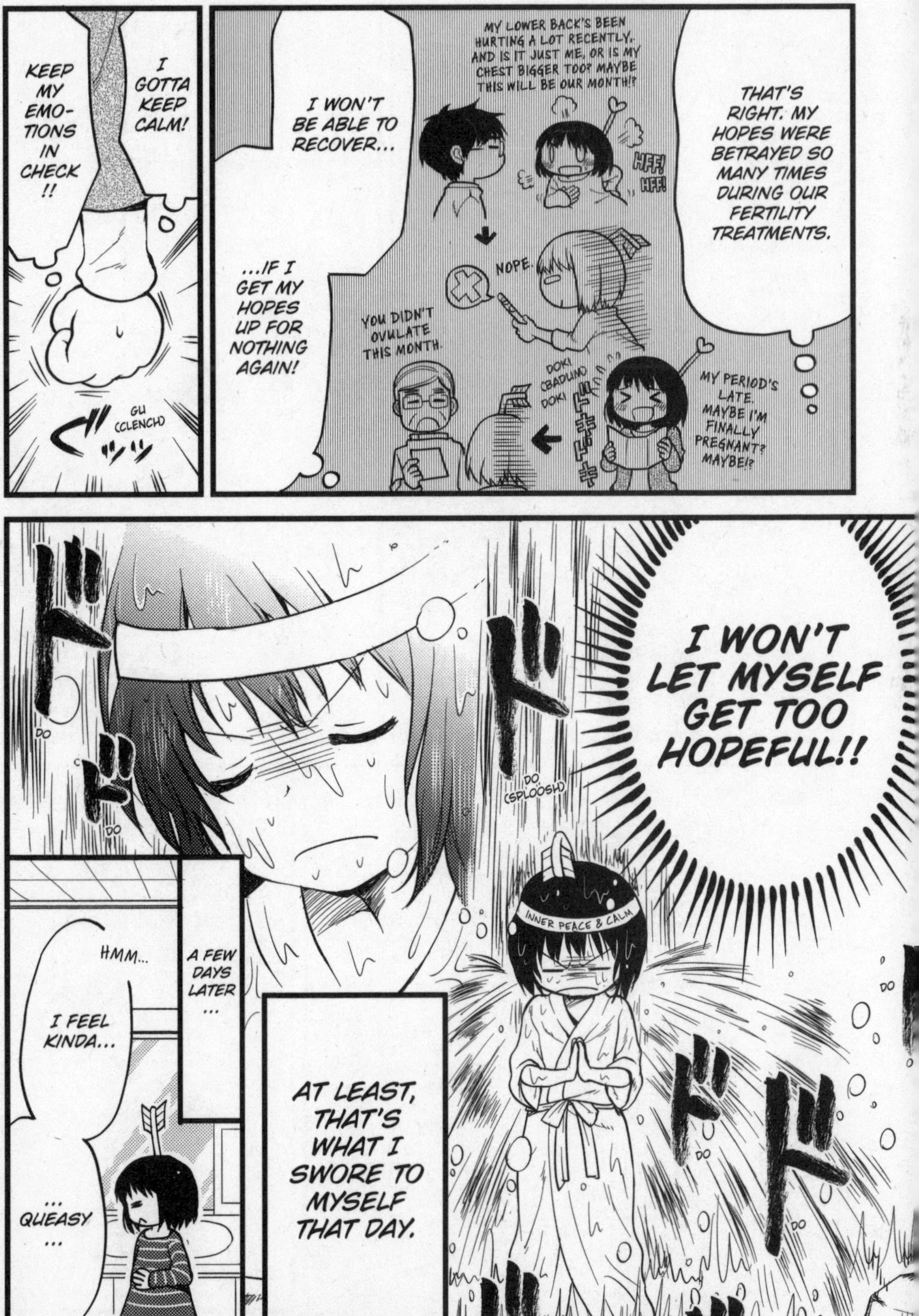
THAT'S RIGHT. MY HOPES WERE BETRAYED SO MANY TIMES DURING OUR FERTILITY TREATMENTS.
MY LOWER BACK'S BEEN HURTING A LOT RECENTLY. AND IS IT JUST ME, OR IS MY CHEST BIGGER TOO? MAYBE THIS WILL BE OUR MONTH!?
HFF! HFF!
NOPE.
MY PERIOD'S LATE. MAYBE I'M FINALLY PREGNANT? MAYBE!?
DOKI (BADUMP) DOKI
YOU DIDN'T OVULATE THIS MONTH.
I WON'T BE ABLE TO RECOVER...
...IF I GET MY HOPES UP FOR NOTHING AGAIN!
I GOTTA KEEP CALM!
KEEP MY EMO-TIONS IN CHECK !!
GU (CLENCH)
I WON'T LET MYSELF GET TOO HOPEFUL!!
DO (SPLOOSH)
DO
DO
INNER PEACE & CALM
DO
DO
DO
DO
DO
AT LEAST, THAT'S WHAT I SWORE TO MYSELF THAT DAY.
A FEW DAYS LATER ...
HMM...
I FEEL KINDA...
... QUEASY ...

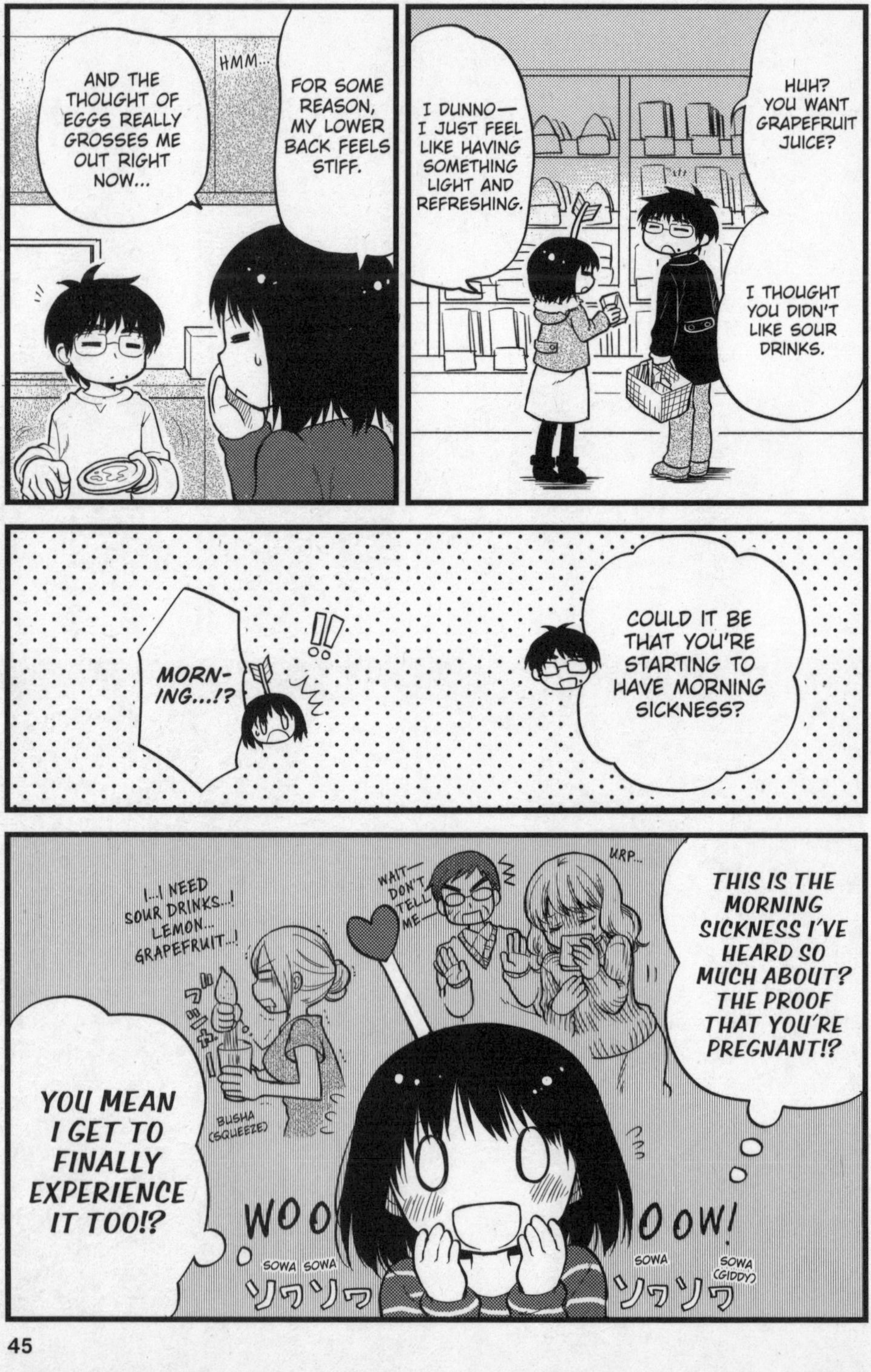
HUH? YOU WANT GRAPEFRUIT JUICE?
I THOUGHT YOU DIDN'T LIKE SOUR DRINKS.
I DUNNO— I JUST FEEL LIKE HAVING SOMETHING LIGHT AND REFRESHING.
HMM...
FOR SOME REASON, MY LOWER BACK FEELS STIFF.
AND THE THOUGHT OF EGGS REALLY GROSSES ME OUT RIGHT NOW...
COULD IT BE THAT YOU'RE STARTING TO HAVE MORNING SICKNESS?
!!
MORN-ING...!?
THIS IS THE MORNING SICKNESS I'VE HEARD SO MUCH ABOUT? THE PROOF THAT YOU'RE PREGNANT!?
URP..
WAIT— DON'T TELL ME—
I...I NEED SOUR DRINKS...! LEMON... GRAPEFRUIT...!
BUSHA (SQUEEZE)
YOU MEAN I GET TO FINALLY EXPERIENCE IT TOO!?
WOO
OOW!
SOWA SOWA
ソワソワ
SOWA SOWA (GIDDY)
ソワソワ

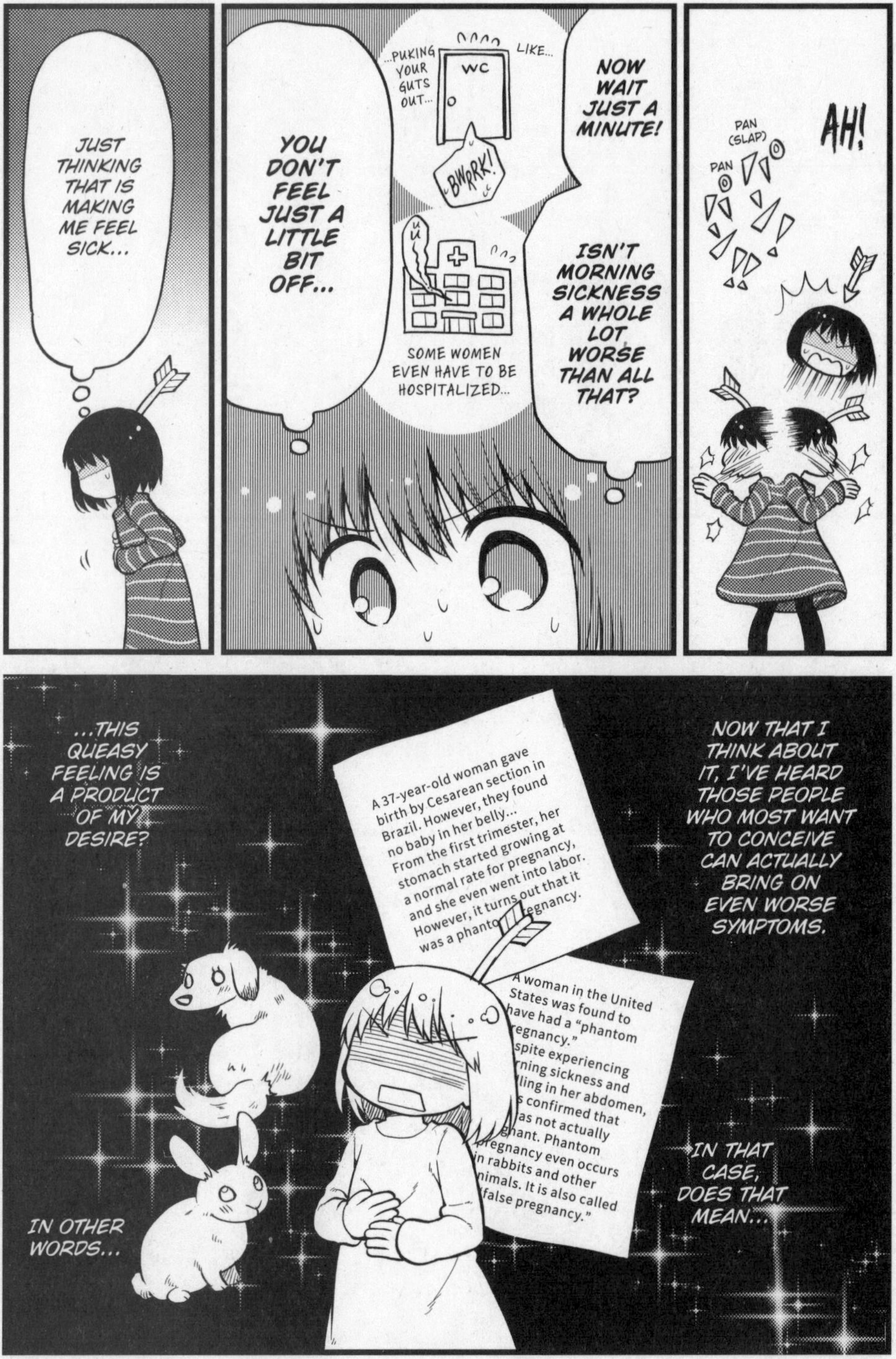
AH!
PAN (SLAP)
PAN
NOW WAIT JUST A MINUTE!
ISN'T MORNING SICKNESS A WHOLE LOT WORSE THAN ALL THAT?
LIKE...
...PUKING YOUR GUTS OUT...
WC
BWRRK!
SOME WOMEN EVEN HAVE TO BE HOSPITALIZED...
YOU DON'T FEEL JUST A LITTLE BIT OFF...
JUST THINKING THAT IS MAKING ME FEEL SICK...
NOW THAT I THINK ABOUT IT, I'VE HEARD THOSE PEOPLE WHO MOST WANT TO CONCEIVE CAN ACTUALLY BRING ON EVEN WORSE SYMPTOMS.
A 37-year-old woman gave birth by Cesarean section in Brazil. However, they found no baby in her belly... From the first trimester, her stomach started growing at a normal rate for pregnancy, and she even went into labor. However, it turns out that it was a phanto egnancy.
A woman in the United States was found to have had a "phantom regnancy." spite experiencing rning sickness and lling in her abdomen, s confirmed that as not actually nant. Phantom pregnancy even occurs in rabbits and other nimals. It is also called false pregnancy."
IN THAT CASE, DOES THAT MEAN...
...THIS QUEASY FEELING IS A PRODUCT OF MY DESIRE?
IN OTHER WORDS...

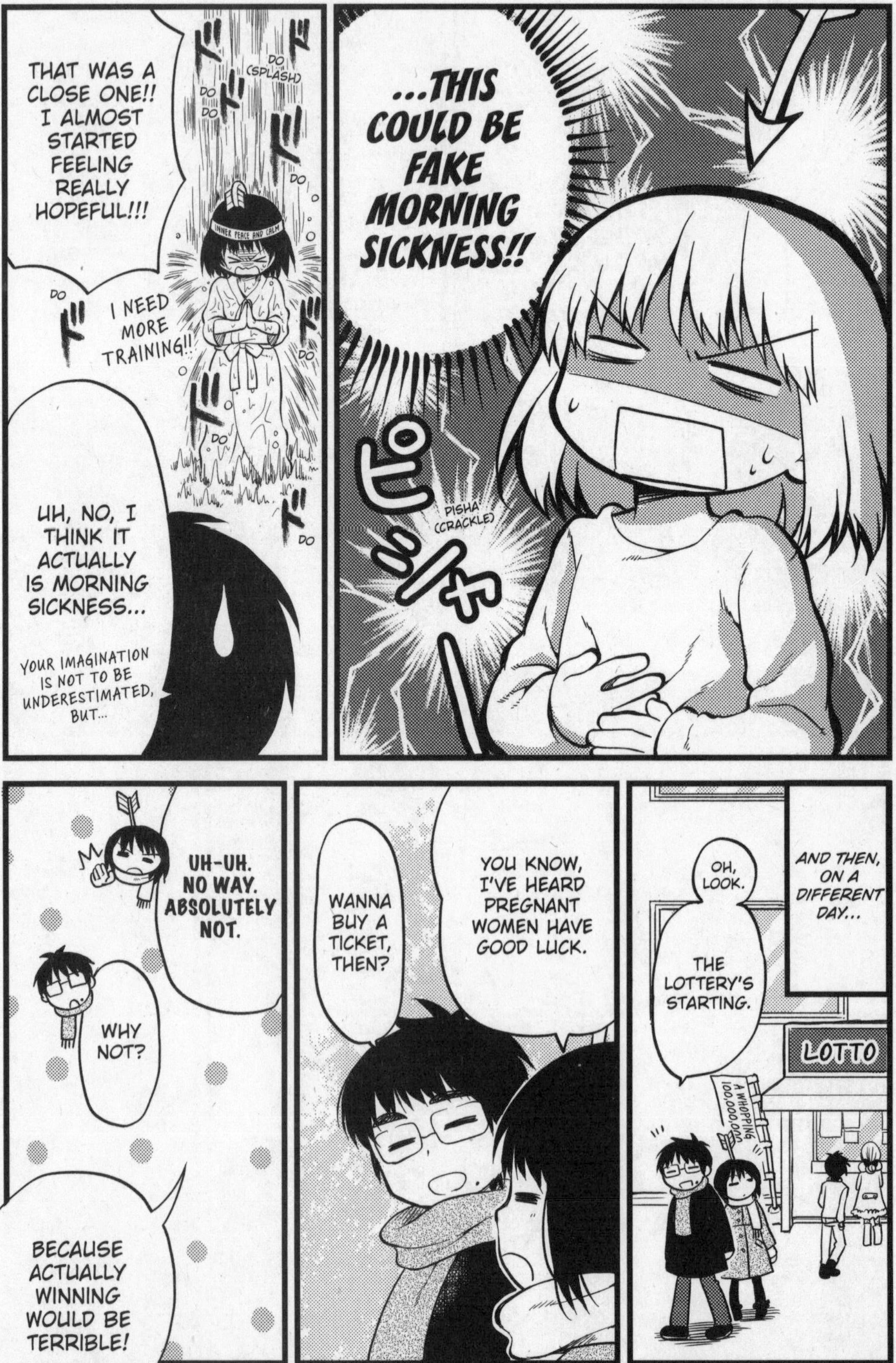
...THIS COULD BE FAKE MORNING SICKNESS!!
PISHA (CRACKLE)
THAT WAS A CLOSE ONE!! I ALMOST STARTED FEELING REALLY HOPEFUL!!!
DO DO DO (SPLASH) DO DO DO
INNER PEACE AND CALM
I NEED MORE TRAINING!!
UH, NO, I THINK IT ACTUALLY IS MORNING SICKNESS...
YOUR IMAGINATION IS NOT TO BE UNDERESTIMATED, BUT...
AND THEN, ON A DIFFERENT DAY...
OH, LOOK.
THE LOTTERY'S STARTING.
LOTTO
A WHOPPING 100,000,000
YOU KNOW, I'VE HEARD PREGNANT WOMEN HAVE GOOD LUCK.
WANNA BUY A TICKET, THEN?
UH-UH. NO WAY. ABSOLUTELY NOT.
WHY NOT?
BECAUSE ACTUALLY WINNING WOULD BE TERRIBLE!

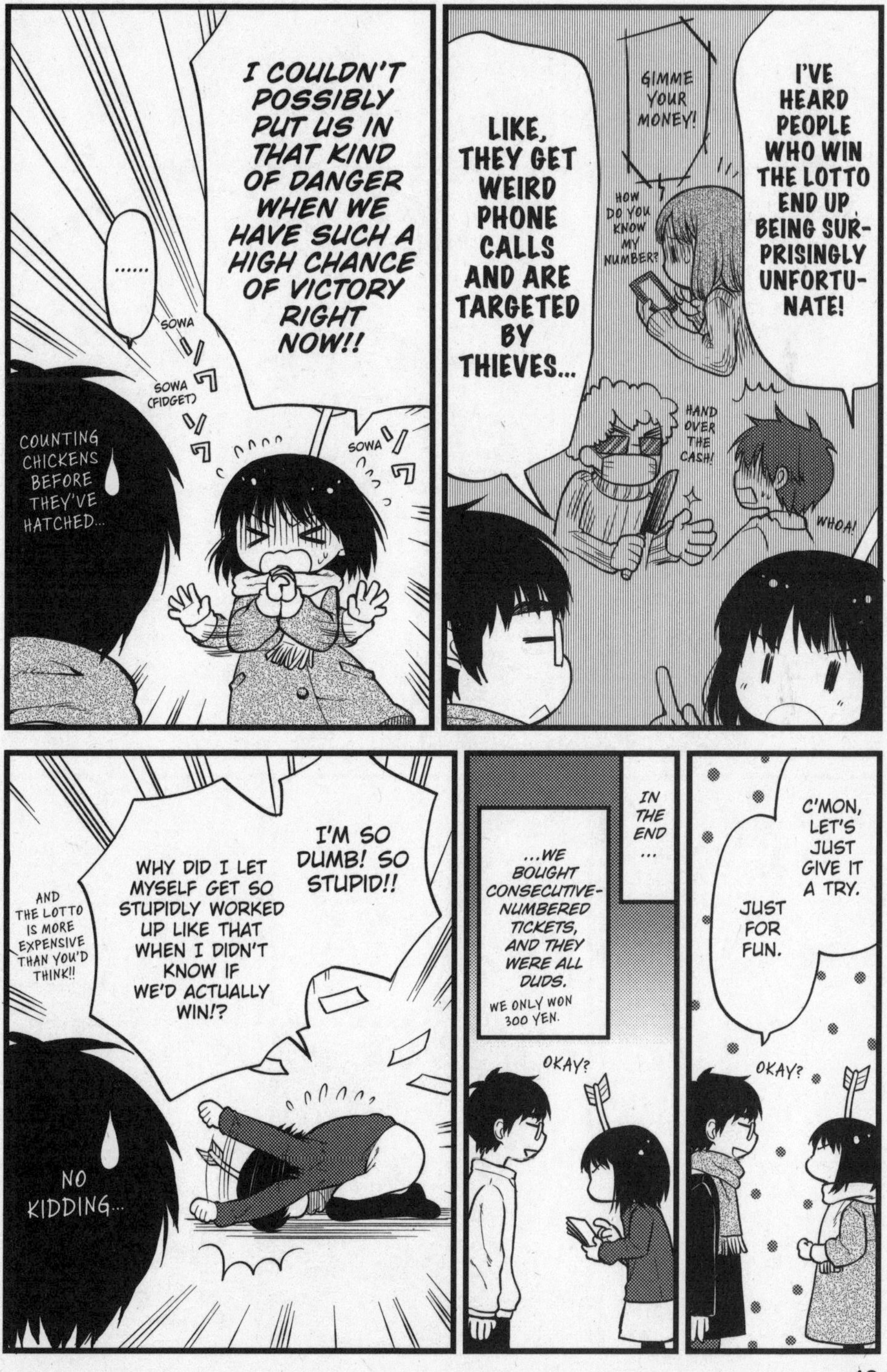
I'VE HEARD PEOPLE WHO WIN THE LOTTO END UP BEING SURPRISINGLY UNFORTUNATE!
LIKE, THEY GET WEIRD PHONE CALLS AND ARE TARGETED BY THIEVES...
GIMME YOUR MONEY!
HOW DO YOU KNOW MY NUMBER?
HAND OVER THE CASH!
WHOA!
I COULDN'T POSSIBLY PUT US IN THAT KIND OF DANGER WHEN WE HAVE SUCH A HIGH CHANCE OF VICTORY RIGHT NOW!!
......
SOWA
SOWA (FIDGET)
SOWA
COUNTING CHICKENS BEFORE THEY'VE HATCHED...
C'MON, LET'S JUST GIVE IT A TRY.
JUST FOR FUN.
OKAY?
IN THE END...
...WE BOUGHT CONSECUTIVE-NUMBERED TICKETS, AND THEY WERE ALL DUDS.
WE ONLY WON 300 YEN.
OKAY?
I'M SO DUMB! SO STUPID!!
WHY DID I LET MYSELF GET SO STUPIDLY WORKED UP LIKE THAT WHEN I DIDN'T KNOW IF WE'D ACTUALLY WIN!?
AND THE LOTTO IS MORE EXPENSIVE THAN YOU'D THINK!!
NO KIDDING...

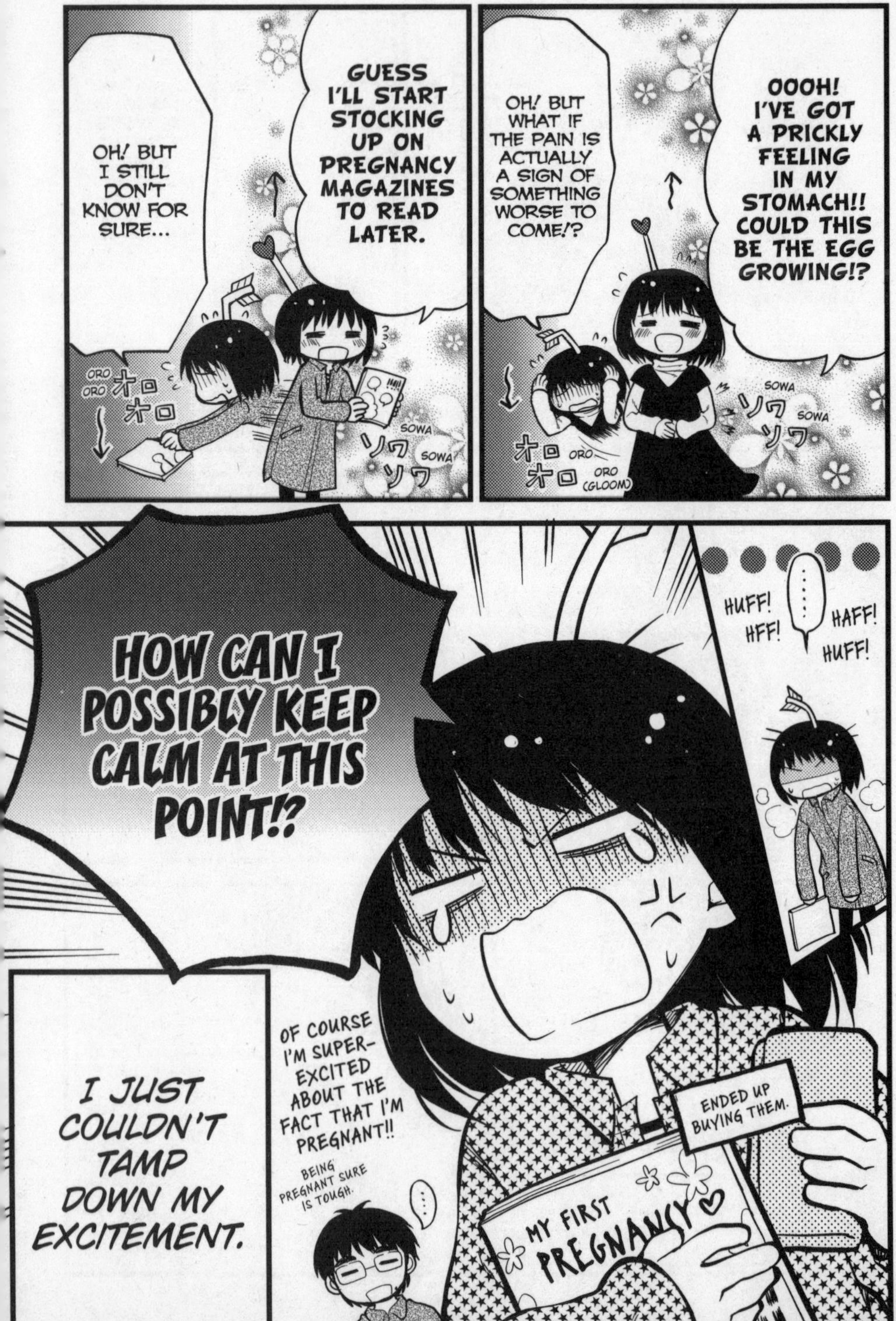
OOOH! I'VE GOT A PRICKLY FEELING IN MY STOMACH!! COULD THIS BE THE EGG GROWING!?
OH! BUT WHAT IF THE PAIN IS ACTUALLY A SIGN OF SOMETHING WORSE TO COME!?
ソワソワ
SOWA SOWA
オロオロ
ORO ORO (GLOOM)
GUESS I'LL START STOCKING UP ON PREGNANCY MAGAZINES TO READ LATER.
OH! BUT I STILL DON'T KNOW FOR SURE...
ソワソワ
SOWA SOWA
オロオロ
ORO ORO
HOW CAN I POSSIBLY KEEP CALM AT THIS POINT!?
HUFF! HFF!
......
HAFF! HUFF!
OF COURSE I'M SUPER-EXCITED ABOUT THE FACT THAT I'M PREGNANT!!
ENDED UP BUYING THEM.
MY FIRST PREGNANCY
BEING PREGNANT SURE IS TOUGH.
...
I JUST COULDN'T TAMP DOWN MY EXCITEMENT.

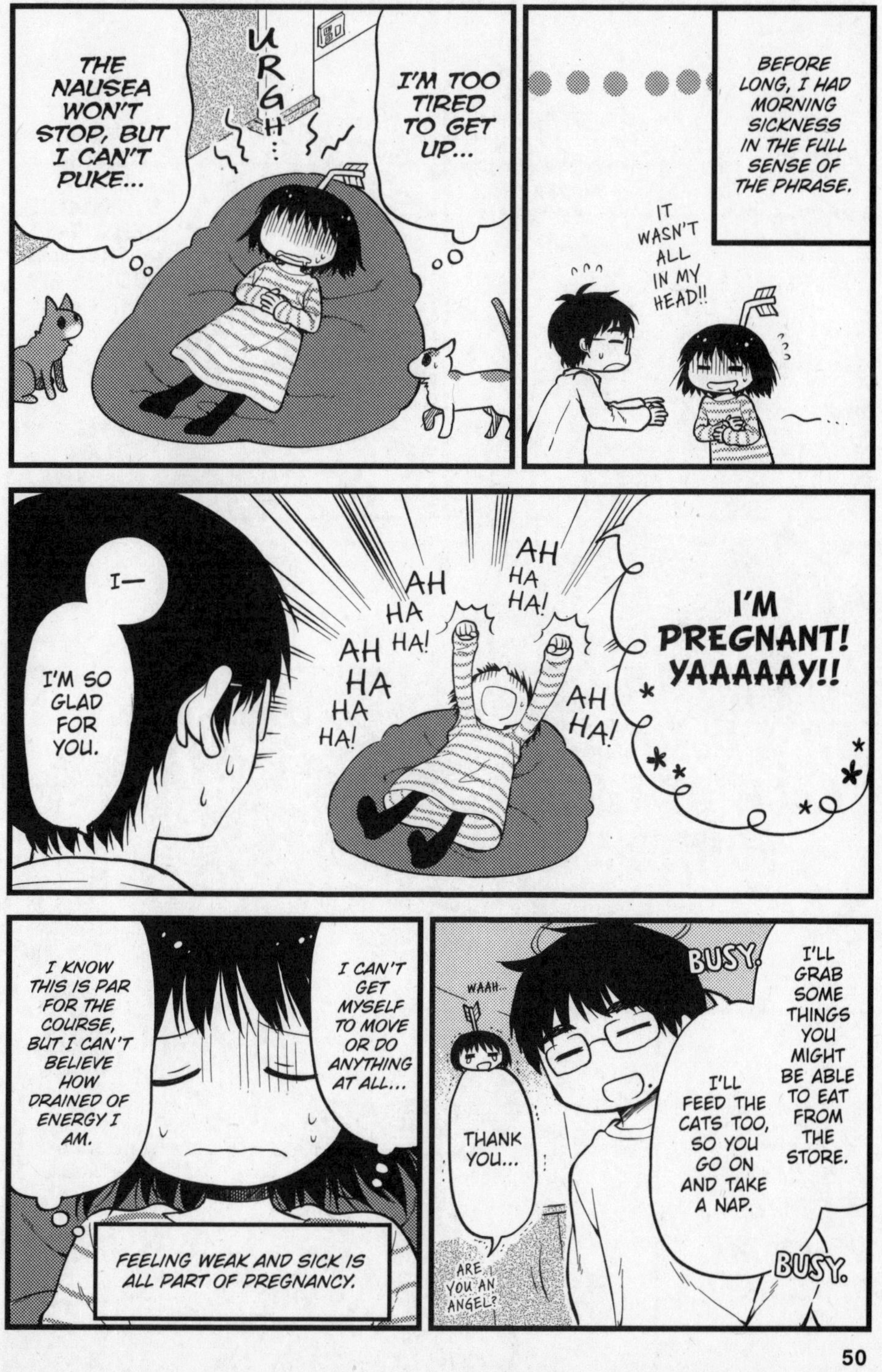
BEFORE LONG, I HAD MORNING SICKNESS IN THE FULL SENSE OF THE PHRASE.
IT WASN'T ALL IN MY HEAD!!
I'M TOO TIRED TO GET UP...
URGH...
THE NAUSEA WON'T STOP, BUT I CAN'T PUKE...
I'M PREGNANT! YAAAAAY!!
AH HA HA!
AH HA HA!
AH HA HA!
AH HA HA HA!
AH HA!
I—
I'M SO GLAD FOR YOU.
BUSY.
I'LL GRAB SOME THINGS YOU MIGHT BE ABLE TO EAT FROM THE STORE.
I'LL FEED THE CATS TOO, SO YOU GO ON AND TAKE A NAP.
BUSY.
WAAH...
THANK YOU...
ARE YOU AN ANGEL?
I CAN'T GET MYSELF TO MOVE OR DO ANYTHING AT ALL...
I KNOW THIS IS PAR FOR THE COURSE, BUT I CAN'T BELIEVE HOW DRAINED OF ENERGY I AM.
FEELING WEAK AND SICK IS ALL PART OF PREGNANCY.

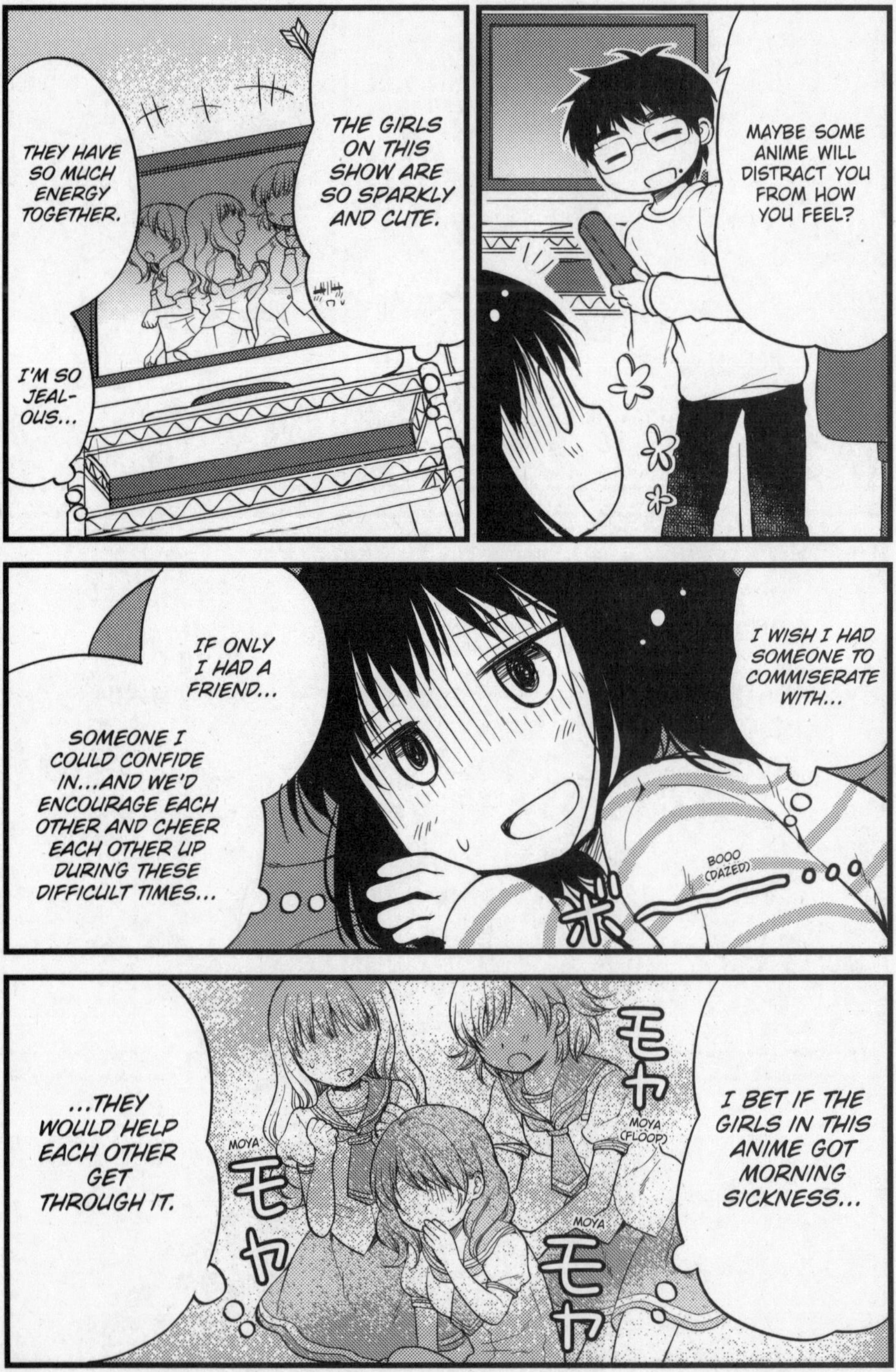
MAYBE SOME ANIME WILL DISTRACT YOU FROM HOW YOU FEEL?
THE GIRLS ON THIS SHOW ARE SO SPARKLY AND CUTE.
THEY HAVE SO MUCH ENERGY TOGETHER.
I'M SO JEAL-OUS...
I WISH I HAD SOMEONE TO COMMISERATE WITH...
IF ONLY I HAD A FRIEND...
SOMEONE I COULD CONFIDE IN...AND WE'D ENCOURAGE EACH OTHER AND CHEER EACH OTHER UP DURING THESE DIFFICULT TIMES...
BOOO (DAZED)
I BET IF THE GIRLS IN THIS ANIME GOT MORNING SICKNESS...
MOYA (FLOOP)
MOYA
MOYA
...THEY WOULD HELP EACH OTHER GET THROUGH IT.

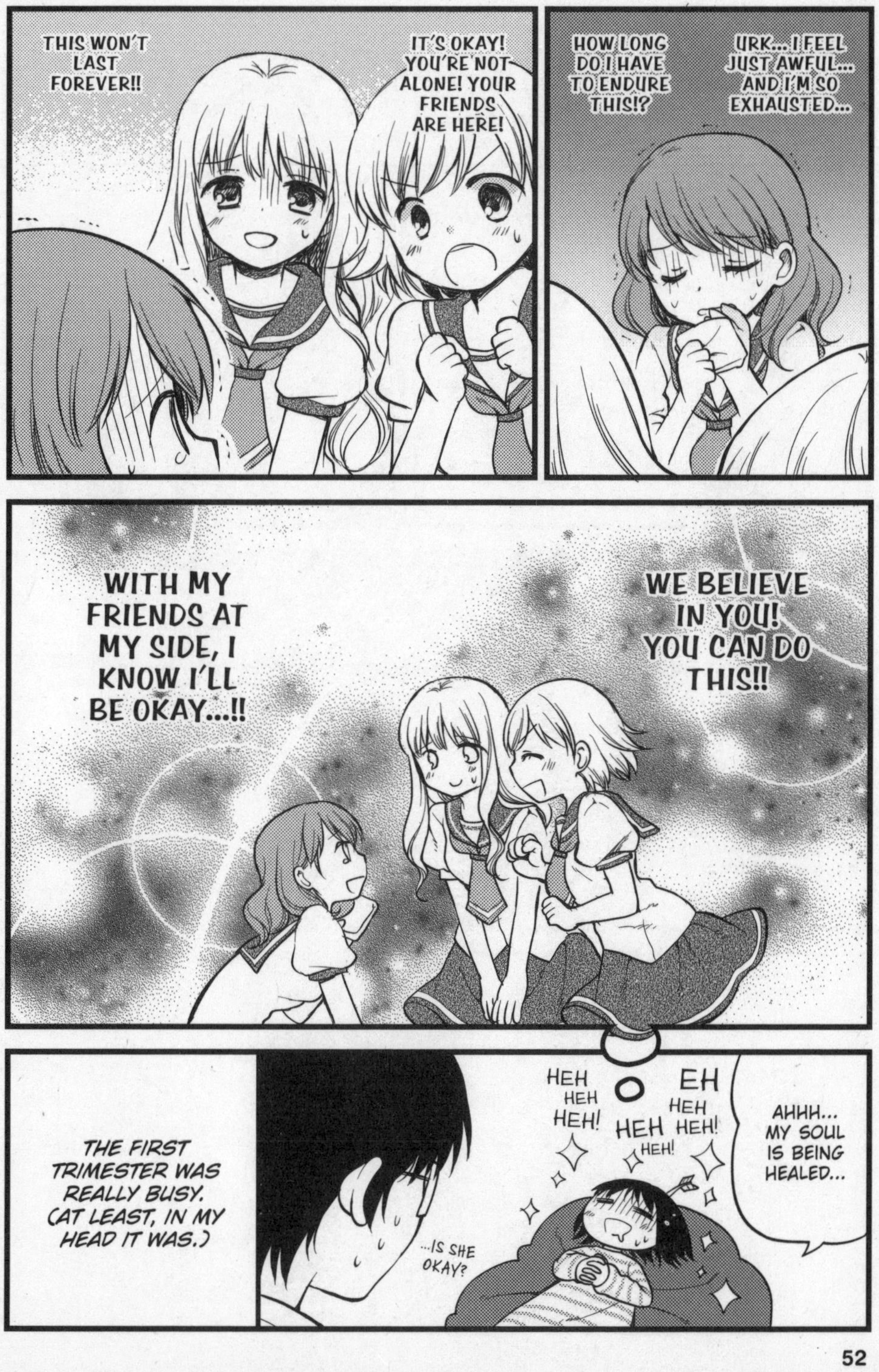
URK... I FEEL JUST AWFUL... AND I'M SO EXHAUSTED...
HOW LONG DO I HAVE TO ENDURE THIS!?
IT'S OKAY! YOU'RE NOT ALONE! YOUR FRIENDS ARE HERE!
THIS WON'T LAST FOREVER!!
WE BELIEVE IN YOU! YOU CAN DO THIS!!
WITH MY FRIENDS AT MY SIDE, I KNOW I'LL BE OKAY...!!
AHHH... MY SOUL IS BEING HEALED...
EH HEH HEH!
HEH HEH HEH!
HEH HEH!
...IS SHE OKAY?
THE FIRST TRIMESTER WAS REALLY BUSY. (AT LEAST, IN MY HEAD IT WAS.)

Chapter 4: I Don't Know If This Is Morning Sickness or Not!

Bonus manga by Azure Konno

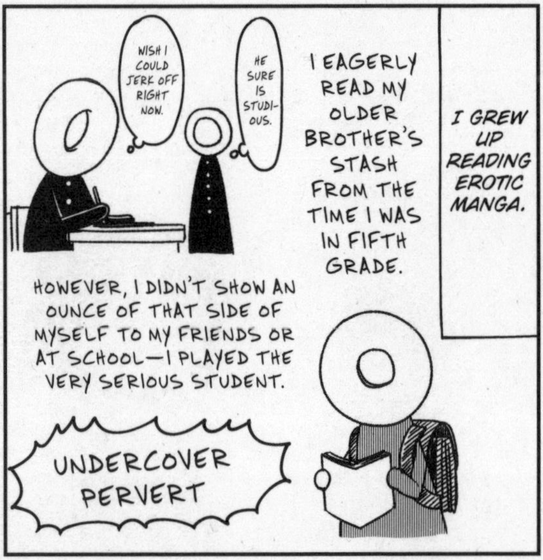

I GREW UP READING EROTIC MANGA.
I EAGERLY READ MY OLDER BROTHER'S STASH FROM THE TIME I WAS IN FIFTH GRADE.
HE SURE IS STUDIOUS.
WISH I COULD JERK OFF RIGHT NOW.
HOWEVER, I DIDN'T SHOW AN OUNCE OF THAT SIDE OF MYSELF TO MY FRIENDS OR AT SCHOOL—I PLAYED THE VERY SERIOUS STUDENT.
UNDERCOVER PERVERT

So, y'know, I just assumed that as long as we didn't use protection, she was guaranteed to get pregnant.

Weirdly, protection is never featured in porn. Like, it doesn't exist. Based on erotic manga, you'd assume you're safe to go without protection.

After ovulation, there's only a twenty-four-hour period when pregnancy can occur. Apparently, sperm can live in the uterus for about three to seven days, so that overlap is when you have a chance of getting pregnant.

Considering that, it's a bit of a surprise to realize there are more safe days than not. I always thought it was the opposite. In fact, I didn't even find out how all that works until I was thirty-five years old. I guess that's kinda bad, huh?

But it's probably not a thing you'd know unless you were thinking about having a kid, right?

Bonus manga by Ayami Kazama

Chapter 4: I Don't Know If This Is Morning Sickness or Not!

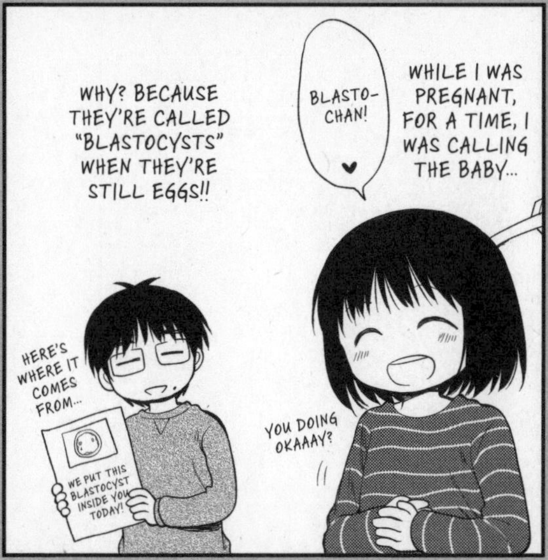
WHILE I WAS PREGNANT, FOR A TIME, I WAS CALLING THE BABY...
BLASTO-CHAN!
WHY? BECAUSE THEY'RE CALLED "BLASTOCYSTS" WHEN THEY'RE STILL EGGS!!
YOU DOING OKAAAY?
HERE'S WHERE IT COMES FROM...
WE PUT THIS BLASTOCYST INSIDE YOU TODAY!

I finally got pregnant!!!
The first IVF transfer didn't work, so at that point, I had lost all hope. When the doctor told me our second transfer had worked, it seemed like a miracle. I cried.
When I told Konno-san I was pregnant, he said, "To tell the truth, I didn't think it would take this time either."
I was reminded of how long and treacherous our road to pregnancy had been.
For convenience's sake, I named the baby in my belly so I could talk to it. I called it "Blasto-chan," since eggs at that stage are called "blastocysts"!!
I'd tell my baby things like, "Blasto-chan, you're so good at cell division! I'm so proud of you!"
I guess knowing the progress of how well your baby's cells have been dividing is one of the good aspects of IVF.
But I know, I know! Blasto-chan had no idea what the heck I was talking about!

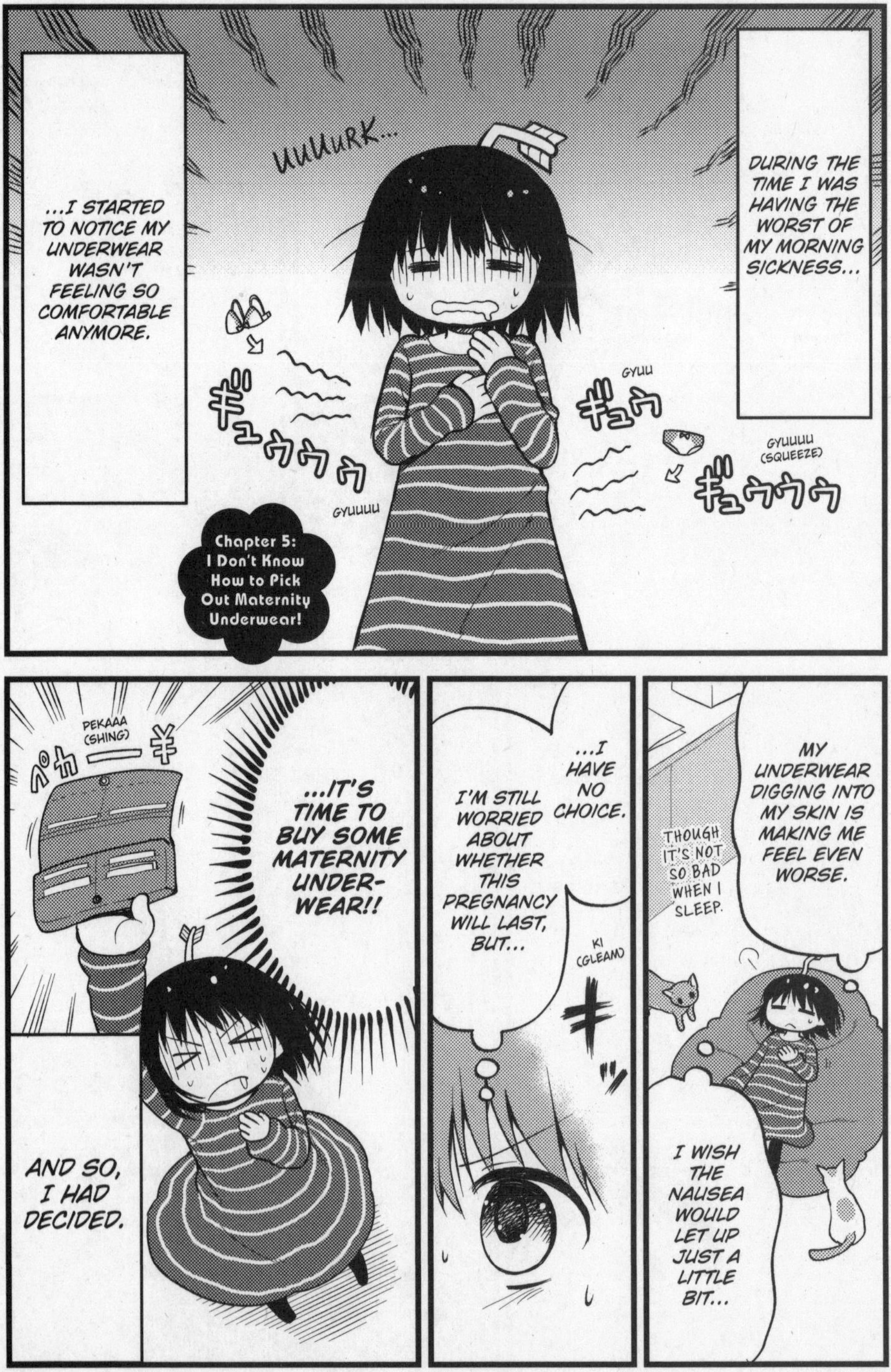
DURING THE TIME I WAS HAVING THE WORST OF MY MORNING SICKNESS...
UUUURK...
GYUU
ギュウ
GYUUUU (SQUEEZE)
ギュウウウ
ギュウウウ
GYUUUU
...I STARTED TO NOTICE MY UNDERWEAR WASN'T FEELING SO COMFORTABLE ANYMORE.
Chapter 5: I Don't Know How to Pick Out Maternity Underwear!
MY UNDERWEAR DIGGING INTO MY SKIN IS MAKING ME FEEL EVEN WORSE.
THOUGH IT'S NOT SO BAD WHEN I SLEEP.
I WISH THE NAUSEA WOULD LET UP JUST A LITTLE BIT...
I'M STILL WORRIED ABOUT WHETHER THIS PREGNANCY WILL LAST, BUT...
...I HAVE NO CHOICE.
KI (GLEAM)
キッ
PEKAAA (SHING)
ペカーッ
...IT'S TIME TO BUY SOME MATERNITY UNDER-WEAR!!
AND SO, I HAD DECIDED.

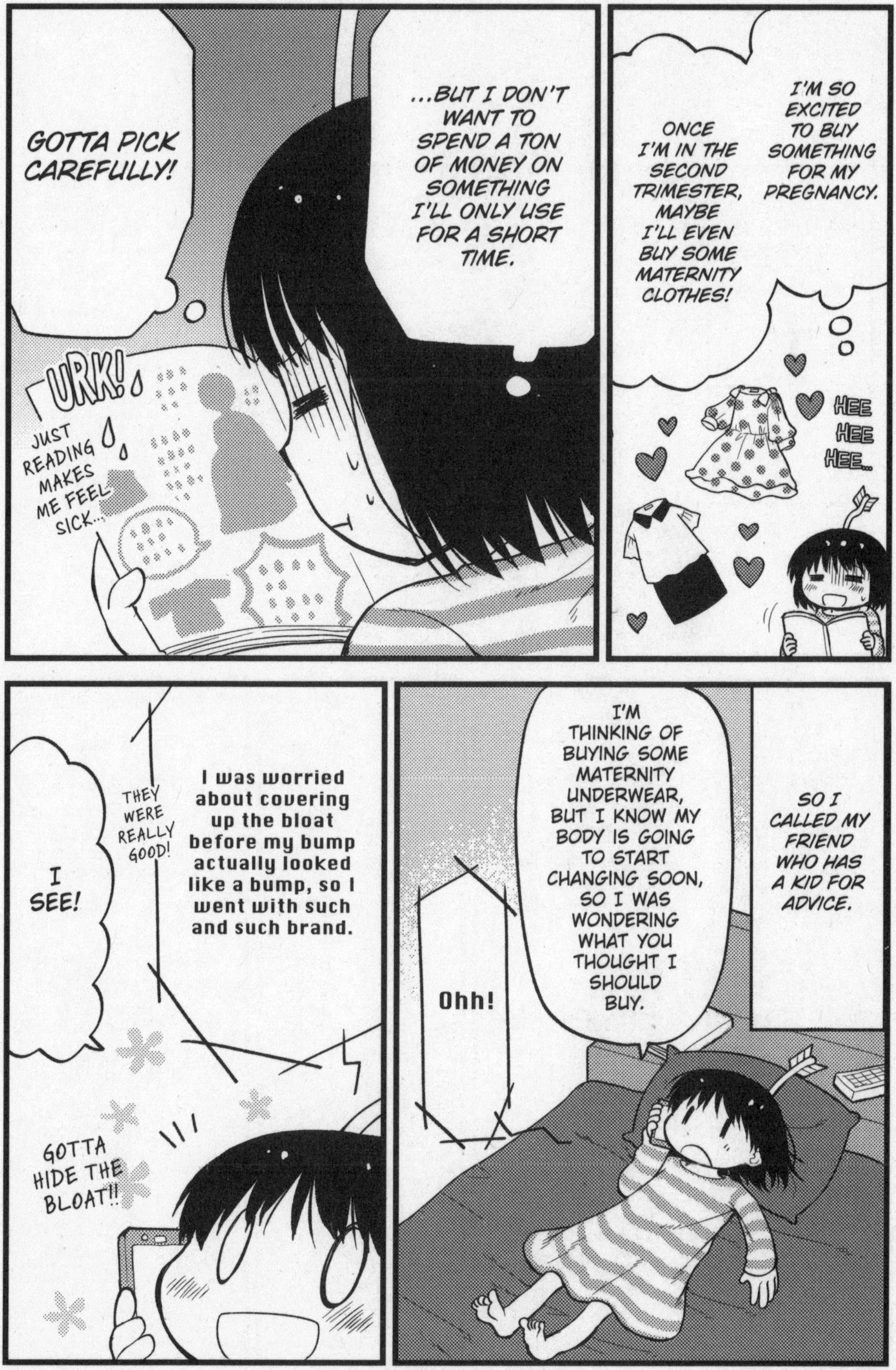
I'M SO EXCITED TO BUY SOMETHING FOR MY PREGNANCY.
ONCE I'M IN THE SECOND TRIMESTER, MAYBE I'LL EVEN BUY SOME MATERNITY CLOTHES!
HEE HEE HEE...
...BUT I DON'T WANT TO SPEND A TON OF MONEY ON SOMETHING I'LL ONLY USE FOR A SHORT TIME.
GOTTA PICK CAREFULLY!
URK!
JUST READING MAKES ME FEEL SICK...
SO I CALLED MY FRIEND WHO HAS A KID FOR ADVICE.
I'M THINKING OF BUYING SOME MATERNITY UNDERWEAR, BUT I KNOW MY BODY IS GOING TO START CHANGING SOON, SO I WAS WONDERING WHAT YOU THOUGHT I SHOULD BUY.
Ohh!
I was worried about covering up the bloat before my bump actually looked like a bump, so I went with such and such brand.
THEY WERE REALLY GOOD!
I SEE!
GOTTA HIDE THE BLOAT!!

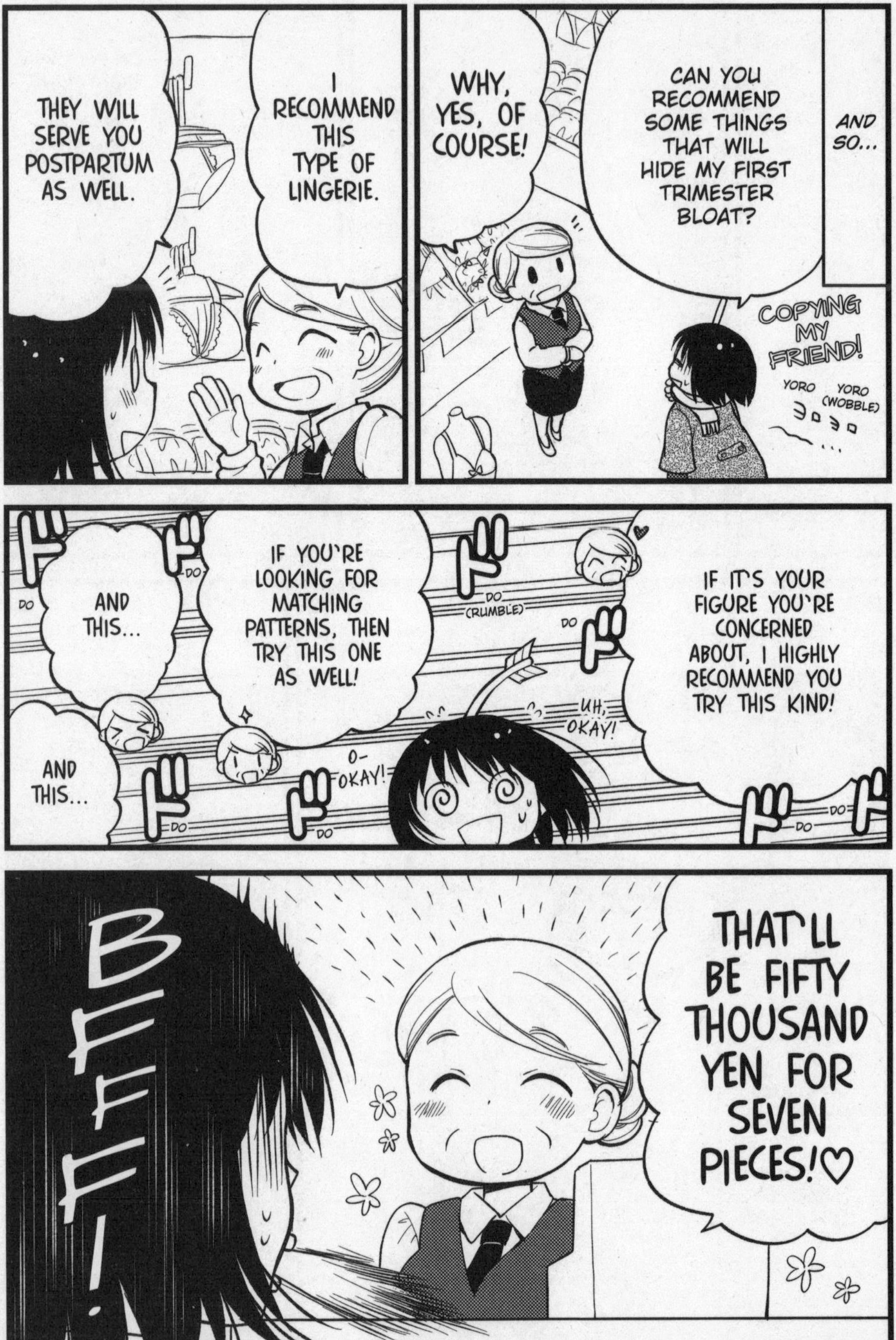

AND SO...
CAN YOU RECOMMEND SOME THINGS THAT WILL HIDE MY FIRST TRIMESTER BLOAT?
COPYING MY FRIEND!
YORO YORO (WOBBLE)
WHY, YES, OF COURSE!
I RECOMMEND THIS TYPE OF LINGERIE.
THEY WILL SERVE YOU POSTPARTUM AS WELL.
DO DO
IF IT'S YOUR FIGURE YOU'RE CONCERNED ABOUT, I HIGHLY RECOMMEND YOU TRY THIS KIND!
UH, OKAY!
DO
DO (CRUMBLE)
IF YOU'RE LOOKING FOR MATCHING PATTERNS, THEN TRY THIS ONE AS WELL!
O-OKAY!
DO
DO
AND THIS...
AND THIS...
DO
DO
THAT'LL BE FIFTY THOUSAND YEN FOR SEVEN PIECES!♡
BFFF!

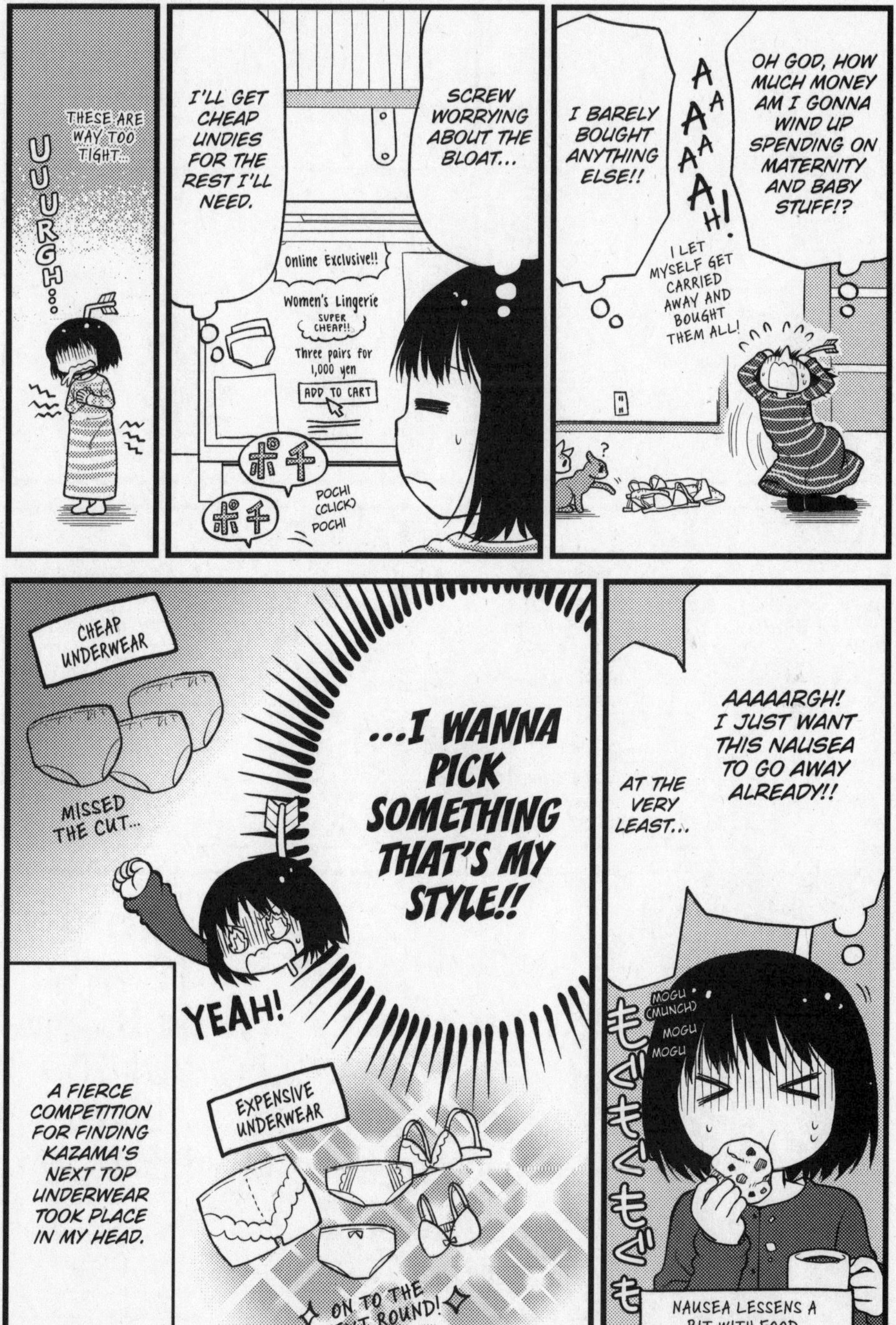
OH GOD, HOW MUCH MONEY AM I GONNA WIND UP SPENDING ON MATERNITY AND BABY STUFF!?
AAAAAH!
I BARELY BOUGHT ANYTHING ELSE!!
I LET MYSELF GET CARRIED AWAY AND BOUGHT THEM ALL!
SCREW WORRYING ABOUT THE BLOAT...
I'LL GET CHEAP UNDIES FOR THE REST I'LL NEED.
Online Exclusive!!
Women's Lingerie
SUPER CHEAP!!
Three pairs for 1,000 yen
ADD TO CART
ポチ
ポチ
POCHI (CLICK) POCHI
THESE ARE WAY TOO TIGHT...
UUURGH...
AT THE VERY LEAST...
AAAAARGH! I JUST WANT THIS NAUSEA TO GO AWAY ALREADY!!
MOGU (MUNCH) MOGU MOGU
もぐもぐもぐ
NAUSEA LESSENS A BIT WITH FOOD.
...I WANNA PICK SOMETHING THAT'S MY STYLE!!
CHEAP UNDERWEAR
MISSED THE CUT...
YEAH!
EXPENSIVE UNDERWEAR
ON TO THE NEXT ROUND!
A FIERCE COMPETITION FOR FINDING KAZAMA'S NEXT TOP UNDERWEAR TOOK PLACE IN MY HEAD.

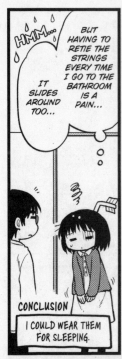

HMMMMMM...
ANYWAY, FOR NOW I WANNA FIND SOMETHING LOOSE THAT'LL HIDE THE BLOAT UNTIL MY STOMACH LOOKS LIKE A BABY BUMP...
Coocle
Underwear that's not tight
KATA (KLAK) KATA
カタ カタ
AH!
LOIN-CLOTHS!!
APPARENTLY THOSE ARE IN STYLE RIGHT NOW!!
CONTESTANT 1
LOINCLOTHS
TWO PAIRS FOR 4,000 YEN!!
POCHI
ポチ
BUT HAVING TO RETIE THE STRINGS EVERY TIME I GO TO THE BATHROOM IS A PAIN...
HMM...
IT SLIDES AROUND TOO...
CONCLUSION
I COULD WEAR THEM FOR SLEEPING.
WANNA WEAR MY BOXER SHORTS?
THEY'RE SUPER-COMFY AND EASY TO WEAR.
HUH!??
CONTESTANT 2
HUBBY'S BOXERS
UHHH... I DUNNO ABOUT THIS...
...
I-I DON'T WANT TO ADMIT IT, BUT...
...THEY'RE NOT BAD...!
SO LOOSE...
YUP!
CONCLUSION
SURPRISINGLY GOOD!

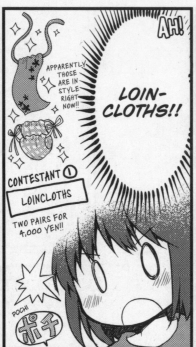

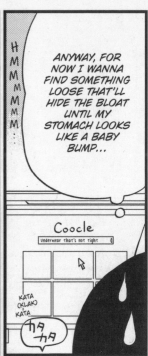

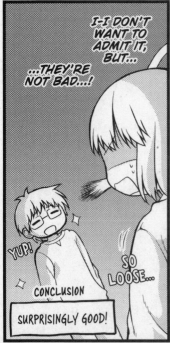

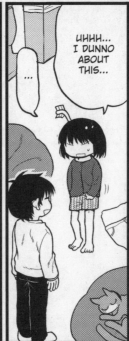

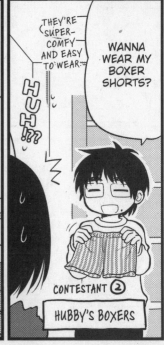

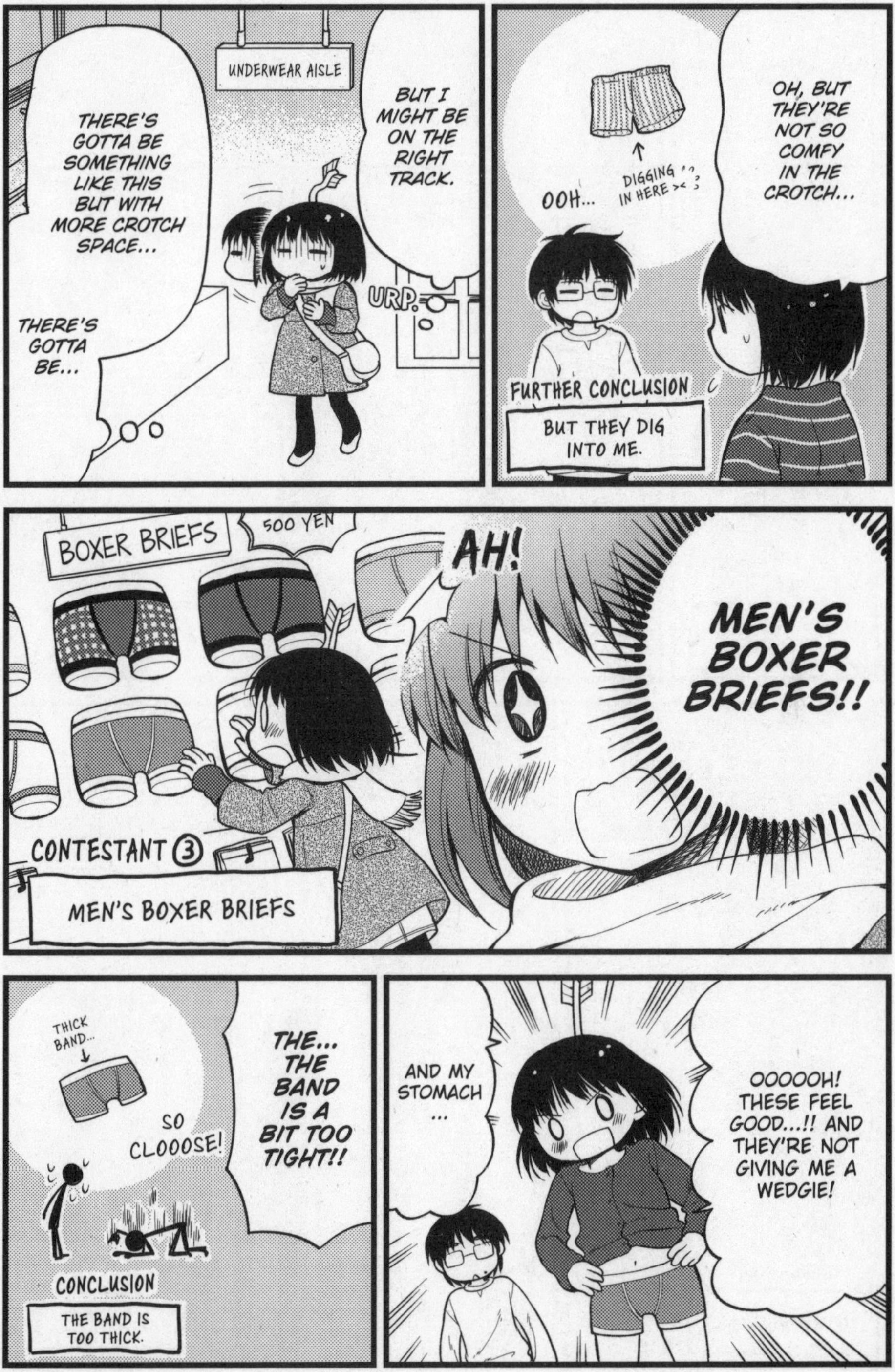

OH, BUT THEY'RE NOT SO COMFY IN THE CROTCH...
OOH...
DIGGING IN HERE ><
FURTHER CONCLUSION
BUT THEY DIG INTO ME.
UNDERWEAR AISLE
BUT I MIGHT BE ON THE RIGHT TRACK.
URP.
THERE'S GOTTA BE SOMETHING LIKE THIS BUT WITH MORE CROTCH SPACE...
THERE'S GOTTA BE...
MEN'S BOXER BRIEFS!!
AH!
500 YEN
BOXER BRIEFS
CONTESTANT 3
MEN'S BOXER BRIEFS
OOOOOH! THESE FEEL GOOD...!! AND THEY'RE NOT GIVING ME A WEDGIE!
AND MY STOMACH ...
THE... THE BAND IS A BIT TOO TIGHT!!
THICK BAND...
SO CLOOOSE!
CONCLUSION
THE BAND IS TOO THICK.

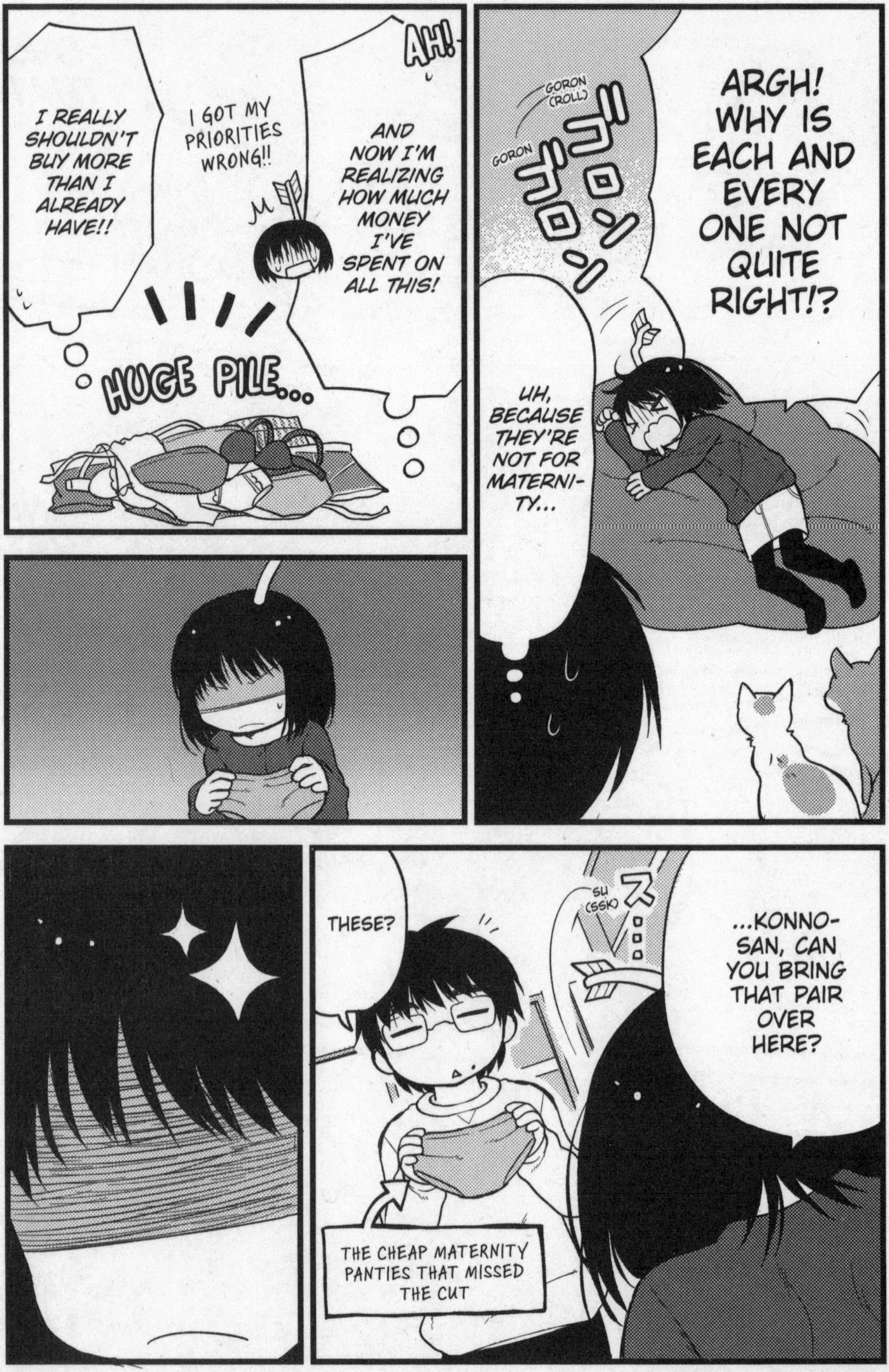
ARGH! WHY IS EACH AND EVERY ONE NOT QUITE RIGHT!?
GORON (ROLL)
GORON
UH, BECAUSE THEY'RE NOT FOR MATERNI-TY...
AH!
AND NOW I'M REALIZING HOW MUCH MONEY I'VE SPENT ON ALL THIS!
I GOT MY PRIORITIES WRONG!!
I REALLY SHOULDN'T BUY MORE THAN I ALREADY HAVE!!
HUGE PILE...
...KONNO-SAN, CAN YOU BRING THAT PAIR OVER HERE?
SU (SSK)
THESE?
THE CHEAP MATERNITY PANTIES THAT MISSED THE CUT

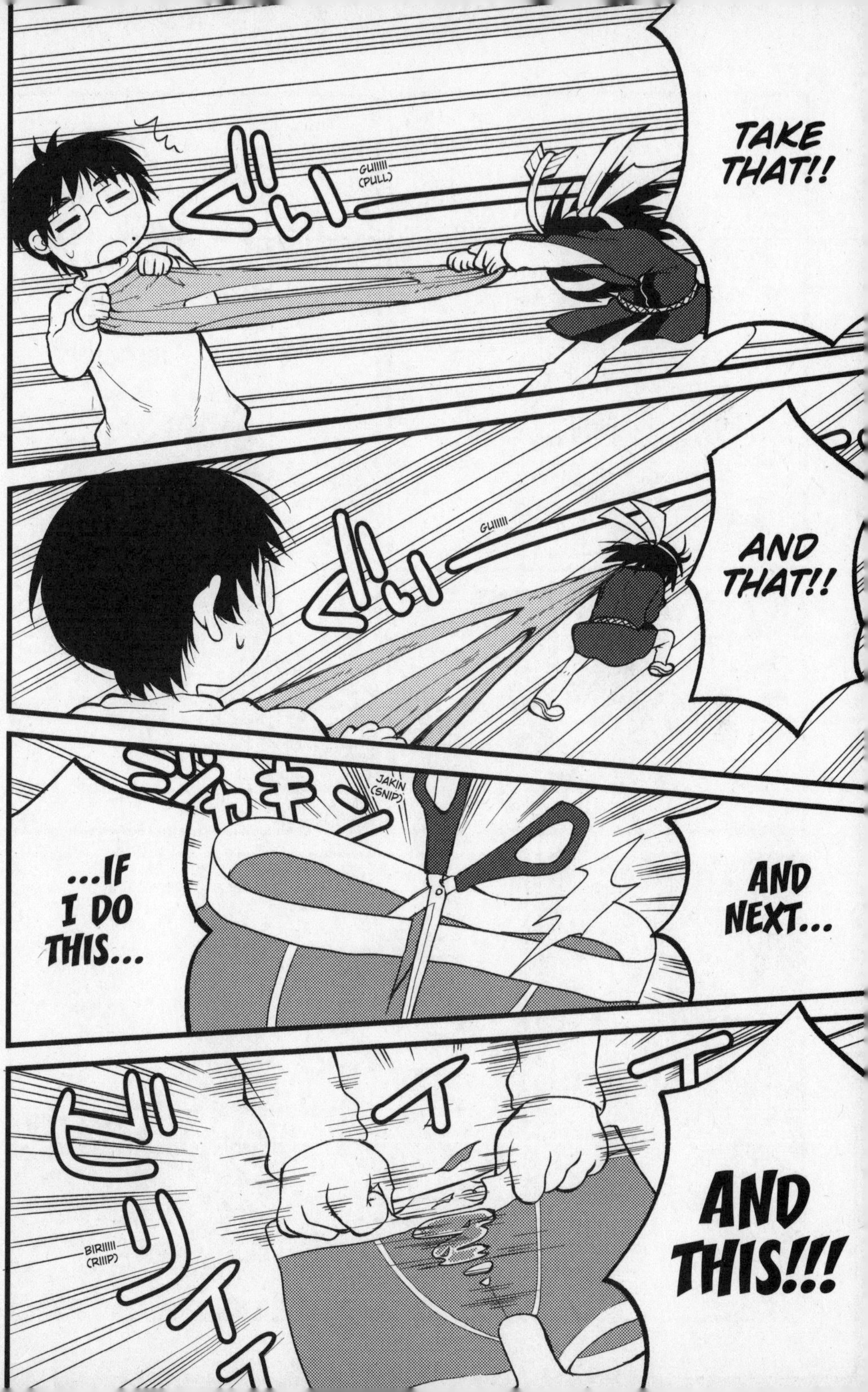
TAKE THAT!!
GUIIIII (PULL)
AND THAT!!
GUIIIII
AND NEXT...
JAKIN (SNIP)
...IF I DO THIS...
AND THIS!!!
BIRIIIII (RIIIP)

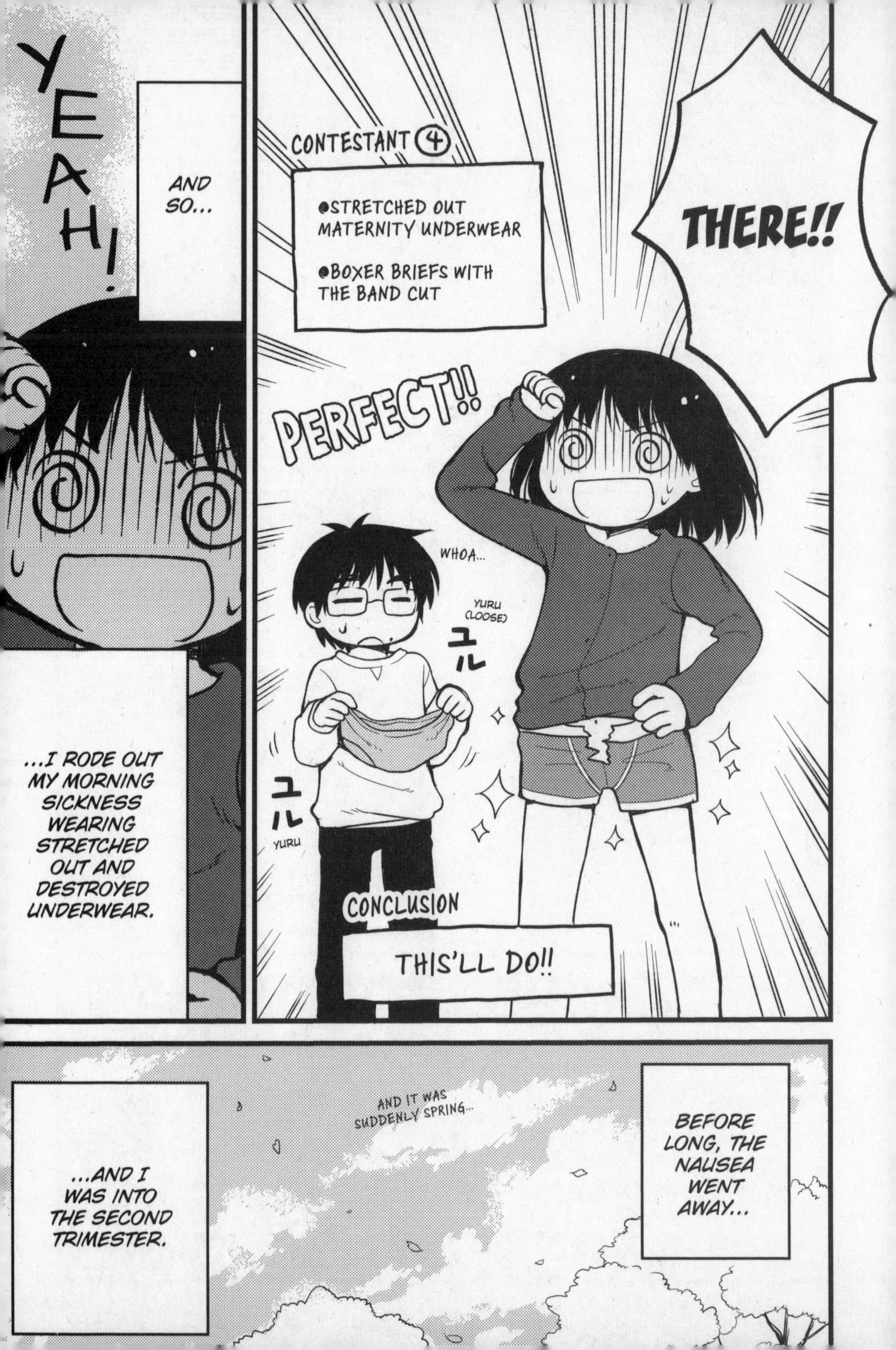
THERE!!
CONTESTANT ④
@STRETCHED OUT MATERNITY UNDERWEAR
@BOXER BRIEFS WITH THE BAND CUT
PERFECT!!
WHOA...
YURU (LOOSE)
ユル
ユル
YURU
CONCLUSION
THIS'LL DO!!
YEAH!
AND SO...
...I RODE OUT MY MORNING SICKNESS WEARING STRETCHED OUT AND DESTROYED UNDERWEAR.
BEFORE LONG, THE NAUSEA WENT AWAY...
AND IT WAS SUDDENLY SPRING...
...AND I WAS INTO THE SECOND TRIMESTER.

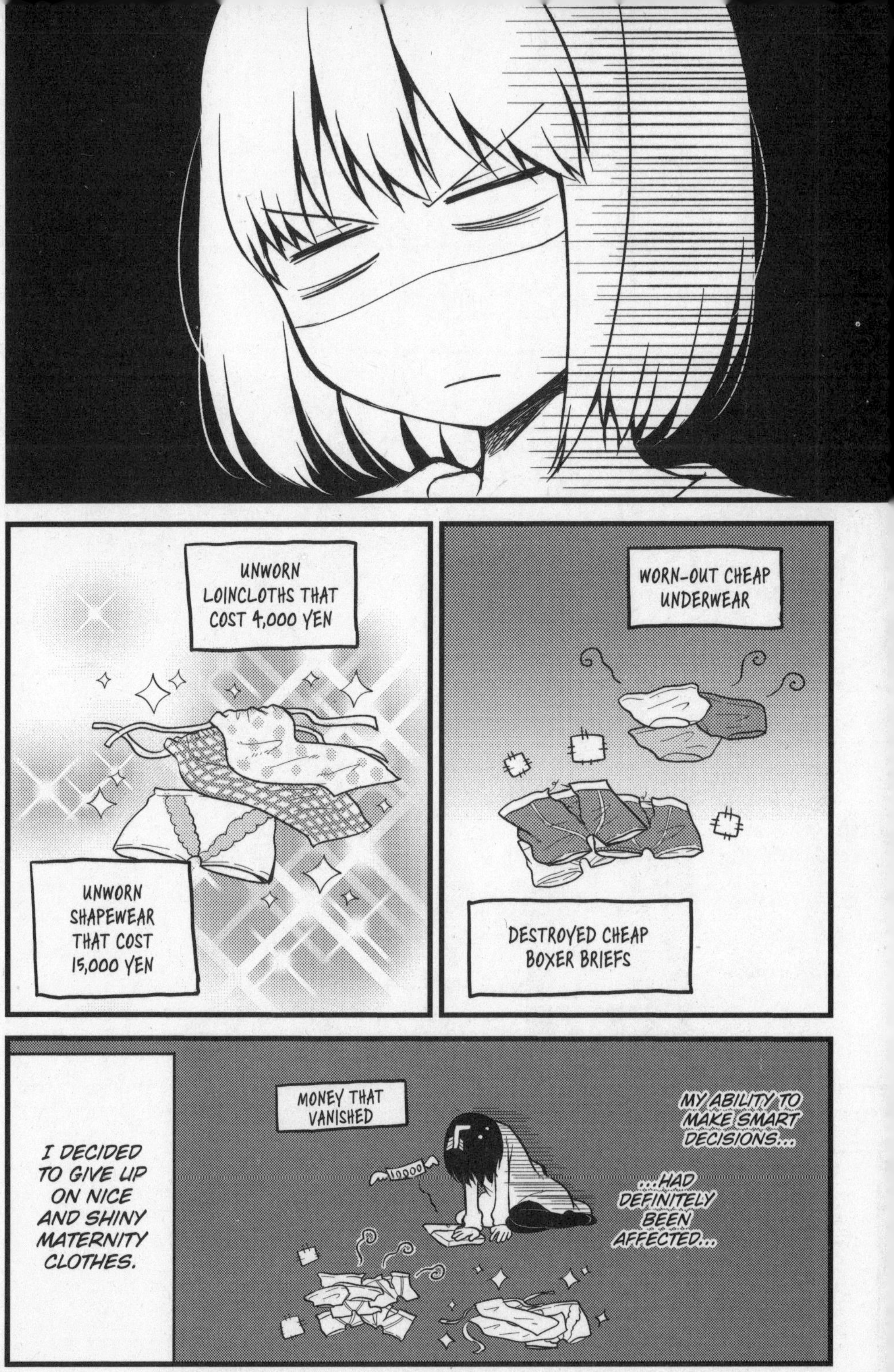
WORN-OUT CHEAP UNDERWEAR
DESTROYED CHEAP BOXER BRIEFS
UNWORN LOINCLOTHS THAT COST 4,000 YEN
UNWORN SHAPEWEAR THAT COST 15,000 YEN
MY ABILITY TO MAKE SMART DECISIONS...
...HAD DEFINITELY BEEN AFFECTED...
MONEY THAT VANISHED
I DECIDED TO GIVE UP ON NICE AND SHINY MATERNITY CLOTHES.

Chapter 5: I Don't Know How to Pick Out Maternity Underwear!

Bonus manga by Azure Konno

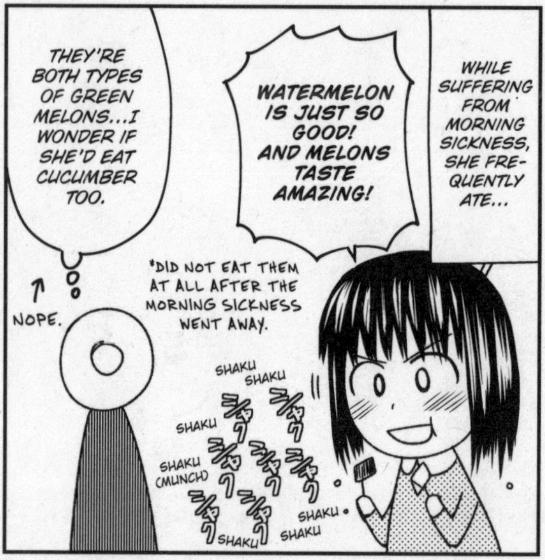
WHILE SUFFERING FROM MORNING SICKNESS, SHE FRE-QUENTLY ATE...
WATERMELON IS JUST SO GOOD! AND MELONS TASTE AMAZING!
THEY'RE BOTH TYPES OF GREEN MELONS...I WONDER IF SHE'D EAT CUCUMBER TOO.
NOPE.
*DID NOT EAT THEM AT ALL AFTER THE MORNING SICKNESS WENT AWAY.
SHAKU SHAKU
SHAKU
SHAKU (MUNCH)
SHAKU
SHAKU
SHAKU

While Kazama-san had morning sickness, she ate a ton of scones. (See page 58—we bought a ton of frozen ones from the bakery Good Day for You.)
Once, she messed up defrosting one of those scones →
It turned completely black, and the room was filled with smoke →
The smoke detector went off, and our neighbors crowded around to see what was going on →
She explained in a tearful voice that there was no fire and she only burned a scone →
I was out at the time, and she sent me teary text messages telling me what had happened →
She was a sobbing mess when I got home.
I comforted her, but I was privately laughing to myself because that's the kind of thing that only happens in manga.
It's still a mystery to me how the microwave managed to scorch the scone black.

Bonus manga by Ayami Kazama

Chapter 5: I Don't Know How to Pick Out Maternity Underwear!

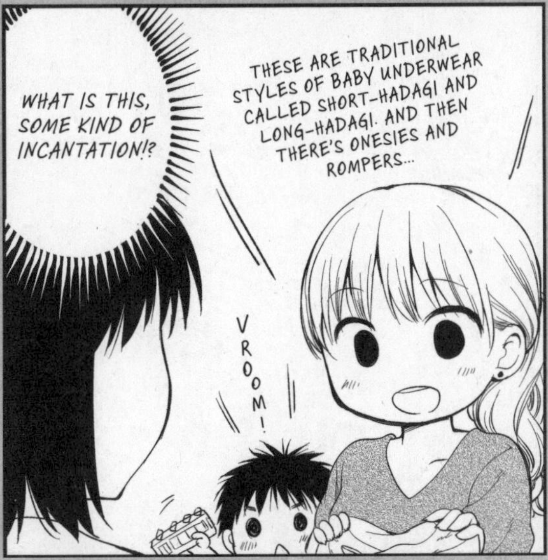
THESE ARE TRADITIONAL STYLES OF BABY UNDERWEAR CALLED SHORT-HADAGI AND LONG-HADAGI. AND THEN THERE'S ONESIES AND ROMPERS...
WHAT IS THIS, SOME KIND OF INCANTATION!?
VROOM!

This chapter describes how confused I was over adult underwear, but there are a ton of different kinds of underwear for babies too!!

My friend explained all the styles to me when she gave me her hand-me-downs, but I had no idea what the heck she was talking about at the time.

What are they called when they have short sleeves? Or buttons on the legs?

I couldn't even work out what their different purposes were. I tried to sort the ones she gave me based on the shapes, but the differences in their designs can be so subtle that I was at a complete loss.

When I asked Konno-san what he thought, he answered, "Can't we just sort them by whether they're for summer or winter and just choose whichever?"

I've always liked how "just do what works" he can be about things.

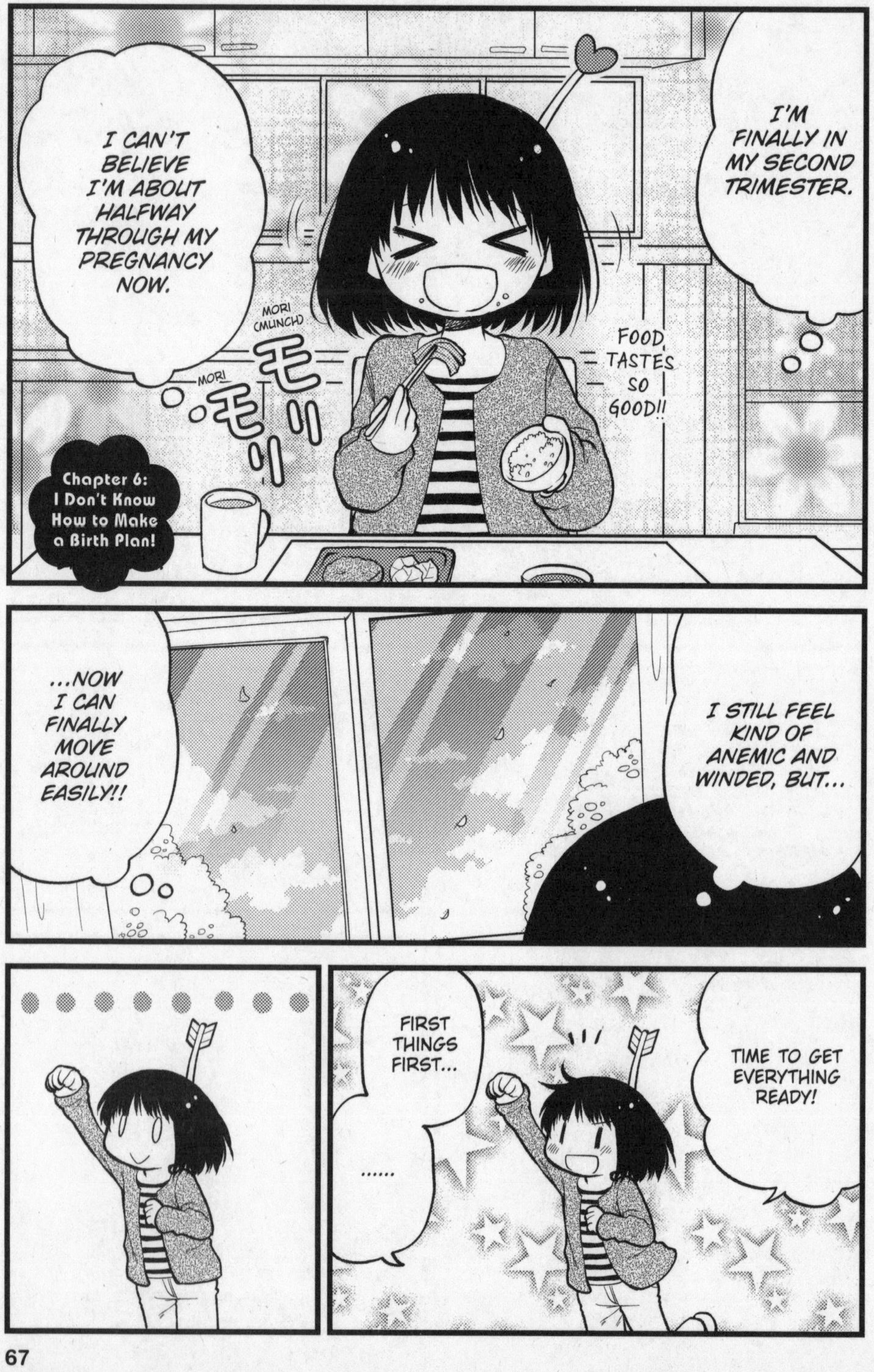
I'M FINALLY IN MY SECOND TRIMESTER.
I CAN'T BELIEVE I'M ABOUT HALFWAY THROUGH MY PREGNANCY NOW.
FOOD TASTES SO GOOD!!
モリ
MORI (MUNCH)
モリ
MORI
Chapter 6: I Don't Know How to Make a Birth Plan!
I STILL FEEL KIND OF ANEMIC AND WINDED, BUT...
...NOW I CAN FINALLY MOVE AROUND EASILY!!
TIME TO GET EVERYTHING READY!
FIRST THINGS FIRST...
......

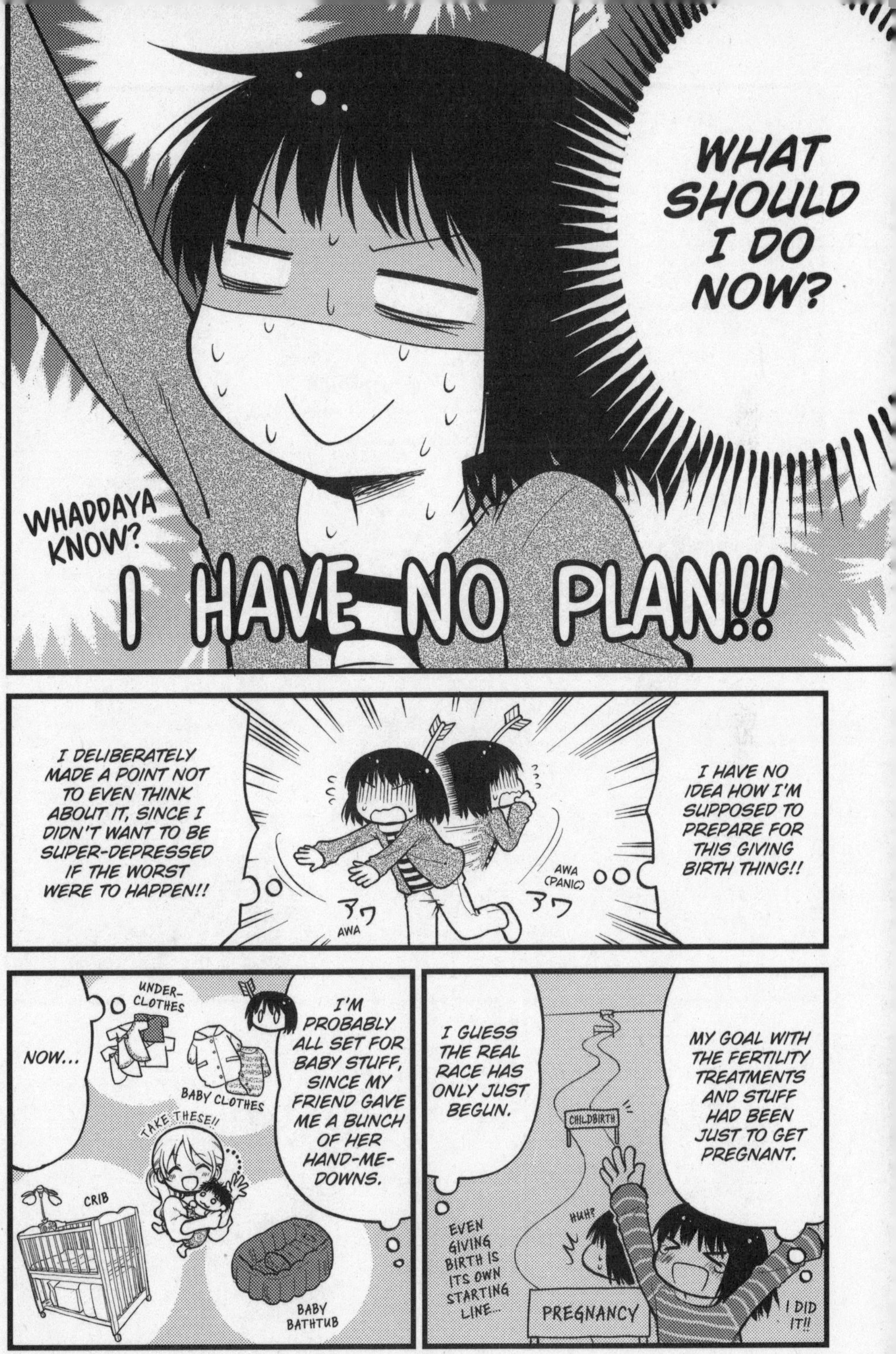
WHAT SHOULD I DO NOW?
WHADDAYA KNOW?
I HAVE NO PLAN!!
I HAVE NO IDEA HOW I'M SUPPOSED TO PREPARE FOR THIS GIVING BIRTH THING!!
AWA (PANIC)
I DELIBERATELY MADE A POINT NOT TO EVEN THINK ABOUT IT, SINCE I DIDN'T WANT TO BE SUPER-DEPRESSED IF THE WORST WERE TO HAPPEN!!
AWA
MY GOAL WITH THE FERTILITY TREATMENTS AND STUFF HAD BEEN JUST TO GET PREGNANT.
I GUESS THE REAL RACE HAS ONLY JUST BEGUN.
CHILDBIRTH
HUH?
EVEN GIVING BIRTH IS ITS OWN STARTING LINE...
I DID IT!!
PREGNANCY
I'M PROBABLY ALL SET FOR BABY STUFF, SINCE MY FRIEND GAVE ME A BUNCH OF HER HAND-ME-DOWNS.
UNDER-CLOTHES
NOW...
BABY CLOTHES
TAKE THESE!!
CRIB
BABY BATHTUB

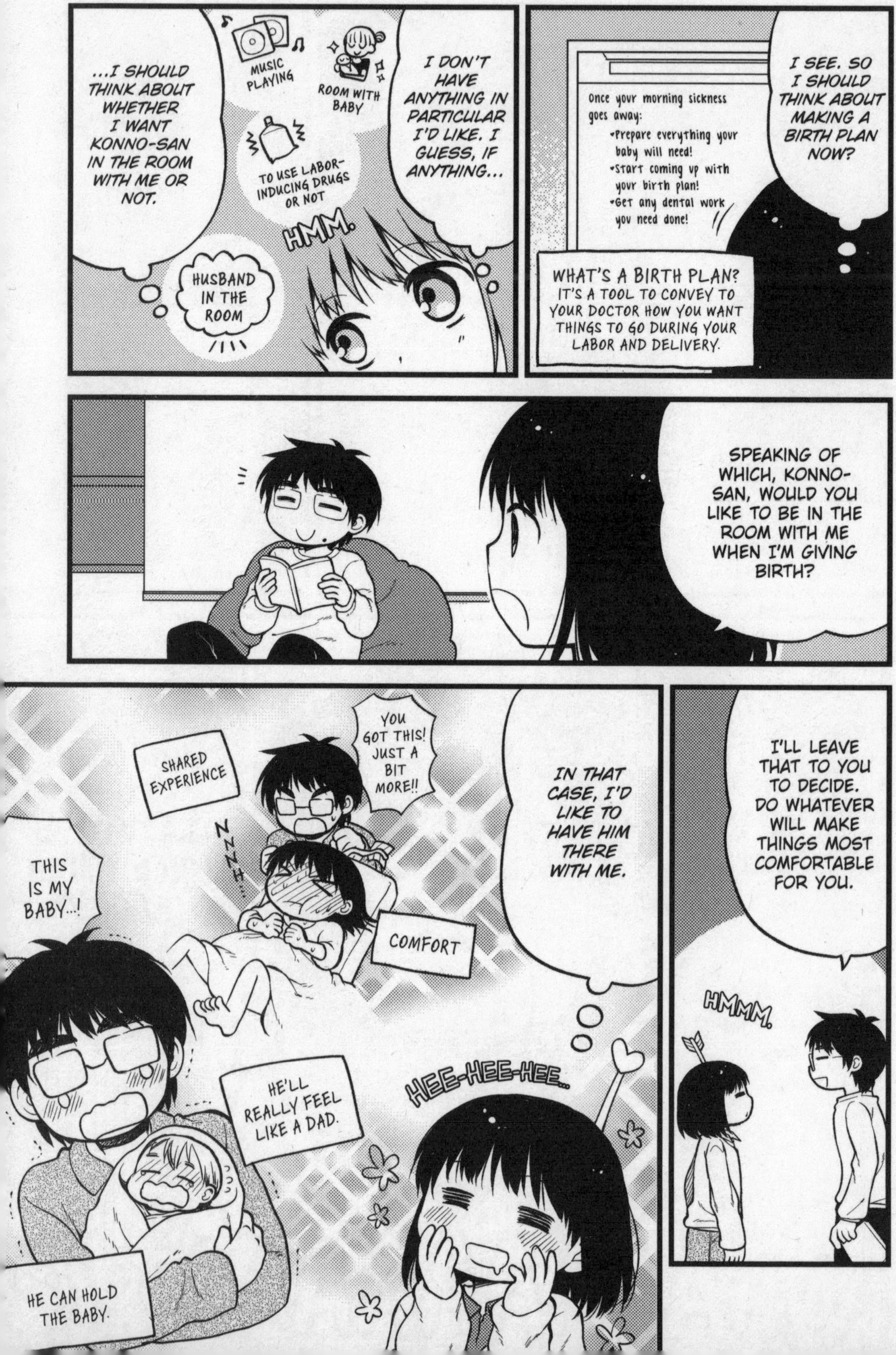
I SEE. SO I SHOULD THINK ABOUT MAKING A BIRTH PLAN NOW?
Once your morning sickness goes away:
•Prepare everything your baby will need!
•Start coming up with your birth plan!
•Get any dental work you need done!
WHAT'S A BIRTH PLAN? IT'S A TOOL TO CONVEY TO YOUR DOCTOR HOW YOU WANT THINGS TO GO DURING YOUR LABOR AND DELIVERY.
I DON'T HAVE ANYTHING IN PARTICULAR I'D LIKE. I GUESS, IF ANYTHING...
ROOM WITH BABY
MUSIC PLAYING
TO USE LABOR-INDUCING DRUGS OR NOT
HMM.
HUSBAND IN THE ROOM
...I SHOULD THINK ABOUT WHETHER I WANT KONNO-SAN IN THE ROOM WITH ME OR NOT.
SPEAKING OF WHICH, KONNO-SAN, WOULD YOU LIKE TO BE IN THE ROOM WITH ME WHEN I'M GIVING BIRTH?
I'LL LEAVE THAT TO YOU TO DECIDE. DO WHATEVER WILL MAKE THINGS MOST COMFORTABLE FOR YOU.
HMMM.
IN THAT CASE, I'D LIKE TO HAVE HIM THERE WITH ME.
YOU GOT THIS! JUST A BIT MORE!!
SHARED EXPERIENCE
NNNH...
COMFORT
THIS IS MY BABY...!
HEE-HEE-HEE...
HE'LL REALLY FEEL LIKE A DAD.
HE CAN HOLD THE BABY.

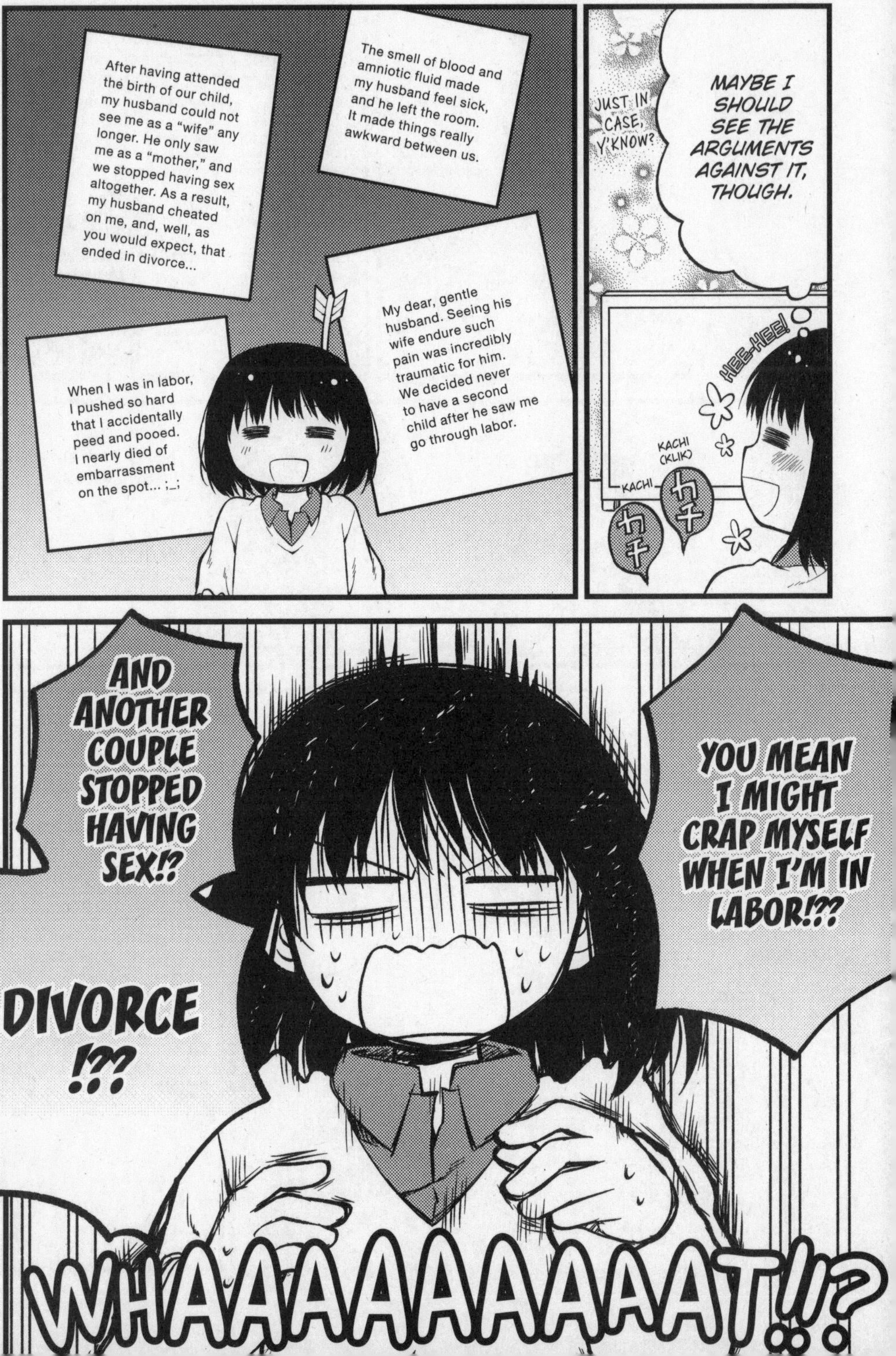
MAYBE I SHOULD SEE THE ARGUMENTS AGAINST IT, THOUGH.
JUST IN CASE, Y'KNOW?
HEE-HEE!
KACHI (KLIK)
KACHI
カチ
カチ
The smell of blood and amniotic fluid made my husband feel sick, and he left the room. It made things really awkward between us.
After having attended the birth of our child, my husband could not see me as a "wife" any longer. He only saw me as a "mother," and we stopped having sex altogether. As a result, my husband cheated on me, and, well, as you would expect, that ended in divorce...
My dear, gentle husband. Seeing his wife endure such pain was incredibly traumatic for him. We decided never to have a second child after he saw me go through labor.
When I was in labor, I pushed so hard that I accidentally peed and pooed. I nearly died of embarrassment on the spot... ;_;
YOU MEAN I MIGHT CRAP MYSELF WHEN I'M IN LABOR!??
AND ANOTHER COUPLE STOPPED HAVING SEX!?
DIVORCE !??
WHAAAAAAAAAAT!!?

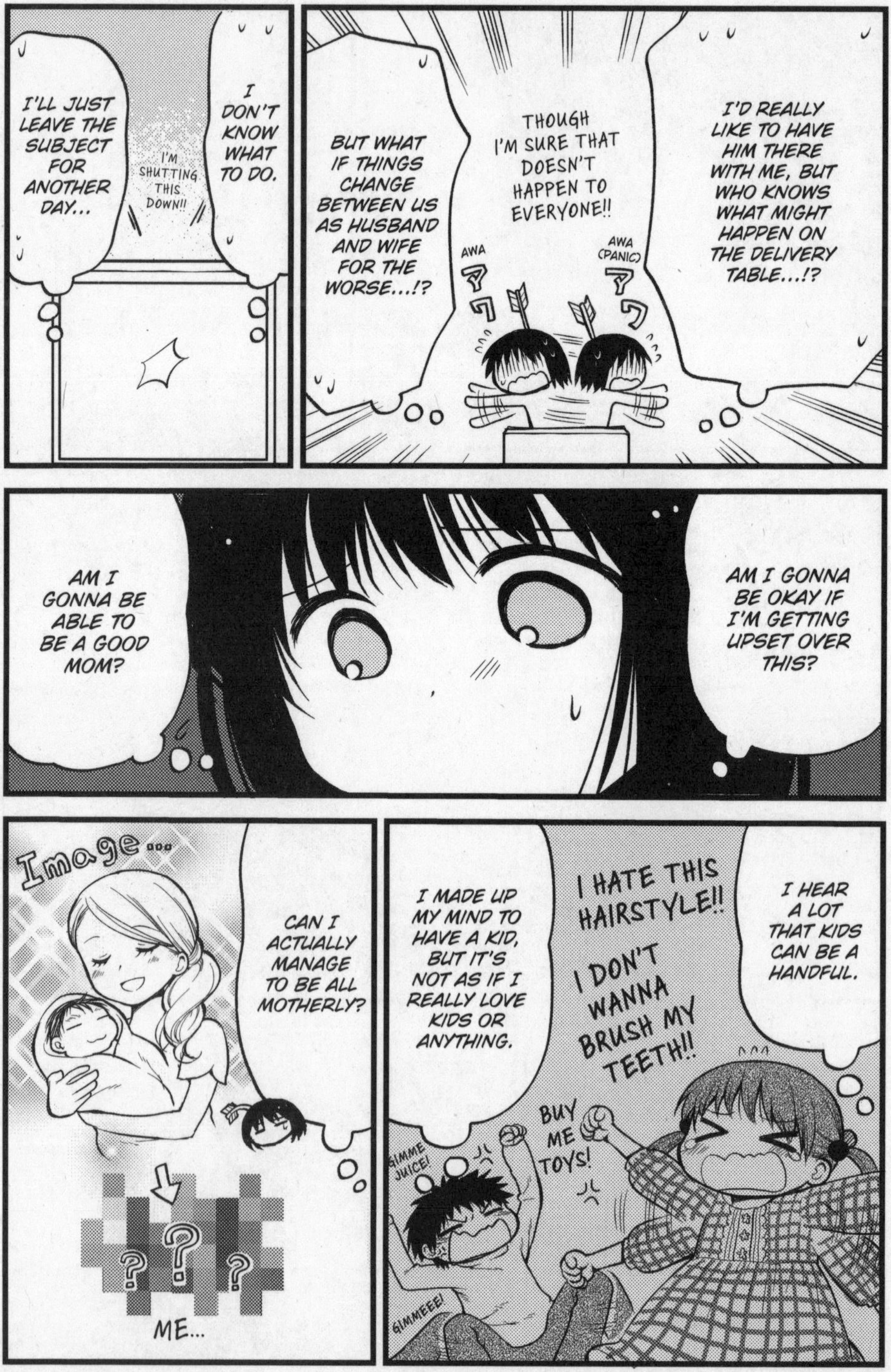
I'D REALLY LIKE TO HAVE HIM THERE WITH ME, BUT WHO KNOWS WHAT MIGHT HAPPEN ON THE DELIVERY TABLE...!?
THOUGH I'M SURE THAT DOESN'T HAPPEN TO EVERYONE!!
AWA (PANIC)
AWA
BUT WHAT IF THINGS CHANGE BETWEEN US AS HUSBAND AND WIFE FOR THE WORSE...!?
I DON'T KNOW WHAT TO DO.
I'M SHUTTING THIS DOWN!!
I'LL JUST LEAVE THE SUBJECT FOR ANOTHER DAY...
AM I GONNA BE OKAY IF I'M GETTING UPSET OVER THIS?
AM I GONNA BE ABLE TO BE A GOOD MOM?
I HEAR A LOT THAT KIDS CAN BE A HANDFUL.
I HATE THIS HAIRSTYLE!!
I DON'T WANNA BRUSH MY TEETH!!
BUY ME TOYS!
GIMME JUICE!
GIMMEEE!
I MADE UP MY MIND TO HAVE A KID, BUT IT'S NOT AS IF I REALLY LOVE KIDS OR ANYTHING.
CAN I ACTUALLY MANAGE TO BE ALL MOTHERLY?
Image...
ME...

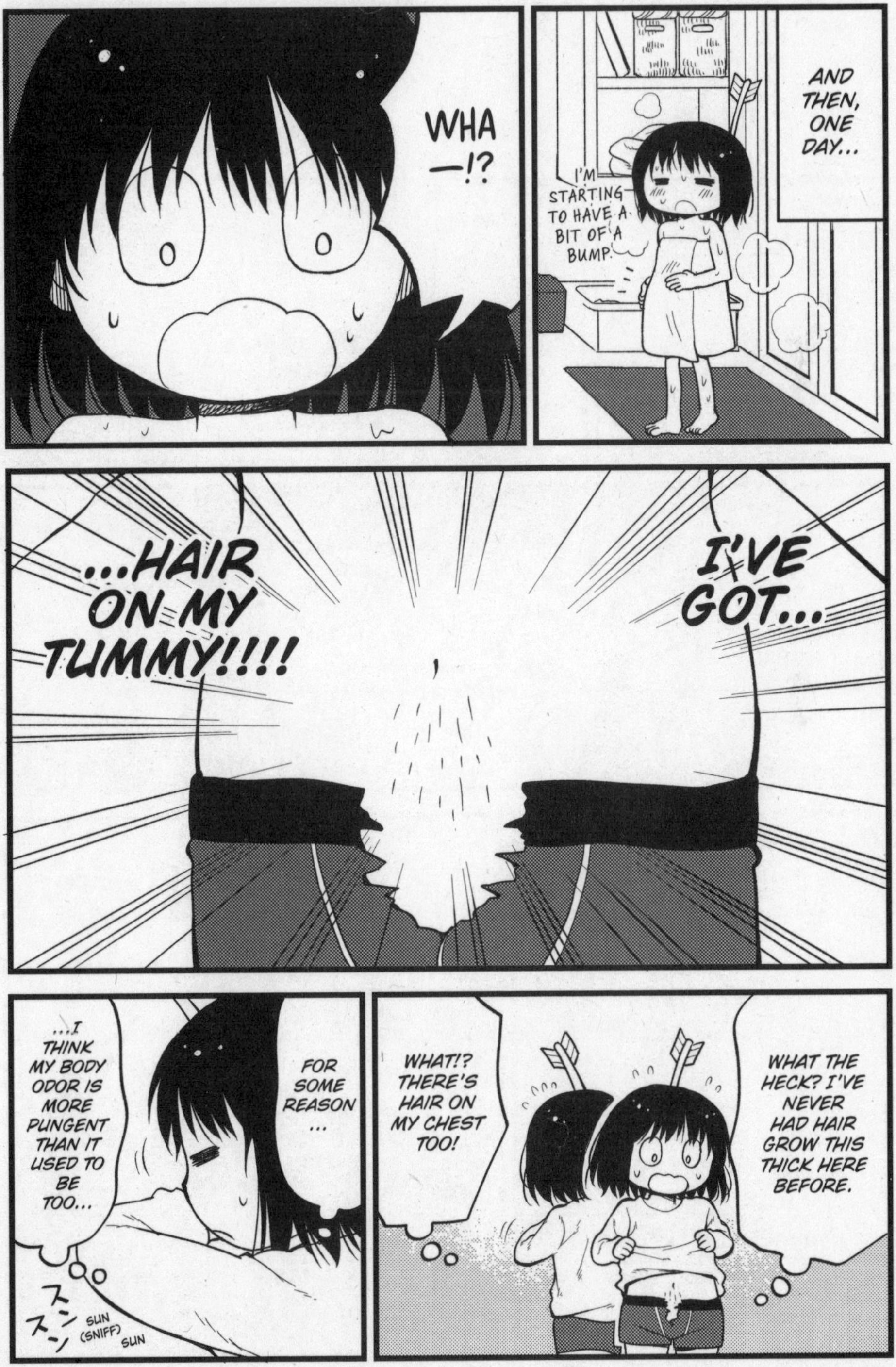
AND THEN, ONE DAY...
I'M STARTING TO HAVE A BIT OF A BUMP.
WHA—!?
I'VE GOT...
...HAIR ON MY TUMMY!!!!
WHAT THE HECK? I'VE NEVER HAD HAIR GROW THIS THICK HERE BEFORE.
WHAT!? THERE'S HAIR ON MY CHEST TOO!
FOR SOME REASON...
...I THINK MY BODY ODOR IS MORE PUNGENT THAN IT USED TO BE TOO...
スンスーン
SUN (SNIFF) SUN

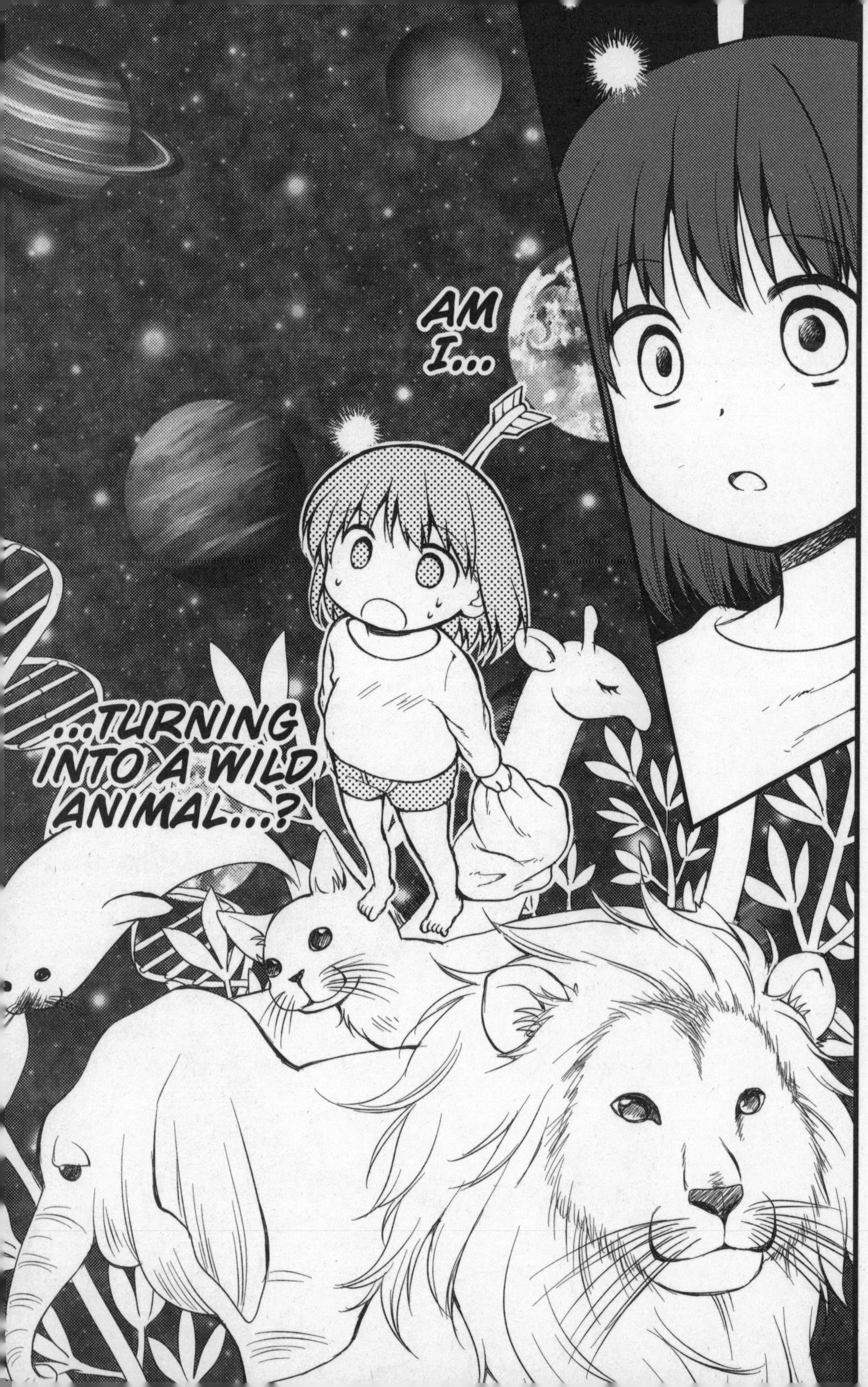
AM I...
...TURNING INTO A WILD ANIMAL...?

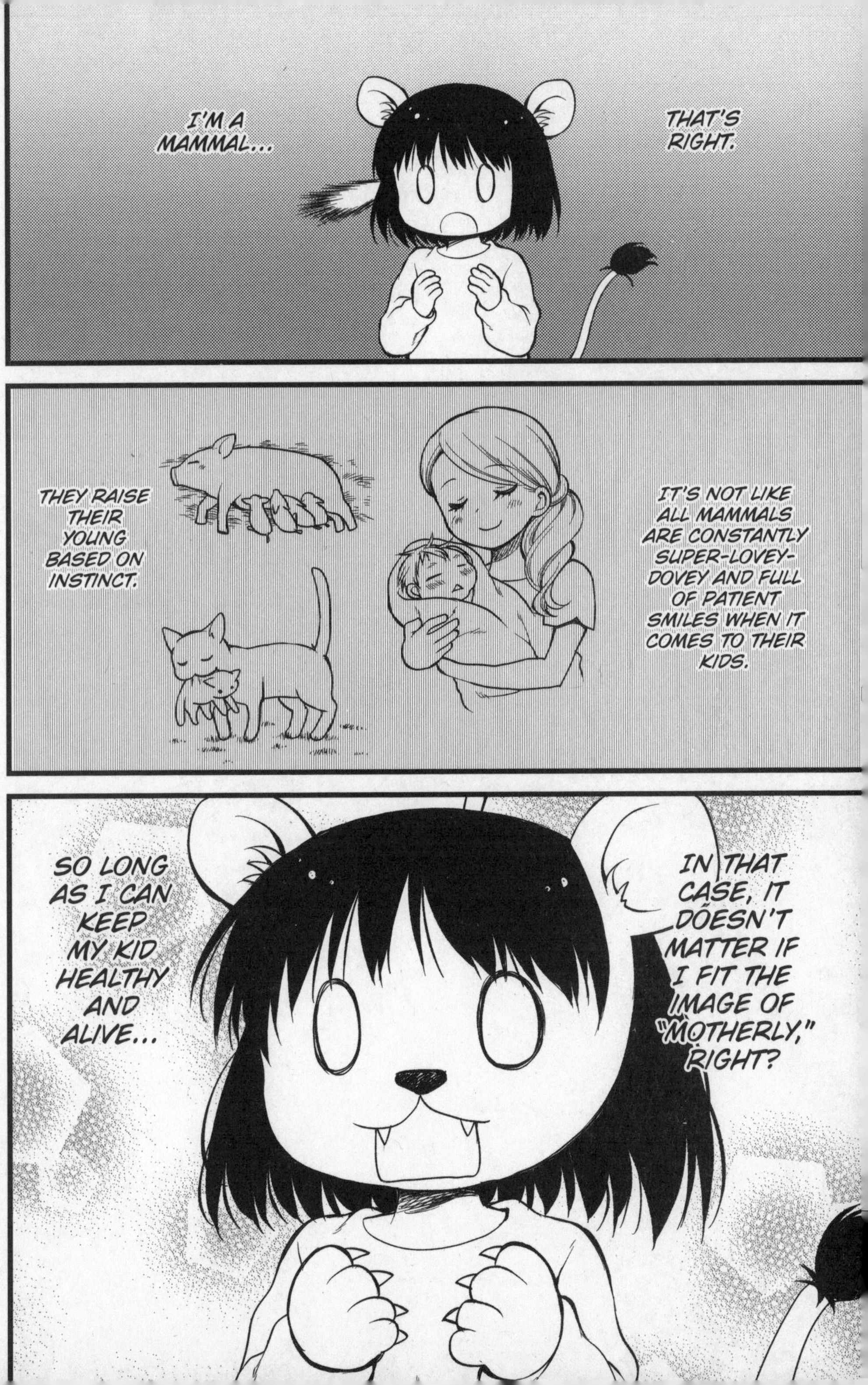
THAT'S RIGHT.
I'M A MAMMAL...
IT'S NOT LIKE ALL MAMMALS ARE CONSTANTLY SUPER-LOVEY-DOVEY AND FULL OF PATIENT SMILES WHEN IT COMES TO THEIR KIDS.
THEY RAISE THEIR YOUNG BASED ON INSTINCT.
IN THAT CASE, IT DOESN'T MATTER IF I FIT THE IMAGE OF "MOTHERLY," RIGHT?
SO LONG AS I CAN KEEP MY KID HEALTHY AND ALIVE...

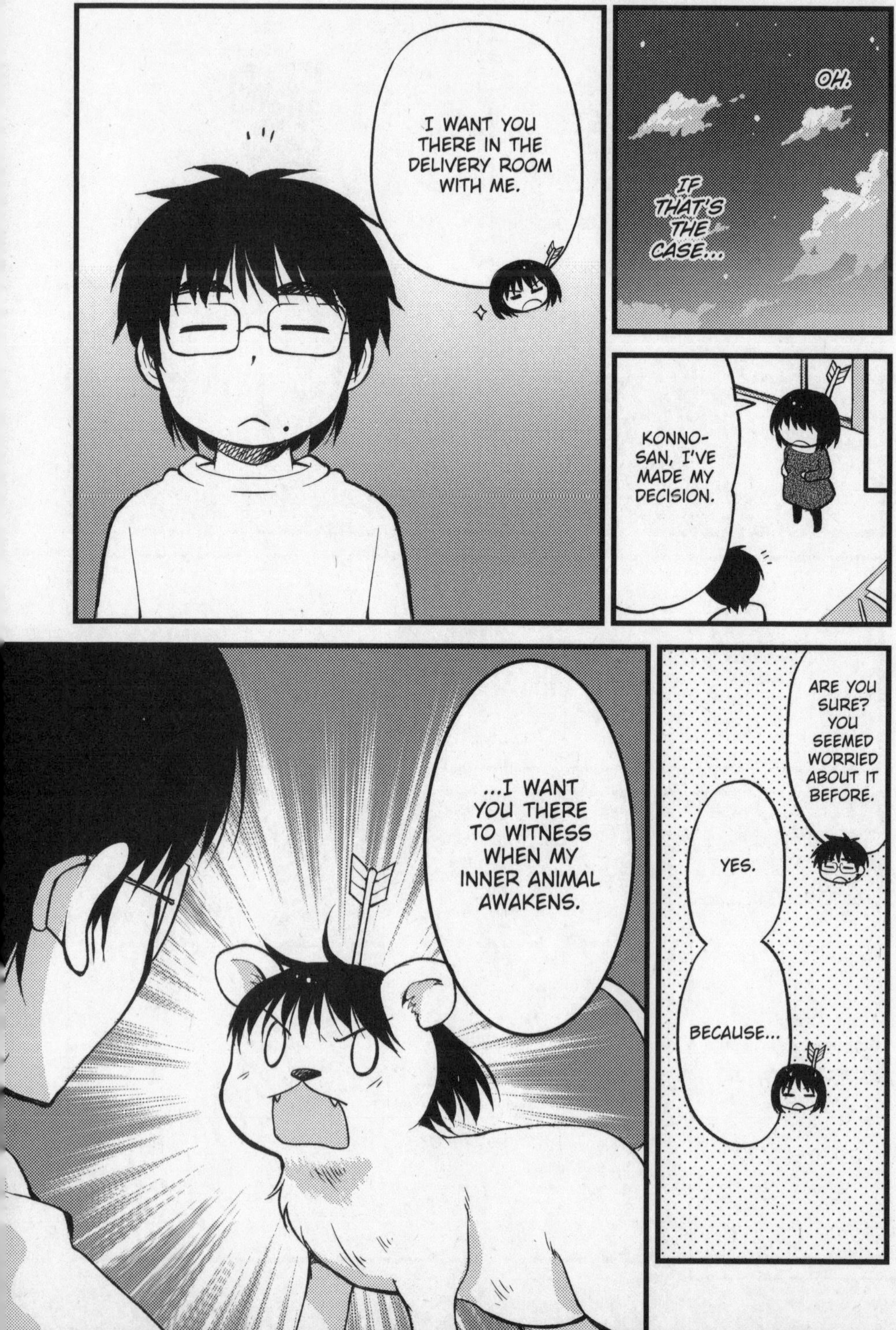
OH.
IF THAT'S THE CASE...
KONNO-SAN, I'VE MADE MY DECISION.
I WANT YOU THERE IN THE DELIVERY ROOM WITH ME.
ARE YOU SURE? YOU SEEMED WORRIED ABOUT IT BEFORE.
YES.
BECAUSE...
...I WANT YOU THERE TO WITNESS WHEN MY INNER ANIMAL AWAKENS.

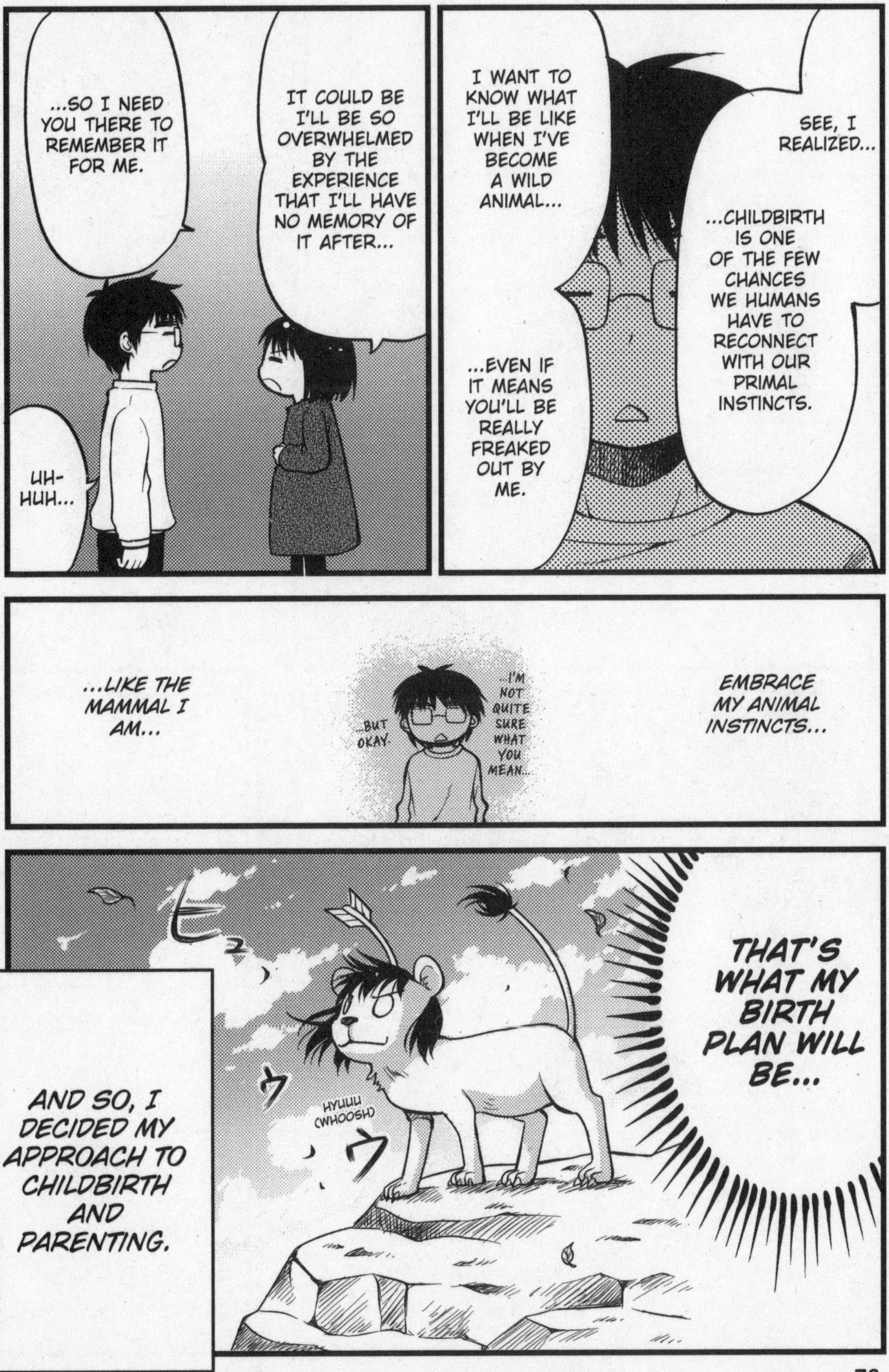
SEE, I REALIZED...
...CHILDBIRTH IS ONE OF THE FEW CHANCES WE HUMANS HAVE TO RECONNECT WITH OUR PRIMAL INSTINCTS.
I WANT TO KNOW WHAT I'LL BE LIKE WHEN I'VE BECOME A WILD ANIMAL...
...EVEN IF IT MEANS YOU'LL BE REALLY FREAKED OUT BY ME.
IT COULD BE I'LL BE SO OVERWHELMED BY THE EXPERIENCE THAT I'LL HAVE NO MEMORY OF IT AFTER...
...SO I NEED YOU THERE TO REMEMBER IT FOR ME.
UH-HUH...
EMBRACE MY ANIMAL INSTINCTS...
...I'M NOT QUITE SURE WHAT YOU MEAN...
...BUT OKAY.
...LIKE THE MAMMAL I AM...
THAT'S WHAT MY BIRTH PLAN WILL BE...
HYUUU (WHOOSH)
AND SO, I DECIDED MY APPROACH TO CHILDBIRTH AND PARENTING.

Chapter 6: I Don't Know How to Make a Birth Plan!

Bonus manga by Azure Konno

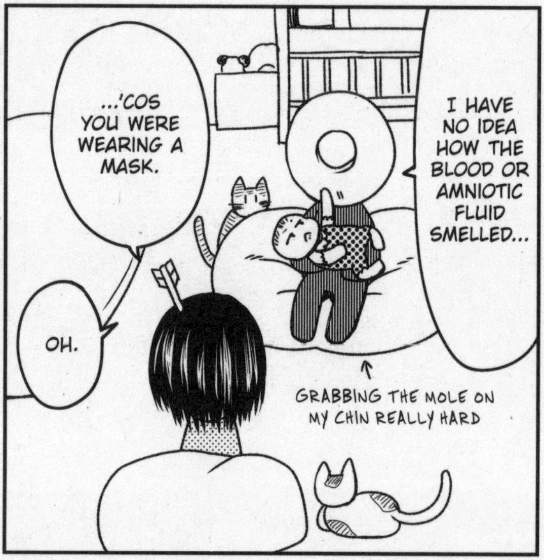
I HAVE NO IDEA HOW THE BLOOD OR AMNIOTIC FLUID SMELLED...
...'COS YOU WERE WEARING A MASK.
OH.
GRABBING THE MOLE ON MY CHIN REALLY HARD

At the time she was going on about wild animals, I thought, "Yet again, I have no idea what she's on about. Ha-ha!"

But I wouldn't say her return to her "inner animal" was too intense or anything.

She didn't have any accidents on the delivery table, we still have a healthy sex life, and we're still married. Thankfully.

And I was fine despite the blood, since I'm one of those people who's always curious about surgeries.

Kazama-san's only request for me in the delivery room was that I wouldn't look between her legs when the baby was coming out.

I think it's probably for the best that I didn't see that.

There are a lot of things in life you're just better off not seeing with your own eyes.

Bonus manga by Ayami Kazama

Chapter 6: I Don't Know How to Make a Birth Plan!

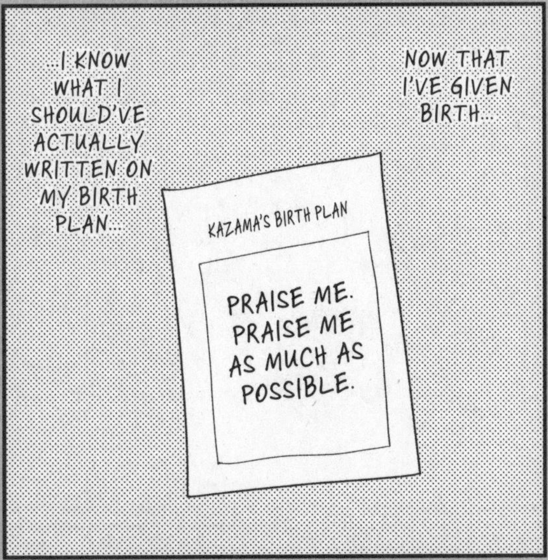
NOW THAT I'VE GIVEN BIRTH...
...I KNOW WHAT I SHOULD'VE ACTUALLY WRITTEN ON MY BIRTH PLAN...
KAZAMA'S BIRTH PLAN
PRAISE ME. PRAISE ME AS MUCH AS POSSIBLE.

I know I really labored trying to come up with something for my birth plan, but when I was screaming, "I can't do this! I can't do thiiiiis!!!" because of the pain of the contractions during the pushing phase, the nurse told me, "Don't say you can't do this! If you can't, then it'll never be over!!!"
It made me wish I had written "praise me as much as possible" on my birth plan.
I know, I know. It wasn't that she was mad or anything. In fact, her words were actually meant to be supportive. But the contractions had made me emotionally very fragile. Anything other than overly kind words really hurt my feelings.
When I was in labor and called one of the nurses, she asked me, "Can you walk to the delivery room? Or do I need to get you a wheelchair?" I was a sobbing mess when I responded, "Why do you have to ask? Just bring iiiit!!"
I know, I know, I was being way too emotional. I was never this bad as a teenager. It's just contractions really are that intense—they take over your entire being...

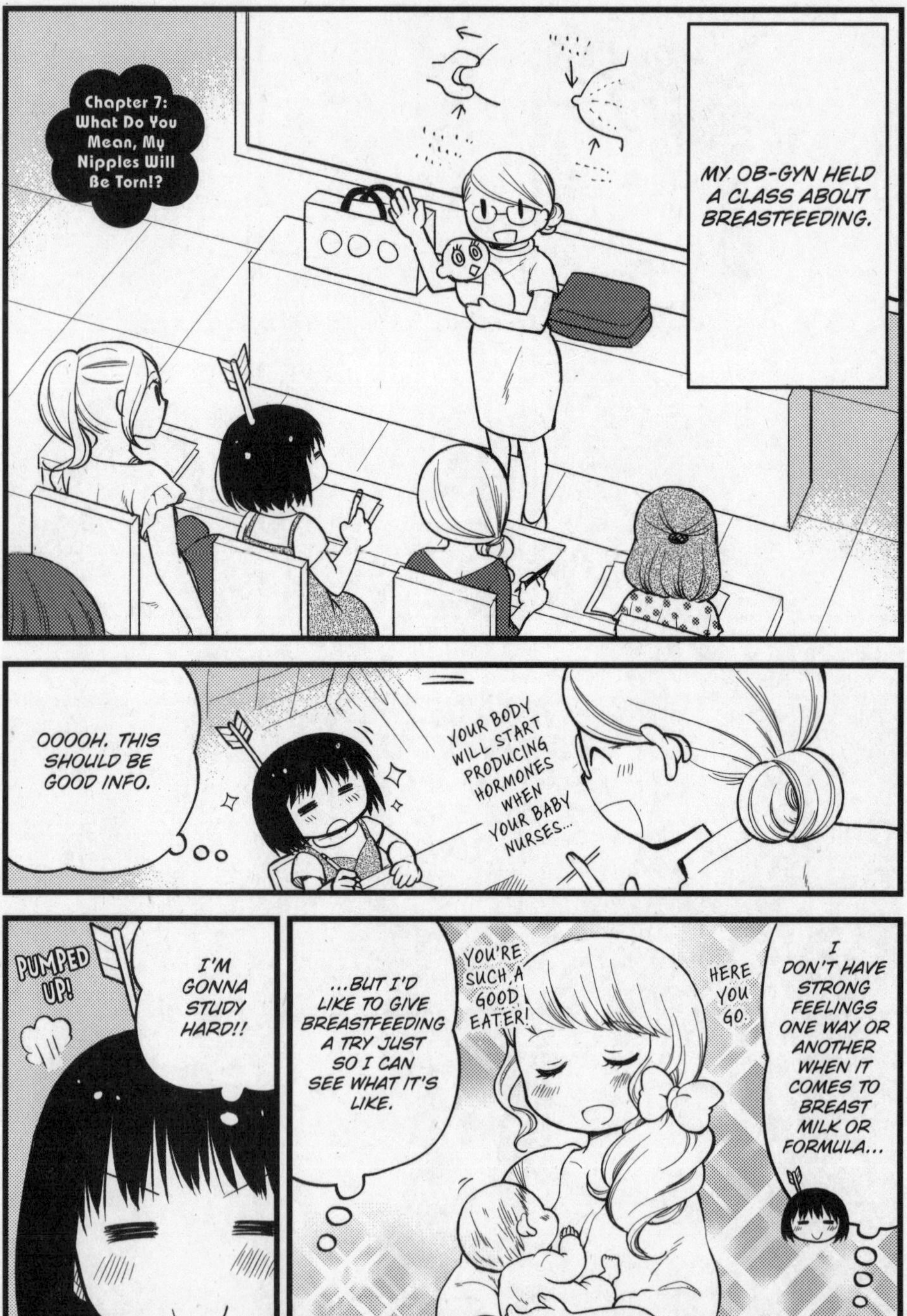
MY OB-GYN HELD A CLASS ABOUT BREASTFEEDING.
Chapter 7: What Do You Mean, My Nipples Will Be Torn!?
YOUR BODY WILL START PRODUCING HORMONES WHEN YOUR BABY NURSES...
OOOOH. THIS SHOULD BE GOOD INFO.
I DON'T HAVE STRONG FEELINGS ONE WAY OR ANOTHER WHEN IT COMES TO BREAST MILK OR FORMULA...
HERE YOU GO.
YOU'RE SUCH A GOOD EATER!
...BUT I'D LIKE TO GIVE BREASTFEEDING A TRY JUST SO I CAN SEE WHAT IT'S LIKE.
COMMUNICATION BETWEEN MOTHER AND CHILD
I'M GONNA STUDY HARD!!
PUMPED UP!

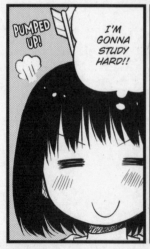

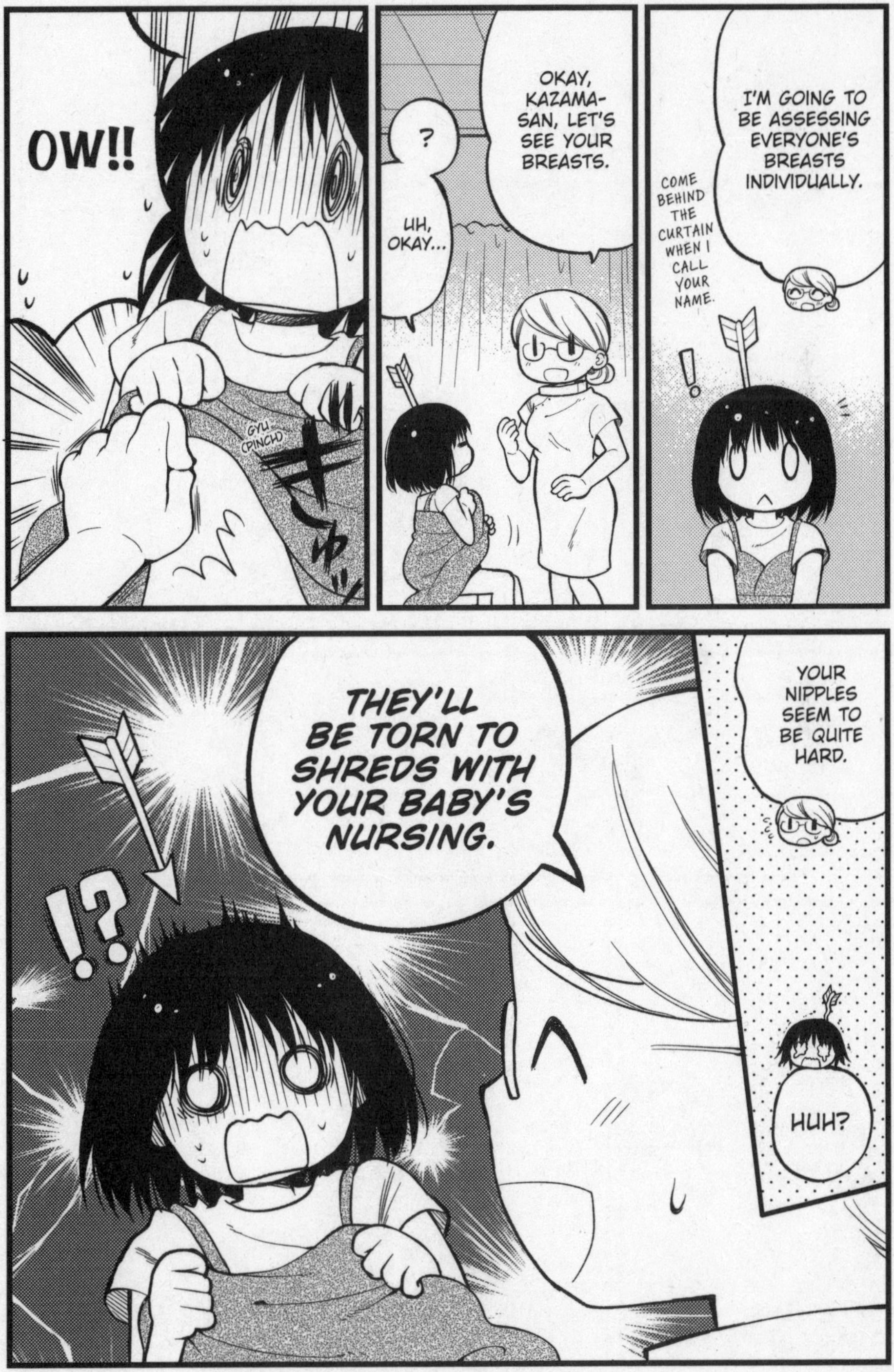
I'M GOING TO BE ASSESSING EVERYONE'S BREASTS INDIVIDUALLY.
COME BEHIND THE CURTAIN WHEN I CALL YOUR NAME.
!
OKAY, KAZAMA-SAN, LET'S SEE YOUR BREASTS.
?
UH, OKAY...
OW!!
GYU (PINCH)
YOUR NIPPLES SEEM TO BE QUITE HARD.
THEY'LL BE TORN TO SHREDS WITH YOUR BABY'S NURSING.
!?
HUH?

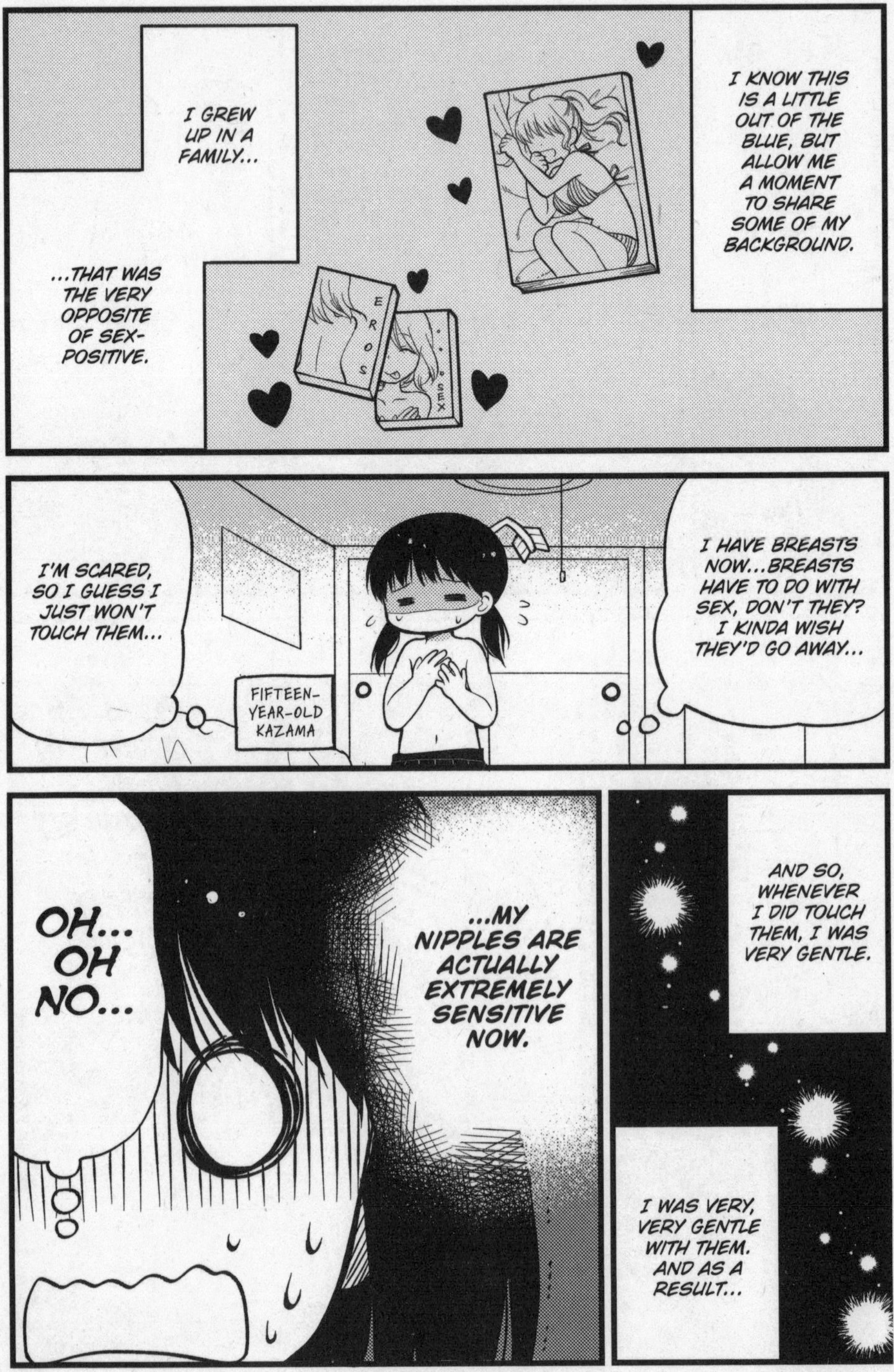
I KNOW THIS IS A LITTLE OUT OF THE BLUE, BUT ALLOW ME A MOMENT TO SHARE SOME OF MY BACKGROUND.
I GREW UP IN A FAMILY...
...THAT WAS THE VERY OPPOSITE OF SEX-POSITIVE.
EROS
SEX
I HAVE BREASTS NOW...BREASTS HAVE TO DO WITH SEX, DON'T THEY? I KINDA WISH THEY'D GO AWAY...
FIFTEEN-YEAR-OLD KAZAMA
I'M SCARED, SO I GUESS I JUST WON'T TOUCH THEM...
AND SO, WHENEVER I DID TOUCH THEM, I WAS VERY GENTLE.
I WAS VERY, VERY GENTLE WITH THEM. AND AS A RESULT...
...MY NIPPLES ARE ACTUALLY EXTREMELY SENSITIVE NOW.
OH... OH NO...

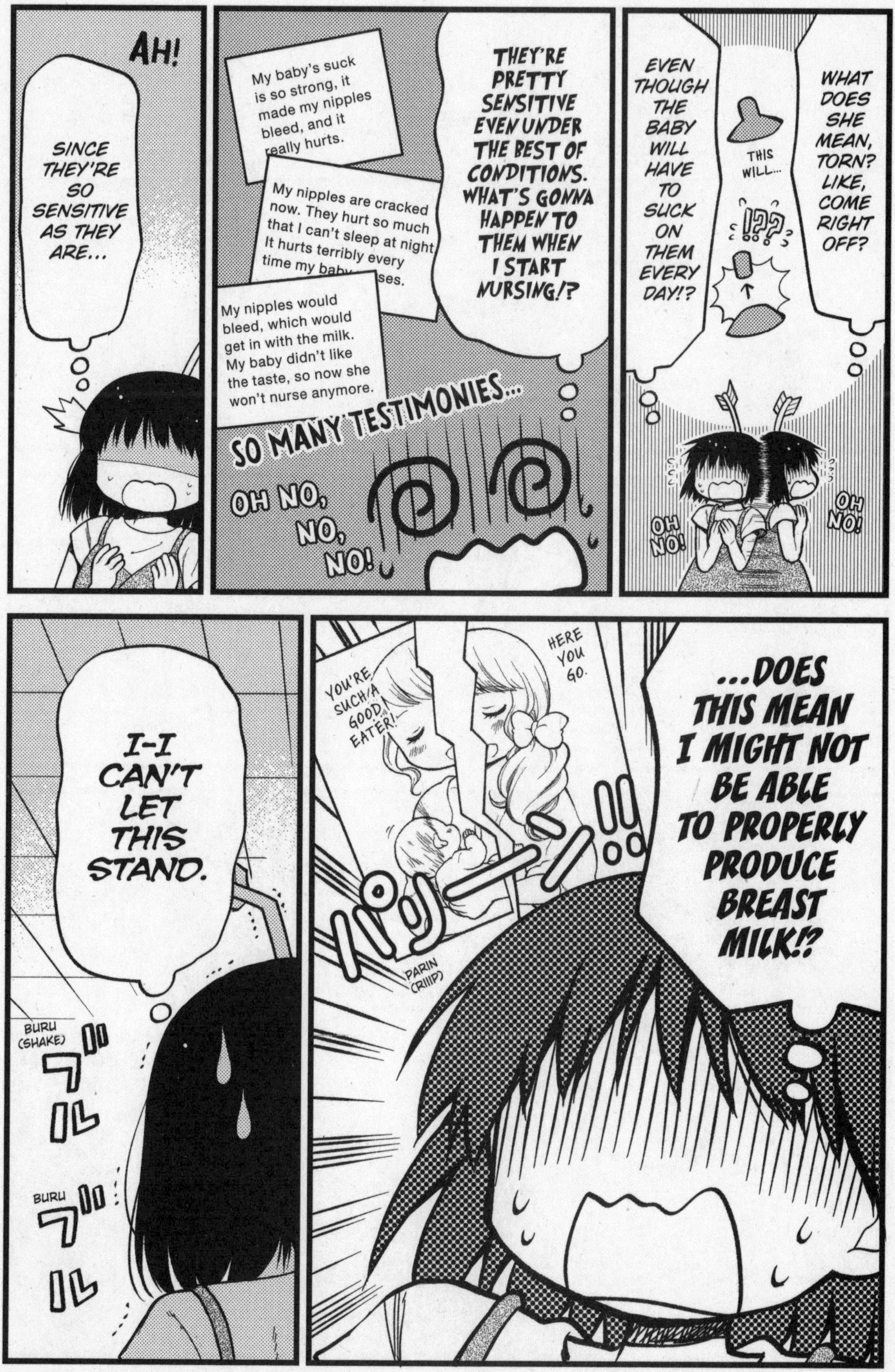
WHAT DOES SHE MEAN, TORN? LIKE, COME RIGHT OFF?
EVEN THOUGH THE BABY WILL HAVE TO SUCK ON THEM EVERY DAY!?
THIS WILL...
!??
OH NO!
OH NO!
THEY'RE PRETTY SENSITIVE EVEN UNDER THE BEST OF CONDITIONS. WHAT'S GONNA HAPPEN TO THEM WHEN I START NURSING!?
My baby's suck is so strong, it made my nipples bleed, and it really hurts.
My nipples are cracked now. They hurt so much that I can't sleep at night. It hurts terribly every time my baby
My nipples would bleed, which would get in with the milk. My baby didn't like the taste, so now she won't nurse anymore.
SO MANY TESTIMONIES...
OH NO, NO, NO!
AH!
SINCE THEY'RE SO SENSITIVE AS THEY ARE...
...DOES THIS MEAN I MIGHT NOT BE ABLE TO PROPERLY PRODUCE BREAST MILK!?
HERE YOU GO.
YOU'RE SUCH A GOOD EATER!
パリーン!!
PARIN (CRIIIP)
I-I CAN'T LET THIS STAND.
BURU (SHAKE)
ブル
BURU
ブル

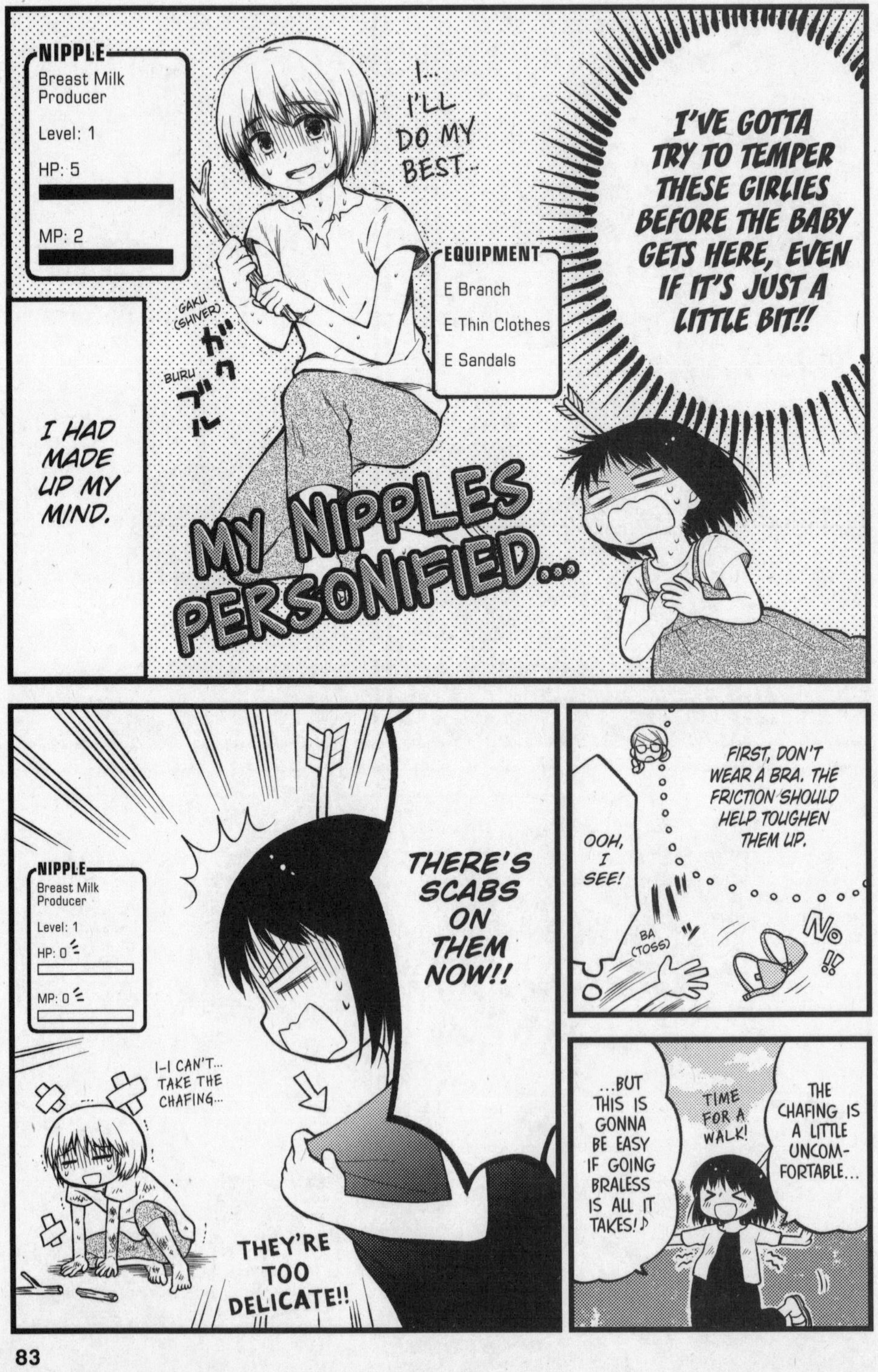
I'VE GOTTA TRY TO TEMPER THESE GIRLIES BEFORE THE BABY GETS HERE, EVEN IF IT'S JUST A LITTLE BIT!!
MY NIPPLES PERSONIFIED...
EQUIPMENT
E Branch
E Thin Clothes
E Sandals
I... I'LL DO MY BEST...
GAKU (SHIVER) ガク
BURU ブル
NIPPLE
Breast Milk Producer
Level: 1
HP: 5
MP: 2
I HAD MADE UP MY MIND.
FIRST, DON'T WEAR A BRA. THE FRICTION SHOULD HELP TOUGHEN THEM UP.
OOH, I SEE!
BA (TOSS)
NO!!
THE CHAFING IS A LITTLE UNCOMFORTABLE...
TIME FOR A WALK!
...BUT THIS IS GONNA BE EASY IF GOING BRALESS IS ALL IT TAKES!♪
THERE'S SCABS ON THEM NOW!!
THEY'RE TOO DELICATE!!
NIPPLE
Breast Milk Producer
Level: 1
HP: 0
MP: 0
I-I CAN'T... TAKE THE CHAFING...

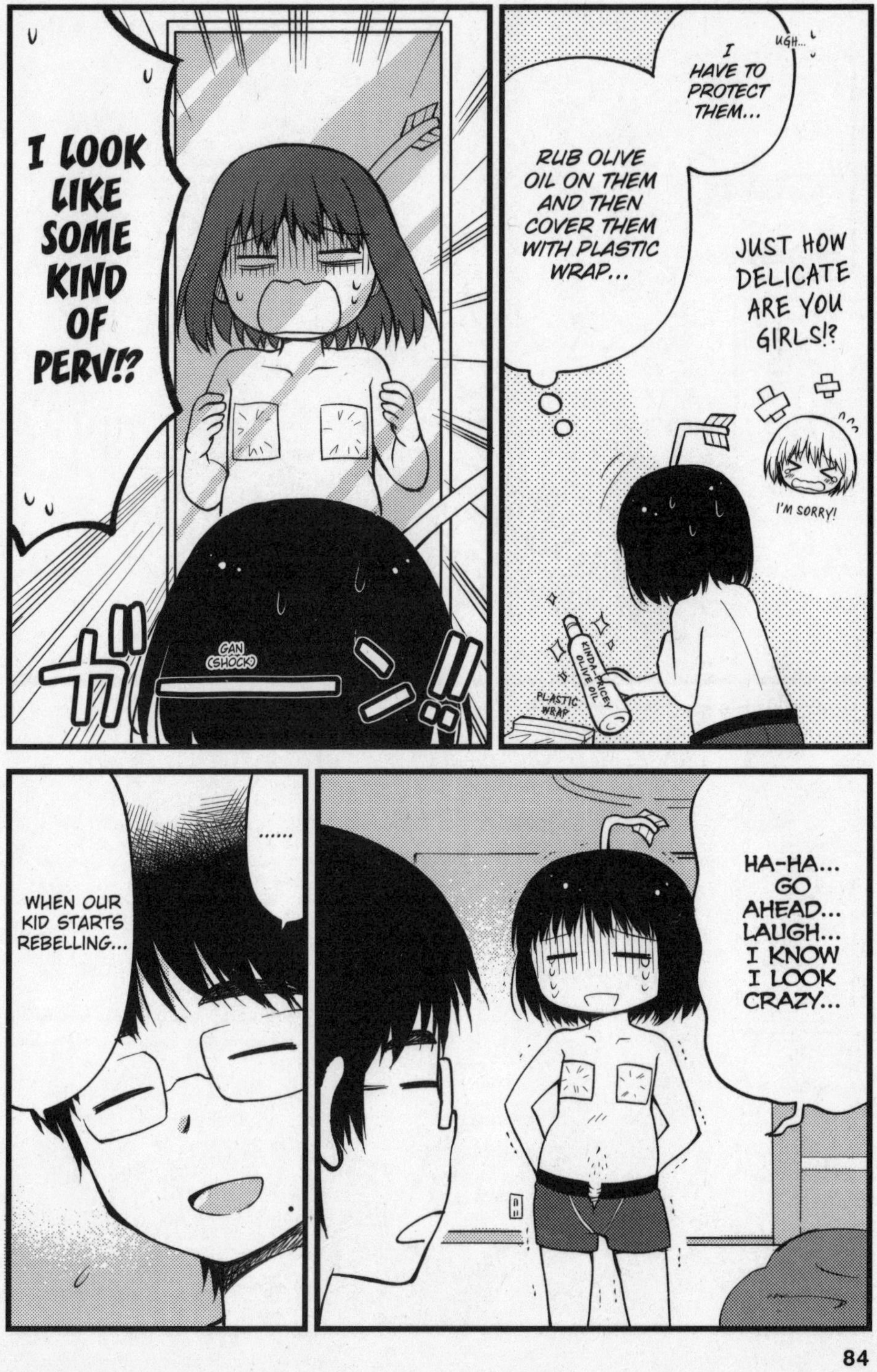
UGH...
I HAVE TO PROTECT THEM...
RUB OLIVE OIL ON THEM AND THEN COVER THEM WITH PLASTIC WRAP...
JUST HOW DELICATE ARE YOU GIRLS!?
I'M SORRY!
KINDA-PRICEY OLIVE OIL
PLASTIC WRAP
I LOOK LIKE SOME KIND OF PERV!?
GAN (SHOCK)
HA-HA... GO AHEAD... LAUGH... I KNOW I LOOK CRAZY...
......
WHEN OUR KID STARTS REBELLING...

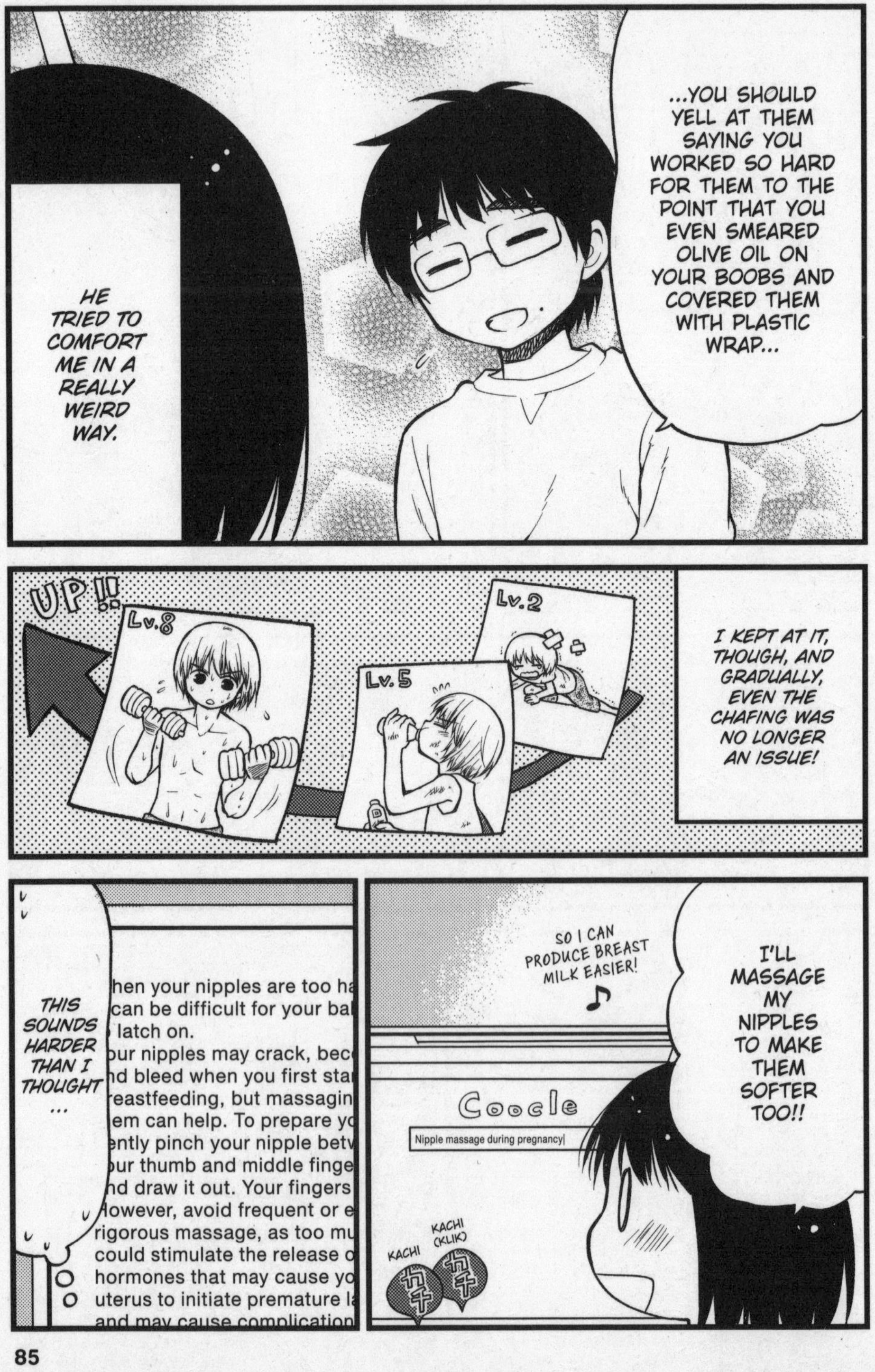
...YOU SHOULD YELL AT THEM SAYING YOU WORKED SO HARD FOR THEM TO THE POINT THAT YOU EVEN SMEARED OLIVE OIL ON YOUR BOOBS AND COVERED THEM WITH PLASTIC WRAP...
HE TRIED TO COMFORT ME IN A REALLY WEIRD WAY.
I KEPT AT IT, THOUGH, AND GRADUALLY, EVEN THE CHAFING WAS NO LONGER AN ISSUE!
Lv.2
Lv.5
Lv.8
UP!!
I'LL MASSAGE MY NIPPLES TO MAKE THEM SOFTER TOO!!
SO I CAN PRODUCE BREAST MILK EASIER! ♪
Coocle
Nipple massage during pregnancy
KACHI (KLIK)
KACHI
THIS SOUNDS HARDER THAN I THOUGHT...
hen your nipples are too ha
can be difficult for your ba
latch on.
our nipples may crack, bec
nd bleed when you first sta
reastfeeding, but massagin
em can help. To prepare yo
ently pinch your nipple betw
our thumb and middle finge
nd draw it out. Your fingers
owever, avoid frequent or e
rigorous massage, as too mu
could stimulate the release o
hormones that may cause yo
uterus to initiate premature la
and may cause complication

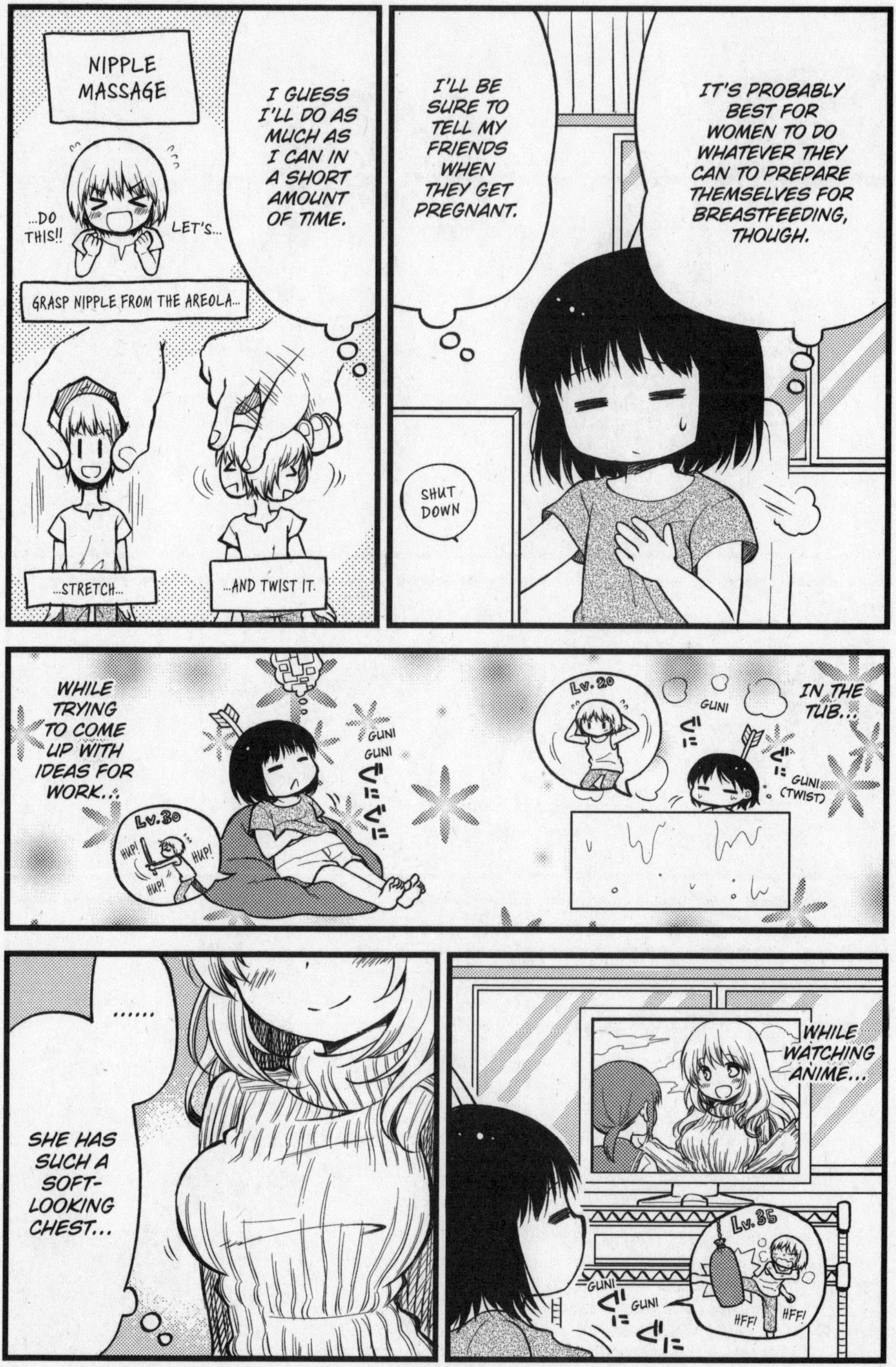
IT'S PROBABLY BEST FOR WOMEN TO DO WHATEVER THEY CAN TO PREPARE THEMSELVES FOR BREASTFEEDING, THOUGH.
I'LL BE SURE TO TELL MY FRIENDS WHEN THEY GET PREGNANT.
SHUT DOWN
I GUESS I'LL DO AS MUCH AS I CAN IN A SHORT AMOUNT OF TIME.
NIPPLE MASSAGE
LET'S...
...DO THIS!!
GRASP NIPPLE FROM THE AREOLA...
...STRETCH...
...AND TWIST IT.
IN THE TUB...
Lv. 20
GUNI
GUNI (TWIST)
WHILE TRYING TO COME UP WITH IDEAS FOR WORK...
GUNI GUNI
Lv. 30
HUP! HUP! HUP!
WHILE WATCHING ANIME...
Lv. 35
HFF! HFF!
GUNI GUNI
......
SHE HAS SUCH A SOFT-LOOKING CHEST...

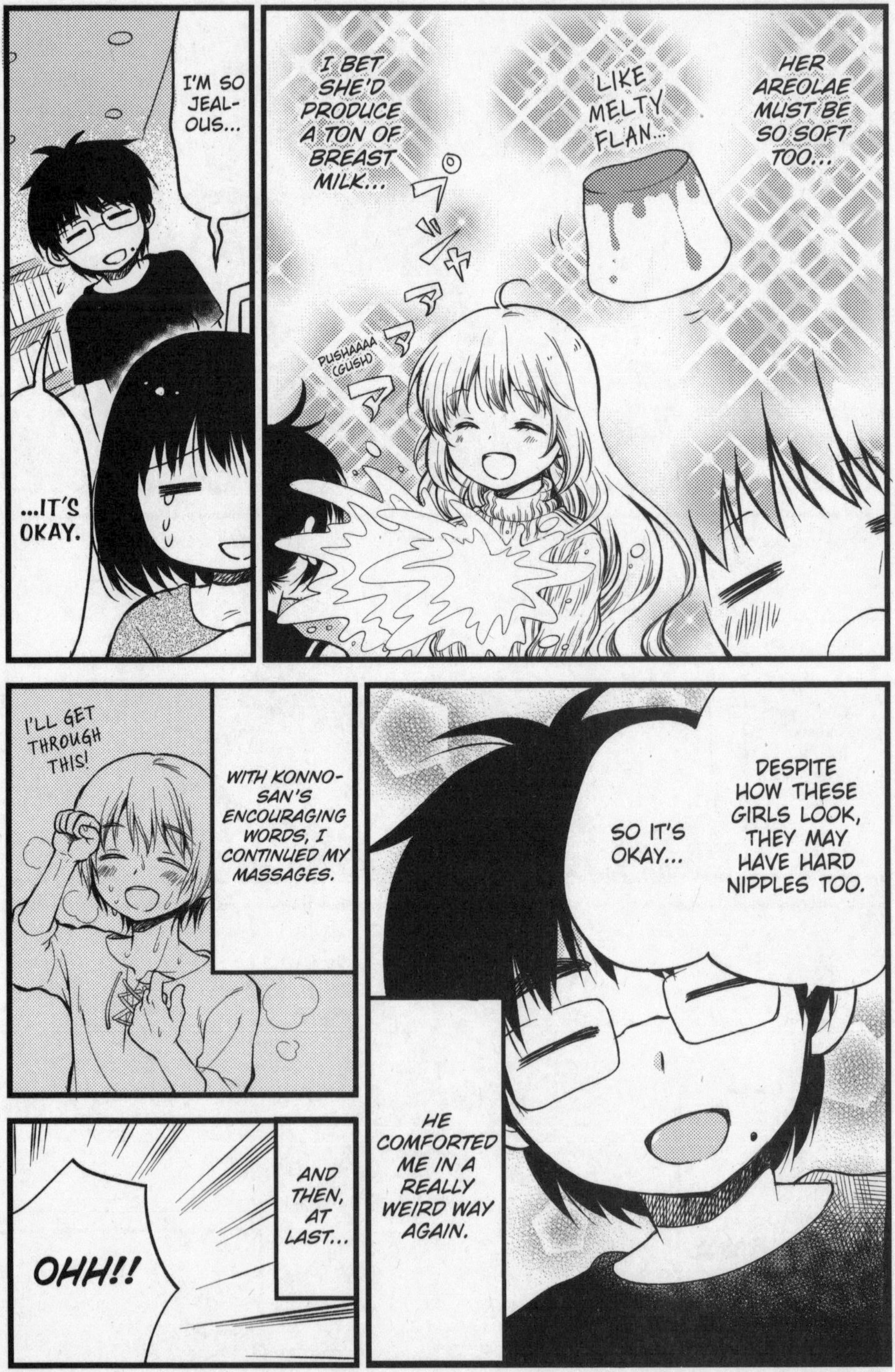
HER AREOLAE MUST BE SO SOFT TOO...
LIKE MELTY FLAN...
I BET SHE'D PRODUCE A TON OF BREAST MILK...
プシャアア
PUSHAAAA (GUSH)
I'M SO JEAL-OUS...
...IT'S OKAY.
DESPITE HOW THESE GIRLS LOOK, THEY MAY HAVE HARD NIPPLES TOO.
SO IT'S OKAY...
HE COMFORTED ME IN A REALLY WEIRD WAY AGAIN.
WITH KONNO-SAN'S ENCOURAGING WORDS, I CONTINUED MY MASSAGES.
I'LL GET THROUGH THIS!
AND THEN, AT LAST...
OHH!!

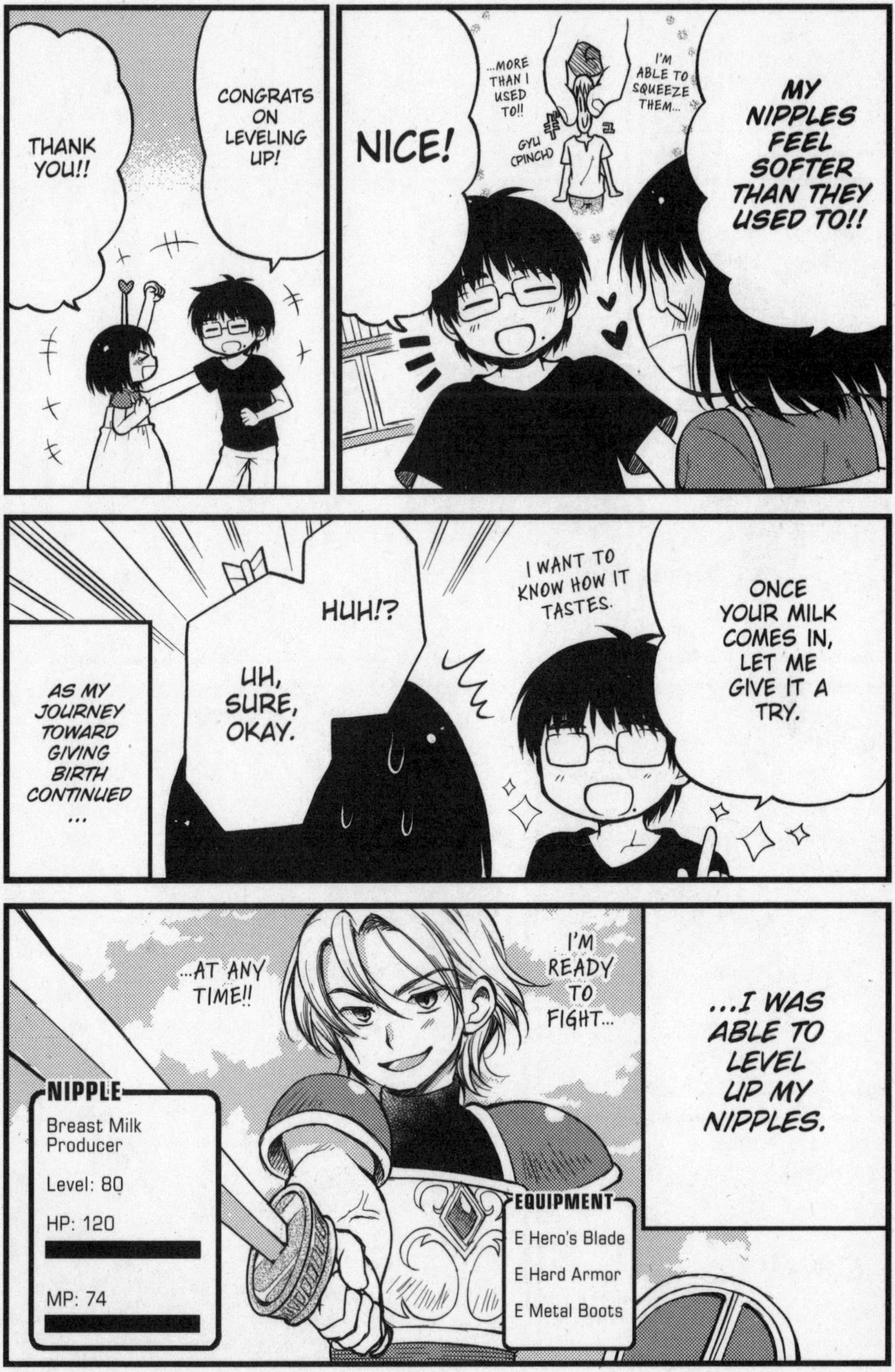
MY NIPPLES FEEL SOFTER THAN THEY USED TO!!
I'M ABLE TO SQUEEZE THEM...
...MORE THAN I USED TO!!
GYU (PINCH)
NICE!
CONGRATS ON LEVELING UP!
THANK YOU!!
ONCE YOUR MILK COMES IN, LET ME GIVE IT A TRY.
I WANT TO KNOW HOW IT TASTES.
HUH!?
UH, SURE, OKAY.
AS MY JOURNEY TOWARD GIVING BIRTH CONTINUED ...
...I WAS ABLE TO LEVEL UP MY NIPPLES.
I'M READY TO FIGHT...
...AT ANY TIME!!
NIPPLE
Breast Milk Producer
Level: 80
HP: 120
MP: 74
EQUIPMENT
E Hero's Blade
E Hard Armor
E Metal Boots

Chapter 7: What Do You Mean, My Nipples Will Be Torn!?

Bonus manga by Azura Konno

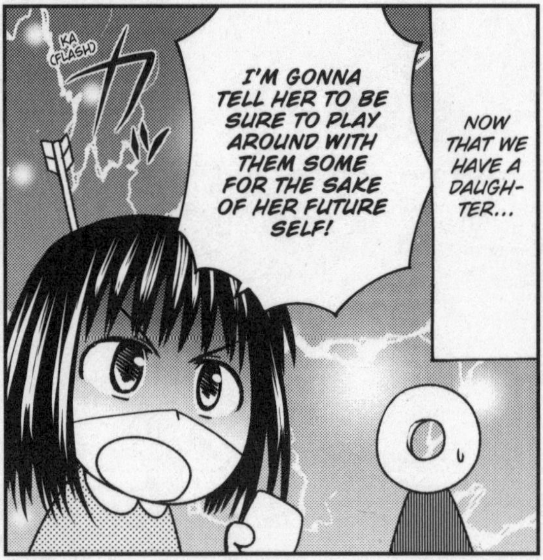
NOW THAT WE HAVE A DAUGH-TER...
I'M GONNA TELL HER TO BE SURE TO PLAY AROUND WITH THEM SOME FOR THE SAKE OF HER FUTURE SELF!
KA (FLASH)

So, uh, I guess I never would've believed that there are people out there with sensitive nipples.
Because mine don't feel a thing.
You'll see people reacting to having their nipples stimulated in a lot of erotic manga, but I never really understood it. As a result, it was a shock when I found out Kazama-san has very sensitive nipples.
Is that normal? I have no idea, since I've never asked another woman.
The opposite sex is shrouded in a veil of mystery to me.
And when it comes to producing breast milk, I assumed women could just make it spurt out on the spot.
Because that's how it is in erotic manga.
I guess manga is just fantasy.

Bonus manga by Ayami Kazama

Chapter 7: What Do You Mean, My Nipples Will Be Torn!?

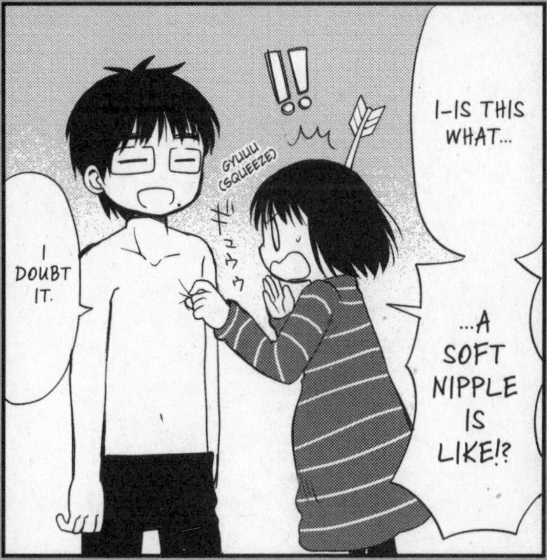
I-IS THIS WHAT...
...A SOFT NIPPLE IS LIKE!?
!!
GYUUU (SQUEEZE)
I DOUBT IT.

When I was told my nipples were hard, I wondered what the heck soft nipples even are.
Just what level of "softness" do they need to be? I was told the ideal is for the areola to be as soft as your earlobes when you pinch to the back, but I don't know what that's supposed to mean at all.
My earlobes? Al dente? Al dente nipples?? I just can't imagine it.
Since I couldn't figure out what kind of nipples I was trying to achieve, I tried pinching Konno-san's.
His were so amazingly soft!!
I'd almost expect him to be better at producing breast milk than me.
To tell the truth, I was really jealous of his nipples.
So I tried to make his nipples my goal, but then I realized men's and women's nipples might be entirely different. So I just kept massaging mine without knowing what the right answer was.
In any case, I'd call Konno-san's nipples "al dente."

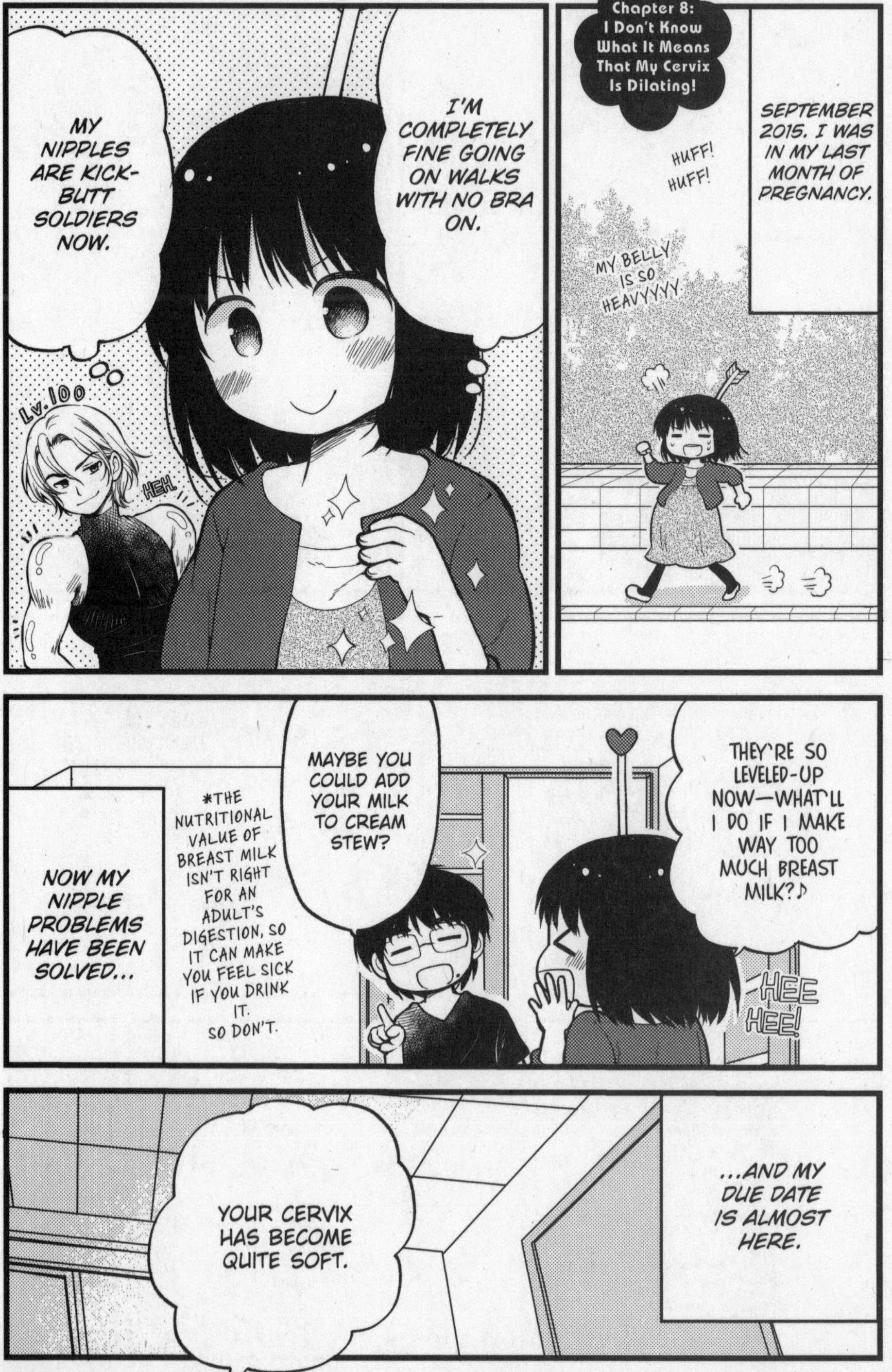
Chapter 8: I Don't Know What It Means That My Cervix Is Dilating!
SEPTEMBER 2015. I WAS IN MY LAST MONTH OF PREGNANCY.
HUFF! HUFF!
MY BELLY IS SO HEAVYYYY.
I'M COMPLETELY FINE GOING ON WALKS WITH NO BRA ON.
MY NIPPLES ARE KICK-BUTT SOLDIERS NOW.
Lv.100
HEH
THEY'RE SO LEVELED-UP NOW—WHAT'LL I DO IF I MAKE WAY TOO MUCH BREAST MILK?♪
HEE HEE!
MAYBE YOU COULD ADD YOUR MILK TO CREAM STEW?
*THE NUTRITIONAL VALUE OF BREAST MILK ISN'T RIGHT FOR AN ADULT'S DIGESTION, SO IT CAN MAKE YOU FEEL SICK IF YOU DRINK IT. SO DON'T.
NOW MY NIPPLE PROBLEMS HAVE BEEN SOLVED...
...AND MY DUE DATE IS ALMOST HERE.
YOUR CERVIX HAS BECOME QUITE SOFT.

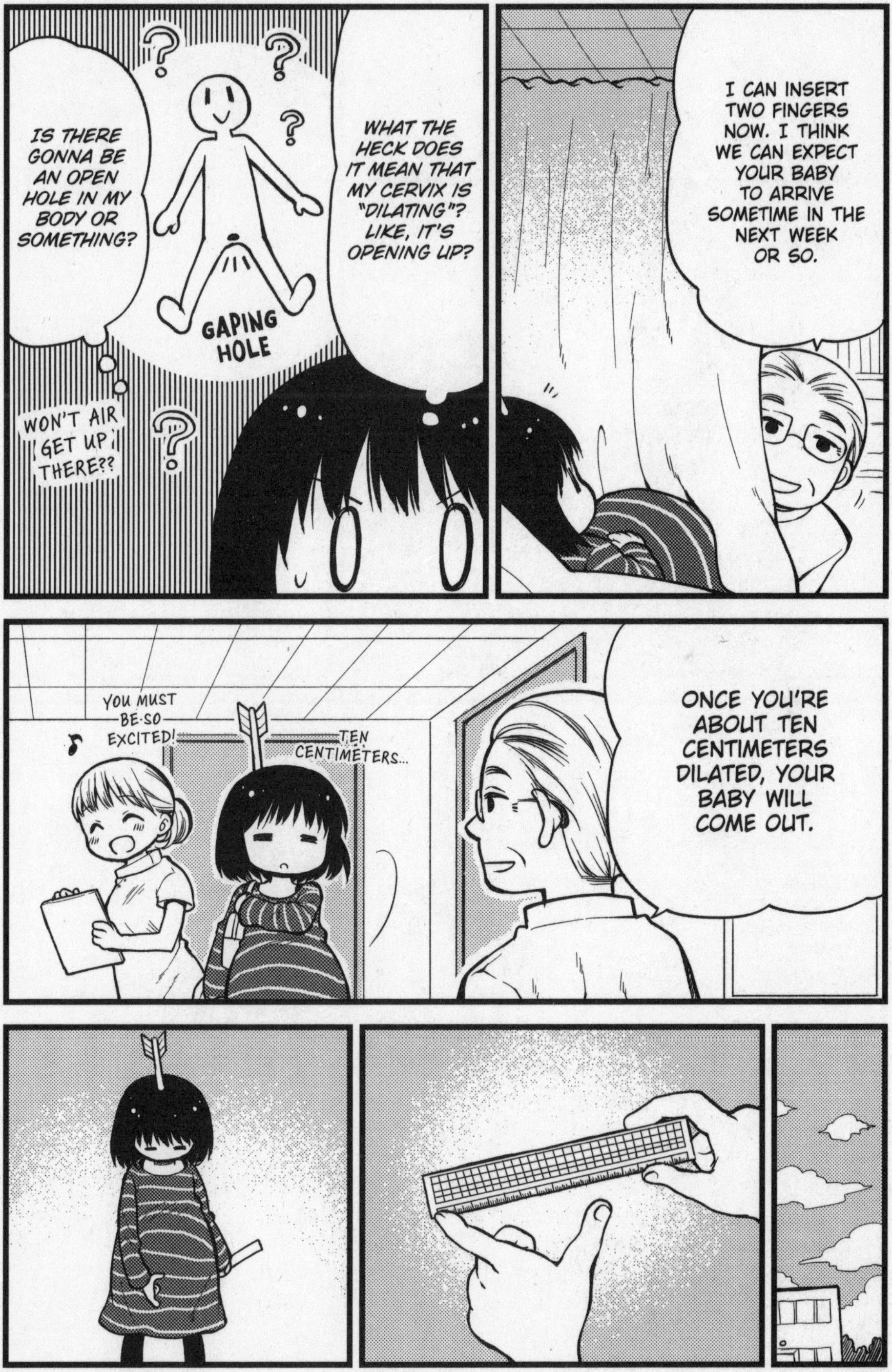
I CAN INSERT TWO FINGERS NOW. I THINK WE CAN EXPECT YOUR BABY TO ARRIVE SOMETIME IN THE NEXT WEEK OR SO.
WHAT THE HECK DOES IT MEAN THAT MY CERVIX IS "DILATING"? LIKE, IT'S OPENING UP?
IS THERE GONNA BE AN OPEN HOLE IN MY BODY OR SOMETHING?
GAPING HOLE
WON'T AIR GET UP THERE??
ONCE YOU'RE ABOUT TEN CENTIMETERS DILATED, YOUR BABY WILL COME OUT.
TEN CENTIMETERS...
YOU MUST BE SO EXCITED!

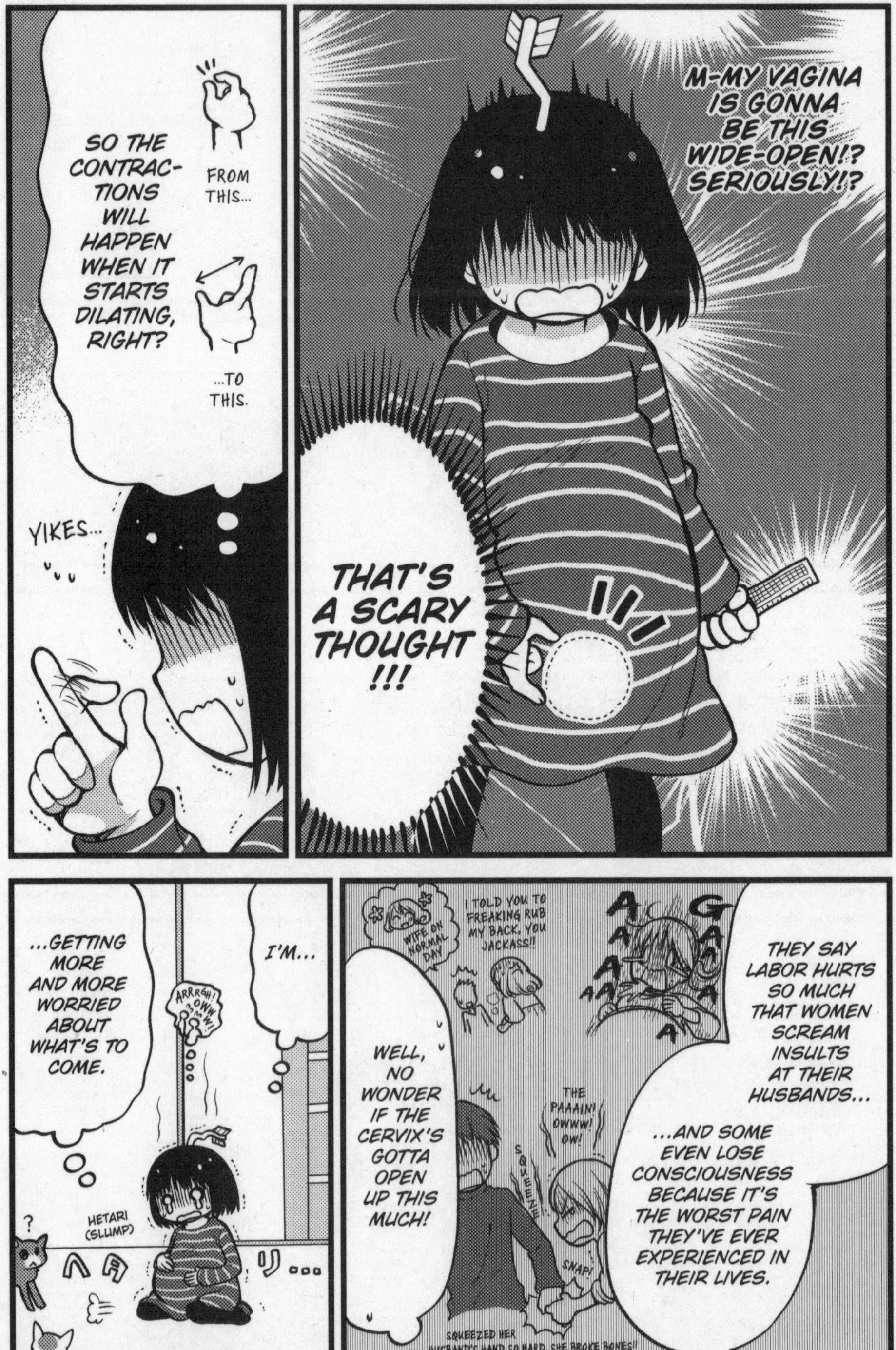
M-MY VAGINA IS GONNA BE THIS WIDE-OPEN!? SERIOUSLY!?
THAT'S A SCARY THOUGHT!!!
SO THE CONTRACTIONS WILL HAPPEN WHEN IT STARTS DILATING, RIGHT?
FROM THIS...
...TO THIS.
YIKES...
THEY SAY LABOR HURTS SO MUCH THAT WOMEN SCREAM INSULTS AT THEIR HUSBANDS...
...AND SOME EVEN LOSE CONSCIOUSNESS BECAUSE IT'S THE WORST PAIN THEY'VE EVER EXPERIENCED IN THEIR LIVES.
GAAAA
AAAAAA
I TOLD YOU TO FREAKING RUB MY BACK, YOU JACKASS!!
WIFE ON NORMAL DAY
THE PAAAIN! OWWW! OW!
SQUEEZE
SNAP!
SQUEEZED HER HUSBAND'S HAND SO HARD, SHE BROKE BONES!!
WELL, NO WONDER IF THE CERVIX'S GOTTA OPEN UP THIS MUCH!
I'M...
...GETTING MORE AND MORE WORRIED ABOUT WHAT'S TO COME.
ARRRGH! OWW!
HETARI (SLUMP)
?

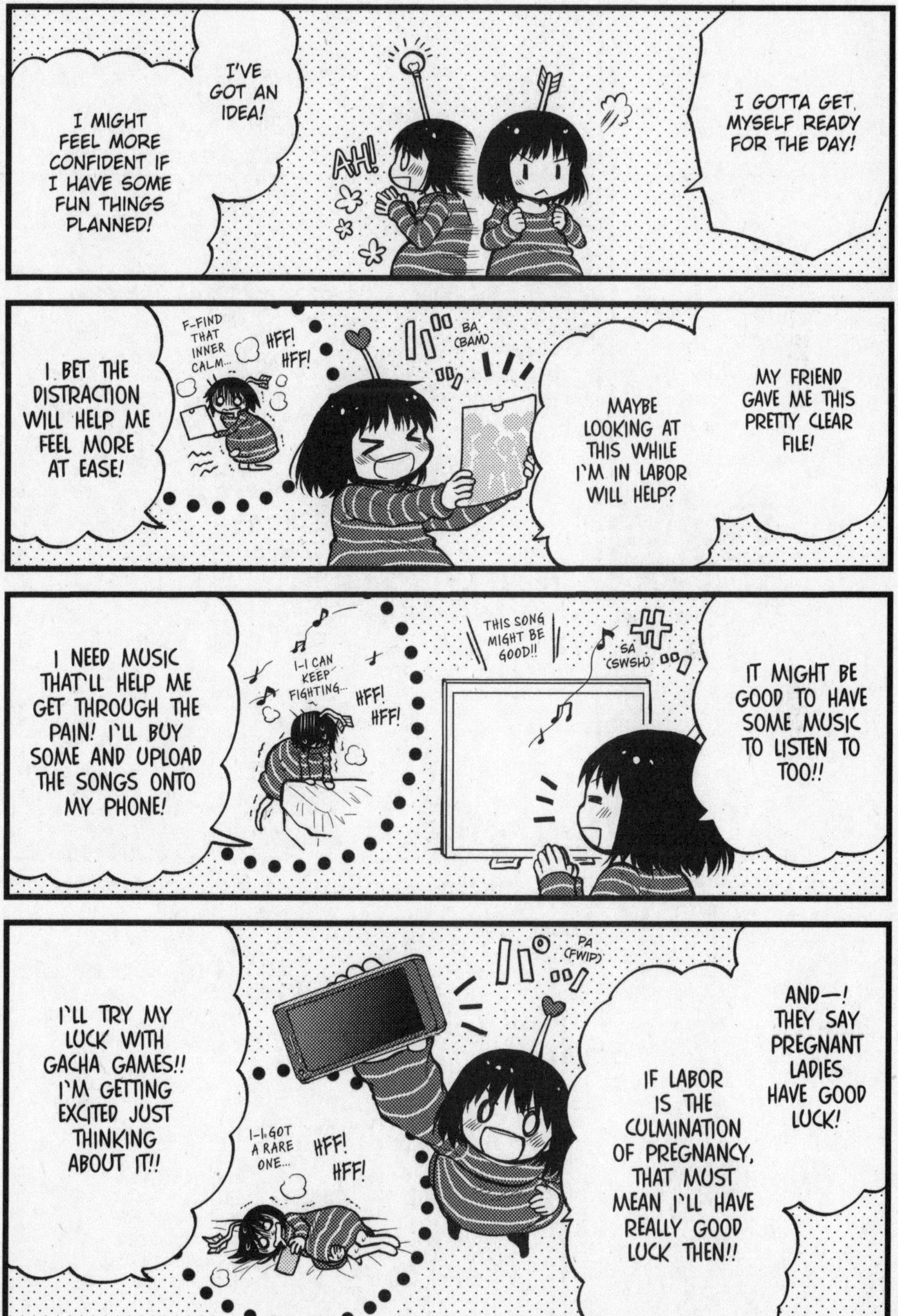
I GOTTA GET MYSELF READY FOR THE DAY!
AH!
I'VE GOT AN IDEA!
I MIGHT FEEL MORE CONFIDENT IF I HAVE SOME FUN THINGS PLANNED!
MY FRIEND GAVE ME THIS PRETTY CLEAR FILE!
MAYBE LOOKING AT THIS WHILE I'M IN LABOR WILL HELP?
BA (BAM)
HFF! HFF!
F-FIND THAT INNER CALM...
I BET THE DISTRACTION WILL HELP ME FEEL MORE AT EASE!
IT MIGHT BE GOOD TO HAVE SOME MUSIC TO LISTEN TO TOO!!
SA (SWSH)
THIS SONG MIGHT BE GOOD!!
HFF! HFF!
I-I CAN KEEP FIGHTING...
I NEED MUSIC THAT'LL HELP ME GET THROUGH THE PAIN! I'LL BUY SOME AND UPLOAD THE SONGS ONTO MY PHONE!
AND—! THEY SAY PREGNANT LADIES HAVE GOOD LUCK!
IF LABOR IS THE CULMINATION OF PREGNANCY, THAT MUST MEAN I'LL HAVE REALLY GOOD LUCK THEN!!
PA (FWIP)
HFF! HFF!
I-I GOT A RARE ONE...
I'LL TRY MY LUCK WITH GACHA GAMES!! I'M GETTING EXCITED JUST THINKING ABOUT IT!!

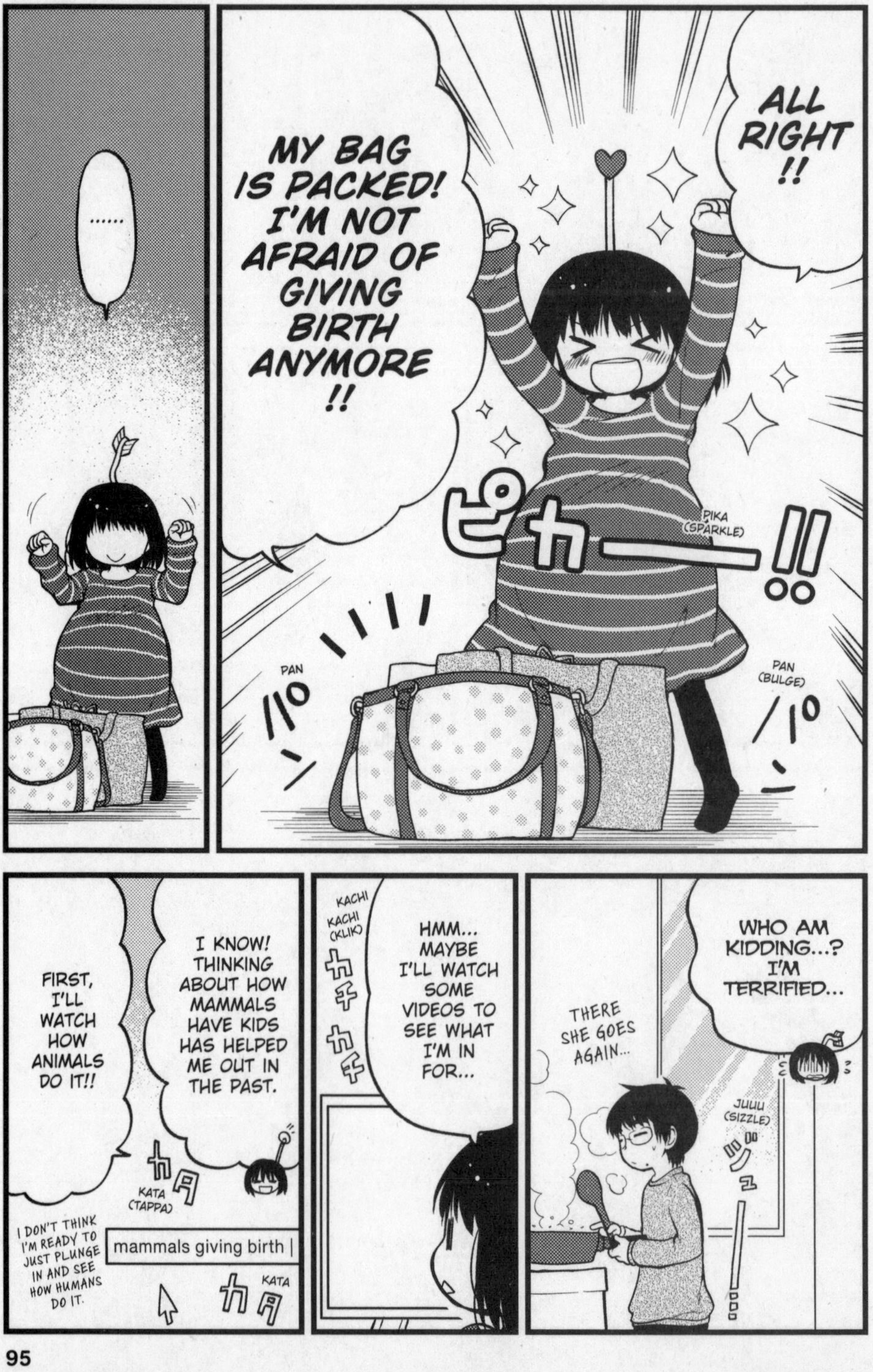
ALL RIGHT!!
MY BAG IS PACKED! I'M NOT AFRAID OF GIVING BIRTH ANYMORE!!
PIKA (SPARKLE)
PAN (BULGE)
PAN
......
WHO AM KIDDING...? I'M TERRIFIED...
THERE SHE GOES AGAIN...
JUUU (SIZZLE)
KACHI KACHI (KLIK)
HMM... MAYBE I'LL WATCH SOME VIDEOS TO SEE WHAT I'M IN FOR...
I KNOW! THINKING ABOUT HOW MAMMALS HAVE KIDS HAS HELPED ME OUT IN THE PAST.
FIRST, I'LL WATCH HOW ANIMALS DO IT!!
KATA (TAPPA)
mammals giving birth |
I DON'T THINK I'M READY TO JUST PLUNGE IN AND SEE HOW HUMANS DO IT.
KATA

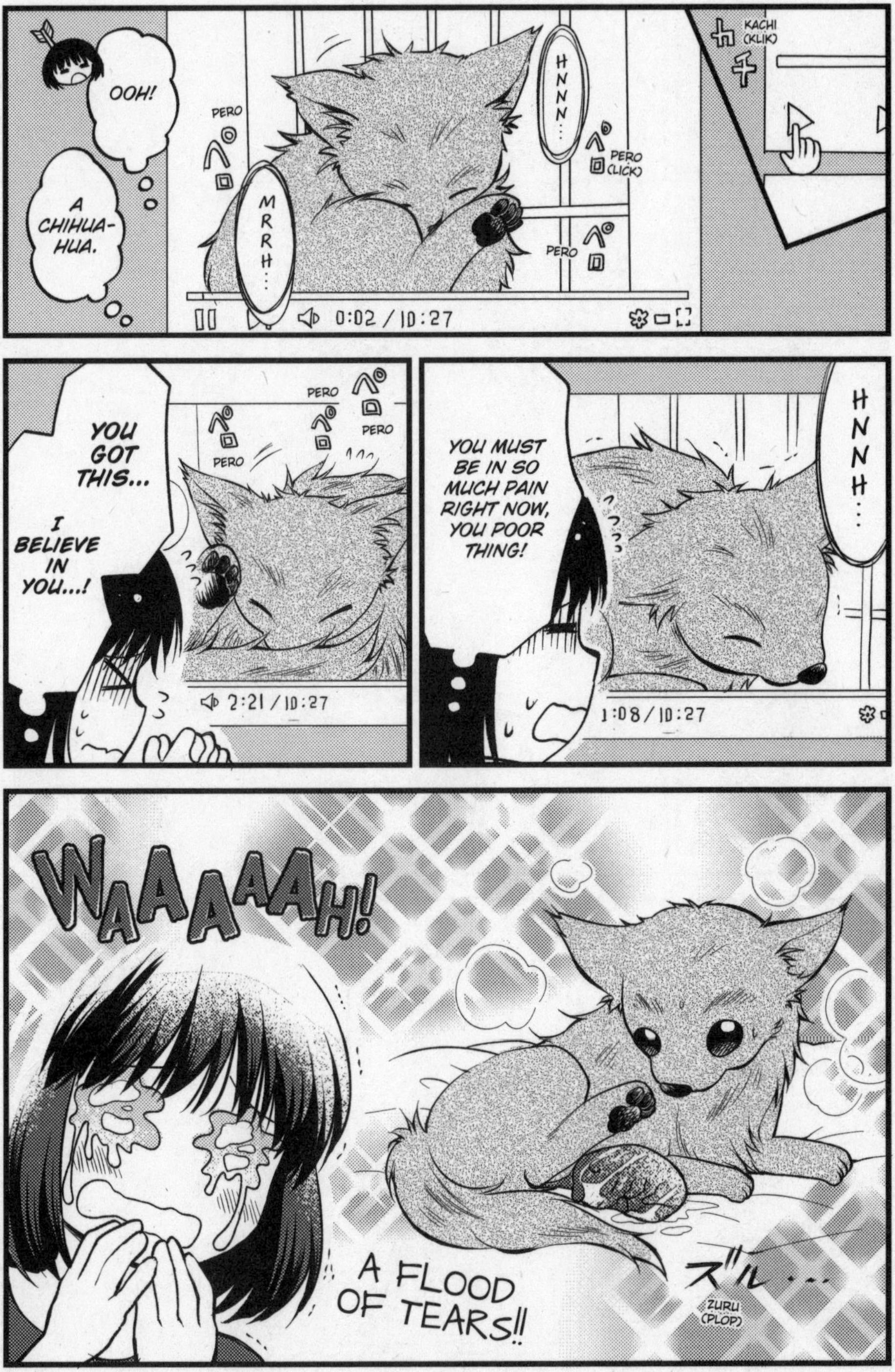
KACHI (KLIK)
HNNN...
PERO (LICK)
PERO
PERO
MRRH...
OOH!
A CHIHUAHUA.
0:02 / 10:27
HNNH...
YOU MUST BE IN SO MUCH PAIN RIGHT NOW, YOU POOR THING!
1:08 / 10:27
PERO
PERO
PERO
YOU GOT THIS...
I BELIEVE IN YOU...!
2:21 / 10:27
WAAAAAH!
ZURU (PLOP)
A FLOOD OF TEARS!!

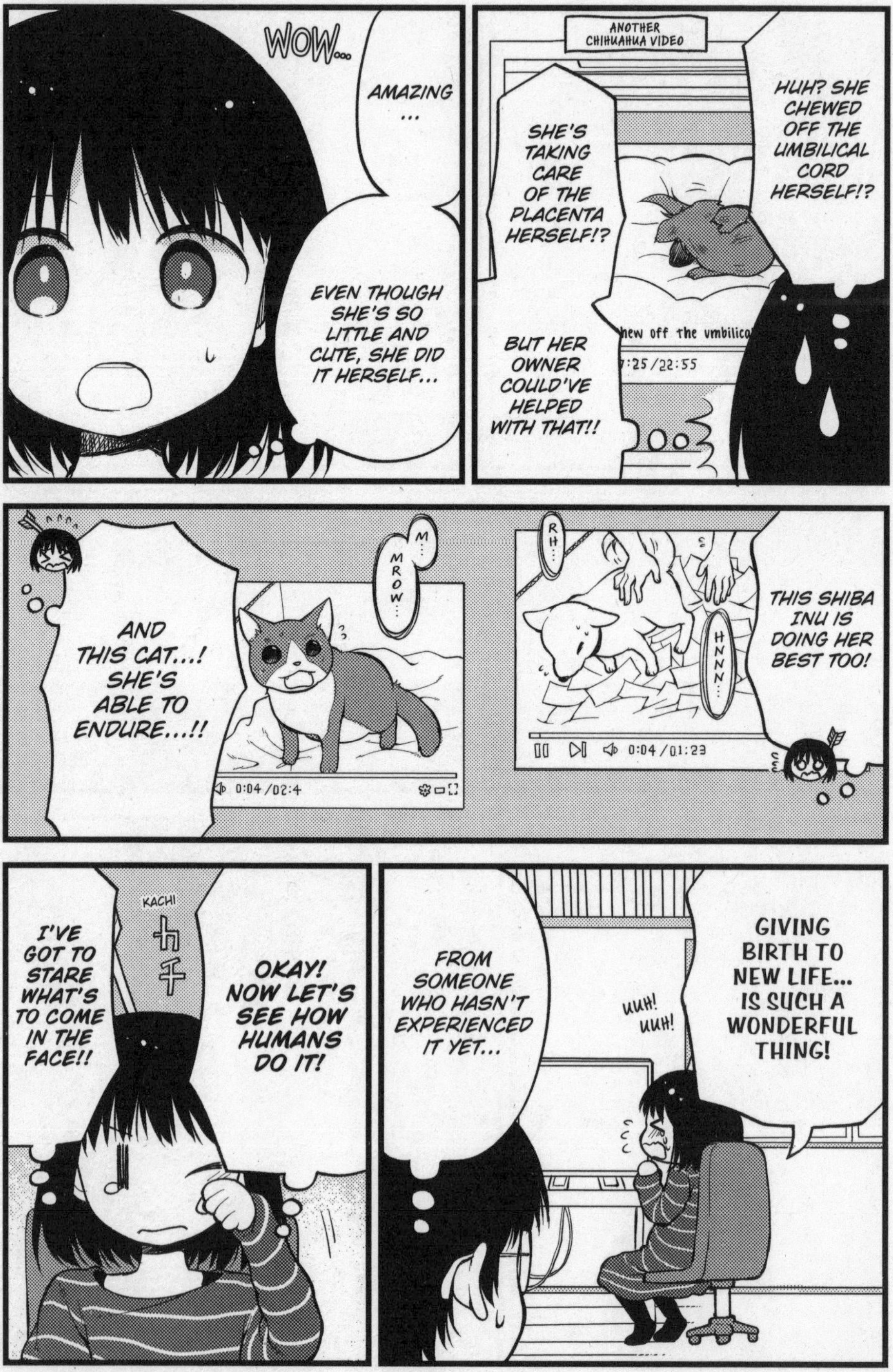
ANOTHER CHIHUAHUA VIDEO
HUH? SHE CHEWED OFF THE UMBILICAL CORD HERSELF!?
SHE'S TAKING CARE OF THE PLACENTA HERSELF!?
hew off the umbilica
7:25/22:55
BUT HER OWNER COULD'VE HELPED WITH THAT!!
WOW...
AMAZING...
EVEN THOUGH SHE'S SO LITTLE AND CUTE, SHE DID IT HERSELF...
THIS SHIBA INU IS DOING HER BEST TOO!
RH...
HNNN...
0:04/01:23
M... MROW...
AND THIS CAT...! SHE'S ABLE TO ENDURE...!!
0:04/02:4
GIVING BIRTH TO NEW LIFE... IS SUCH A WONDERFUL THING!
UUH! UUH!
FROM SOMEONE WHO HASN'T EXPERIENCED IT YET...
OKAY! NOW LET'S SEE HOW HUMANS DO IT!
KACHI
カチ
I'VE GOT TO STARE WHAT'S TO COME IN THE FACE!!

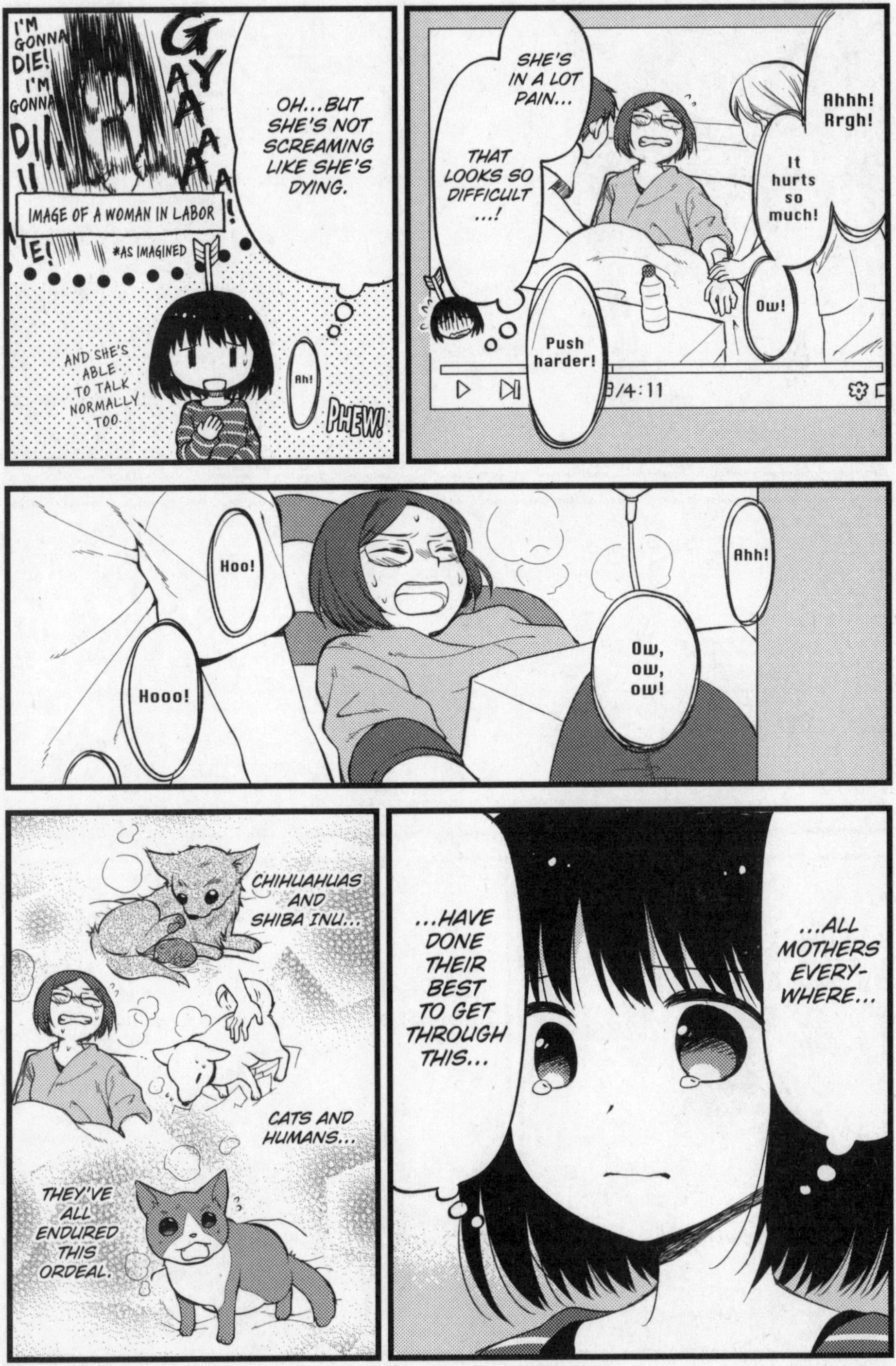
Ahhh! Rrgh!
It hurts so much!
SHE'S IN A LOT PAIN...
THAT LOOKS SO DIFFICULT ...!
Ow!
Push harder!
OH...BUT SHE'S NOT SCREAMING LIKE SHE'S DYING.
GYAAAAA!
I'M GONNA DIE! I'M GONNA DI...
IMAGE OF A WOMAN IN LABOR
*AS IMAGINED
Ah!
PHEW!
AND SHE'S ABLE TO TALK NORMALLY TOO.
Ahh!
Ow, ow, ow!
Hoo!
Hooo!
...ALL MOTHERS EVERY-WHERE...
...HAVE DONE THEIR BEST TO GET THROUGH THIS...
CHIHUAHUAS AND SHIBA INU...
CATS AND HUMANS...
THEY'VE ALL ENDURED THIS ORDEAL.

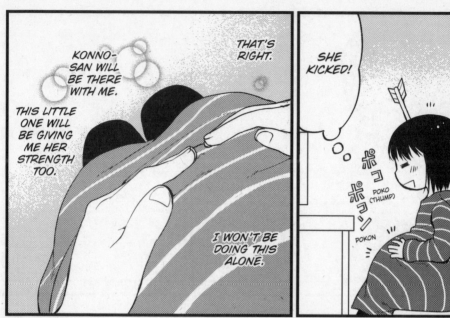

KONNO-SAN WILL BE THERE WITH ME.

THAT'S RIGHT.

THIS LITTLE ONE WILL BE GIVING ME HER STRENGTH TOO.

I WON'T BE DOING THIS ALONE.

SHE KICKED!

POKO
(THUMP)

POKON

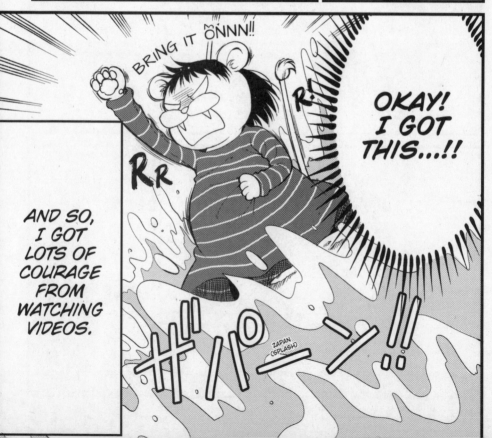

BRING IT ONNN!!

OKAY! I GOT THIS...!!

Rr

Rr

AND SO, I GOT LOTS OF COURAGE FROM WATCHING VIDEOS.

ZAPAN
(SPLASH)

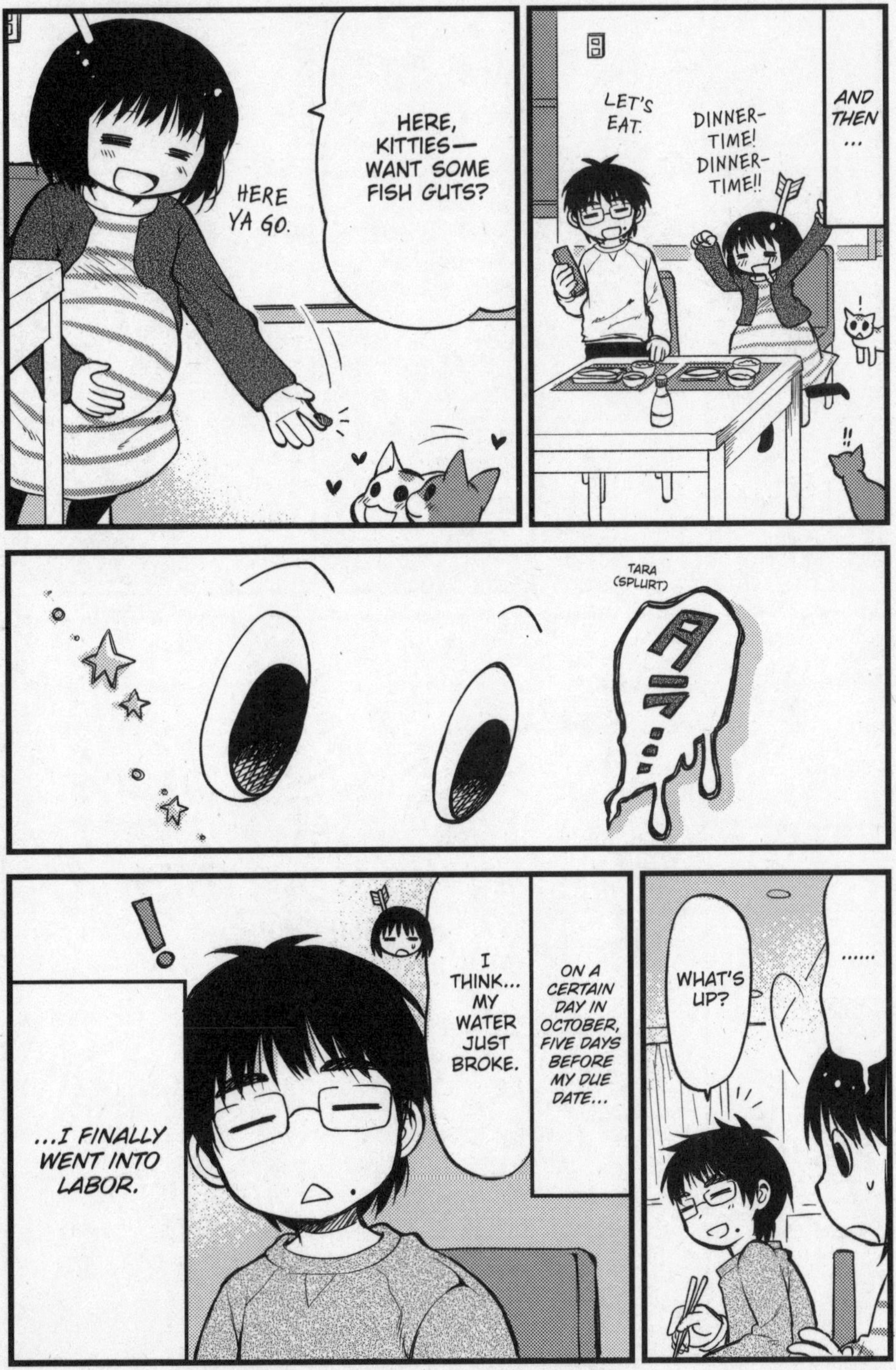
AND THEN...
DINNER-TIME! DINNER-TIME!!
LET'S EAT.
!
!!
HERE, KITTIES—WANT SOME FISH GUTS?
HERE YA GO.
TARA (SPLURT)
......
WHAT'S UP?
ON A CERTAIN DAY IN OCTOBER, FIVE DAYS BEFORE MY DUE DATE...
I THINK... MY WATER JUST BROKE.
!
...I FINALLY WENT INTO LABOR.

Chapter 8: I Don't Know What It Means That My Cervix Is Dilating!

Bonus manga by Azure Konno

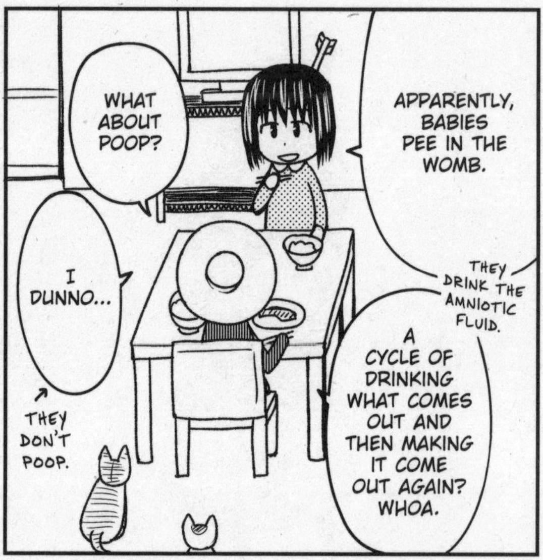
APPARENTLY, BABIES PEE IN THE WOMB.
THEY DRINK THE AMNIOTIC FLUID.
WHAT ABOUT POOP?
I DUNNO...
THEY DON'T POOP.
A CYCLE OF DRINKING WHAT COMES OUT AND THEN MAKING IT COME OUT AGAIN? WHOA.

When she told me the doctor could insert two fingers into her cervix, I wondered to myself, "Fingers...? It's some distance to reach the cervix...Did he put his whole hand in there?"
I still don't know the answer.
What I assume is that the cervix moved lower in her body.
She talked a lot about how much her nipples hurt when she went walking around without a bra, but then she got excited because it reminded her of what most girls feel during adolescence. She told me that from the time we started dating, she's been getting to experience all at once the sorts of things most teenagers experience. I always had sex on the brain when I was a teenager, but it seems Kazama-san was quite the opposite. It was really shocking to learn.

Bonus manga by Ayami Kazama

Chapter 8: I Don't Know What It Means That My Cervix Is Dilating!

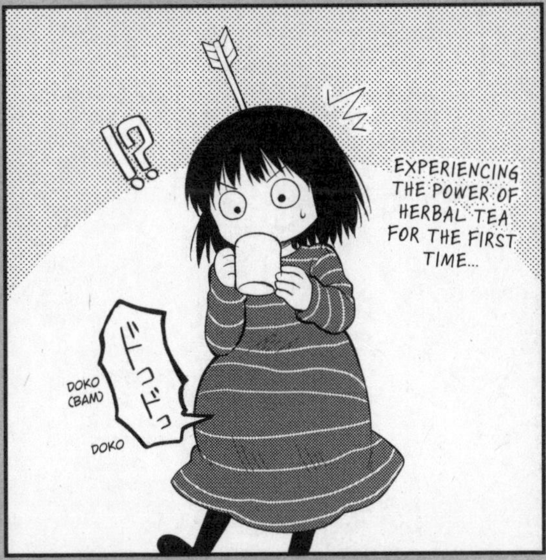
!?
EXPERIENCING THE POWER OF HERBAL TEA FOR THE FIRST TIME...
ドコドコ
DOKO (BAM)
DOKO

As my due date got closer, I started drinking raspberry leaf tea pretty regularly.
It's an herbal tea that's said to help soften your cervix.
I had practically no confidence in the softness of my cervix, so I started drinking it when I reached full term. It certainly seemed to have an effect on my body because my uterus instantly contracted and started going *Bam-Bam!* like the beat of a taiko drum. It was amazing!
Herbal tea was never something I had much interest in before, but it's not to be underestimated!
Anyway, it started going *Bam-Bam!* so much, I started worrying if my baby was going to be okay. I wonder how it must have felt inside there.
Maybe it felt like an earthquake was happening? Must have been a really big earthquake, then.

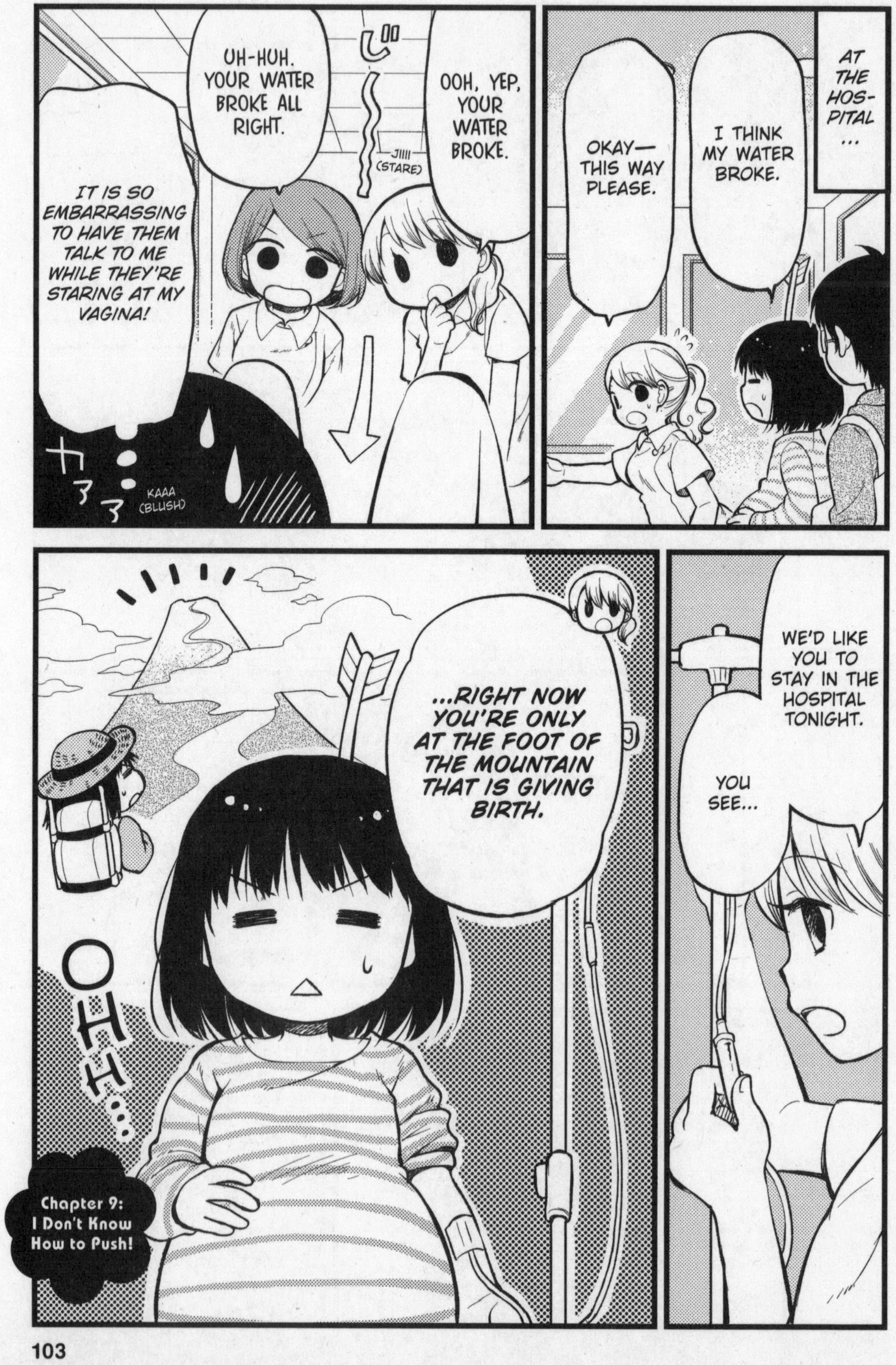
AT THE HOS-PITAL...
I THINK MY WATER BROKE.
OKAY—THIS WAY PLEASE.
OOH, YEP, YOUR WATER BROKE.
JIIII (STARE)
UH-HUH. YOUR WATER BROKE ALL RIGHT.
IT IS SO EMBARRASSING TO HAVE THEM TALK TO ME WHILE THEY'RE STARING AT MY VAGINA!
KAAA (BLUSH)
WE'D LIKE YOU TO STAY IN THE HOSPITAL TONIGHT.
YOU SEE...
...RIGHT NOW YOU'RE ONLY AT THE FOOT OF THE MOUNTAIN THAT IS GIVING BIRTH.
OHH...
Chapter 9: I Don't Know How to Push!

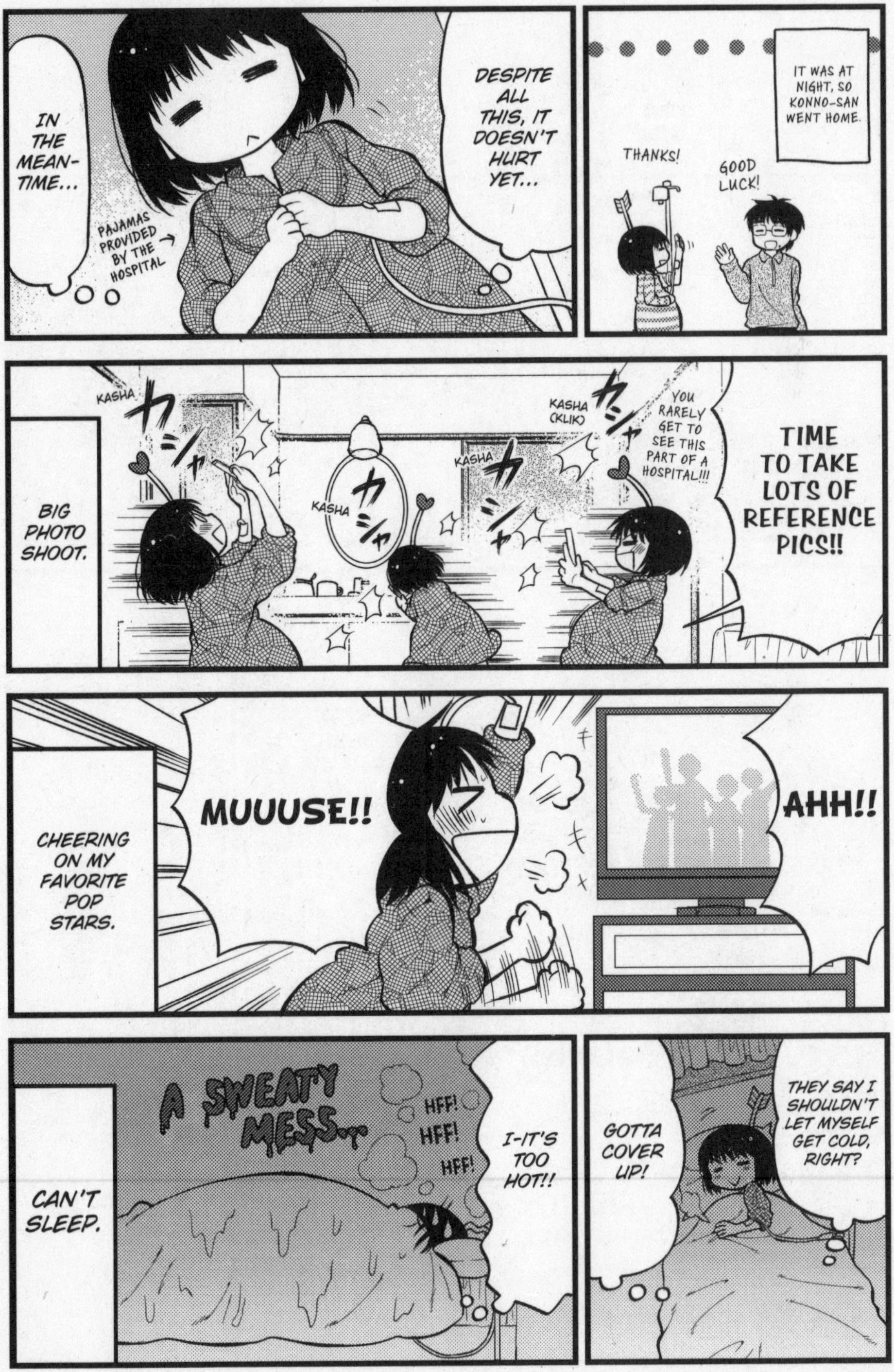
IT WAS AT NIGHT, SO KONNO-SAN WENT HOME.
GOOD LUCK!
THANKS!
DESPITE ALL THIS, IT DOESN'T HURT YET...
IN THE MEAN-TIME...
PAJAMAS PROVIDED BY THE HOSPITAL
TIME TO TAKE LOTS OF REFERENCE PICS!!
YOU RARELY GET TO SEE THIS PART OF A HOSPITAL!!!
KASHA (KLIK)
KASHA
KASHA
KASHA
BIG PHOTO SHOOT.
AHH!!
MUUUSE!!
CHEERING ON MY FAVORITE POP STARS.
THEY SAY I SHOULDN'T LET MYSELF GET COLD, RIGHT?
GOTTA COVER UP!
I-IT'S TOO HOT!!
HFF! HFF! HFF!
A SWEATY MESS...
CAN'T SLEEP.

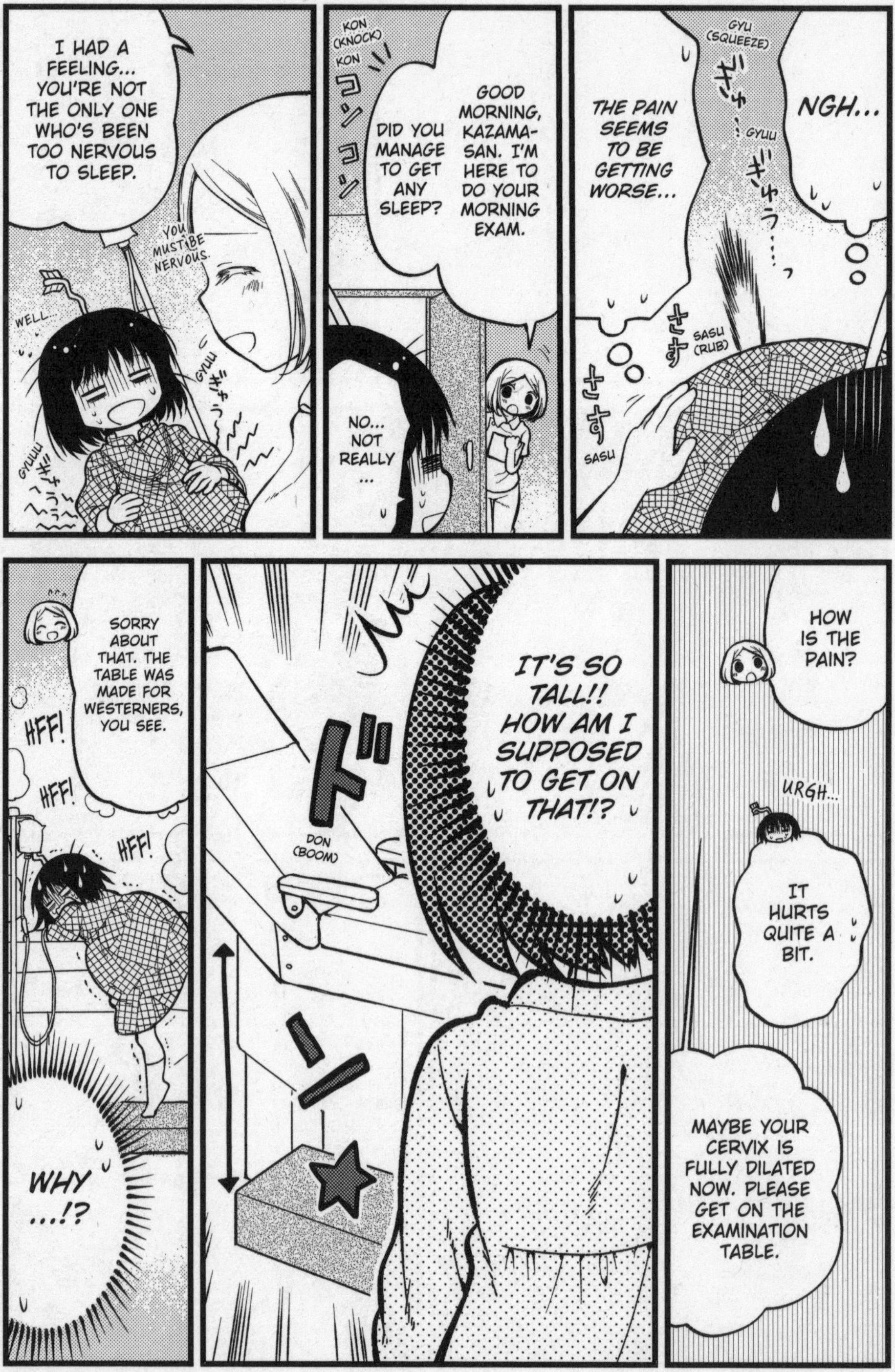
NGH...
GYU (SQUEEZE)
THE PAIN SEEMS TO BE GETTING WORSE...
GYUU
SASU (RUB)
SASU
KON (KNOCK)
KON
GOOD MORNING, KAZAMA-SAN. I'M HERE TO DO YOUR MORNING EXAM.
DID YOU MANAGE TO GET ANY SLEEP?
NO... NOT REALLY...
I HAD A FEELING... YOU'RE NOT THE ONLY ONE WHO'S BEEN TOO NERVOUS TO SLEEP.
YOU MUST BE NERVOUS.
WELL...
GYUU
GYUUU
HOW IS THE PAIN?
URGH...
IT HURTS QUITE A BIT.
MAYBE YOUR CERVIX IS FULLY DILATED NOW. PLEASE GET ON THE EXAMINATION TABLE.
IT'S SO TALL!! HOW AM I SUPPOSED TO GET ON THAT!?
DON (BOOM)
SORRY ABOUT THAT. THE TABLE WAS MADE FOR WESTERNERS, YOU SEE.
HFF!
HFF!
HFF!
WHY ...!?

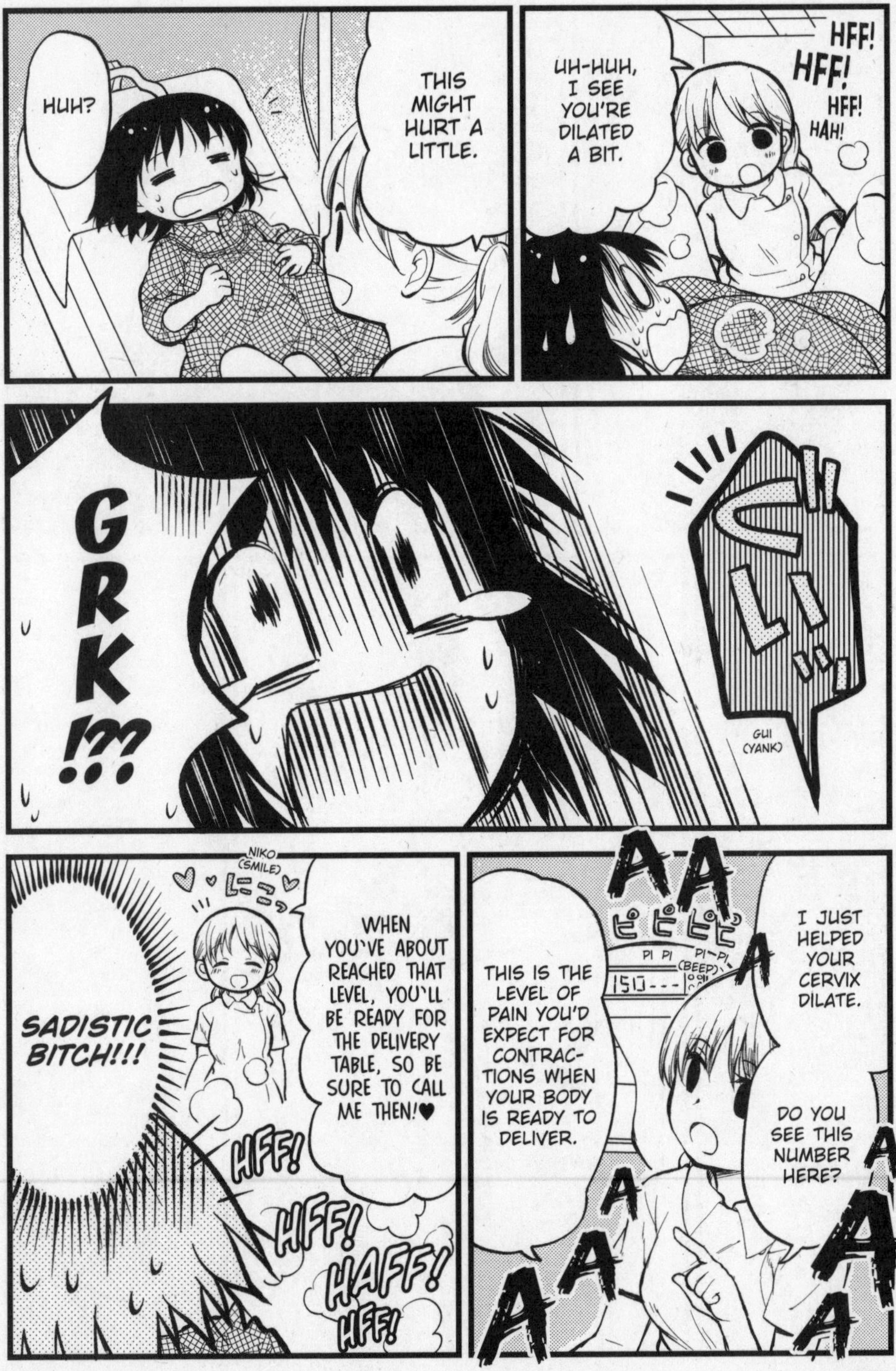
HFF! HFF! HFF! HAH!
UH-HUH, I SEE YOU'RE DILATED A BIT.
THIS MIGHT HURT A LITTLE.
HUH?
ぐい!!
GUI (YANK)
GRK!??
I JUST HELPED YOUR CERVIX DILATE.
DO YOU SEE THIS NUMBER HERE?
ピピピピ
PI PI PI~PI (BEEP)
THIS IS THE LEVEL OF PAIN YOU'D EXPECT FOR CONTRAC-TIONS WHEN YOUR BODY IS READY TO DELIVER.
AAAAAAAAAA
WHEN YOU'VE ABOUT REACHED THAT LEVEL, YOU'LL BE READY FOR THE DELIVERY TABLE, SO BE SURE TO CALL ME THEN!♥
にこっ
NIKO (SMILE)
SADISTIC BITCH!!!
HFF! HFF! HAFF! HFF!

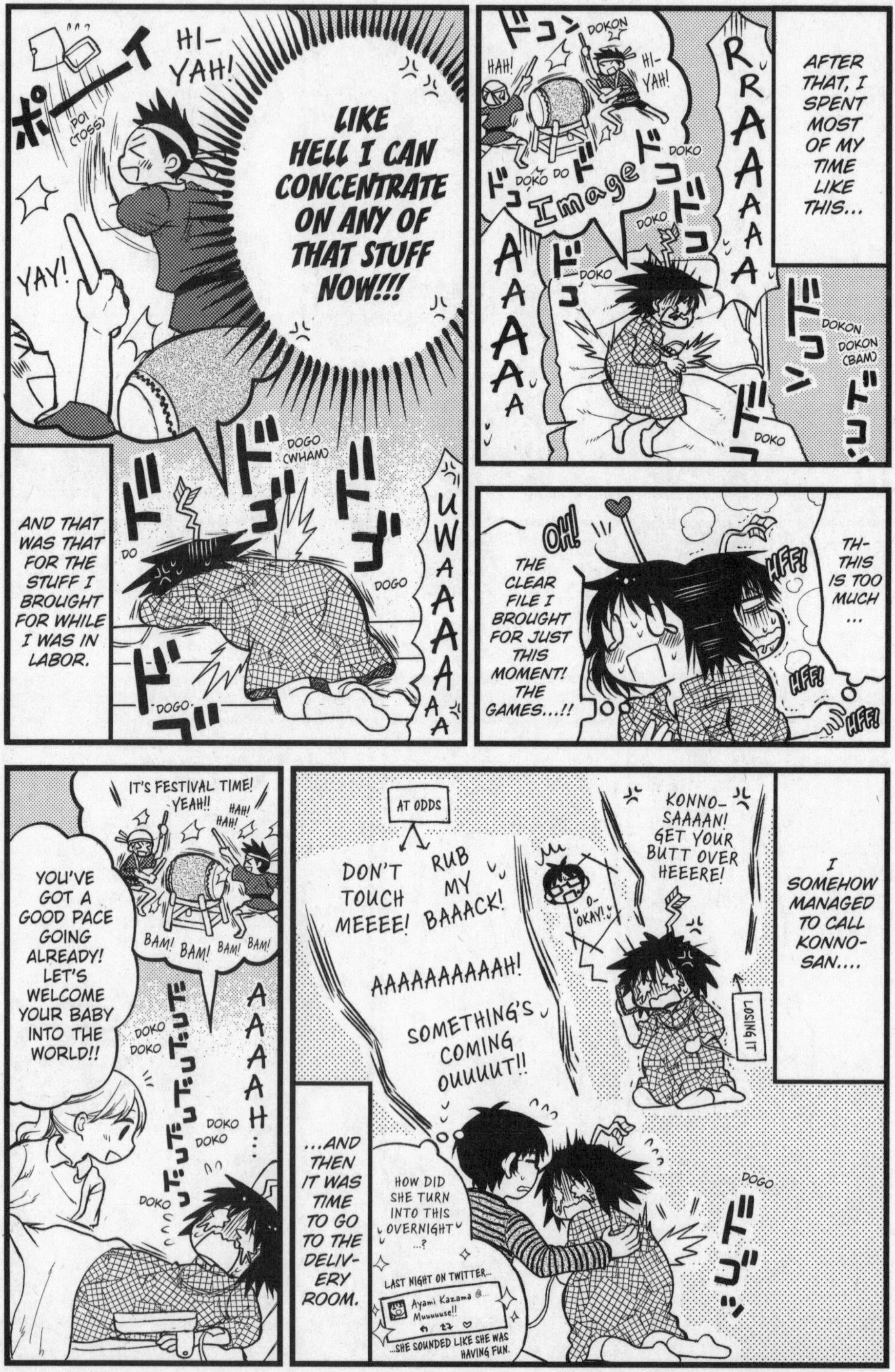
AFTER THAT, I SPENT MOST OF MY TIME LIKE THIS…
RAAAAAAA
DOKON
HI-YAH!
HAH!
Image
DOKO DO DOKO DOKO DOKO
DOKON DOKON (BAM)
DOKO
AAAAAAA
TH-THIS IS TOO MUCH…
HFF! HFF! HFF!
OH!
THE CLEAR FILE I BROUGHT FOR JUST THIS MOMENT! THE GAMES…!!
HI-YAH!
POI (TOSS)
YAY!
LIKE HELL I CAN CONCENTRATE ON ANY OF THAT STUFF NOW!!!
DOGO (WHAM)
UWAAAAAAAAA
DOGO
DO
DOGO
AND THAT WAS THAT FOR THE STUFF I BROUGHT FOR WHILE I WAS IN LABOR.
I SOMEHOW MANAGED TO CALL KONNO-SAN….
KONNO-SAAAAN! GET YOUR BUTT OVER HEEERE!
O-OKAY!
LOSING IT
AT ODDS
RUB MY BAAACK!
DON'T TOUCH MEEEE!
AAAAAAAAAH!
SOMETHING'S COMING OUUUUT!!
DOGO
HOW DID SHE TURN INTO THIS OVERNIGHT…?
LAST NIGHT ON TWITTER…
Ayami Kazama
Muuuuuse!!
…SHE SOUNDED LIKE SHE WAS HAVING FUN.
…AND THEN IT WAS TIME TO GO TO THE DELIVERY ROOM.
IT'S FESTIVAL TIME! YEAH!!
HAH! HAH!
BAM! BAM! BAM! BAM!
YOU'VE GOT A GOOD PACE GOING ALREADY! LET'S WELCOME YOUR BABY INTO THE WORLD!!
AAAAAH…
DOKO DOKO
DOKO DOKO
DOKO

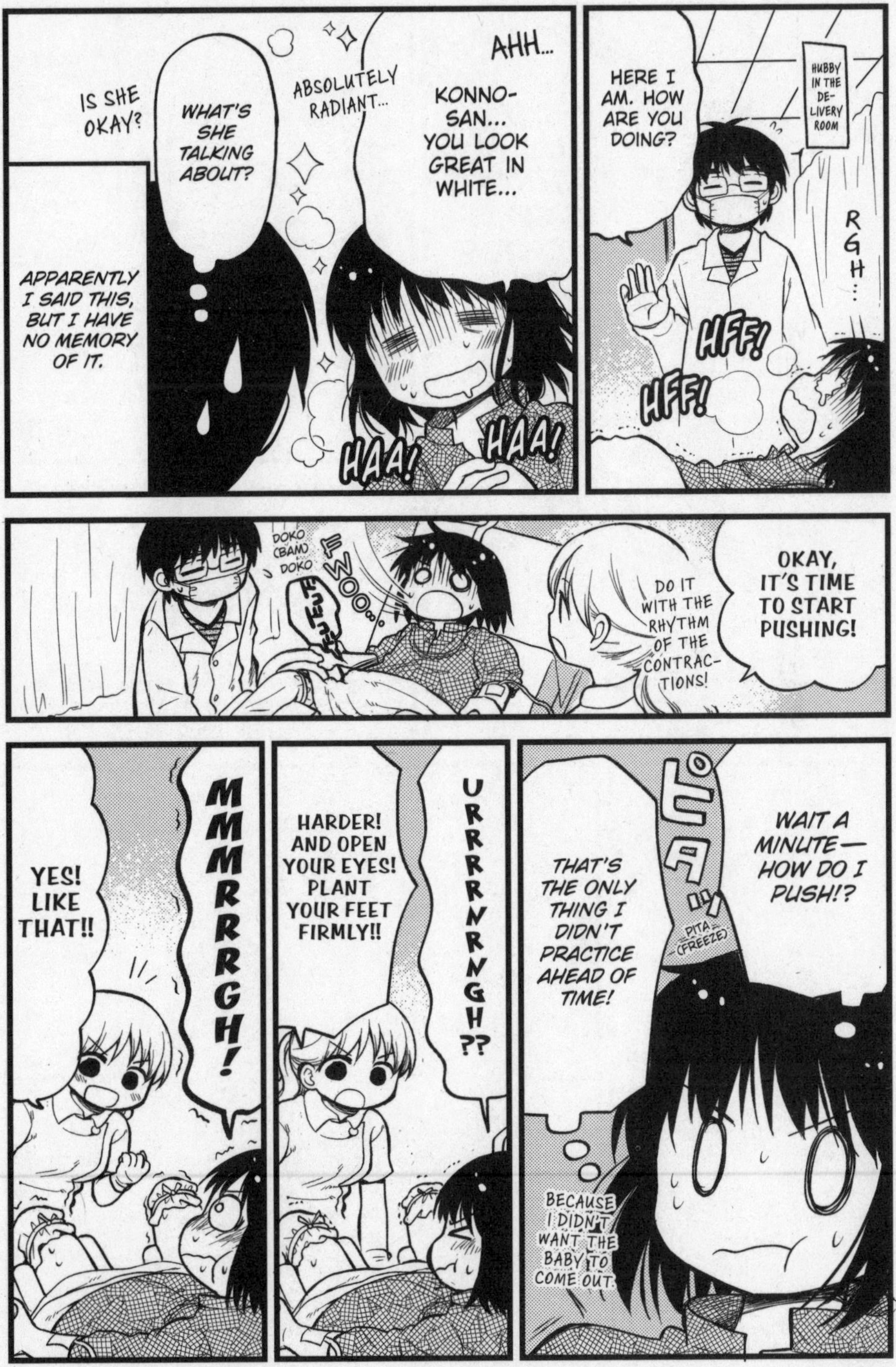
HUBBY IN THE DELIVERY ROOM
HERE I AM. HOW ARE YOU DOING?
RGH...
HFF!
HFF!
AHH...
KONNO-SAN... YOU LOOK GREAT IN WHITE...
ABSOLUTELY RADIANT...
HAA!
HAA!
WHAT'S SHE TALKING ABOUT?
IS SHE OKAY?
APPARENTLY I SAID THIS, BUT I HAVE NO MEMORY OF IT.
OKAY, IT'S TIME TO START PUSHING!
DO IT WITH THE RHYTHM OF THE CONTRACTIONS!
FWOO...
DOKO (BAM) DOKO
WAIT A MINUTE— HOW DO I PUSH!?
PITA (FREEZE)
THAT'S THE ONLY THING I DIDN'T PRACTICE AHEAD OF TIME!
BECAUSE I DIDN'T WANT THE BABY TO COME OUT.
URRRRNRNGH??
HARDER! AND OPEN YOUR EYES! PLANT YOUR FEET FIRMLY!!
MMMRRRGH!
YES! LIKE THAT!!

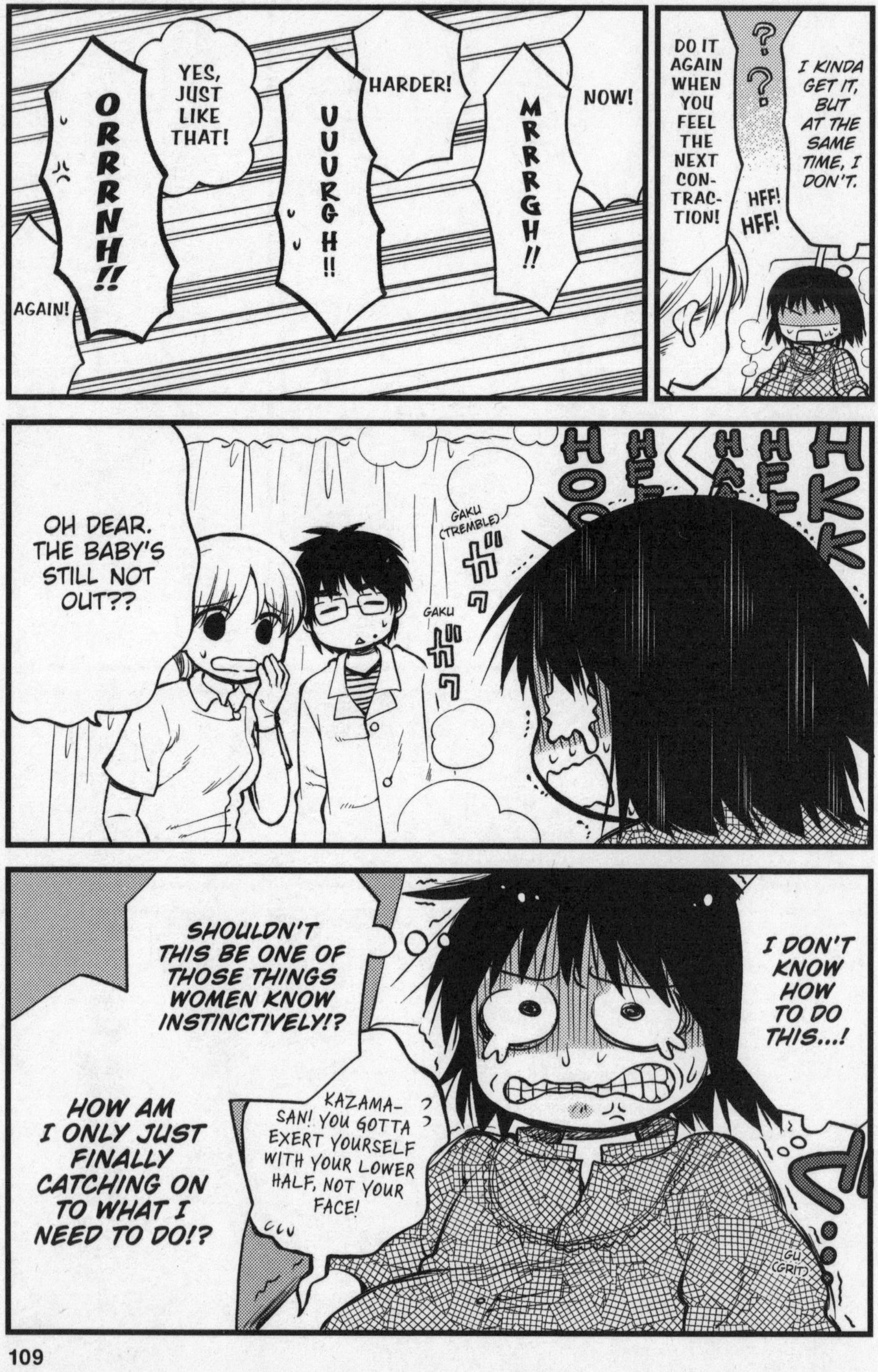
I KINDA GET IT, BUT AT THE SAME TIME, I DON'T.
??
HFF! HFF!
DO IT AGAIN WHEN YOU FEEL THE NEXT CON-TRAC-TION!
NOW!
MRRRGH!!
HARDER!
UUURGH!!
YES, JUST LIKE THAT!
ORRRNH!!
AGAIN!
HKKK
GAKU (TREMBLE)
GAKU
OH DEAR. THE BABY'S STILL NOT OUT??
I DON'T KNOW HOW TO DO THIS...!
SHOULDN'T THIS BE ONE OF THOSE THINGS WOMEN KNOW INSTINCTIVELY!?
KAZAMA-SAN! YOU GOTTA EXERT YOURSELF WITH YOUR LOWER HALF, NOT YOUR FACE!
HOW AM I ONLY JUST FINALLY CATCHING ON TO WHAT I NEED TO DO!?
GU (GRIT)

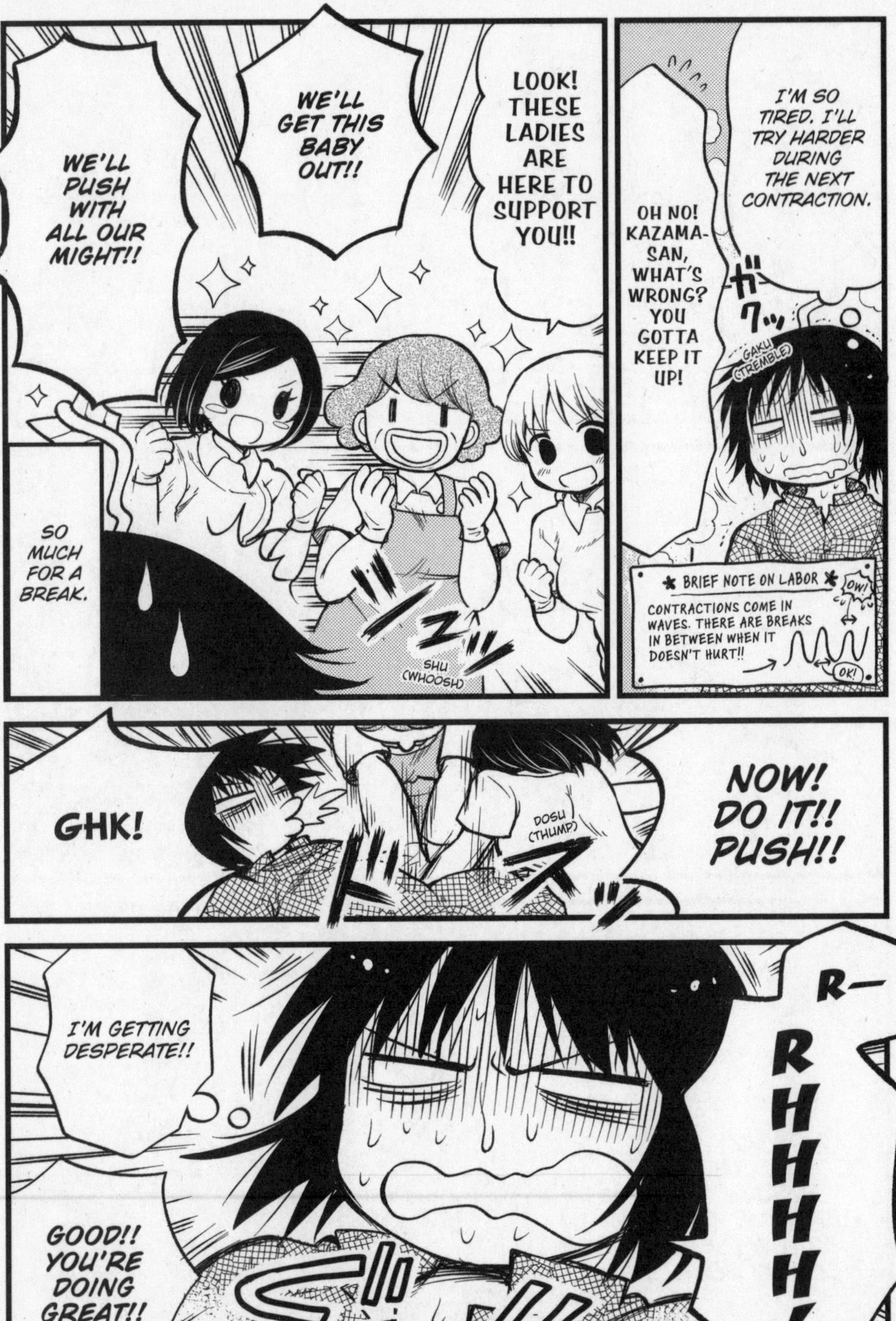
I'M SO TIRED. I'LL TRY HARDER DURING THE NEXT CONTRACTION.
OH NO! KAZAMA-SAN, WHAT'S WRONG? YOU GOTTA KEEP IT UP!
GAKU (TREMBLE)
BRIEF NOTE ON LABOR
CONTRACTIONS COME IN WAVES. THERE ARE BREAKS IN BETWEEN WHEN IT DOESN'T HURT!!
OW!
OK!
LOOK! THESE LADIES ARE HERE TO SUPPORT YOU!!
WE'LL GET THIS BABY OUT!!
WE'LL PUSH WITH ALL OUR MIGHT!!
SO MUCH FOR A BREAK.
SHU (WHOOSH)
NOW! DO IT!! PUSH!!
DOSU (THUMP)
GHK!
R— RHHHHH!
I'M GETTING DESPERATE!!
GOOD!! YOU'RE DOING GREAT!!
GU (CLENCH)

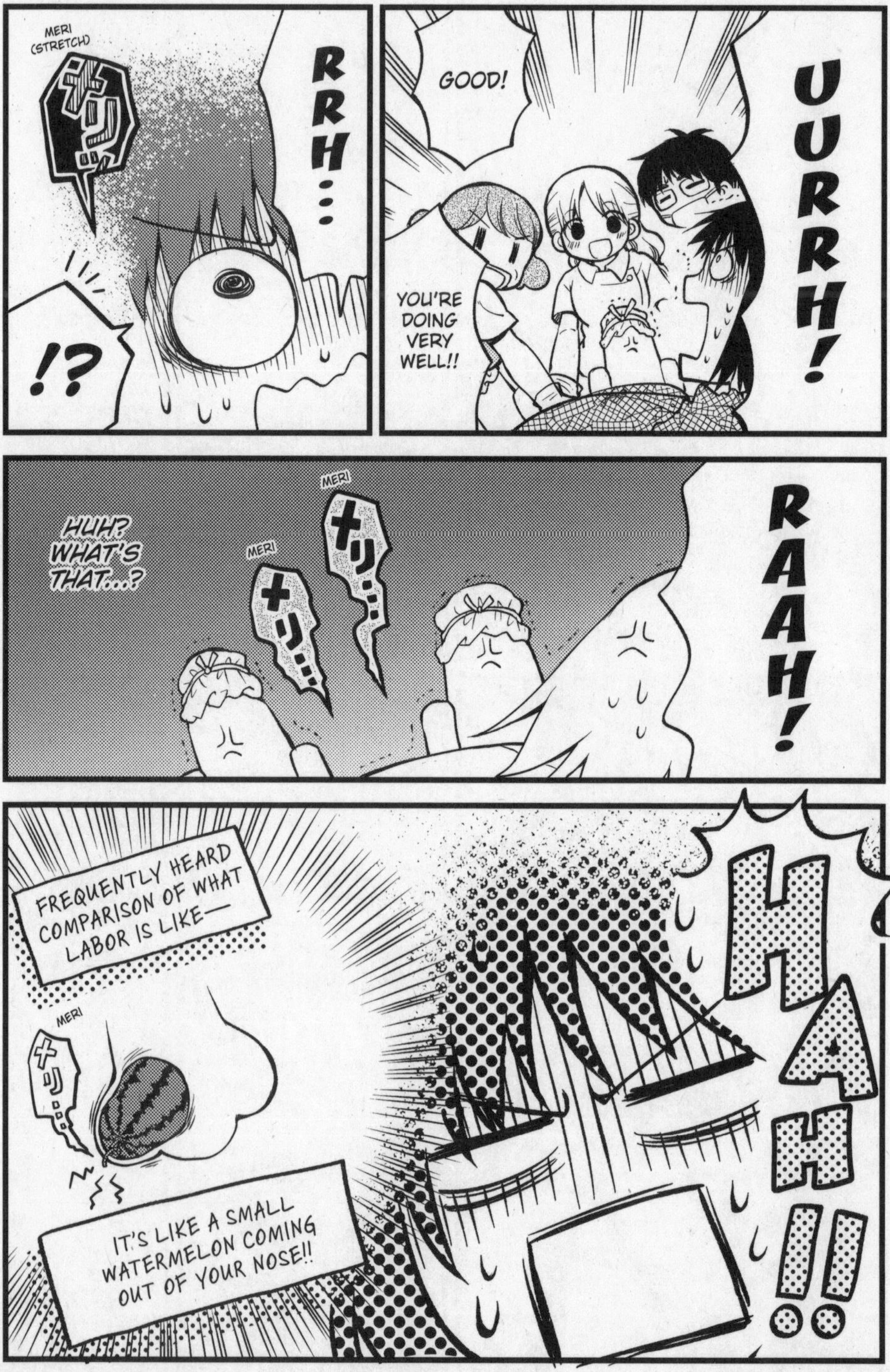
UURRH!
GOOD!
YOU'RE DOING VERY WELL!!
RRRH...
MERI (STRETCH)
!?
RAAAH!
MERI
MERI
HUH? WHAT'S THAT...?
HAH!!
FREQUENTLY HEARD COMPARISON OF WHAT LABOR IS LIKE—
MERI
IT'S LIKE A SMALL WATERMELON COMING OUT OF YOUR NOSE!!

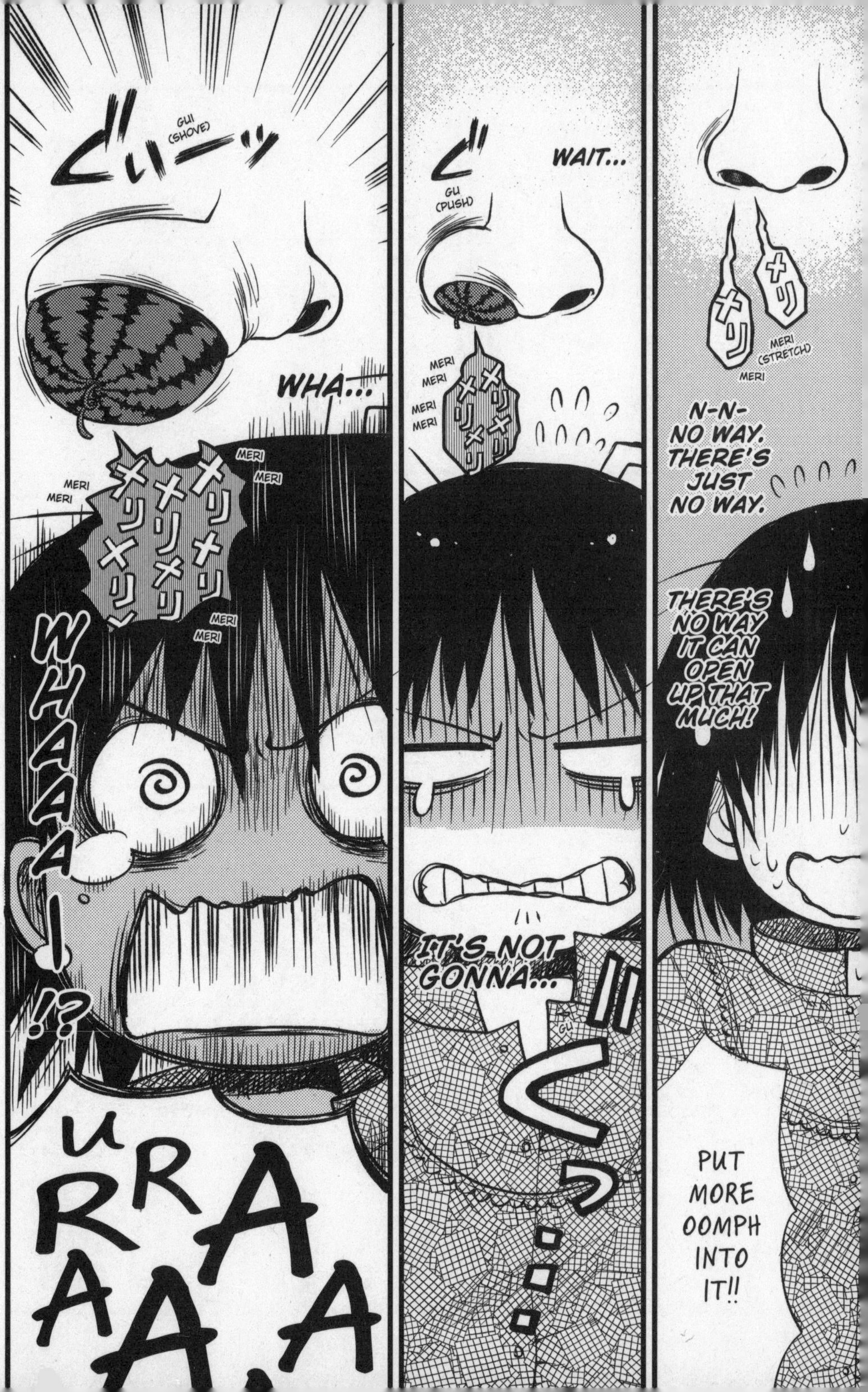
MERI (STRETCH)
MERI
N-N-NO WAY. THERE'S JUST NO WAY.
THERE'S NO WAY IT CAN OPEN UP THAT MUCH!
PUT MORE OOMPH INTO IT!!
WAIT...
GU (PUSH)
MERI MERI MERI MERI
IT'S NOT GONNA...
GU
GUI (SHOVE)
WHA...
MERI MERI
MERI MERI
MERI MERI
WHAAAA!!?
URRAAAA

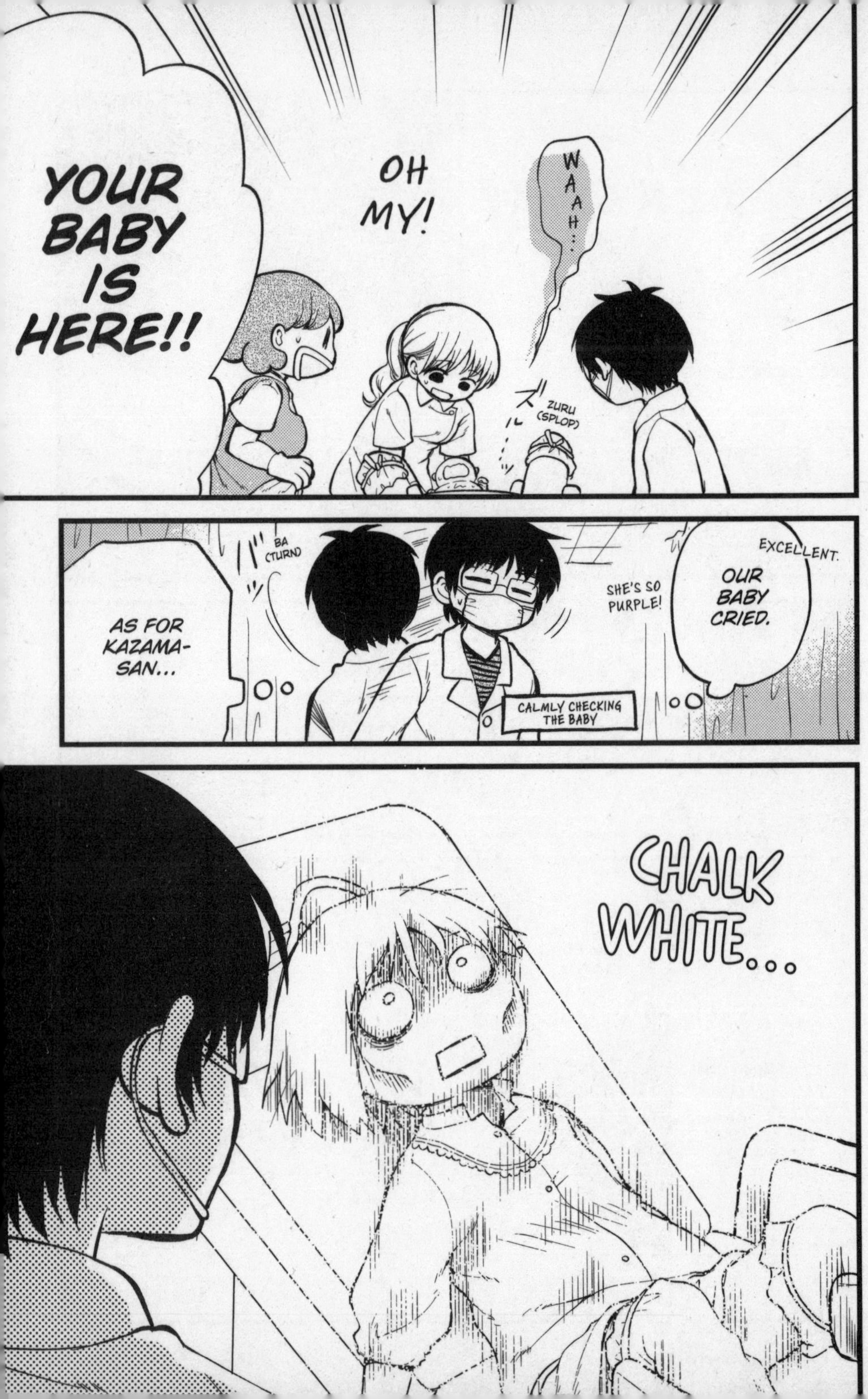
WAAH...
OH MY!
YOUR BABY IS HERE!!
ZURU (SPLOP)
EXCELLENT.
OUR BABY CRIED.
SHE'S SO PURPLE!
BA (TURN)
AS FOR KAZAMA-SAN...
CALMLY CHECKING THE BABY
CHALK WHITE...

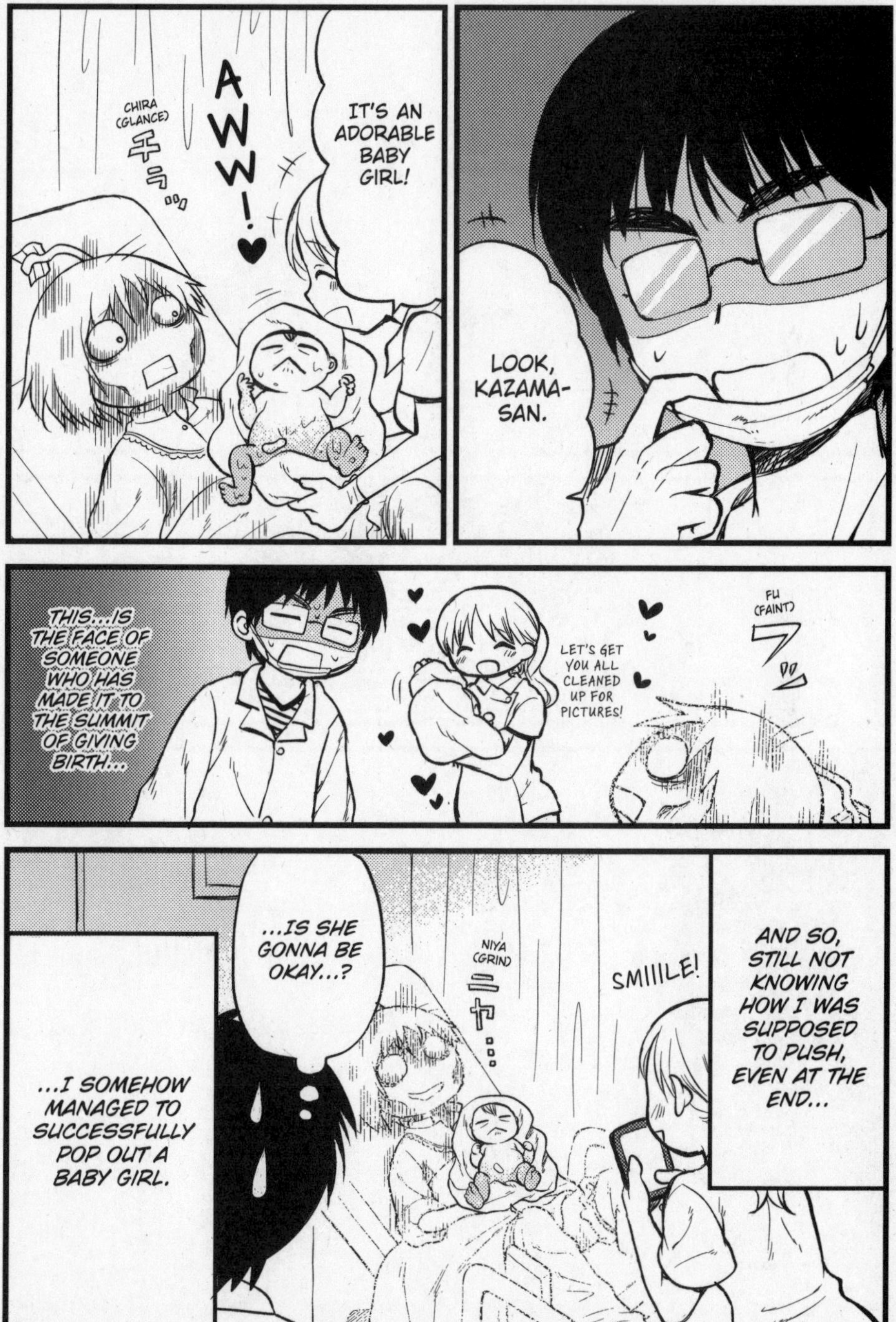
LOOK, KAZAMA-SAN.
IT'S AN ADORABLE BABY GIRL!
AWW!
CHIRA (GLANCE)
チラ
FU (FAINT)
フ
LET'S GET YOU ALL CLEANED UP FOR PICTURES!
THIS...IS THE FACE OF SOMEONE WHO HAS MADE IT TO THE SUMMIT OF GIVING BIRTH...
AND SO, STILL NOT KNOWING HOW I WAS SUPPOSED TO PUSH, EVEN AT THE END...
SMIIILE!
NIYA (GRIN)
ニヤ
...IS SHE GONNA BE OKAY...?
...I SOMEHOW MANAGED TO SUCCESSFULLY POP OUT A BABY GIRL.

Chapter 9: I Don't Know How to Push!

Bonus manga by Azure Konno

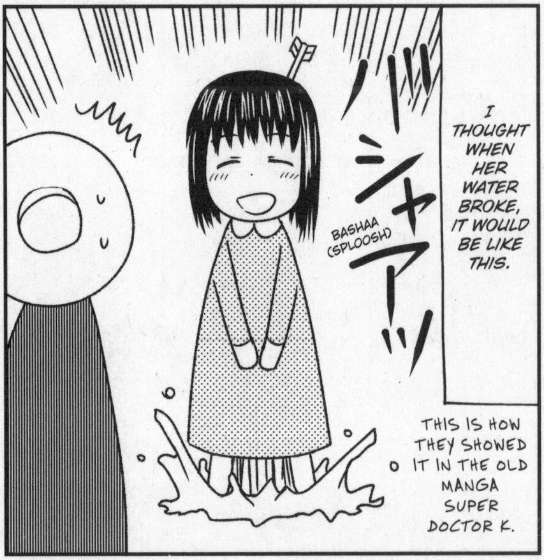
I THOUGHT WHEN HER WATER BROKE, IT WOULD BE LIKE THIS.
BASHAA (SPLOOSH)
THIS IS HOW THEY SHOWED IT IN THE OLD MANGA SUPER DOCTOR K.

When we went to the hospital, she still felt fine and didn't feel any pain yet, so I was chilling out and snacking on Karamucho chips, thinking it would take quite a while—maybe not even until the next evening.

But then, early in the morning, I was taken by surprise when she called me in tears. How had her condition changed so fast?

At first, Kazama-san said she wanted an epidural, but the nearest hospital that offered them was twenty minutes away by car, so she gave up on the idea and settled on a natural birth at a place that was only five minutes away.

When it finally came time for the delivery, there's not much a man can do—I could only give her encouragement.

I thought if I said something like "Keep going! You got this!" she would yell back at me with something like, "I am going, you moron!!" So I encouraged her by just saying, "You're doing great! Yeah! You're doing great!"

Bonus manga by Ayami Kazama

Chapter 9: I Don't Know How to Push!

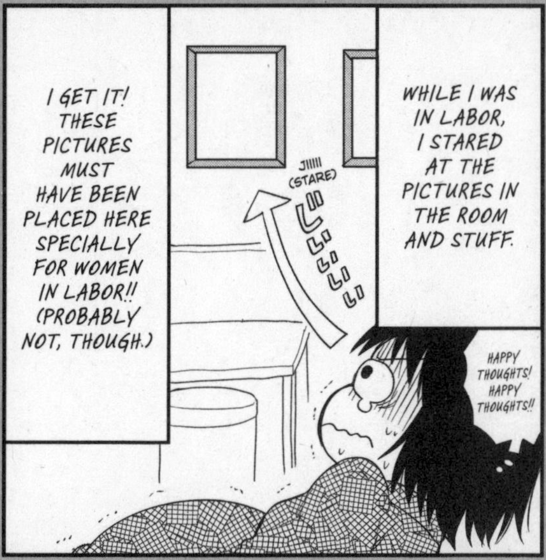
WHILE I WAS IN LABOR, I STARED AT THE PICTURES IN THE ROOM AND STUFF.
JIIII (STARE)
I GET IT! THESE PICTURES MUST HAVE BEEN PLACED HERE SPECIALLY FOR WOMEN IN LABOR!! (PROBABLY NOT, THOUGH.)
HAPPY THOUGHTS! HAPPY THOUGHTS!!

Not only am I not athletic in the least, but because I was incredibly out of shape, my body was inflexible and stiff.
I was expecting labor to last quite a while.
Once it finally started, I forced myself to eat all of my breakfast—despite feeling like I was gonna die—so that I'd have the energy to endure this very long battle. I also made sure to take lots of photos for reference later and slept through most of it, even when my contractions were five minutes apart. When I was awake, I stared at the pictures on the walls and just endured.
But it was a relatively easy birth—I was only in labor about nine hours despite this being my first birth, so maybe it doesn't really have anything to do with how athletic you are.

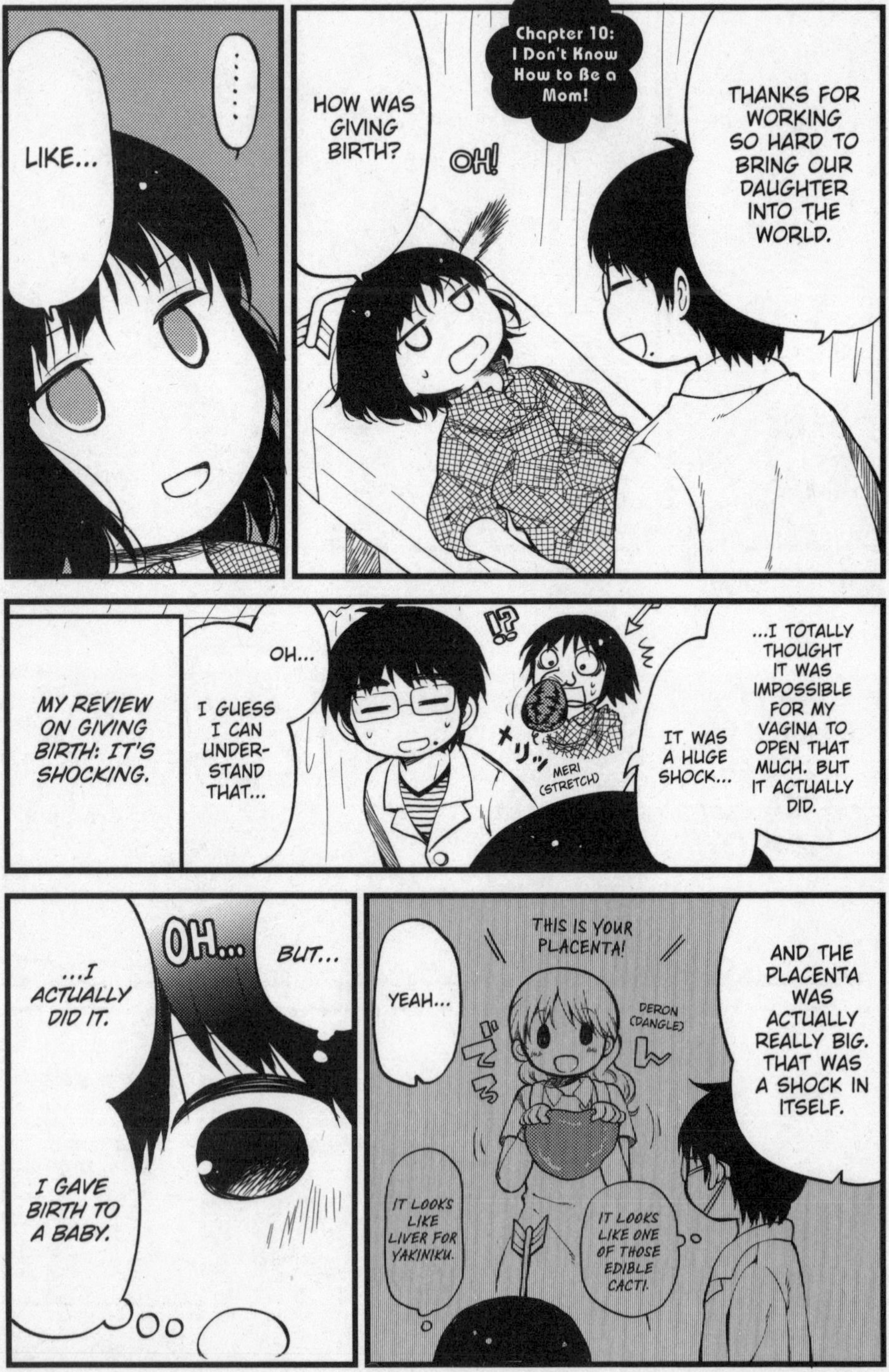
Chapter 10: I Don't Know How to Be a Mom!
THANKS FOR WORKING SO HARD TO BRING OUR DAUGHTER INTO THE WORLD.
OH!
HOW WAS GIVING BIRTH?
......
LIKE...
...I TOTALLY THOUGHT IT WAS IMPOSSIBLE FOR MY VAGINA TO OPEN THAT MUCH. BUT IT ACTUALLY DID.
IT WAS A HUGE SHOCK...
!?
MERI (STRETCH)
OH...
I GUESS I CAN UNDER-STAND THAT...
MY REVIEW ON GIVING BIRTH: IT'S SHOCKING.
AND THE PLACENTA WAS ACTUALLY REALLY BIG. THAT WAS A SHOCK IN ITSELF.
THIS IS YOUR PLACENTA!
DERON (DANGLE)
YEAH...
IT LOOKS LIKE ONE OF THOSE EDIBLE CACTI.
IT LOOKS LIKE LIVER FOR YAKINIKU.
BUT...
OH...
...I ACTUALLY DID IT.
I GAVE BIRTH TO A BABY.

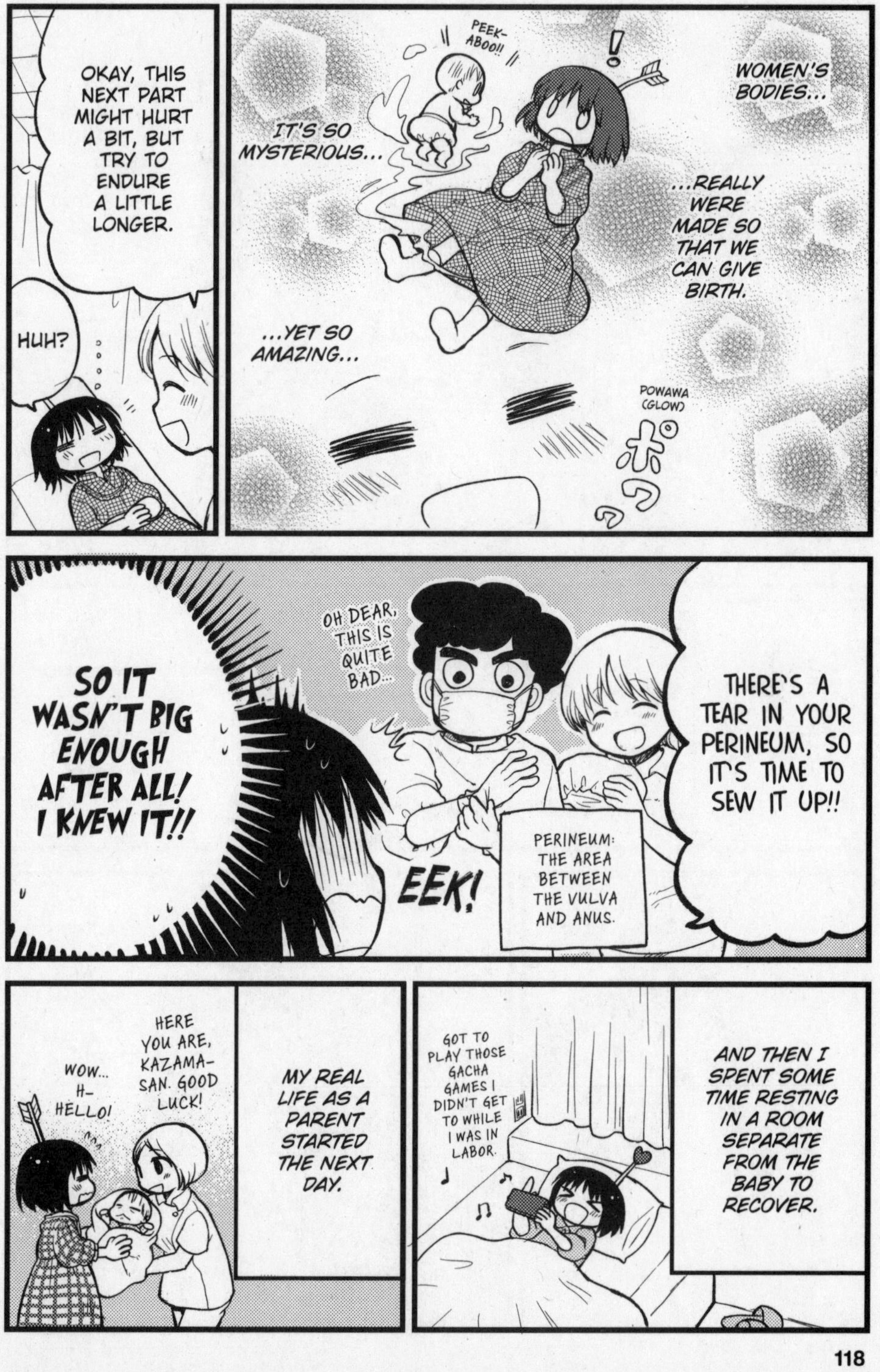

WOMEN'S BODIES...
PEEK-ABOO!!
...REALLY WERE MADE SO THAT WE CAN GIVE BIRTH.
IT'S SO MYSTERIOUS...
...YET SO AMAZING...
POWAWA (GLOW)
OKAY, THIS NEXT PART MIGHT HURT A BIT, BUT TRY TO ENDURE A LITTLE LONGER.
HUH?
THERE'S A TEAR IN YOUR PERINEUM, SO IT'S TIME TO SEW IT UP!!
PERINEUM: THE AREA BETWEEN THE VULVA AND ANUS.
OH DEAR, THIS IS QUITE BAD...
EEK!
SO IT WASN'T BIG ENOUGH AFTER ALL! I KNEW IT!!
AND THEN I SPENT SOME TIME RESTING IN A ROOM SEPARATE FROM THE BABY TO RECOVER.
GOT TO PLAY THOSE GACHA GAMES I DIDN'T GET TO WHILE I WAS IN LABOR.
MY REAL LIFE AS A PARENT STARTED THE NEXT DAY.
HERE YOU ARE, KAZAMA-SAN. GOOD LUCK!
WOW... H- HELLO!

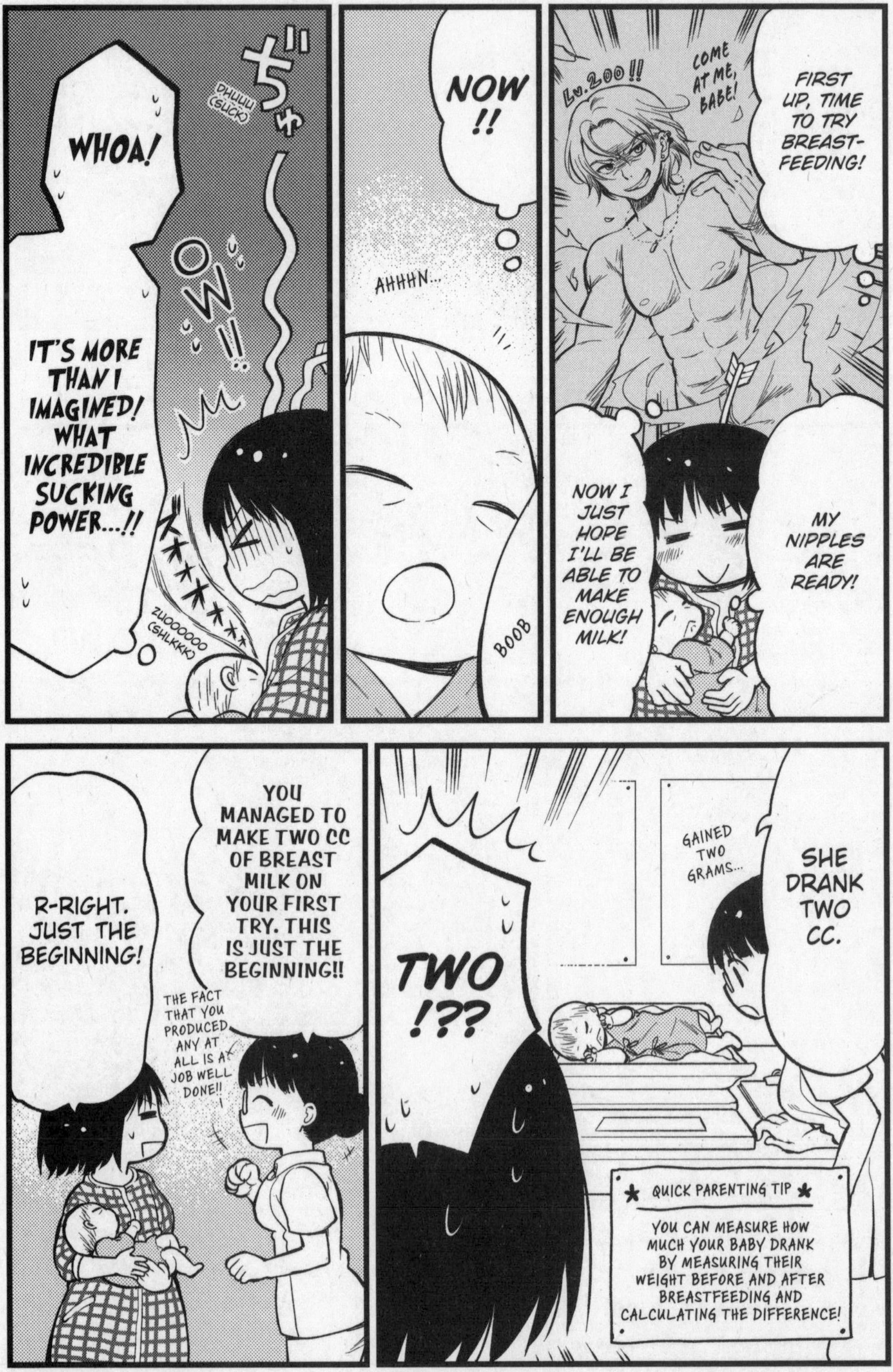
FIRST UP, TIME TO TRY BREAST-FEEDING!
COME AT ME, BABE!
Lv.200!!
MY NIPPLES ARE READY!
NOW I JUST HOPE I'LL BE ABLE TO MAKE ENOUGH MILK!
NOW!!
AHHHN...
BOOB
ぢゅ
DHUUU (SUCK)
WHOA!
OW!!
IT'S MORE THAN I IMAGINED! WHAT INCREDIBLE SUCKING POWER...!!
ZUOOOOOO (SHLKKK)
SHE DRANK TWO CC.
GAINED TWO GRAMS...
TWO!??
QUICK PARENTING TIP
YOU CAN MEASURE HOW MUCH YOUR BABY DRANK BY MEASURING THEIR WEIGHT BEFORE AND AFTER BREASTFEEDING AND CALCULATING THE DIFFERENCE!
YOU MANAGED TO MAKE TWO CC OF BREAST MILK ON YOUR FIRST TRY. THIS IS JUST THE BEGINNING!!
R-RIGHT. JUST THE BEGINNING!
THE FACT THAT YOU PRODUCED ANY AT ALL IS A JOB WELL DONE!!

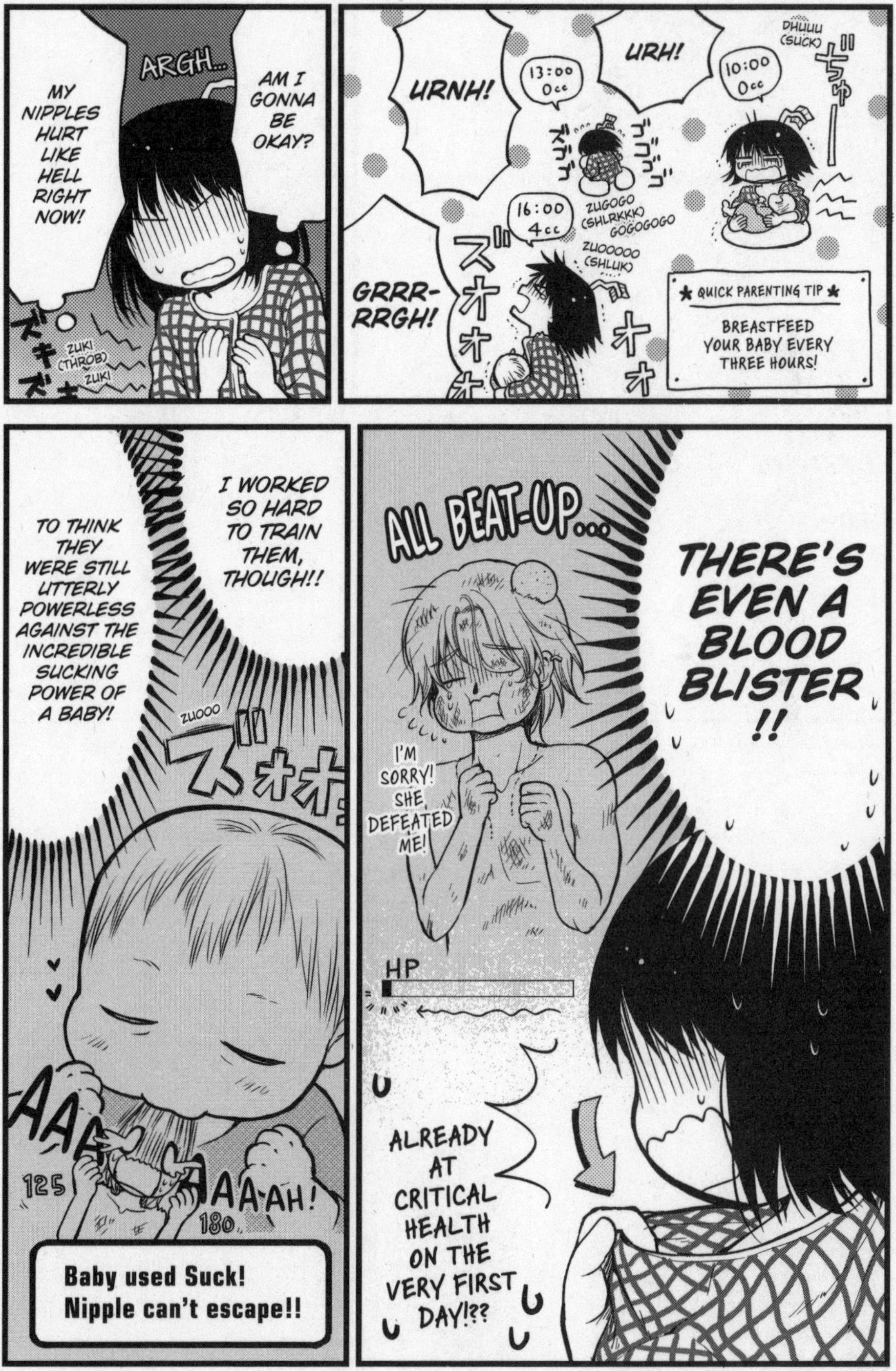
DHUUU (SUCK)
10:00 0cc
URH!
13:00 0cc
URNH!
ZUGOGO (SHLRKKK) GOGOGOGO
16:00 4cc
ZUOOOOO (SHLUK)
GRRR-RRGH!
QUICK PARENTING TIP
BREASTFEED YOUR BABY EVERY THREE HOURS!
AM I GONNA BE OKAY?
ARGH...
MY NIPPLES HURT LIKE HELL RIGHT NOW!
ZUKI (THROB) ZUKI
THERE'S EVEN A BLOOD BLISTER!!
ALL BEAT-UP...
I'M SORRY! SHE DEFEATED ME!
HP
ALREADY AT CRITICAL HEALTH ON THE VERY FIRST DAY!??
I WORKED SO HARD TO TRAIN THEM, THOUGH!!
TO THINK THEY WERE STILL UTTERLY POWERLESS AGAINST THE INCREDIBLE SUCKING POWER OF A BABY!
ZUOOO
AAAAAAH!
125
180
Baby used Suck! Nipple can't escape!!

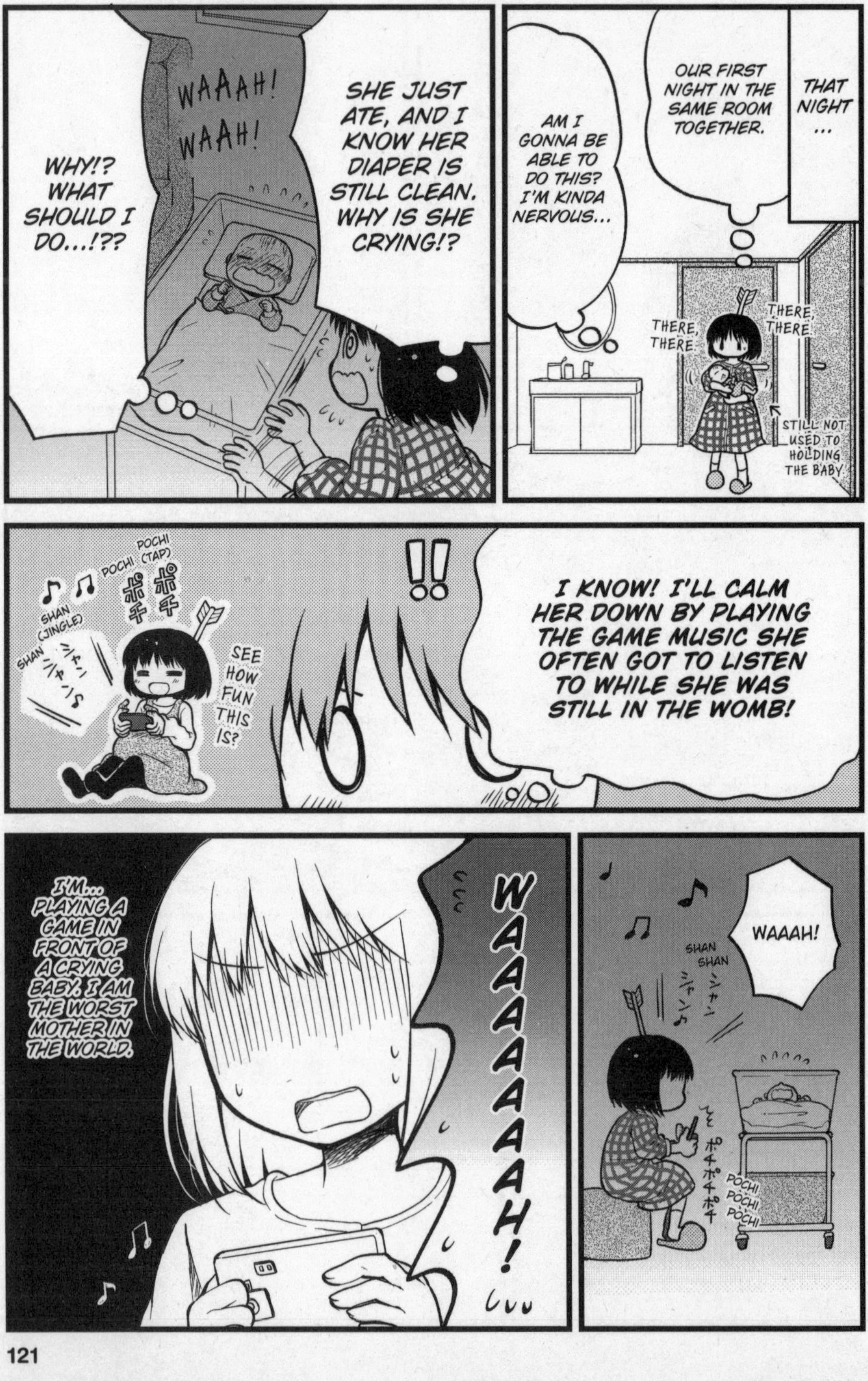
THAT NIGHT ...
OUR FIRST NIGHT IN THE SAME ROOM TOGETHER.
AM I GONNA BE ABLE TO DO THIS? I'M KINDA NERVOUS...
THERE, THERE
THERE, THERE
STILL NOT USED TO HOLDING THE BABY.
SHE JUST ATE, AND I KNOW HER DIAPER IS STILL CLEAN. WHY IS SHE CRYING!?
WAAAH! WAAH!
WHY!? WHAT SHOULD I DO...!??
!!
I KNOW! I'LL CALM HER DOWN BY PLAYING THE GAME MUSIC SHE OFTEN GOT TO LISTEN TO WHILE SHE WAS STILL IN THE WOMB!
POCHI POCHI (TAP)
SEE HOW FUN THIS IS?
SHAN SHAN (JINGLE)
WAAAH!
SHAN SHAN
POCHI POCHI POCHI
WAAAAAAAAAAH!
I'M... PLAYING A GAME IN FRONT OF A CRYING BABY. I AM THE WORST MOTHER IN THE WORLD.

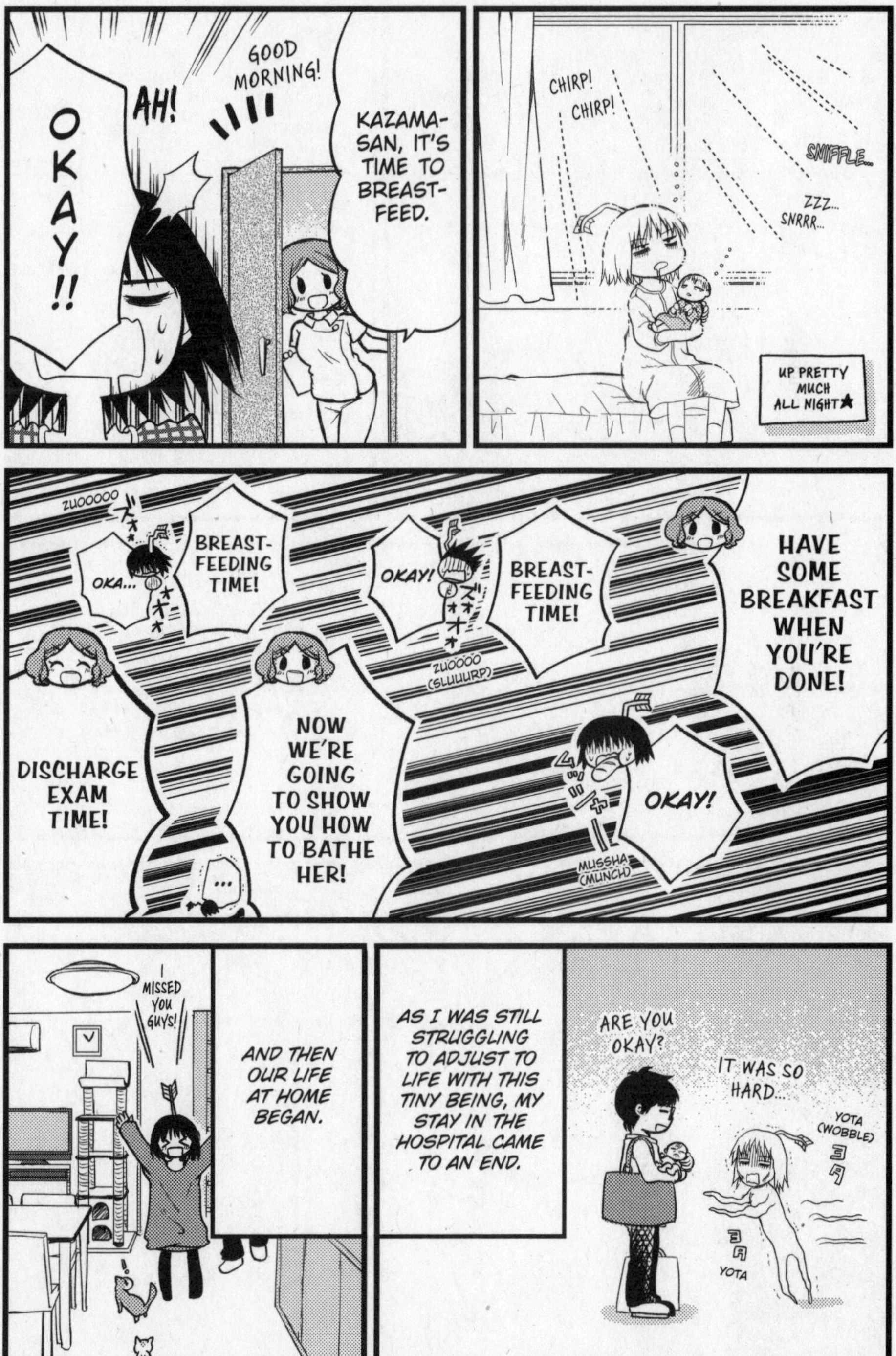
CHIRP!
CHIRP!
SNIFFLE...
ZZZ... SNRRR...
UP PRETTY MUCH ALL NIGHT★
KAZAMA-SAN, IT'S TIME TO BREAST-FEED.
GOOD MORNING!
AH!
OKAY!!
HAVE SOME BREAKFAST WHEN YOU'RE DONE!
BREAST-FEEDING TIME!
OKAY!
ZUOOOO (SLUUURP)
BREAST-FEEDING TIME!
ZUOOOOO
OKA...
OKAY!
MUSSHA (MUNCH)
NOW WE'RE GOING TO SHOW YOU HOW TO BATHE HER!
DISCHARGE EXAM TIME!
...
ARE YOU OKAY?
IT WAS SO HARD...
YOTA (WOBBLE)
YOTA
AS I WAS STILL STRUGGLING TO ADJUST TO LIFE WITH THIS TINY BEING, MY STAY IN THE HOSPITAL CAME TO AN END.
AND THEN OUR LIFE AT HOME BEGAN.
I MISSED YOU GUYS!

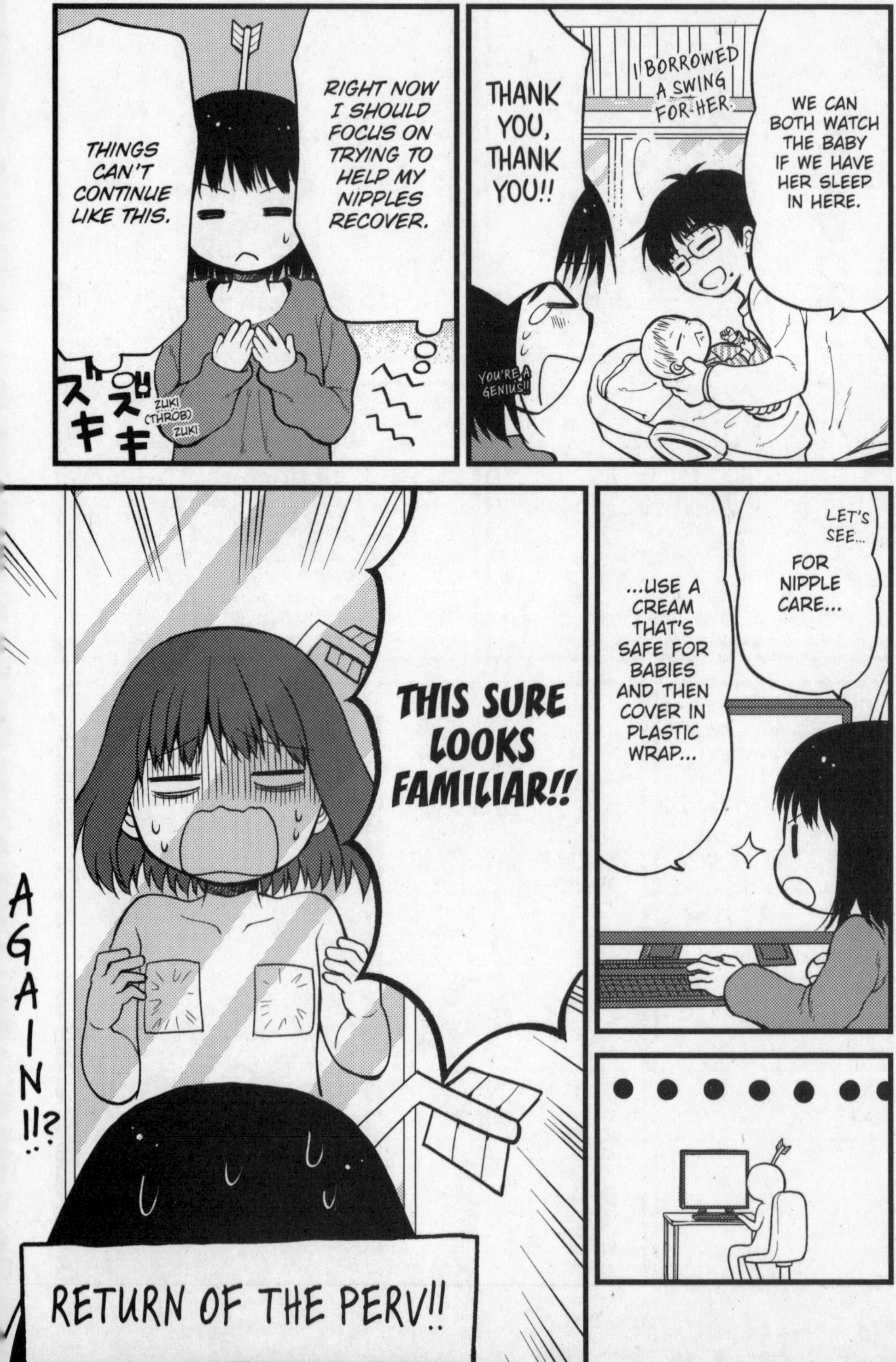
I BORROWED A SWING FOR HER.
WE CAN BOTH WATCH THE BABY IF WE HAVE HER SLEEP IN HERE.
THANK YOU, THANK YOU!!
YOU'RE A GENIUS!!
THINGS CAN'T CONTINUE LIKE THIS.
RIGHT NOW I SHOULD FOCUS ON TRYING TO HELP MY NIPPLES RECOVER.
ZUKI (THROB) ZUKI
LET'S SEE...
FOR NIPPLE CARE...
...USE A CREAM THAT'S SAFE FOR BABIES AND THEN COVER IN PLASTIC WRAP...
THIS SURE LOOKS FAMILIAR!!
AGAIN!!?
RETURN OF THE PERV!!

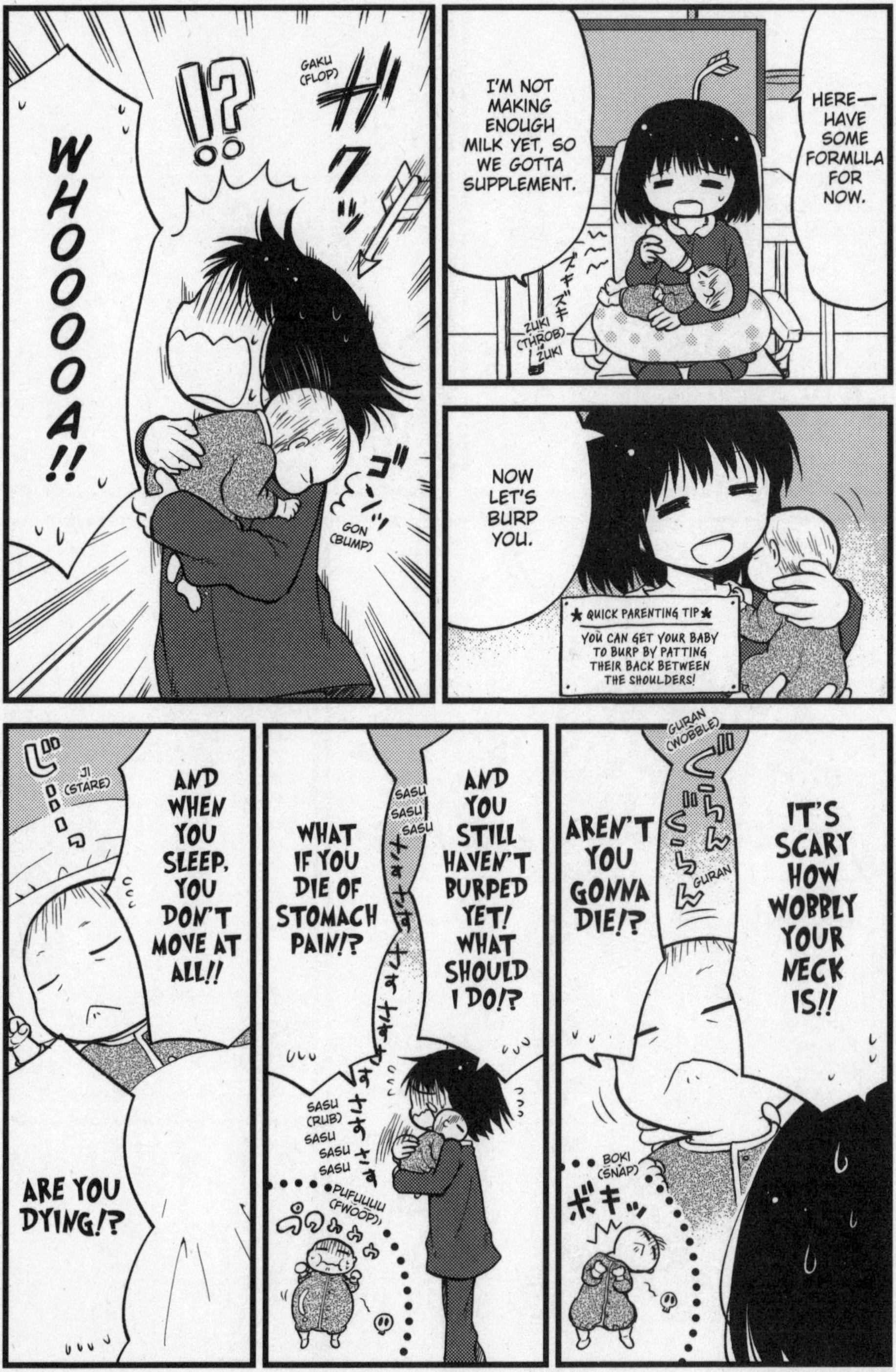
HERE—HAVE SOME FORMULA FOR NOW.
I'M NOT MAKING ENOUGH MILK YET, SO WE GOTTA SUPPLEMENT.
ZUKI (THROB) ZUKI
NOW LET'S BURP YOU.
★ QUICK PARENTING TIP ★
YOU CAN GET YOUR BABY TO BURP BY PATTING THEIR BACK BETWEEN THE SHOULDERS!
GAKU (FLOP)
!?
WHOOOOOA!!
GON (BUMP)
IT'S SCARY HOW WOBBLY YOUR NECK IS!!
GURAN (WOBBLE) GURAN
AREN'T YOU GONNA DIE!?
BOKI (SNAP)
AND YOU STILL HAVEN'T BURPED YET! WHAT SHOULD I DO!?
SASU SASU SASU
WHAT IF YOU DIE OF STOMACH PAIN!?
SASU (RUB) SASU SASU SASU
PUFUUUU (FWOOP)
JI (STARE)
AND WHEN YOU SLEEP, YOU DON'T MOVE AT ALL!!
ARE YOU DYING!?

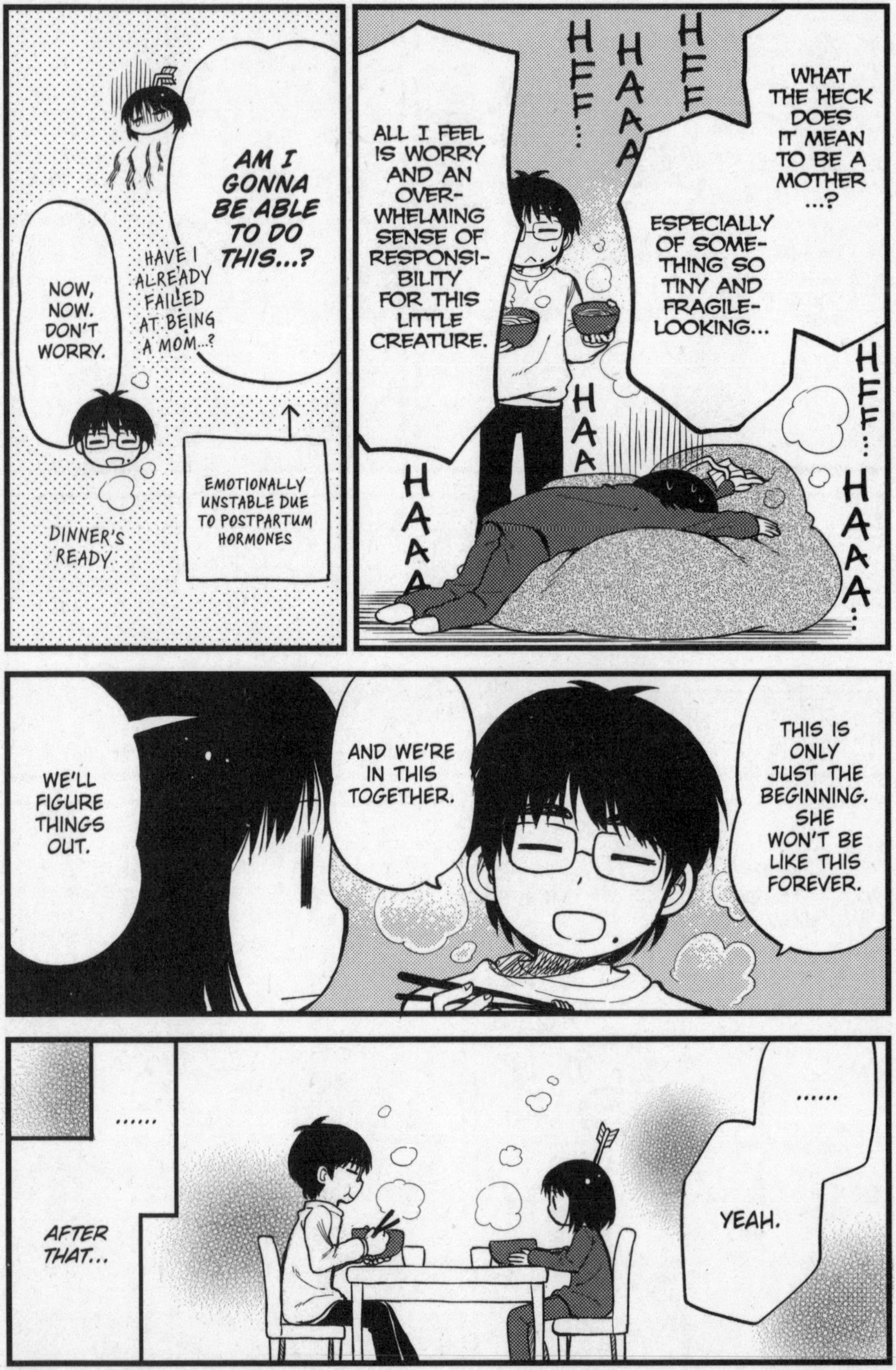
HFF... HAAA HFF...
WHAT THE HECK DOES IT MEAN TO BE A MOTHER ...?
ESPECIALLY OF SOME-THING SO TINY AND FRAGILE-LOOKING...
ALL I FEEL IS WORRY AND AN OVER-WHELMING SENSE OF RESPONSI-BILITY FOR THIS LITTLE CREATURE.
HFF... HAAAA...
HAA
HAAA
AM I GONNA BE ABLE TO DO THIS...?
HAVE I ALREADY FAILED AT BEING A MOM...?
EMOTIONALLY UNSTABLE DUE TO POSTPARTUM HORMONES
NOW, NOW. DON'T WORRY.
DINNER'S READY
THIS IS ONLY JUST THE BEGINNING. SHE WON'T BE LIKE THIS FOREVER.
AND WE'RE IN THIS TOGETHER.
WE'LL FIGURE THINGS OUT.
......
YEAH.
......
AFTER THAT...

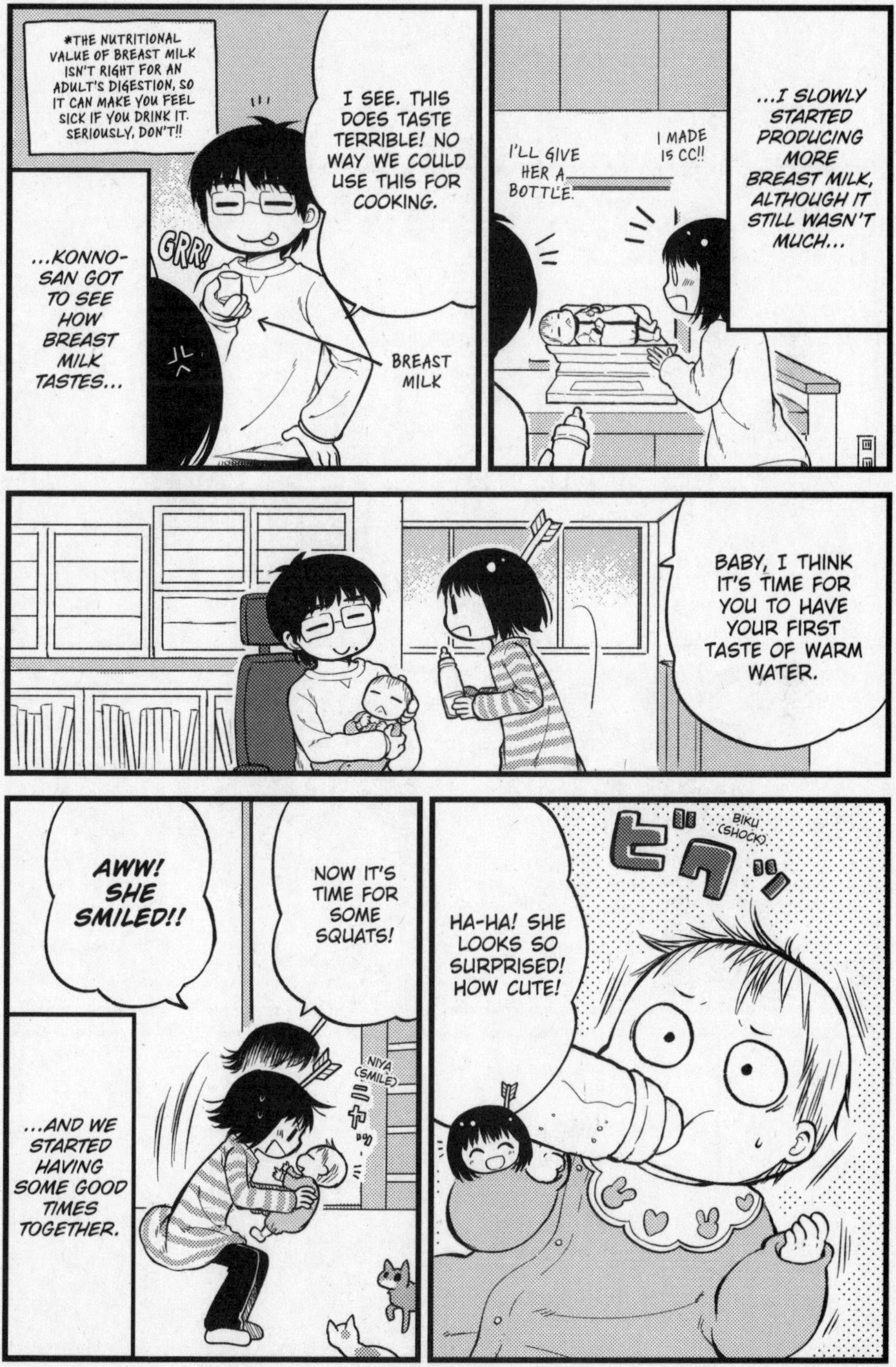
...I SLOWLY STARTED PRODUCING MORE BREAST MILK, ALTHOUGH IT STILL WASN'T MUCH...
I MADE 15 CC!!
I'LL GIVE HER A BOTTLE.
I SEE. THIS DOES TASTE TERRIBLE! NO WAY WE COULD USE THIS FOR COOKING.
*THE NUTRITIONAL VALUE OF BREAST MILK ISN'T RIGHT FOR AN ADULT'S DIGESTION, SO IT CAN MAKE YOU FEEL SICK IF YOU DRINK IT. SERIOUSLY, DON'T!!
GRR!
BREAST MILK
...KONNO-SAN GOT TO SEE HOW BREAST MILK TASTES...
BABY, I THINK IT'S TIME FOR YOU TO HAVE YOUR FIRST TASTE OF WARM WATER.
BIKU (SHOCK)
HA-HA! SHE LOOKS SO SURPRISED! HOW CUTE!
NOW IT'S TIME FOR SOME SQUATS!
AWW! SHE SMILED!!
NIYA (SMILE)
...AND WE STARTED HAVING SOME GOOD TIMES TOGETHER.

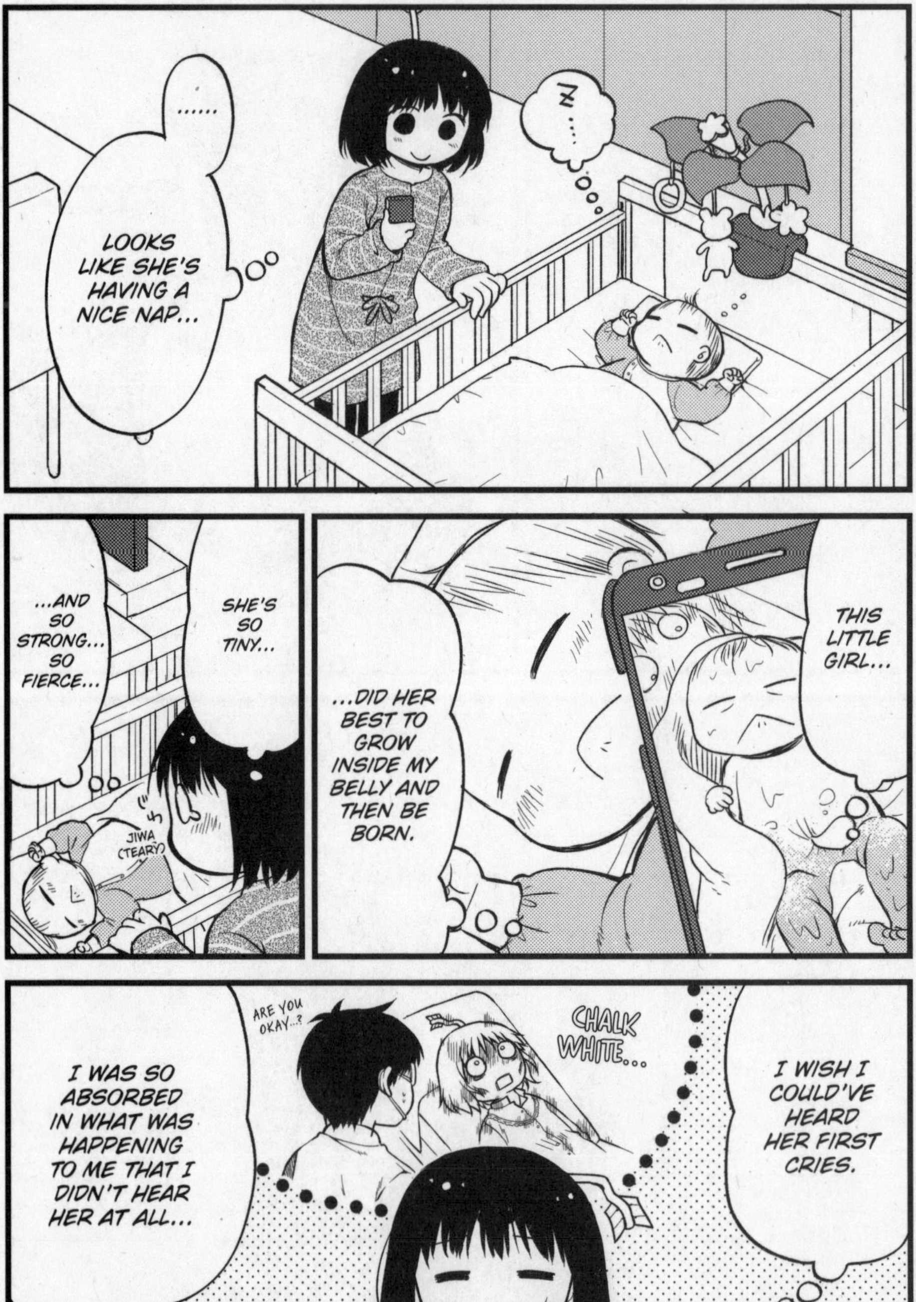
Z...
......
LOOKS LIKE SHE'S HAVING A NICE NAP...
THIS LITTLE GIRL...
...DID HER BEST TO GROW INSIDE MY BELLY AND THEN BE BORN.
SHE'S SO TINY...
...AND SO STRONG... SO FIERCE...
JIWA (TEARY)
I WISH I COULD'VE HEARD HER FIRST CRIES.
CHALK WHITE...
ARE YOU OKAY...?
I WAS SO ABSORBED IN WHAT WAS HAPPENING TO ME THAT I DIDN'T HEAR HER AT ALL...

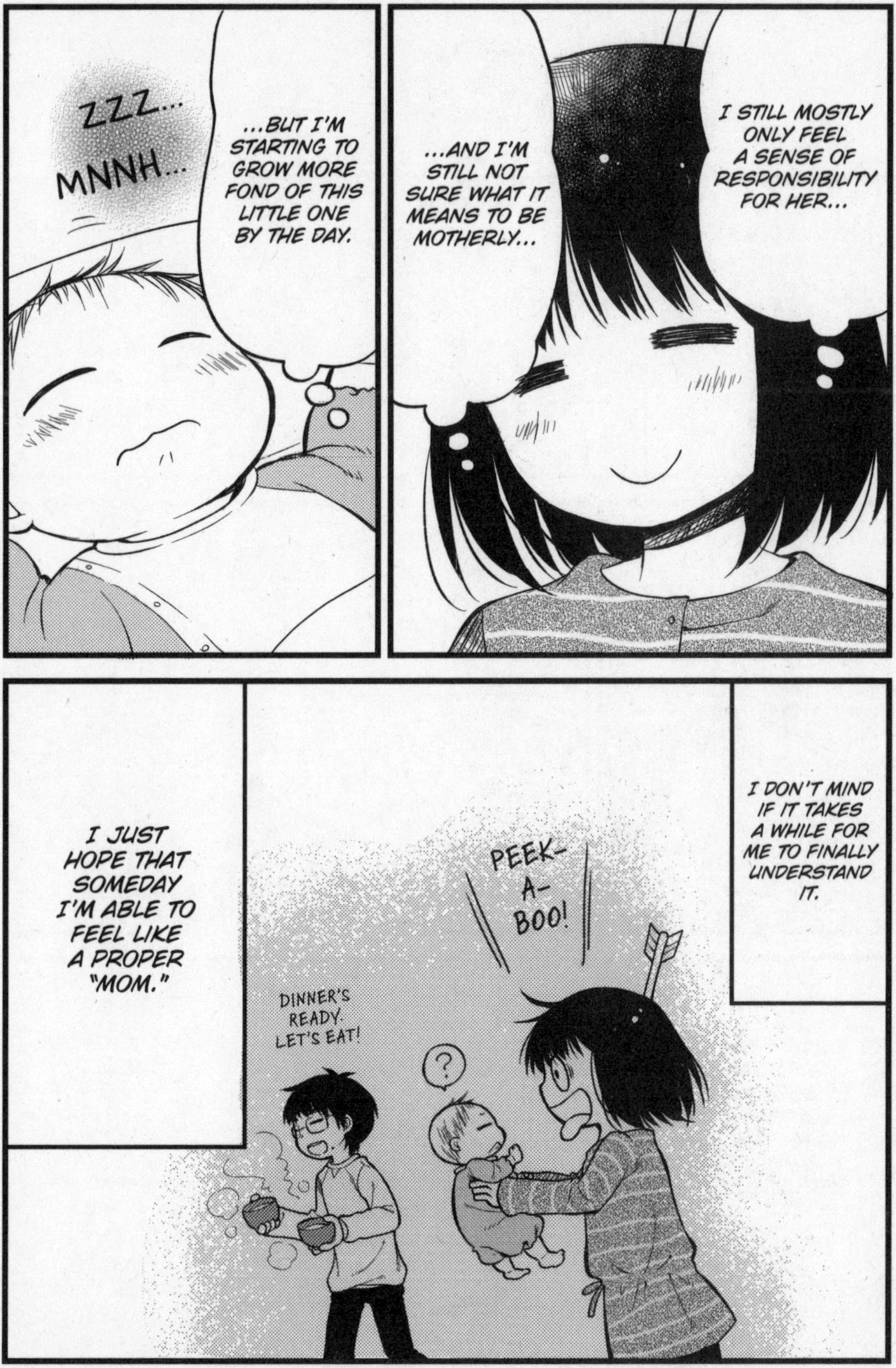
I STILL MOSTLY ONLY FEEL A SENSE OF RESPONSIBILITY FOR HER...
...AND I'M STILL NOT SURE WHAT IT MEANS TO BE MOTHERLY...
...BUT I'M STARTING TO GROW MORE FOND OF THIS LITTLE ONE BY THE DAY.
ZZZ... MNNH...
I DON'T MIND IF IT TAKES A WHILE FOR ME TO FINALLY UNDERSTAND IT.
PEEK-A-BOO!
I JUST HOPE THAT SOMEDAY I'M ABLE TO FEEL LIKE A PROPER "MOM."
DINNER'S READY. LET'S EAT!
?

Bonus manga by Azure Konno

Chapter 10: I Don't Know How to Be a Mom!

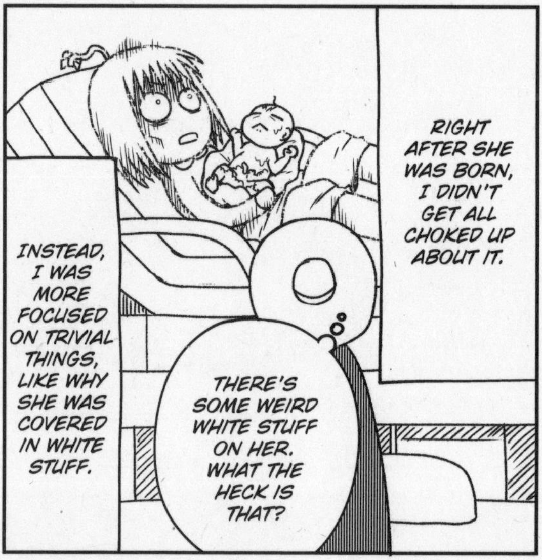
RIGHT AFTER SHE WAS BORN, I DIDN'T GET ALL CHOKED UP ABOUT IT.
INSTEAD, I WAS MORE FOCUSED ON TRIVIAL THINGS, LIKE WHY SHE WAS COVERED IN WHITE STUFF.
THERE'S SOME WEIRD WHITE STUFF ON HER. WHAT THE HECK IS THAT?

And so we became a happy family of three. I've always wanted a kid, so I'm pretty happy about it.
It's something I couldn't have done myself, so I'm incredibly grateful to Kazama-san for enduring all she went through in order to make it happen.
Kazama-san's nipples hurt terribly, and she wanted me to experience what it felt like as well, so she tried to get me to let the baby suck on my nipples too.
But I'm not into that sort of thing.
And I feel that would be weird as a dad.
I can just imagine how my daughter would avoid me one day if she found out that she had sucked on my nipples when she was an infant.
I know Kazama-san just wanted me to know what she was feeling, but that just wasn't happening.

Bonus manga by Ayami Kazama

Chapter 10: I Don't Know How to Be a Mom!

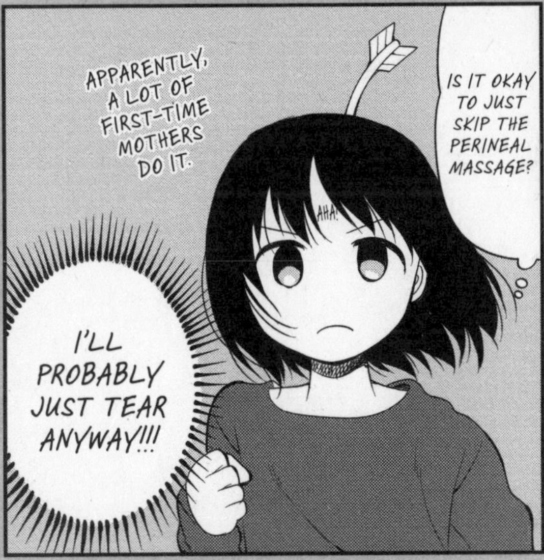
IS IT OKAY TO JUST SKIP THE PERINEAL MASSAGE?
APPARENTLY, A LOT OF FIRST-TIME MOTHERS DO IT.
AHA!
I'LL PROBABLY JUST TEAR ANYWAY!!!

*AND... I DID TEAR...

In addition to nipple massages, there are also perineal massages. You stretch the perineum so to prevent it from tearing and reduce pain during childbirth.
I thought that my nipples would be the bigger problem for me, so I didn't bother at all.
At the childbirth info session I went to, they told us most women either get an incision or tear, so I just assumed it was inevitable.
Sure enough, it tore.
After that, I couldn't sit down anywhere unless I put a donut pillow down first.

Postpartum Anecdote: Breastfeeding

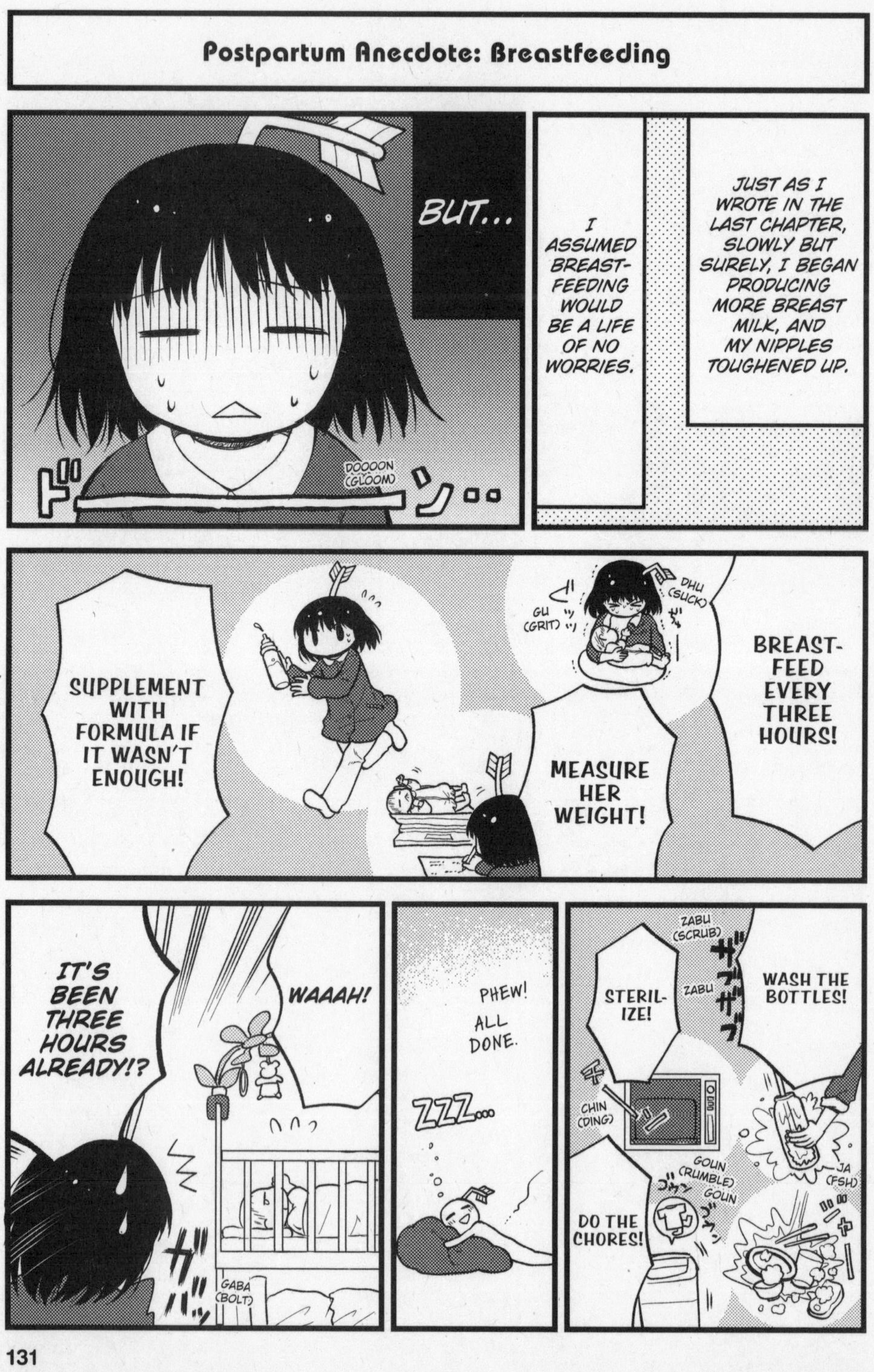
JUST AS I WROTE IN THE LAST CHAPTER, SLOWLY BUT SURELY, I BEGAN PRODUCING MORE BREAST MILK, AND MY NIPPLES TOUGHENED UP.
I ASSUMED BREAST-FEEDING WOULD BE A LIFE OF NO WORRIES.
BUT...
DOOOON (GLOOM)
BREAST-FEED EVERY THREE HOURS!
DHU (SUCK)
GU (GRIT)
MEASURE HER WEIGHT!
SUPPLEMENT WITH FORMULA IF IT WASN'T ENOUGH!
WASH THE BOTTLES!
ZABU (SCRUB)
ZABU
JA (FSH)
STERIL-IZE!
CHIN (DING)
GOUN (RUMBLE)
GOUN
DO THE CHORES!
PHEW!
ALL DONE.
ZZZ...
WAAAH!
IT'S BEEN THREE HOURS ALREADY!?
GABA (BOLT)

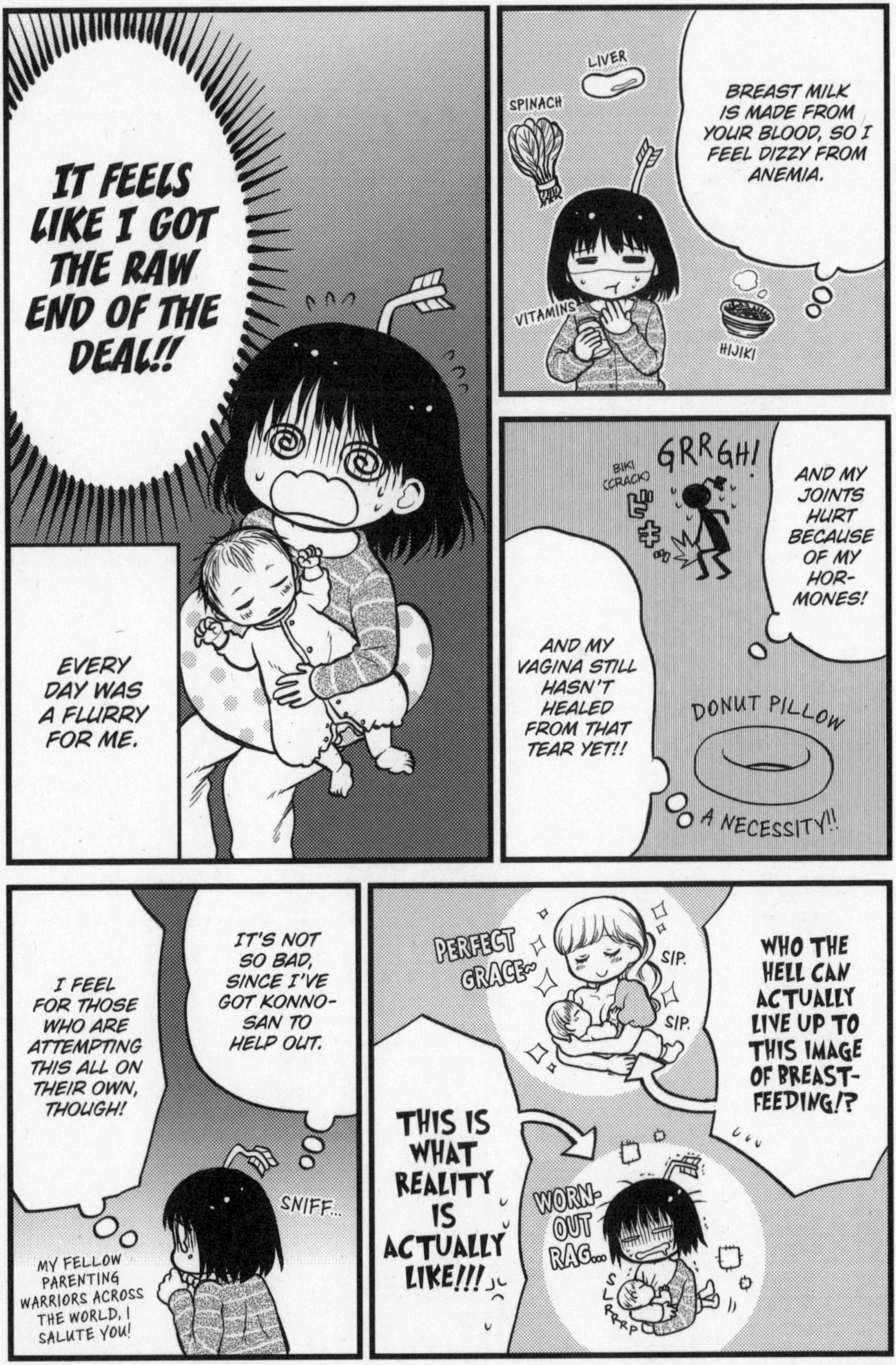
LIVER
BREAST MILK IS MADE FROM YOUR BLOOD, SO I FEEL DIZZY FROM ANEMIA.
SPINACH
VITAMINS
HIJIKI
AND MY JOINTS HURT BECAUSE OF MY HOR-MONES!
GRRGH!
BIKI (CRACK)
ビキッ
AND MY VAGINA STILL HASN'T HEALED FROM THAT TEAR YET!!
DONUT PILLOW
A NECESSITY!!
IT FEELS LIKE I GOT THE RAW END OF THE DEAL!!
EVERY DAY WAS A FLURRY FOR ME.
WHO THE HELL CAN ACTUALLY LIVE UP TO THIS IMAGE OF BREAST-FEEDING!?
SIP.
SIP.
PERFECT GRACE~
THIS IS WHAT REALITY IS ACTUALLY LIKE!!!
WORN-OUT RAG...
SLRRRRP
IT'S NOT SO BAD, SINCE I'VE GOT KONNO-SAN TO HELP OUT.
I FEEL FOR THOSE WHO ARE ATTEMPTING THIS ALL ON THEIR OWN, THOUGH!
SNIFF...
MY FELLOW PARENTING WARRIORS ACROSS THE WORLD, I SALUTE YOU!

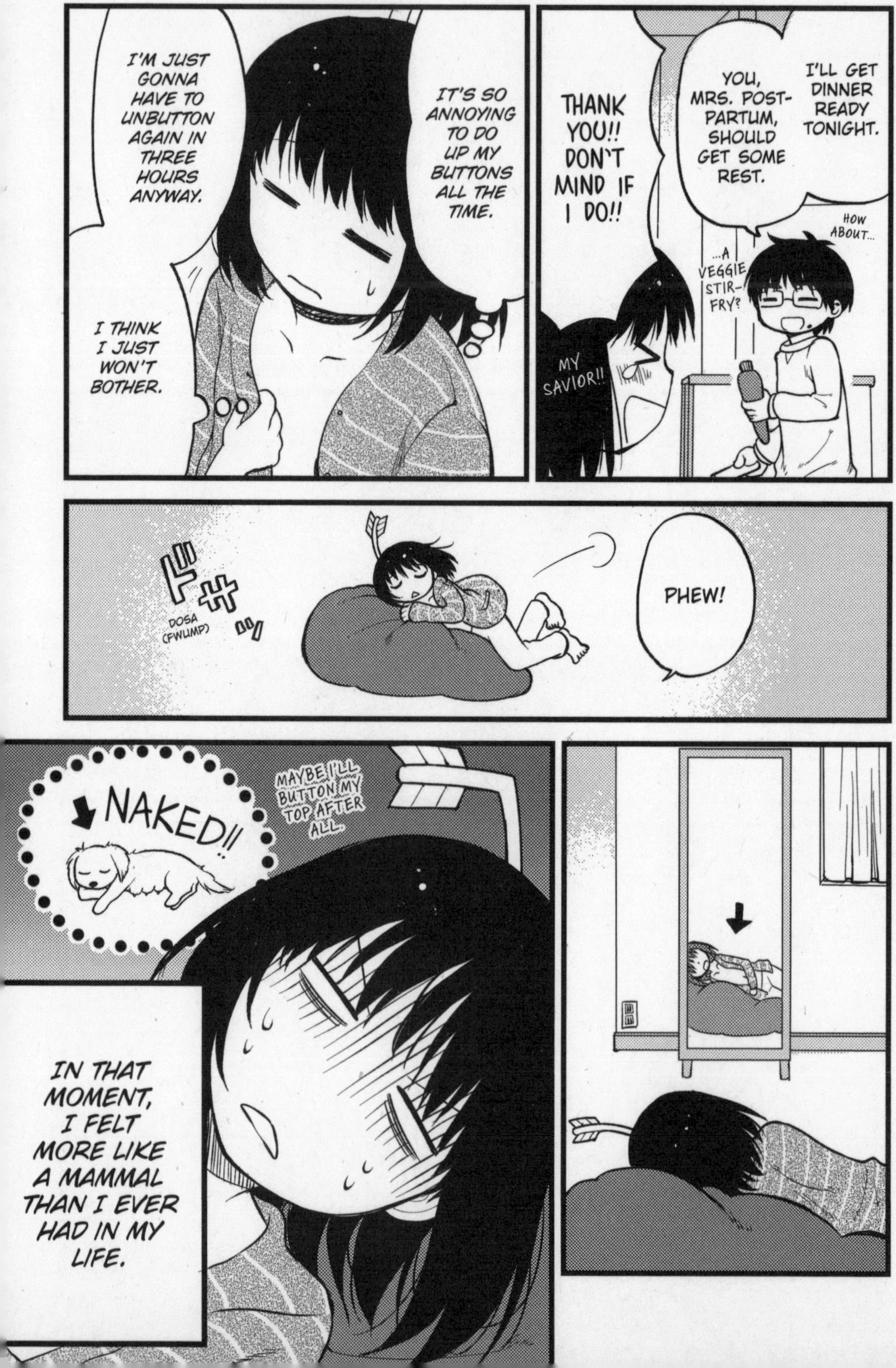
I'LL GET DINNER READY TONIGHT.
YOU, MRS. POST-PARTUM, SHOULD GET SOME REST.
HOW ABOUT...
...A VEGGIE STIR-FRY?
THANK YOU!! DON'T MIND IF I DO!!
MY SAVIOR!!
IT'S SO ANNOYING TO DO UP MY BUTTONS ALL THE TIME.
I'M JUST GONNA HAVE TO UNBUTTON AGAIN IN THREE HOURS ANYWAY.
I THINK I JUST WON'T BOTHER.
PHEW!
DOSA (FWUMP)
MAYBE I'LL BUTTON MY TOP AFTER ALL.
NAKED!!
IN THAT MOMENT, I FELT MORE LIKE A MAMMAL THAN I EVER HAD IN MY LIFE.

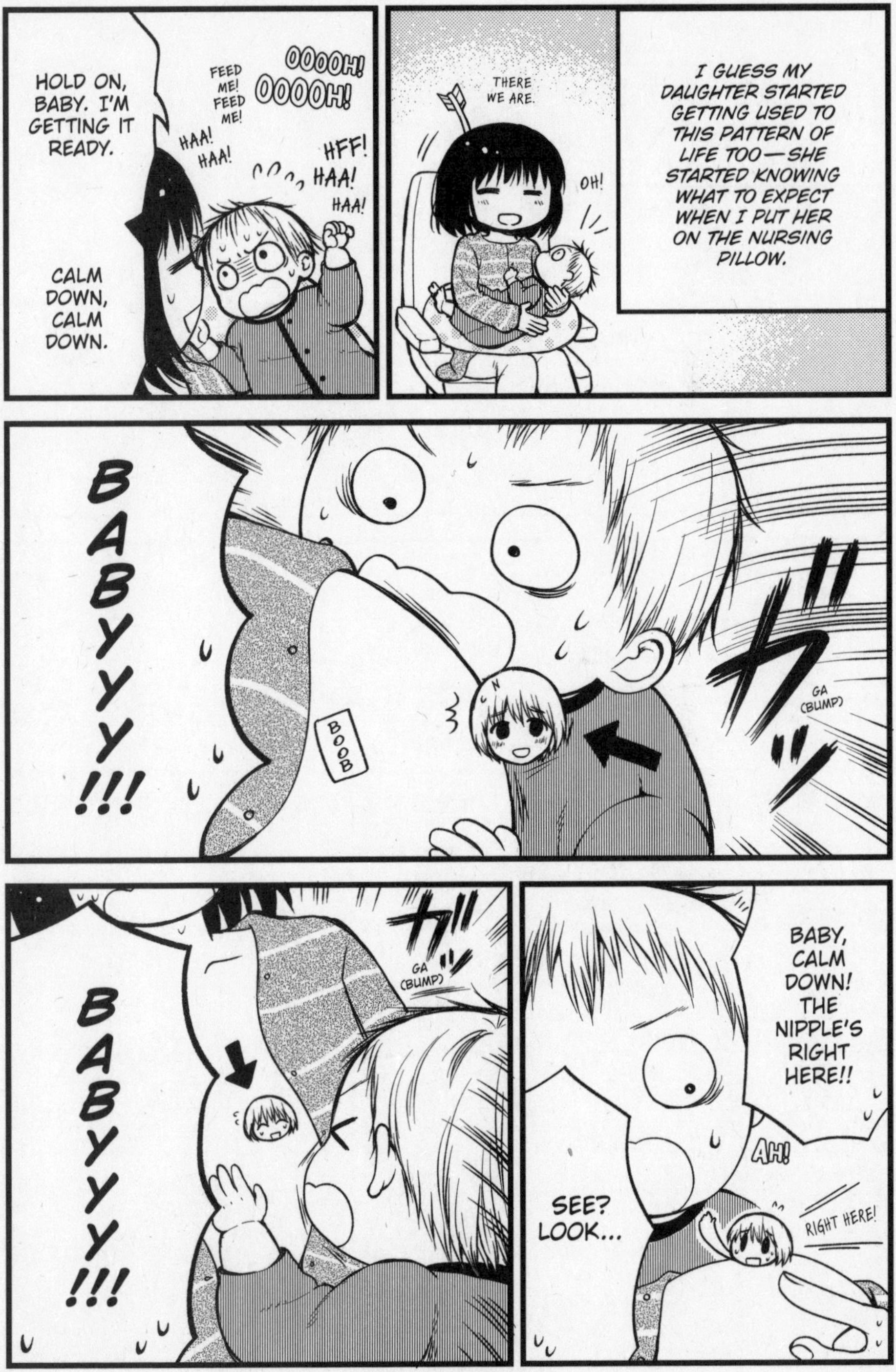
HOLD ON, BABY. I'M GETTING IT READY.
FEED ME! FEED ME!
OOOOH! OOOOH!
HAA! HAA!
HFF! HAA! HAA!
CALM DOWN, CALM DOWN.
THERE WE ARE.
OH!
I GUESS MY DAUGHTER STARTED GETTING USED TO THIS PATTERN OF LIFE TOO—SHE STARTED KNOWING WHAT TO EXPECT WHEN I PUT HER ON THE NURSING PILLOW.
BABYYY!!!
BOOB
GA (BUMP)
BABYYY!!!
GA (BUMP)
BABY, CALM DOWN! THE NIPPLE'S RIGHT HERE!!
AH!
SEE? LOOK...
RIGHT HERE!

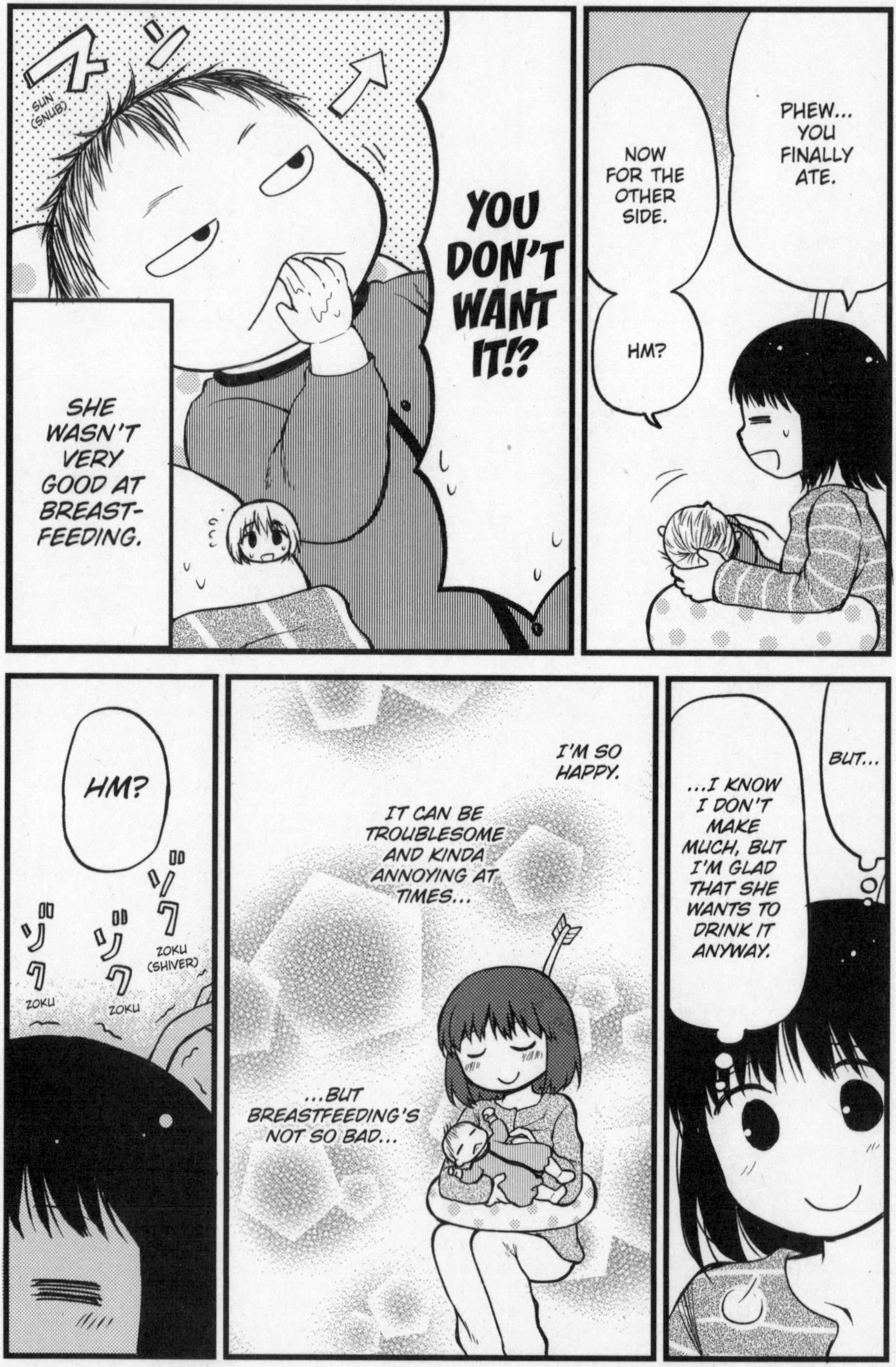
PHEW... YOU FINALLY ATE.
NOW FOR THE OTHER SIDE.
HM?
スン
SUN (SNUB)
YOU DON'T WANT IT!?
SHE WASN'T VERY GOOD AT BREAST-FEEDING.
BUT...
...I KNOW I DON'T MAKE MUCH, BUT I'M GLAD THAT SHE WANTS TO DRINK IT ANYWAY.
I'M SO HAPPY.
IT CAN BE TROUBLESOME AND KINDA ANNOYING AT TIMES...
...BUT BREASTFEEDING'S NOT SO BAD...
HM?
ゾク
ZOKU (SHIVER)
ゾク
ZOKU
ゾク
ZOKU

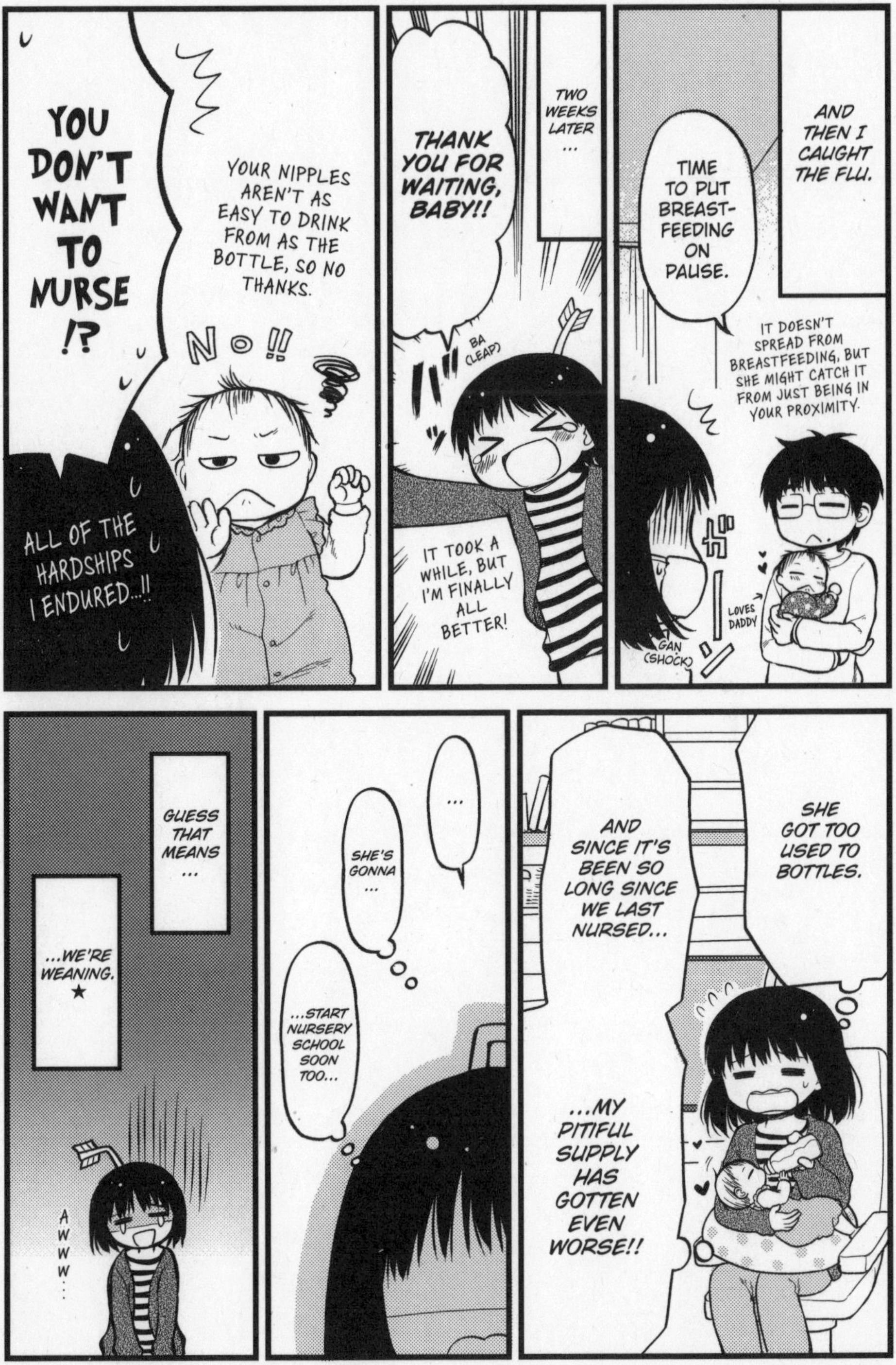
AND THEN I CAUGHT THE FLU.
TIME TO PUT BREAST-FEEDING ON PAUSE.
IT DOESN'T SPREAD FROM BREASTFEEDING, BUT SHE MIGHT CATCH IT FROM JUST BEING IN YOUR PROXIMITY.
LOVES DADDY
GAN (SHOCK)
TWO WEEKS LATER ...
THANK YOU FOR WAITING, BABY!!
BA (LEAP)
IT TOOK A WHILE, BUT I'M FINALLY ALL BETTER!
YOUR NIPPLES AREN'T AS EASY TO DRINK FROM AS THE BOTTLE, SO NO THANKS.
YOU DON'T WANT TO NURSE !?
No!!
ALL OF THE HARDSHIPS I ENDURED...!!
SHE GOT TOO USED TO BOTTLES.
AND SINCE IT'S BEEN SO LONG SINCE WE LAST NURSED...
...MY PITIFUL SUPPLY HAS GOTTEN EVEN WORSE!!
...
SHE'S GONNA ...
...START NURSERY SCHOOL SOON TOO...
GUESS THAT MEANS ...
...WE'RE WEANING. ★
AWWW...

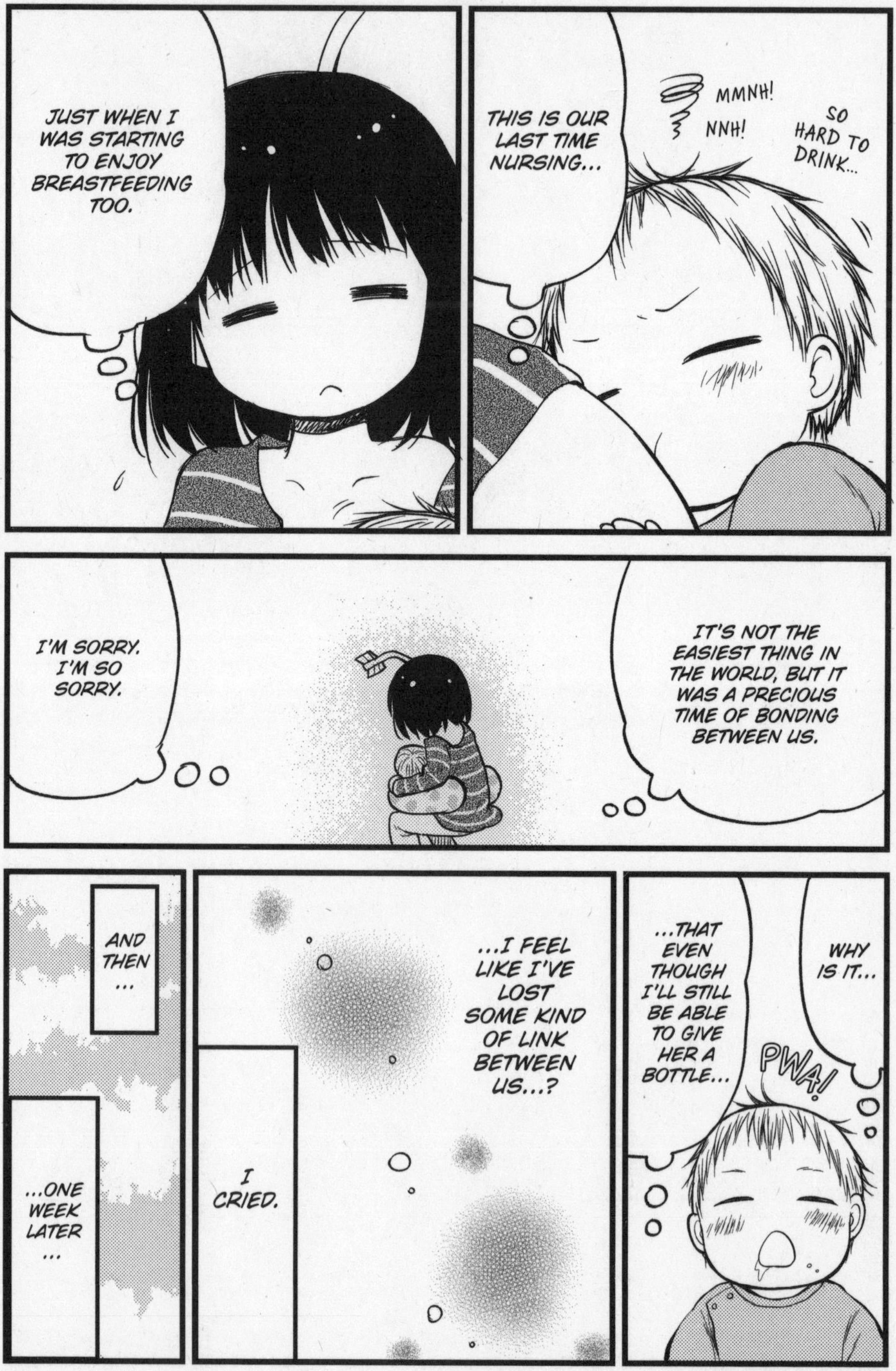
THIS IS OUR LAST TIME NURSING...
MMNH!
NNH!
SO HARD TO DRINK...
JUST WHEN I WAS STARTING TO ENJOY BREASTFEEDING TOO.
IT'S NOT THE EASIEST THING IN THE WORLD, BUT IT WAS A PRECIOUS TIME OF BONDING BETWEEN US.
I'M SORRY. I'M SO SORRY.
WHY IS IT...
...THAT EVEN THOUGH I'LL STILL BE ABLE TO GIVE HER A BOTTLE...
PWA!
...I FEEL LIKE I'VE LOST SOME KIND OF LINK BETWEEN US...?
I CRIED.
AND THEN...
...ONE WEEK LATER...

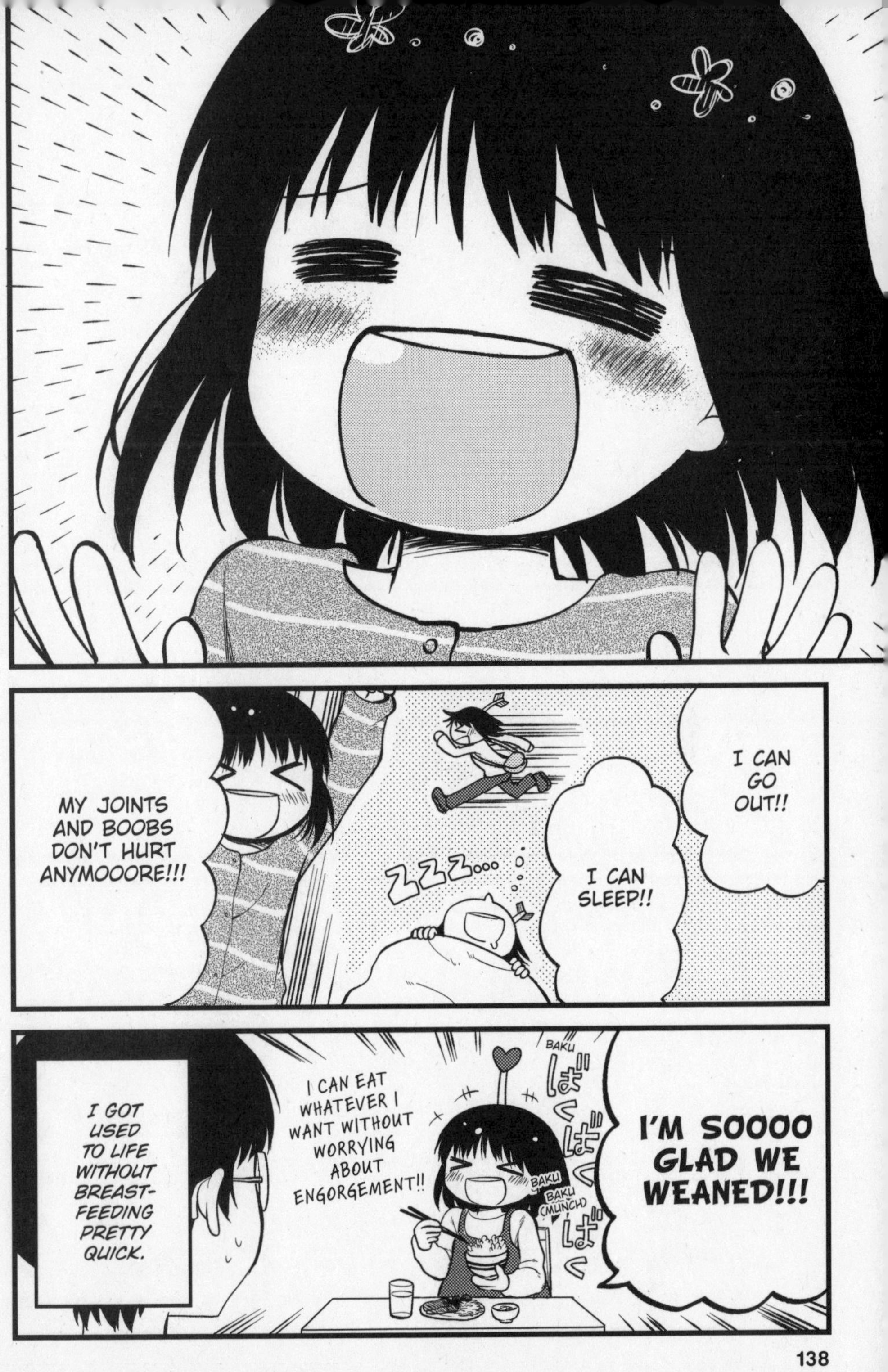
I CAN GO OUT!!
I CAN SLEEP!!
ZZZ...
MY JOINTS AND BOOBS DON'T HURT ANYMOOORE!!!
I'M SOOOO GLAD WE WEANED!!!
BAKU ばくばく
BAKU BAKU (MUNCH) ばくばく
I CAN EAT WHATEVER I WANT WITHOUT WORRYING ABOUT ENGORGEMENT!!
I GOT USED TO LIFE WITHOUT BREAST-FEEDING PRETTY QUICK.

Postpartum Anecdote: Breastfeeding

Bonus manga by Azure Konno

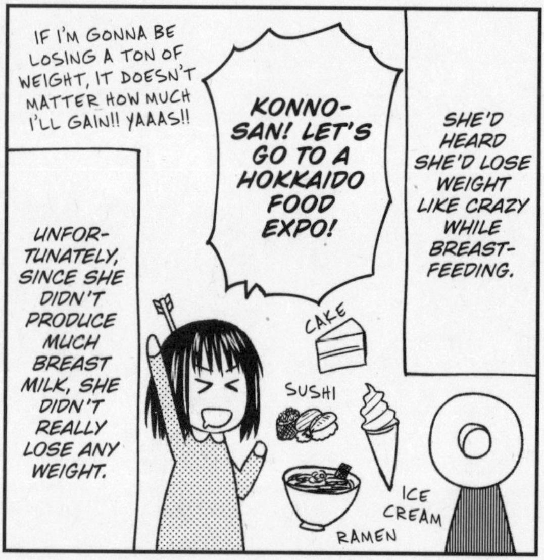
SHE'D HEARD SHE'D LOSE WEIGHT LIKE CRAZY WHILE BREAST-FEEDING.
KONNO-SAN! LET'S GO TO A HOKKAIDO FOOD EXPO!
IF I'M GONNA BE LOSING A TON OF WEIGHT, IT DOESN'T MATTER HOW MUCH I'LL GAIN!! YAAAS!!
UNFOR-TUNATELY, SINCE SHE DIDN'T PRODUCE MUCH BREAST MILK, SHE DIDN'T REALLY LOSE ANY WEIGHT.
CAKE
SUSHI
ICE CREAM
RAMEN

They say that when breastfeeding, a woman's calcium leaves through her breast milk, and her joints start to hurt.
Women really have to undergo some incredible hardships in order to raise children.
It would be better if all fathers in the world could take paternity leave. Our wives desperately need us. I was really grateful to be a manga artist, as I was able to be at home to support my wife.
Ladies who aren't married yet, I highly recommend getting a husband who draws comics for a living. Though you'll have to ignore the fact that most of us are big pervs.

Bonus manga by Ayami Kazama

Postpartum Anecdote: Breastfeeding

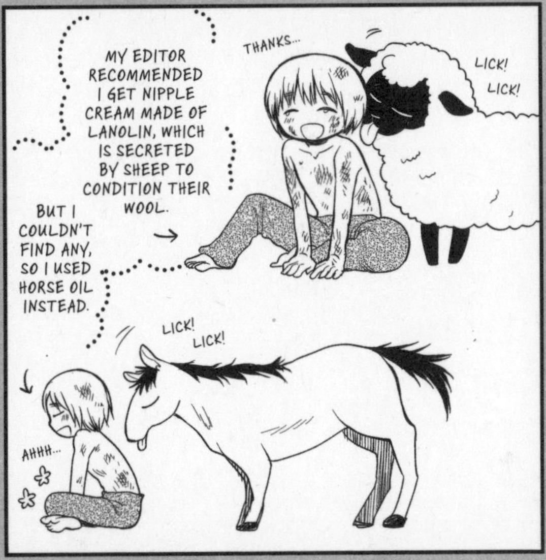
MY EDITOR RECOMMENDED I GET NIPPLE CREAM MADE OF LANOLIN, WHICH IS SECRETED BY SHEEP TO CONDITION THEIR WOOL.
THANKS...
LICK!
LICK!
BUT I COULDN'T FIND ANY, SO I USED HORSE OIL INSTEAD.
LICK!
LICK!
AHHH...

When searching for a cream I could use on my nipples that would be safe for my baby, I was told to look for lanolin. When I couldn't find any, I had to rely on horse oil instead.
It was a lot more effective than I thought it would be. Thank you, horses..And sheep too...
But even though it's the 21st century and we've been to the moon and back, the fact that we still have to go down the path of a perv in order to help our nipples recover seems to show we haven't evolved all that much, huh?
Surely there could be a better way by now...
I mean, we've been giving birth since the beginning of time...!
Is it just that simple is best?
I guess it is true that out of all ways of perversion, using cream on nipples isn't the worst visually...

Postpartum Anecdote: The Worry

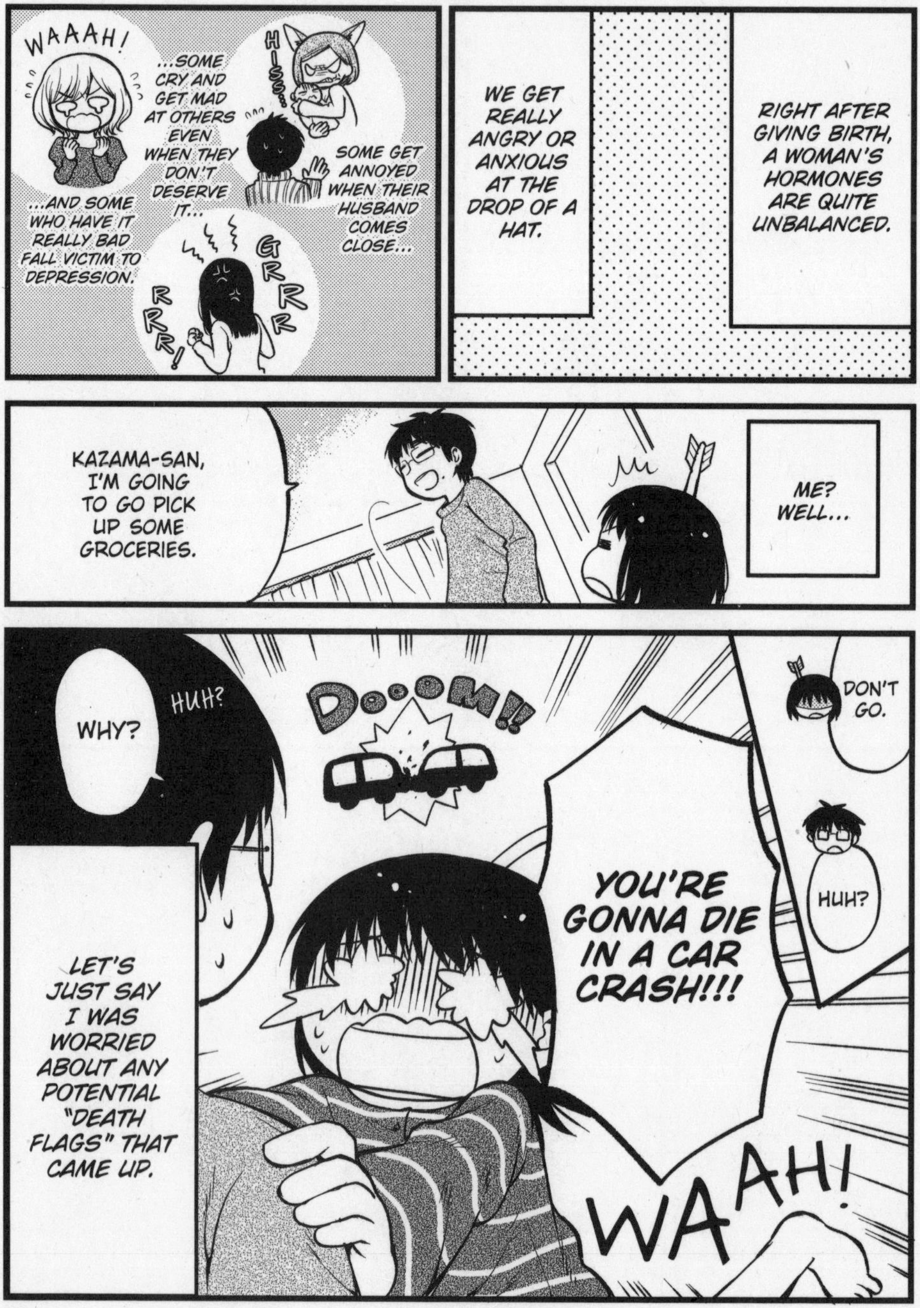
RIGHT AFTER GIVING BIRTH, A WOMAN'S HORMONES ARE QUITE UNBALANCED.
WE GET REALLY ANGRY OR ANXIOUS AT THE DROP OF A HAT.
SOME GET ANNOYED WHEN THEIR HUSBAND COMES CLOSE...
HISS...
...SOME CRY AND GET MAD AT OTHERS EVEN WHEN THEY DON'T DESERVE IT...
WAAAH!
...AND SOME WHO HAVE IT REALLY BAD FALL VICTIM TO DEPRESSION.
GRRRRRR!
ME? WELL...
KAZAMA-SAN, I'M GOING TO GO PICK UP SOME GROCERIES.
DON'T GO.
HUH?
DOOOM!!
YOU'RE GONNA DIE IN A CAR CRASH!!!
WAAH!
HUH?
WHY?
LET'S JUST SAY I WAS WORRIED ABOUT ANY POTENTIAL "DEATH FLAGS" THAT CAME UP.

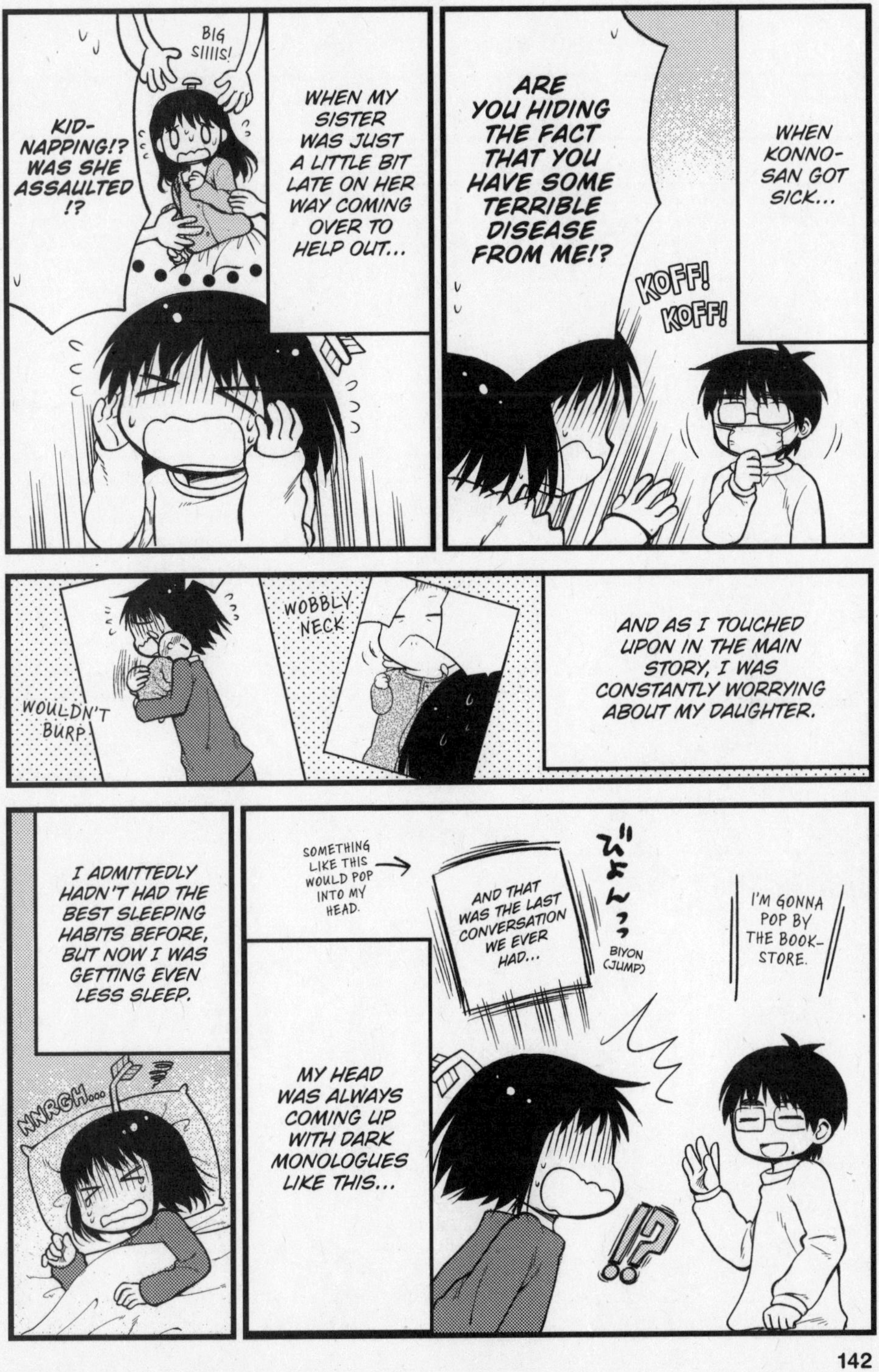

WHEN KONNO-SAN GOT SICK...
KOFF! KOFF!
ARE YOU HIDING THE FACT THAT YOU HAVE SOME TERRIBLE DISEASE FROM ME!?
WHEN MY SISTER WAS JUST A LITTLE BIT LATE ON HER WAY COMING OVER TO HELP OUT...
BIG SIIIIS!
KID-NAPPING!? WAS SHE ASSAULTED !?
AND AS I TOUCHED UPON IN THE MAIN STORY, I WAS CONSTANTLY WORRYING ABOUT MY DAUGHTER.
WOBBLY NECK
WOULDN'T BURP
I'M GONNA POP BY THE BOOK-STORE.
びよんっ
BIYON (JUMP)
AND THAT WAS THE LAST CONVERSATION WE EVER HAD...
SOMETHING LIKE THIS WOULD POP INTO MY HEAD.
!?
MY HEAD WAS ALWAYS COMING UP WITH DARK MONOLOGUES LIKE THIS...
I ADMITTEDLY HADN'T HAD THE BEST SLEEPING HABITS BEFORE, BUT NOW I WAS GETTING EVEN LESS SLEEP.
NNRGH...

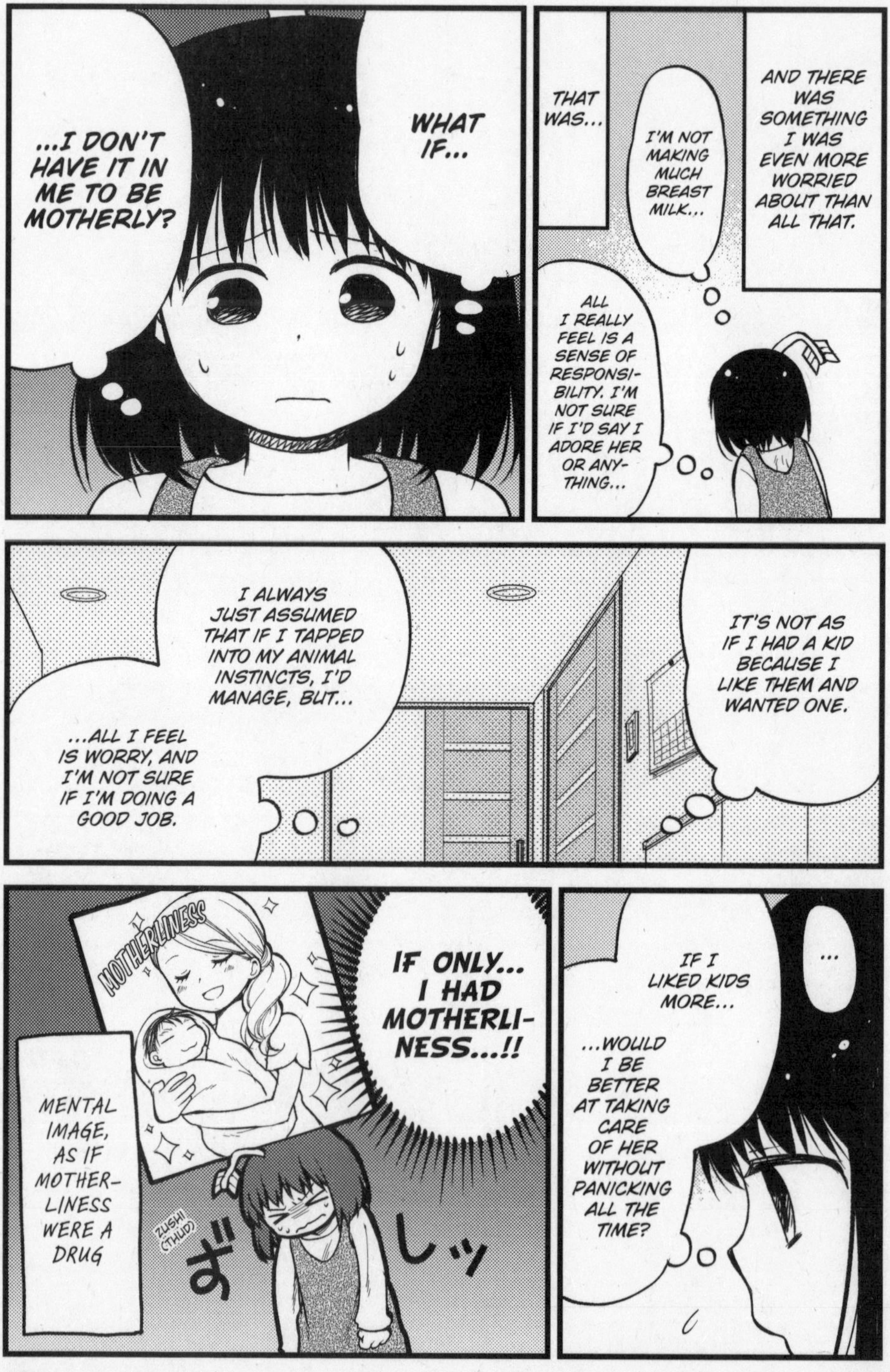
AND THERE WAS SOMETHING I WAS EVEN MORE WORRIED ABOUT THAN ALL THAT.
THAT WAS...
I'M NOT MAKING MUCH BREAST MILK...
ALL I REALLY FEEL IS A SENSE OF RESPONSIBILITY. I'M NOT SURE IF I'D SAY I ADORE HER OR ANYTHING...
WHAT IF...
...I DON'T HAVE IT IN ME TO BE MOTHERLY?
IT'S NOT AS IF I HAD A KID BECAUSE I LIKE THEM AND WANTED ONE.
I ALWAYS JUST ASSUMED THAT IF I TAPPED INTO MY ANIMAL INSTINCTS, I'D MANAGE, BUT...
...ALL I FEEL IS WORRY, AND I'M NOT SURE IF I'M DOING A GOOD JOB.
...
IF I LIKED KIDS MORE...
...WOULD I BE BETTER AT TAKING CARE OF HER WITHOUT PANICKING ALL THE TIME?
IF ONLY... I HAD MOTHERLINESS...!!
MOTHERLINESS
MENTAL IMAGE, AS IF MOTHERLINESS WERE A DRUG
ずしッ
ZUSHI (THUD)

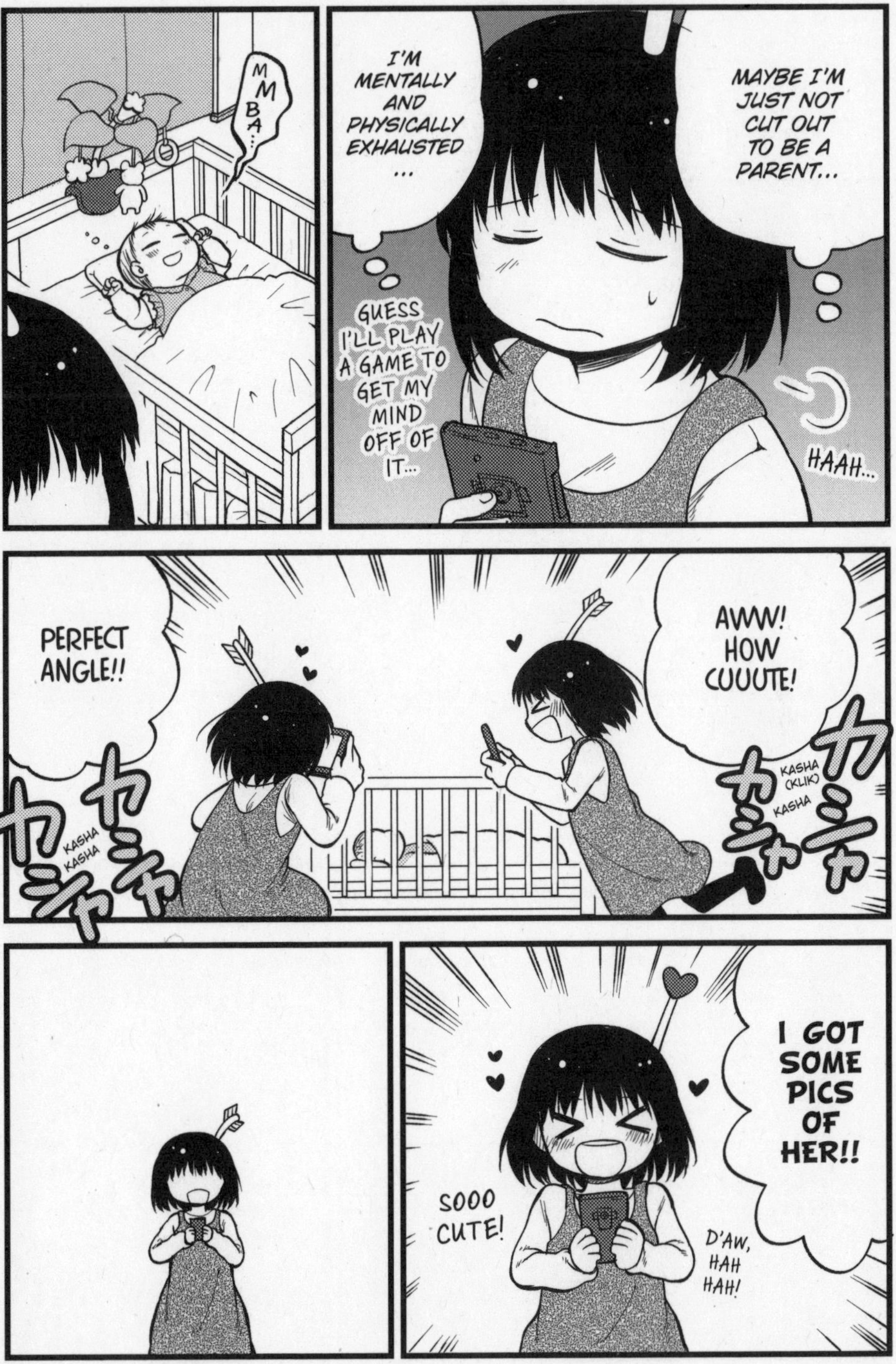
MAYBE I'M JUST NOT CUT OUT TO BE A PARENT...
I'M MENTALLY AND PHYSICALLY EXHAUSTED...
HAAH...
GUESS I'LL PLAY A GAME TO GET MY MIND OFF OF IT...
MMBA...
AWW! HOW CUUUTE!
カシャカシャ
KASHA (KLIK) KASHA
PERFECT ANGLE!!
カシャカシャ
KASHA KASHA
I GOT SOME PICS OF HER!!
D'AW, HAH HAH!
SOOO CUTE!

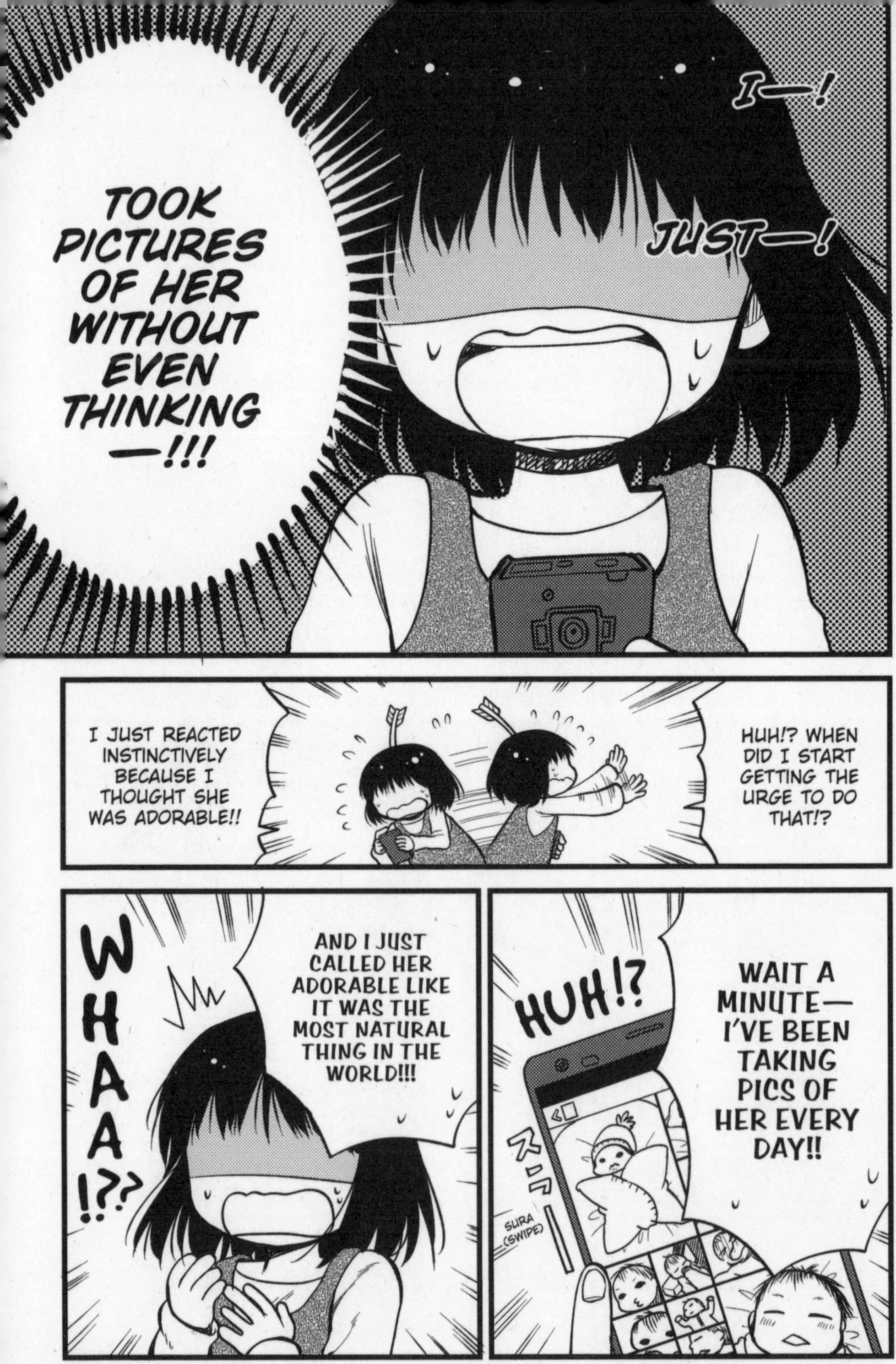
I—!
JUST—!
TOOK PICTURES OF HER WITHOUT EVEN THINKING—!!!
HUH!? WHEN DID I START GETTING THE URGE TO DO THAT!?
I JUST REACTED INSTINCTIVELY BECAUSE I THOUGHT SHE WAS ADORABLE!!
HUH!?
WAIT A MINUTE— I'VE BEEN TAKING PICS OF HER EVERY DAY!!
SURA (SWIPE)
AND I JUST CALLED HER ADORABLE LIKE IT WAS THE MOST NATURAL THING IN THE WORLD!!!
WHAA!??

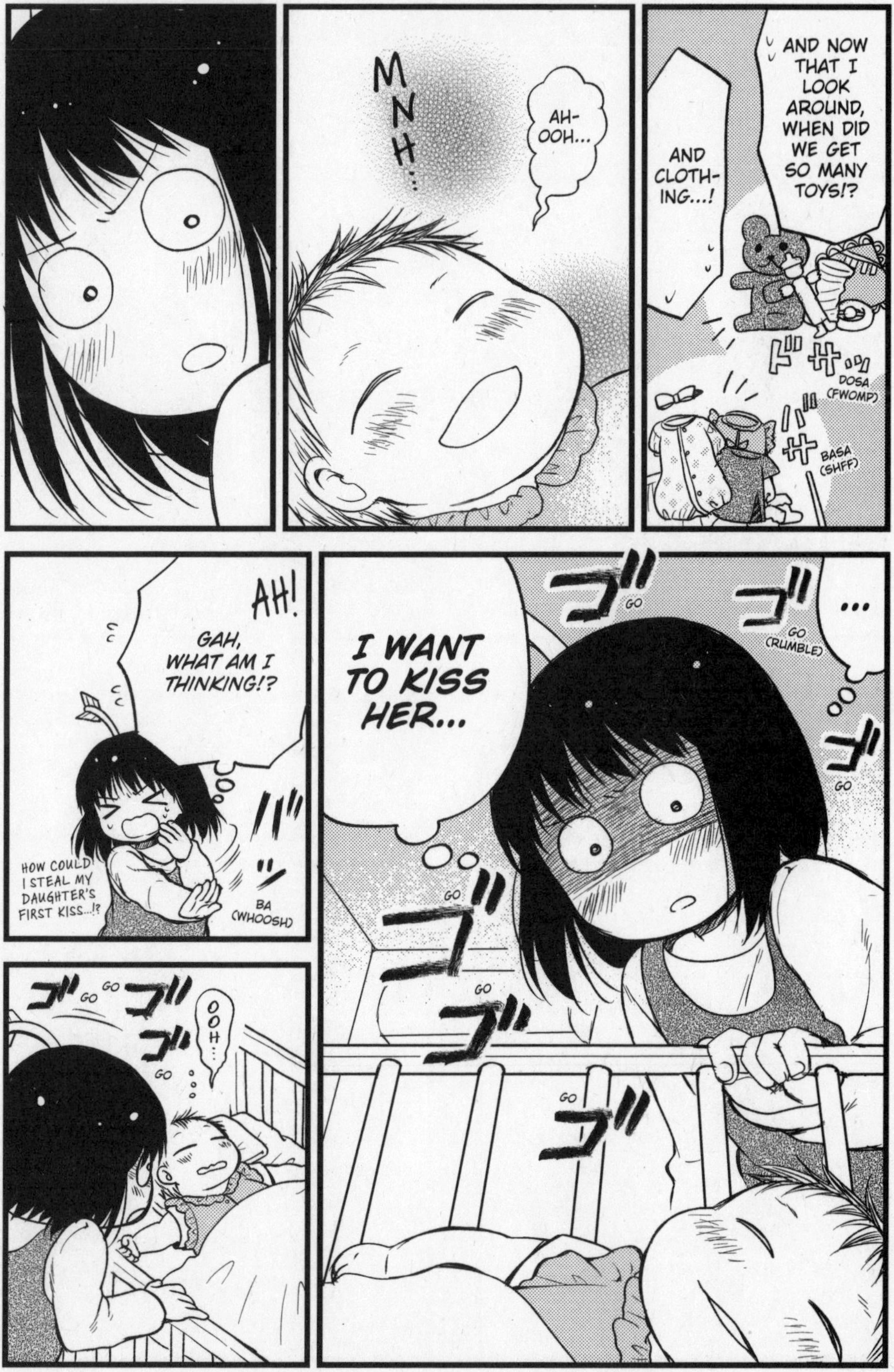
AND NOW THAT I LOOK AROUND, WHEN DID WE GET SO MANY TOYS!?
AND CLOTHING...!
DOSA (FWOMP)
BASA (SHFF)
MNH...
AH-OOH...
GO (RUMBLE)
...
I WANT TO KISS HER...
GO
AH!
GAH, WHAT AM I THINKING!?
HOW COULD I STEAL MY DAUGHTER'S FIRST KISS...!?
BA (WHOOSH)
GO GO
OOH...

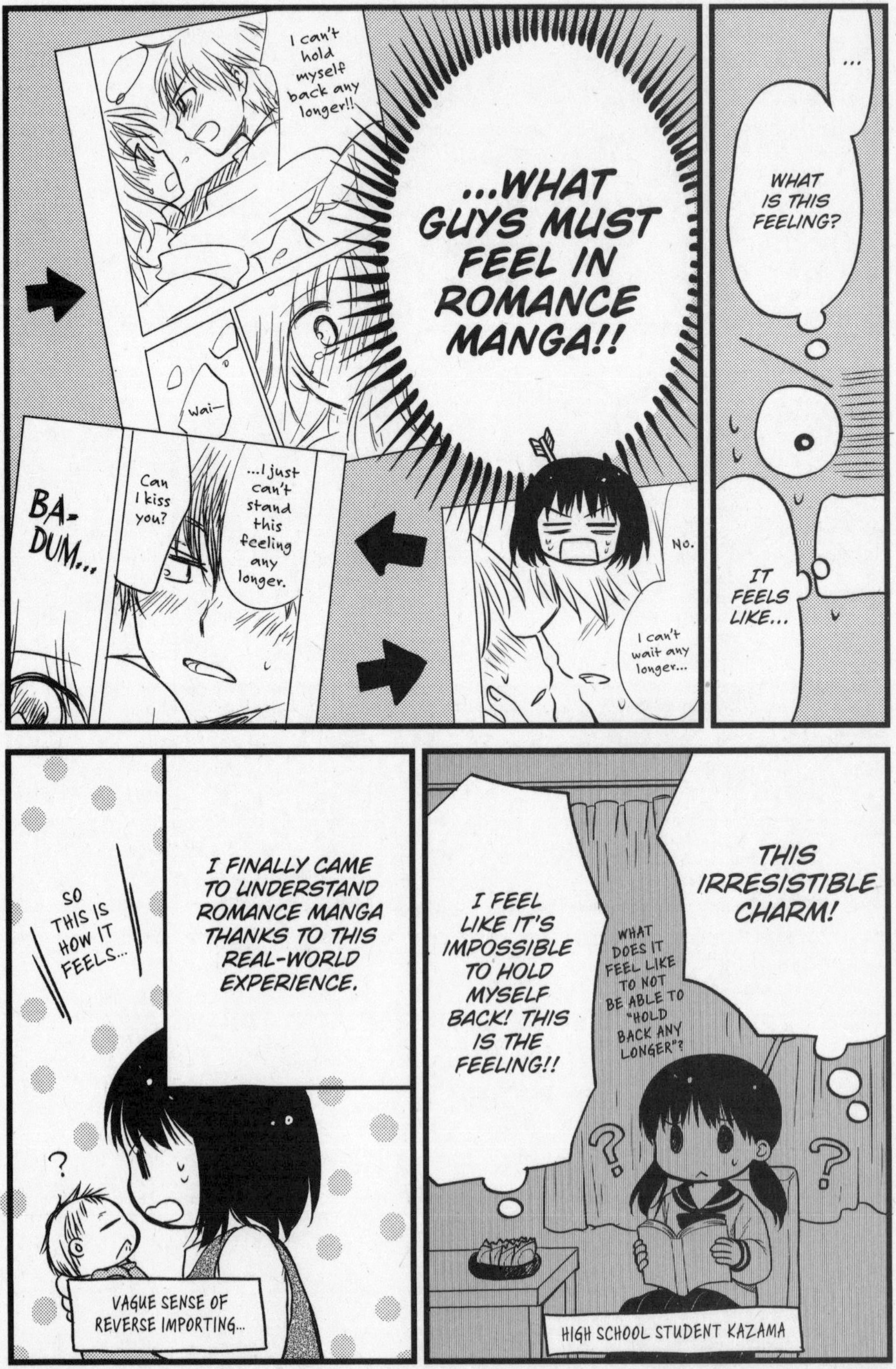
...
WHAT IS THIS FEELING?
IT FEELS LIKE...
...WHAT GUYS MUST FEEL IN ROMANCE MANGA!!
I can't hold myself back any longer!!
wai-
...I just can't stand this feeling any longer.
Can I kiss you?
BA-DUM...
No.
I can't wait any longer...
THIS IRRESISTIBLE CHARM!
I FEEL LIKE IT'S IMPOSSIBLE TO HOLD MYSELF BACK! THIS IS THE FEELING!!
WHAT DOES IT FEEL LIKE TO NOT BE ABLE TO "HOLD BACK ANY LONGER"?
HIGH SCHOOL STUDENT KAZAMA
I FINALLY CAME TO UNDERSTAND ROMANCE MANGA THANKS TO THIS REAL-WORLD EXPERIENCE.
SO THIS IS HOW IT FEELS...
?
VAGUE SENSE OF REVERSE IMPORTING...

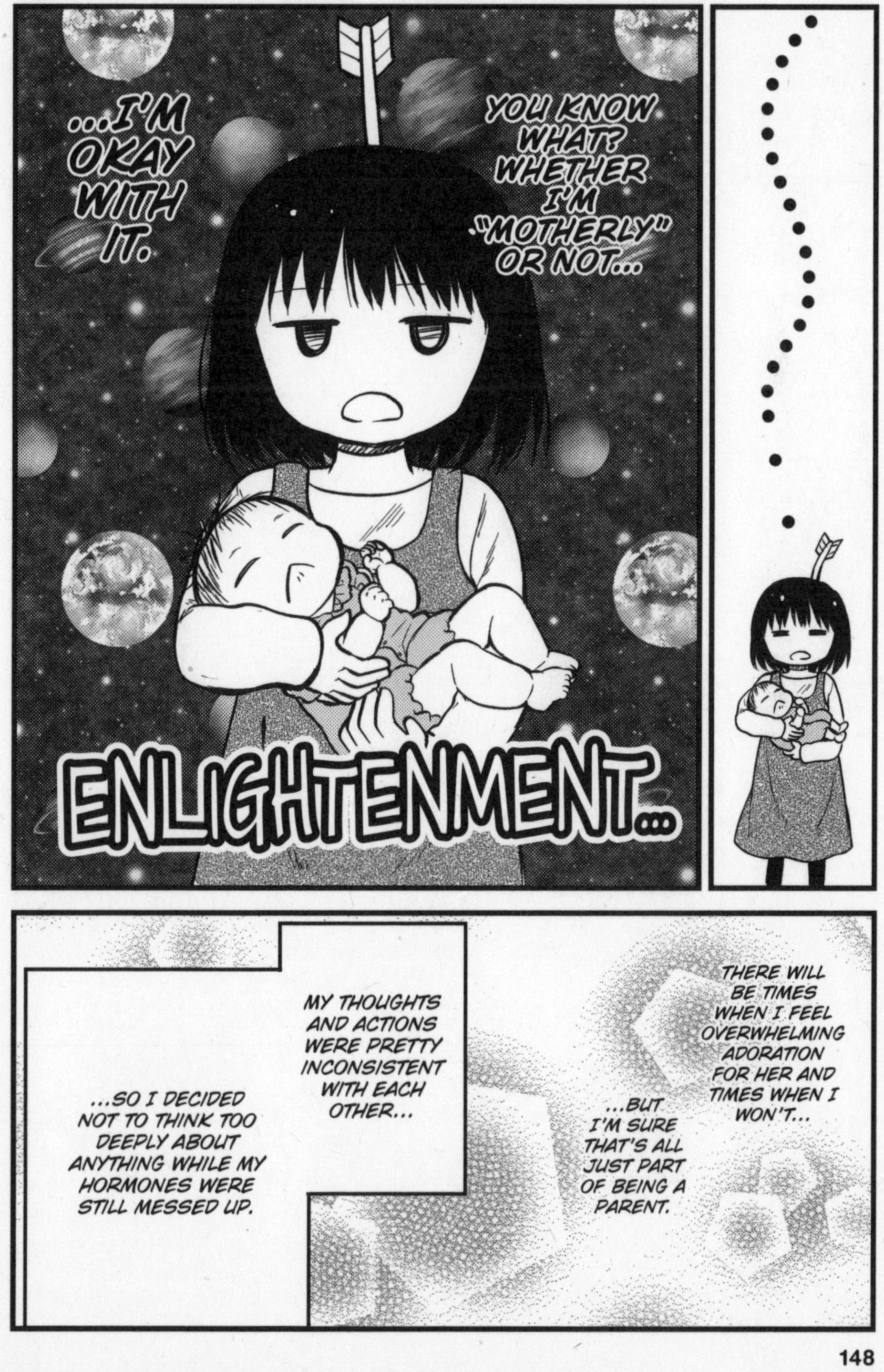
YOU KNOW WHAT? WHETHER I'M "MOTHERLY" OR NOT...
...I'M OKAY WITH IT.
ENLIGHTENMENT...
THERE WILL BE TIMES WHEN I FEEL OVERWHELMING ADORATION FOR HER AND TIMES WHEN I WON'T...
...BUT I'M SURE THAT'S ALL JUST PART OF BEING A PARENT.
MY THOUGHTS AND ACTIONS WERE PRETTY INCONSISTENT WITH EACH OTHER...
...SO I DECIDED NOT TO THINK TOO DEEPLY ABOUT ANYTHING WHILE MY HORMONES WERE STILL MESSED UP.

Postpartum Anecdote: The Worry

Bonus manga by Azure Konno

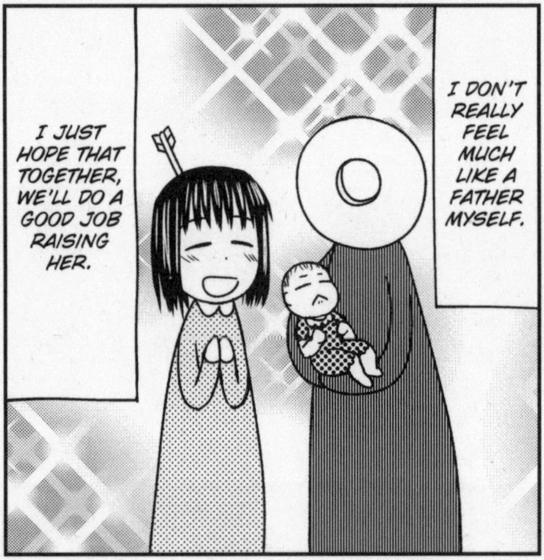
I DON'T REALLY FEEL MUCH LIKE A FATHER MYSELF.
I JUST HOPE THAT TOGETHER, WE'LL DO A GOOD JOB RAISING HER.

When Kazama-san and I started dating, I realized just how much changes in hormones can affect women.
Men really don't experience that sort of thing, so we can be pretty insensitive to it.
I guess Kazama-san was able to understand the hormonal changes, since she'd experienced it herself.
Kids are so cute that there are times when you're overwhelmed by the desire to hug them tight. Who would have thought that a guy like me, who never gets overly emotional, would feel that kind of impulse?
All I know is, I should probably stop saying embarrassing things like, "I'ma squeezey-weezey you now!" or, "C'mere, I'ma scoop you right up now!" whenever I go to pick her up.
(And it's not just me—Kazama-san says this to her too.)
In any case, I think there are gonna be lots of fun times ahead for our family!

Bonus manga by Ayami Kazama

Postpartum Anecdote: The Worry

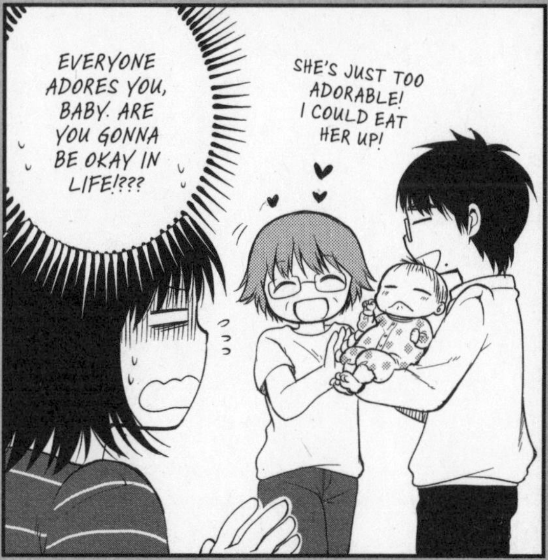
SHE'S JUST TOO ADORABLE! I COULD EAT HER UP!
EVERYONE ADORES YOU, BABY. ARE YOU GONNA BE OKAY IN LIFE!???

My daughter's popularity was one of my concerns.
Every day she's adored and showered with love by her parents.
Her parents' friends also tell her how cute she is.
And of course, her grandparents are crazy about her.
They say you're only popular three times in your life, and now she's already used up one of those times!!!
But when I wrote about this on Twitter, one of my followers assured me, "Children are like treasures to everyone, so of course people are gonna go gaga over them. I'm sure this doesn't count!"
Isn't that great? I accepted this notion without question.
I hope my daughter is popular and adored for the rest of her life.

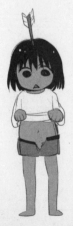

*I Don't Know
How to Give Birth!*
Presented by
Ayami Kazama

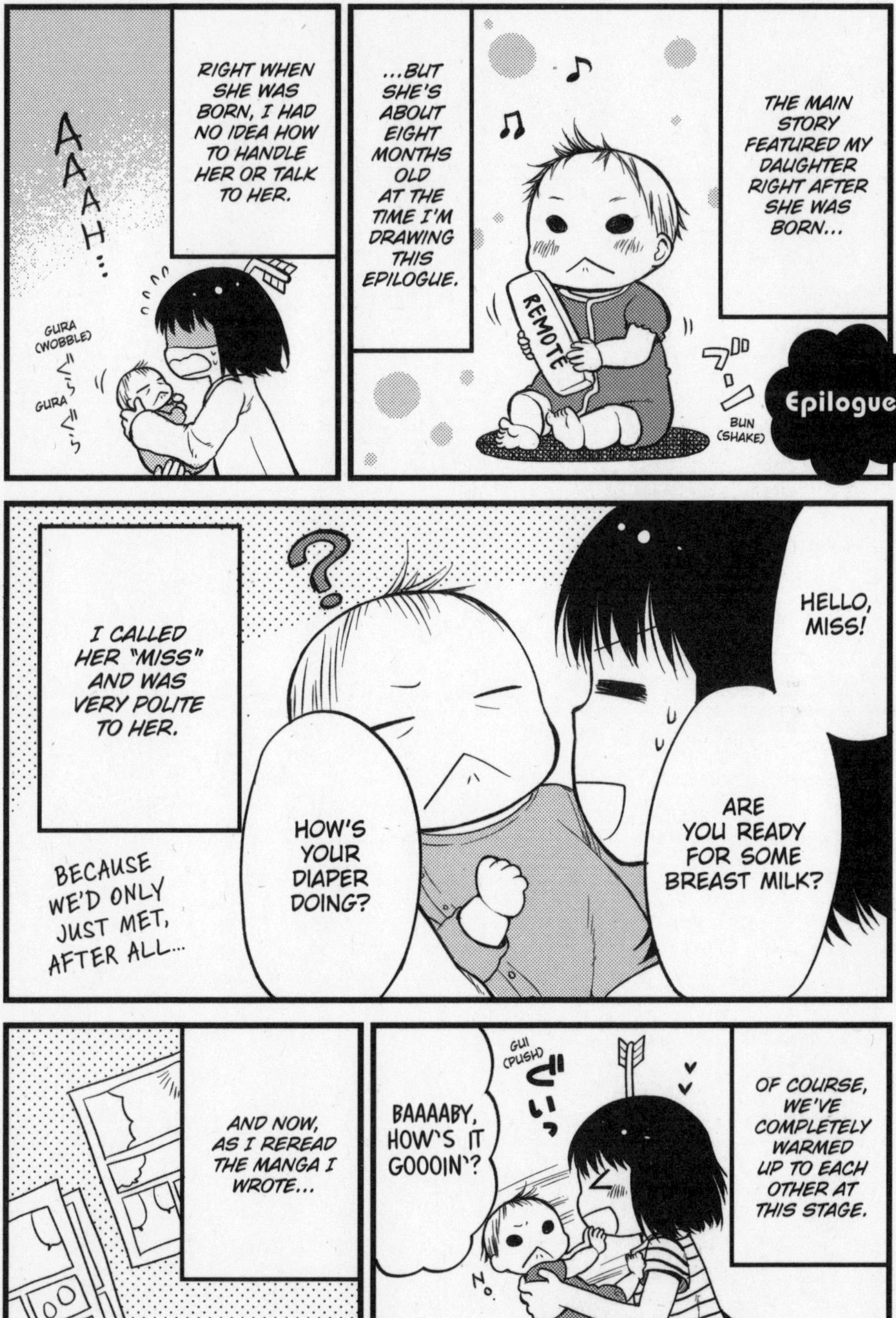
Epilogue
THE MAIN STORY FEATURED MY DAUGHTER RIGHT AFTER SHE WAS BORN...
BUN (SHAKE)
REMOTE
...BUT SHE'S ABOUT EIGHT MONTHS OLD AT THE TIME I'M DRAWING THIS EPILOGUE.
RIGHT WHEN SHE WAS BORN, I HAD NO IDEA HOW TO HANDLE HER OR TALK TO HER.
AAAH...
GURA (WOBBLE)
GURA
HELLO, MISS!
ARE YOU READY FOR SOME BREAST MILK?
HOW'S YOUR DIAPER DOING?
I CALLED HER "MISS" AND WAS VERY POLITE TO HER.
BECAUSE WE'D ONLY JUST MET, AFTER ALL...
OF COURSE, WE'VE COMPLETELY WARMED UP TO EACH OTHER AT THIS STAGE.
GUI (PUSH)
BAAAABY, HOW'S IT GOOOIN'?
AND NOW, AS I REREAD THE MANGA I WROTE...

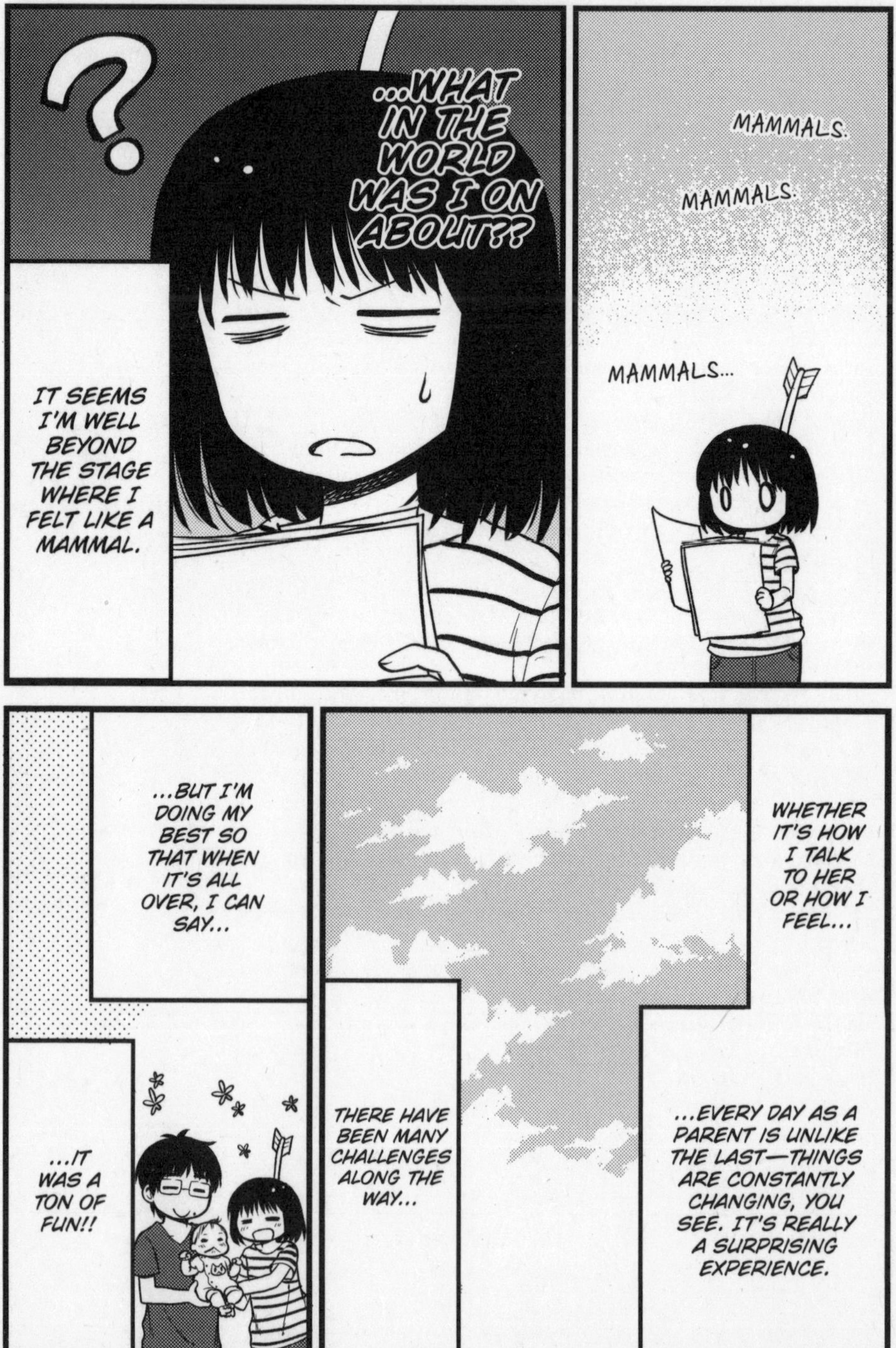
MAMMALS.
MAMMALS.
MAMMALS...
...WHAT IN THE WORLD WAS I ON ABOUT??
IT SEEMS I'M WELL BEYOND THE STAGE WHERE I FELT LIKE A MAMMAL.
WHETHER IT'S HOW I TALK TO HER OR HOW I FEEL...
...EVERY DAY AS A PARENT IS UNLIKE THE LAST—THINGS ARE CONSTANTLY CHANGING, YOU SEE. IT'S REALLY A SURPRISING EXPERIENCE.
THERE HAVE BEEN MANY CHALLENGES ALONG THE WAY...
...BUT I'M DOING MY BEST SO THAT WHEN IT'S ALL OVER, I CAN SAY...
...IT WAS A TON OF FUN!!

AFTERWORD

Thank you so much for reading to the end.

I recorded my real-life experiences in this autobiographical comic essay of my journey to having a baby—from getting fertility treatments, to being pregnant, to giving birth. What did you think of it?

I had a lot of fun writing and drawing this manga.

The reason why it was fun was because working on the pages allowed me to reflect on the worries and problems I had during pregnancy and early parenting. It helped me realize I didn't need to overthink things or that I could approach them in other ways.

They say it's best to write your worries to paper, but in my case, I guess that drawing what I'm going through as a manga helps me to look at my problems objectively and think them over calmly.

And now that I've given birth to my daughter and am in the midst of raising her, I looked over what I had drawn before for the first time in a while when I was putting this book together. I found myself awfully surprised at my line of reasoning back when I was receiving the treatments and was pregnant. Forgetting is my special skill, you see.

I like to draw my problems and worries in manga form, and then I immediately forget them!

I'm doing well so we can progress toward the future in the world.

We haven't had any major problems, and my daughter's growing fast.

She's going to nursery school now, and I've started to see glimpses of what kind of unique individual she might be growing to become.

As I wrote in this manga, I didn't particularly like children or anything before choosing to become a mother. While there are days when parenting can be hard, I really enjoy taking care of my daughter, who grows and changes with every passing day.

I still doubt myself and worry a lot, but I think with Konno-san here to help out, we'll be able to get through any challenge. Also, babies have the most amazing skin, don't you think? Their chubby little cheeks, thighs, and belly...They're just so squeezable!

Lastly, I'd like to thank:
- Editor in Chief Matsuda, who gave me her valuable feedback despite being so busy when I was going crazy with work and giving birth
- Shirashima-san, who so kindly adjusted the schedule to accommodate me
- Tsuchihashi-san from Hive (whose designs are amazing! Drool!!)
- Azure Konno-san (Thank you for always cooking and for helping out with my manga!)
- My daughter (She's adorable!)
- My friends and acquaintances who gave me their feedback
- And you, who read this book!

I hope reading this manga gave you the strength you may need, invoked some kind of emotion in you, or even was just entertaining.

Ayami Kazama

TRANSLATION NOTES

Common Honorifics

no honorific: Indicates familiarity or closeness; if used without permission or reason, addressing someone in this manner would constitute an insult.

-*san*: The Japanese equivalent of Mr./Mrs./Miss. If a situation calls for politeness, this is the fail-safe honorific.

-*chan*: An affectionate honorific indicating familiarity used mostly in reference to girls; also used in reference to cute persons or animals of either gender.

Currency Conversion

While conversion rates fluctuate, an easy estimate for Japanese yen conversion is ¥100 to 1 USD.

Page 41

Okonomiyaki is a savory pancake. It can be made with a variety of different toppings but commonly includes shredded cabbage, grated yam, eggs, green onion, and pork belly.

Page 92

Dilation of the cervix is often measured in centimeters, even in the US, but for an idea of how wide 10 cm is (approximately 4 inches), it's about the width of the average fist.

Page 94

Gacha machines are vending machines that dispense a variety of toys, often part of a collectible set, each contained within a plastic capsule. The phone game Ayami is playing employs the same random mechanic as the capsule machines as players try to collect their desired rewards. Luck is often the only factor in getting the item you really want!

Page 102

A *taiko* drum is a traditional Japanese percussion instrument, of which there are a wide variety of types. The kind brought to mind here are the large, barrel-sized drums hit with wide drumsticks, often seen in festival performances.

Page 104

The band Ayami is watching and cheering for while in the hospital is μ's (pronounced Muse), an idol group popularized by the *Love Live! School Idol Project* anime.

Page 115

Konno mentions *Super Doctor K*, a 1988 manga by Kazuo Mafune that tells the tale of Doctor Kazuka, a surgeon who travels the world to help anyone who may need him.

Karamucho is a brand of spicy potato snacks. They are available as either chips or sticks.

Page 117

Yakiniku is grilled meat or offal. At *yakiniku* restaurants, diners can cook their own portions over small wood-charcoal fires set up on the table.

Page 119

Cubic centimeters, or cc, are a unit of measurement for volume. Approximately 30 cc is equal to 1 fluid oz, so 2 cc is about half a teaspoon!

Page 132

Hijiki, a brown sea vegetable, is a Japanese dietary staple. Rich in fiber and minerals like calcium, magnesium, and iron, it's not surprising Ayami is eating it along with other mineral-dense health foods.

Page 152

In the original, Ayami uses the term "*senpai*" in reference to her daughter, which is an honorific generally used for upperclassmen or more senior coworkers.

I Don't Know How to Give Birth!

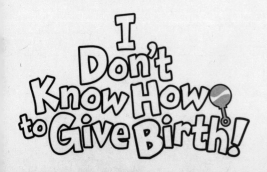

I Don't Know How to

Ayami Kazama

Translation by **JULIE GONIWICH** • Lettering by **ABIGAIL BLACKMAN**

SHUSSAN NO SHIKATA GA WAKARANAI !
©Ayami Kazama 2016
First published in Japan in 2016 by KADOKAWA CORPORATION, Tokyo.
English translation rights arranged with KADOKAWA CORPORATION, Tokyo through TUTTLE-MORI AGENCY, INC., Tokyo.

English translation © 2020 by Yen Press, LLC

Yen Press
150 West 30th Street, 19th Floor
New York, NY 10001

Visit us at yenpress.com • facebook.com/yenpress • twitter.com/yenpress
yenpress.tumblr.com • instagram.com/yenpress

First Yen Press Edition: August 2020

Yen Press is an imprint of Yen Press, LLC.
The Yen Press name and logo are trademarks of Yen Press, LLC.

The publisher is not responsible for websites
(or their content) that are not owned by the publisher.

Library of Congress Control Number: 2019953325

ISBNs: 978-1-9753-3288-4 (paperback)
        978-1-9753-3305-8 (ebook)

10 9 8 7 6 5 4 3 2 1

WOR

Printed in the United States of America

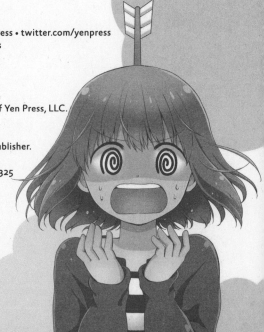